Father Involvement in Canada

Edited by Jessica Ball and Kerry Daly

Father Involvement in Canada
Diversity, Renewal, and Transformation

© UBC Press 2012

All rights reserved. No part of this publication may be reproduced, stored in a retrieval system, or transmitted, in any form or by any means, without prior written permission of the publisher, or, in Canada, in the case of photocopying or other reprographic copying, a licence from Access Copyright, www.accesscopyright.ca.

21 20 19 18 17 16 15 14 13 12   5 4 3 2 1

Printed in Canada on FSC-certified ancient-forest-free paper (100% post-consumer recycled) that is processed chlorine- and acid-free.

Library and Archives Canada Cataloguing in Publication

Father involvement in Canada : diversity, renewal, and tranformation / edited by Jessica Ball and Kerry Daly.

Includes bibliographical references and index.
Also issued in electronic format.
ISBN 978-0-7748-2400-2 (bound); ISBN 978-0-7748-2401-9 (pbk.)

1. Fatherhood – Canada. 2. Fathers – Canada. I. Ball, Jessica II. Daly, Kerry J.E. (Kerry Joseph Eugene)

HQ756.F374 2012   306.874′20971   C2012-903635-8

Canadä

UBC Press gratefully acknowledges the financial support for our publishing program of the Government of Canada (through the Canada Book Fund), the Canada Council for the Arts, and the British Columbia Arts Council.

This book has been published with the help of a grant from the Canadian Federation for the Humanities and Social Sciences, through the Awards to Scholarly Publications Program, using funds provided by the Social Sciences and Humanities Research Council of Canada.

Printed and bound in Canada by Friesens
Set in Stone by Artegraphica Design Co. Ltd.
Copy editor: Joyce Hildebrand
Proofreader: Grace Yaginuma
Indexer: Heather Ebbs

UBC Press
The University of British Columbia
2029 West Mall
Vancouver, BC V6T 1Z2
www.ubcpress.ca

Dedicated to the generations of fathers who went before and will come after ...

JB – To my father, Ernie Ball, who embodied an enigmatic unity of the masculine and feminine in the focused and multi-dimensional way he raised his children.

KD – To my son, Ben Daly, who fulfills with dedication and tenderness the promise of the next generation of men to be loving and caring dads.

Contents

List of Tables / ix

Acknowledgments / xi

Foreword / xiii
Joseph H. Pleck

Part 1: Trends and Perspectives: An Overview of Father Involvement

1 Father Involvement in Canada: A Transformative Approach / 1
Jessica Ball and Kerry Daly

2 Canadian Fathers: Demographic and Socio-Economic Profiles
from Census and National Surveys / 26
Zenaida R. Ravanera and John Hoffman

3 Fathers Make a Difference in Their Children's Lives: A Review
of the Research Evidence / 50
Sarah Allen, Kerry Daly, and Jessica Ball

4 Feminist Mothers Researching Fathering: Advocates, Contributors,
and Dissenters / 89
Andrea Doucet and Linda Hawkins

Part 2: The Diversity of Fathering Experiences: Contested Terrain

5 Young Fatherhood, Generativity, and Men's Development: Travelling
a Two-Way Street to Maturity / 107
Michael W. Pratt, Heather L. Lawford, and James W. Allen

6 Aboriginal Fathers in Canada through Time / 126
Jessica Ball

7 The Short End of the Stick? Fatherhood in the Wake of Separation
and Divorce / 149
Denise L. Whitehead and Nicholas Bala

8 Fathering within Child Welfare / 171
*Susan Strega, Leslie Brown, Elizabeth Manning, Christopher Walmsley,
Lena Dominelli, and Marilyn Callahan*

9 The Experiences of Fathers of a Child with a Chronic Health Condition:
Caregiving Experiences and Potential Support Interventions / 190
John Beaton, David Nicholas, Ted McNeill, and Lisa Wenger

Part 3: Toward Social Change: Policy and Practice Issues for Fathers

10 Fathers and Parental Leave in Canada: Policies and Practices / 207
Lindsey McKay, Katherine Marshall, and Andrea Doucet

11 Looking Forward: Father Involvement and Changing Forms
of Masculine Care / 224
Kerry Daly and Jessica Ball

List of Contributors / 238

Index / 243

Tables

2.1 Living arrangements of all men aged 15 to 64 and marital status of fathers, by age groups, 2006 / 28

2.2 Median age at parenthood, by 5-year birth cohorts / 29

2.3 Socio-economic characteristics of men, by age groups and fatherhood status, 2006 / 31

2.4 Average hours per day of paid and unpaid work, men and women aged 25 to 54 with children under 19 years old / 33

2.5 Participation in and time spent on paid work, housework, and other unpaid work, men aged 25 to 54 living with children under 19 years old / 33

2.6 Informal network indicators by fatherhood status, Canadian men aged 30 to 64, 2003 / 35

2.7 Socio-economic characteristics of fathers aged 15 to 64, by immigration status, 2006 / 36

2.8 Demographic and socio-economic characteristics of fathers aged 15 to 64, by Aboriginal status, 2006 / 38

2.9 Full-time school attendance, men aged 15 to 29, by fatherhood status, 2006 / 39

2.10 Marital status of lone fathers aged 15 to 64, by age group, 2006 / 40

2.11 Socio-economic characteristics of fathers aged 15 to 64, by marital status, 2006 / 41

2.12 Percentage of dependents involving custody orders, by party granted custody, 1995-2003 / 42

2.13 Demographic characteristics of fathers with children of any age, by type of father, 2006 / 44

x *List of Tables*

10.1 Comparison of Canada (EI) and Québec (QPIP) parental leave benefit plans since 2006 / 210

10.2 Take-up rate and average weeks taken among eligible fathers of paid paternity or parental leave / 215

Appendix

3.1 Impact of positive father involvement on child development outcomes / 69

Acknowledgments

First we wish to acknowledge with thanks the generosity of fathers and their partners across Canada who shared their experiences of father involvement with researchers whose work is represented in the chapters of this book. It has been a privilege for all of the research team members to hear, reflect on, and interpret their stories, challenges, and aspirations.

Bringing together the diverse talents and interests of the research teams that contributed chapters in this book required some extraordinarily capable and tenacious support. Lisa Wenger, a doctoral candidate in Family Relations and Human Development at the University of Guelph, accompanied us every step of the way on this book-making journey. Lisa managed communications with chapter authors, demonstrated a breadth of knowledge and skill in her canny editorial feedback that was at times quite breathtaking, and greased the wheels of the book project with grace and humour. We also wish to thank Darcy Cullen of UBC Press for welcoming a volume on father involvement that could begin to fill a gap in understanding parenting in Canada and for providing valuable feedback and advice as the book evolved.

Impetus for this book grew out of an eight-year research project funded by the Social Sciences and Humanities Research Council of Canada and its Community-University Research Alliances program. This complex, nationally networked investigation was deftly managed by Linda Hawkins, director of the Institute for Community Engaged Scholarship at the University of Guelph. Her critical commentaries and enthusiasm fuelled our efforts to bring together authors who could convey the complexity and heterogeneity of fathers' roles in caring for children. Funding for the networking process that led to this volume was also provided by the Public Health Agency of Canada. The agency's interest in father involvement was stimulated and informed by the tireless work of Fernand Lozier, who dedicated much of his career to animating the father involvement movement in Canada. He was a pioneer in calling for more focused research and public advocacy to illuminate, stimulate, and recognize the varied roles that fathers play in the lives of their children, young and old.

Foreword

By Joseph H. Pleck

From the perspective of someone who began working on fathering research in the 1970s, the way that the landscape of fatherhood, both scholarly and cultural, has changed over the last four decades is remarkable. When I started out, "fatherhood research" meant the investigation of the consequences of father absence. Through the early 1970s, it seemed that in psychological theory, fathers were towering figures in child development – but towering only by their absence. That changed, of course, and new research subsequently emerged that focused instead on what fathers do when they are present. It is now over 35 years since the onset of this contemporary study of fatherhood, an onset marked by the publication in 1974 of the first edition of Michael Lamb's *Role of the Father in Child Development*. And over 25 years have passed since the explicit formulation of the foundational construct of "father involvement" (Lamb, Pleck, Charnov, & Levine, 1985; Pleck, Lamb, & Levine, 1985). From one perspective, the study of fatherhood and father involvement in the modern sense has been going on for a long time, but from another vantage point, it is historically quite recent.

Today, the father involvement concept is taken for granted and is deeply embedded in current thinking. At the same time, it is contested. Like most constructs in the social sciences, the concept has come in for its share of criticism. Doesn't the construct of father involvement imply a "maternal template"? A deficit perspective on fathers? A feminist-oriented assumption that there should be gender equity in parenting? Doesn't it ignore fathers' thoughts and feelings, and fail to recognize, and even devalue, fathers' economic support for their children? Isn't the concept based on the experience of only white middle-class fathers, thereby defining fathering in a way that makes fathers belonging to minorities and lower socio-economic classes appear deficient? And isn't the notion that father involvement is increasing only "media hype"? The lively debates ensuing from these important challenges have pressed scholars to refine their thinking and their research methods. Even more important, they have led researchers and practitioners to broaden the scope of what they include in "fathering" and who they study as "fathers" (Pleck, 2010b).

Besides the evolution of academic research and theory, another crucial part of the changing landscape of fatherhood over recent decades is the shift in public perceptions about fathers and in fathers' views of themselves. I can offer some data from a Pew Research Center (2007) national survey in the United States. About three fifths of adult men and women surveyed said that they think it is harder to be a father now than it was 20 or 30 years ago. And how well does the US public think today's fathers are doing in the face of this increased "paternal challenge"? Of women surveyed, 56% said today's dads are doing as good a job or a better job raising their kids compared with fathers a generation ago. Intriguingly, married working mothers' assessments of fathers' performance were especially positive: 72% of those working at least part-time and raising young children said dads today are doing as good a job or better.

But here's the rub: among US men, there appears to be a crisis of paternal self-confidence. Only 41% of men in the Pew survey thought contemporary fathers are doing better or even as well as fathers in the past. The majority of men (55%) said today's dads are actually doing a worse job. The need for books like *Father Involvement in Canada: Diversity, Renewal, and Transformation* lies precisely in the intersection of today's increased paternal challenges and the rising crisis in paternal self-confidence.

In their introductory and concluding essays, Jessica Ball and Kerry Daly clearly articulate the multiple themes underlying the book, so I will not try to recapitulate them. Perhaps especially important are the themes of diversity in fathering and the embeddedness of fathering in masculinity and gender. *Father Involvement in Canada* is fundamentally grounded in the recognition of diversity and the valorization of inclusiveness. As applied to fatherhood, the principles of diversity and inclusiveness are far-reaching, addressing multiple domains: fathers' backgrounds and life histories, the social and institutional contexts in which they father, and the ways in which they enact fathering. These multiple backgrounds, contexts, and modes of fathering may vary profoundly. As the ethic of diversity and inclusiveness seems to be under attack in so many cultures today (especially my own, that of the United States), this book's steadfast affirmation of these values is especially important.

A particularly notable way in which *Father Involvement in Canada* reflects and fosters new thinking in fatherhood research and practice is the attention its chapters give to the multiple ways in which fathering is intertwined with masculinity and gender. Although to say that fathering is gendered may seem a commonplace, the book brings new insight into gender's crucial role and explores a central dialectic. On the one hand, institutions, social services, and policies too often reflect the stereotypical assumption that as parents, fathers are "second class." The long-standing cultural equations of "woman = mother" and "mother = parent" leave little place for men in the lives of their children. On the other hand, the belief that fathers are essential, making a unique contribution to children's development, is increasingly prevalent. (An Internet search on "fathers" and "essential" jointly yielded 5.4 million web pages in May 2009; the same search in September 2010 produced 17.9 million web pages.) What is believed to make fathers' contributions so essential is that it is uniquely male.

Rigorous evidence that good fathering makes an independent, causal contribution to child development has indeed begun to accumulate. This evidence derives from investigations addressing the methodological weaknesses plaguing so much past research, weaknesses such as failure to control for confounding variables – in particular, mothering (since good fathering and good mothering are correlated), same-informant bias in assessments of fathering and child outcomes, and the need to take into account children's reciprocal influence on fathering (Pleck, 2010b). This research confirmation of independent paternal effects provides a rationale for fathering practice. At the same time, however, evidence is lacking that fathers' contributions occur *specifically because* their parenting is uniquely masculine (Pleck, 2010a). This latter conclusion is challenging since for so many fathers, and for so many practitioners serving them, the idea of an essential, unique paternal contribution is inspirational and motivating. In a cultural context in which fathers' roles are less socially valued than those of mothers, this belief may seem to be the only one available that fathers can use to construct a narrative explaining why they want to and should be involved, and that justifies to fatherhood practitioners why they work so hard to help.

Whatever the research findings, it is unlikely that the words "essential" and "unique" will disappear in public discourse about fathers. Fathers and fatherhood practitioners need not get stuck on these words, however. Nearly all who say that fathers are "essential" do not mean this in a literal sense, for that would mean that it is impossible for any child raised without a father, or without a good father, to develop successfully. Most of those using the rhetoric of paternal essentiality know of too many disconfirming examples; what they mean by "essential" is something more like "really important." And there is indeed a sense in which, for many children, their father's contribution is unique. Children benefit by having more than one adult who raises and is deeply committed to them. For most children, their father is unique in being the only adult besides their mother who is potentially available and potentially motivated to be a parent to them in this way. (And for some children, their father has a unique availability to be the child's *only* parent.) Whether or not fathering has a unique effect on children in general, for a particular child, her or his individual father is highly likely to be "one of a kind" in his availability and motivation to be a co-parent or sole parent.

Fathers need support to fulfill the unique potential they have to parent their children. *Father Involvement in Canada* – encompassing the diversity in fathers' backgrounds, in their current contexts, and in how they father – points the way to how scholars can better understand the varying ways in which fathers realize this potential, and how practitioners can better help them to do so.

References

Lamb, M. E. (Ed.). (1974). *The role of the father in child development*. New York, NY: Wiley.

Lamb, M. E., Pleck, J. H., Charnov, E. L., & Levine, J. A. (1985). Paternal behavior in humans. *American Zoologist, 25*, 883-894.

Pew Research Center. (2007). *Being Dad may be tougher these days, but working moms are among their biggest fans*. Retrieved from http://pewsocialtrends.org/pubs/510/fathers-day.

Pleck, J. H. (2010a). Fatherhood and masculinity. In M. E. Lamb (Ed.), *The role of the father in child development* (5th ed., pp. 32-66). New York, NY: Wiley.

Pleck, J. H. (2010b). Paternal involvement: Revised conceptualization and theoretical linkages with child outcomes. In M. E. Lamb (Ed.), *The role of the father in child development* (5th ed., pp. 67-107). New York, NY: Wiley.

Pleck, J. H., Lamb, M. E., & Levine, J. A. (1985). Facilitating future change in men's family roles. *Marriage and Family Review, 9*(3-4), 11-16.

Part 1
Trends and Perspectives:
An Overview of Father Involvement

1
Father Involvement in Canada: A Transformative Approach

Jessica Ball and Kerry Daly

There is an extraordinary range of possibilities for being a father in Canada today: biological paternity in the context of heterosexual marriage, adoption of a child with one's same-sex partner, sperm donation, step-parenting, lone parenting, co-parenting with an ex-partner, and myriad other ways. A father's contribution to his child may be primarily financial. He may have little or no contact with some or all of his children, whether by choice or by circumstance. Or he may be directly involved in every aspect of his child's care.

This multitude of options parallels significant and concurrent challenges to dominant cultural constructions of masculinity in Canada. Increasingly, embodiments of masculinity are visibly diverse. Popular media tend to catastrophize this multiplicity. Census findings that show a rising prevalence of lone-parent households tend to be seen as indicative of a crisis in family life. The decline of lasting heterosexual marriage and the rise in unfamiliar patterns of father involvement are often read as signs that traditional masculinity and the patriarchal heritage are under attack. Theories of fatherhood are proving to be less useful than they were when they had to account for findings of research that focused mainly on quantitative measurements of father involvement in European-heritage, nuclear families. Practitioners in health and social services find themselves on uncertain ground as their understandings, skills, and program models seem inadequate to reach out to fathers in ways that fathers respond to and find helpful.

If Canadian society is to keep step with and support men on their various paths to becoming fathers and in their diverse family constellations and father-child relationships, research is sorely needed that can inform guiding concepts, professional education curricula, policy decisions, and community program development. This book is a compilation of discussions about twenty-first century research by Canadian scholars who are part of an emerging movement to understand and support father involvement in its many forms. Canadian investigators and practitioners who are advancing understandings and outreach regarding fathers cut across many disciplines, including child and youth care, family studies, psychology, sociology, social work, public policy, and law. Thus, a number of theoretical lenses are being used to examine fathers' involvement, and a number of professions and service sectors are exploring how practices need to be revised or refined to support fathers' involvement.

Against a background of, until recently, a paucity of research and theory on Canadian fathers' involvement, this book provides a status update on the nascent and growing movement in Canada to understand and support fathers' involvement with their children; it offers a multi-layered reading of the personal and social systems that are shaping father involvement within and across diverse populations in Canadian society. Each of the contributing authors approaches fathers' experiences from a slightly different angle. By bringing these approaches together, the book creates a map of the interlocking individual, familial, institutional, socio-cultural, political, and material systems in which fathers are embedded. In this way, it provides a baseline for tracking the experiences of populations of fathers that vary by ethnicity, age, marital status, and context. It explores fathers' relative vulnerability as a result of poverty, access to paternity leave, and the degree of support they receive from the health sector, child welfare, other institutions, and communities. These critical dimensions of the ecological embeddedness of father involvement tend to be disregarded in normative, universalistic concepts of fatherhood. The book's contributors also identify some of the gaps that remain in our understandings, policies, and practice competencies, and offer directions for future research and policy work to reduce barriers and improve community-based supports for fathers.

As research on father involvement in Canada has grown over the past decades from a scattering of disparate studies to a developing body of knowledge, several unifying themes can be discerned. These include ecological embeddedness; diversity and social inclusion; visibility, outreach, and engagement; and reconceptualization of masculinity in the context of involved fatherhood. The emerging salience of these four themes, combined with increasingly vocal calls for more nuanced public understanding and more concerted program efforts to recognize and encourage positive father involvement, provided the impetus for this book. Following an overview of changing patterns of father involvement in Canada, this chapter takes up these key themes, which are also developed by the authors that follow.

The Shifting Terrain of Fatherhood in Canada

In 2006, Statistics Canada (2006a) counted 8.1 million fathers in Canada. Among these, just under half (3.8 million) were biological, adoptive, or step-parent fathers living with children under 18 years of age.[1] Married-couple families accounted for 68% of all families in Canada (down from 80% two decades ago). The proportion of families headed by common-law couples (15.5%) and lone-parent families (15.9%) increased from the 2001 census (Statistics Canada, 2001, 2006a). According to Statistics Canada (2006a), of the 1.4 million lone-parent families with at least one child under age 16 at home, 20% involved single fathers. Based on these data, between 2001 and 2006, the growth of lone-male-headed families (14.6%) was more than twice the rate of growth (6.3%) of lone-female-headed families.

Time and money are basic resources for family life. Large inequalities of wealth and income between the richest and poorest 20% of Canadian families are enduring and prominent features of the Canadian social landscape. Particularly vulnerable are Aboriginal families, newcomers, and families that rely on a single earner. In addition, the experience of a mild to severe disability is a common one for Canadians, who have a disability rate of 14.3%, including 3.7% of children under 15 years old (Statistics Canada, 2007). Disability can contribute to vulnerability and to poverty due to costs incurred in meeting exceptional needs. All these conditions call for supports and services for affected children, fathers, and mothers, which are in short supply, especially in rural areas and in the North.

The past 30 years have seen profound shifts in how families try to provide economic security for family members. Changes in family functioning and dynamics have occurred in the gender division of paid and unpaid labour, the division of household labour and distribution of care responsibilities, and decisions about who will work what hours or take parental leave upon the birth or adoption of a child. There has been a steady rise in labour market participation of women, along with a growing number of two-parent families with dual earners. In 1976, less than half (46%) of all women aged 15 and over were in the paid labour force, compared to 63% in 2009 (Statistics Canada, 2009). Compared to what is often referred to as the "traditional" family model of male breadwinner/female homemaker (Pleck, 1979), the gap between the labour force participation of men and women has narrowed from 40 percentage points in 1976 to 9 percentage points in 2009. In 2006, 73% of all women with children under 16 years old living at home were employed on a full- or part-time basis, up from 39% in 1976. While pay equity remains an elusive goal for Canadian women, 28% of women earned more than their male spouse in 2007, up from 12% in 1976 (Statistics Canada, 2009). Taken together, fathers put in an average of two more hours of paid work per week compared to mothers. However, an increasing number of fathers also work part-time, and 10% of stay-at-home parents are fathers (Statistics Canada, 2006a). The reported number of same-sex couples has surged over the past decade, growing at five times the pace of heterosexual couples between 2001 and 2006; the 2006 census counted 45,345 same-sex couples (Statistics Canada, 2006c). Reflecting the legalization of same-sex marriages in Canada in July 2005, 16.5% of these were married couples. A majority of these couples were male. A small but significant number of same-sex married and common-law couples (9%) had children under 25 living with them; a minority of these couples were men. These and other important shifts in the composition and contexts of families are described in more detail by Ravanera and Hoffman later in this volume.

As patterns of family relationships involving children become more diversified in the early twenty-first century, stable nuclear families headed by one father and one mother are becoming ever more rare, both as a goal for adults and as a reality for children and families. More fathers are involved as their children's lone caregiver – either full-time as lone parents or part-time when they care for their children in joint-custody arrangements. Increasing numbers of fathers are involved in more than one family. Along with these changes and shifting gender expectations regarding parenting in general, there is dawning awareness that sustained, positive involvement of fathers with their children must be encouraged and supported by media, public policies, child care programs, schools, social programs, child health services, and workplaces. Popular culture in Canada tends to see diverse groups of men as enjoying certain patriarchal dividends. For example, although women are increasingly taking up traditionally male roles as co-providers for their children, caring for children continues to be publicly depicted, and frequently experienced, as more of a choice for fathers and a necessity for mothers. Images of fathers eager to shed their parenting responsibilities in favour of work, sports, or personal gratification persist in popular media, and while women are frequently depicted as calling for more father involvement in direct child care activities, some studies point to some ambivalence on the parts of mothers about how much and in what aspects of child care they want fathers to share (Cannon, Schoppe-Sullivan, Mangelsdorf, Brown, & Sokolowski, 2009; Gaunt, 2008; Schoppe-Sullivan, Brown, Cannon, Mangelsdorf, & Szewczyk Sokolowski, 2008). Policies are needed to promote gender equity in opportunities to develop knowledge, skills, and commitment to care for children and to be fully engaged as parents.

Popular media in Canada is replete with negative representations of fathers as less competent than mothers when it comes to caring for children; fathers are also portrayed as more likely to be violent in the domestic sphere. The fact that some men are violent in family contexts also tends to be culturally depicted as an expression of patriarchal dividends accruing to fathers in a male-dominated, traditional society. While domestic violence is found in a small minority of (but still too many) Canadian families, in 2004 an estimated 7% of women (653,000 women) and 6% of men (546,000) over 14 years old reported some form of spousal violence in the context of a current or previous marital or common-law relationship in the previous five years (Statistics Canada, 2005). Other studies have similarly suggested a relative equivalence between Canadian men and women in their propensity to perpetrate violence in family contexts (Dutton & Nicholls, 2005; Grandin, Lupri, & Brinkerhoff, 1998).[2] In the face of such portrayals, an apparent groundswell of fathers is critically resisting both dominant discourses of normative gendered parenting (Doucet, 2009) and popular images of the "deadbeat dad" and family buffoon. A stroll through grocery stores, city parks, and community recreation centres would certainly suggest that droves of Canadian fathers reject essentialized masculine parenting roles and are involved in personal care routines, coaching, guiding, teaching, driving, and generally sharing time with their youngsters, with and without adult partners. The influx of new Canadians is also shaping the social landscape, contributing a complex and varied array of ideals about family life and a father's responsibilities, roles, needs, and goals. The persistence of negative expectations and images in popular media appears to be based, in part, on mother-centric and dominant cultural ideas of what counts as a loving, meaningful contribution to caring for and supporting the health and development of children and youth.

Among scholars, the forms and meanings of father involvement – as well as how we measure, interpret, and conceptualize father involvement – are being questioned (Day & Lamb, 2004; Palkovitz, 1997; Parke, 2004). Some investigators are beginning to deal with the practical difficulty but conceptual necessity of capturing the multi-dimensionality of father involvement measurement tools (Schoppe-Sullivan, McBride, & Ho, 2004). Investigators are also recognizing that not all fathers experience the birth or adoption of their child as a seminal moment when they don the mantle of fatherhood; rather, some fathers grow into the role gradually, and the nature, extent, meaning, and impacts of different forms of father-child interaction vary as their children change over time (Amato, 1998).

Advocates of increased father involvement in child care (e.g., Kershaw, Pulkingham, & Fuller, 2008) must grapple not only with an ideological commitment to equality of opportunities, if not expectations, for men and women to play significant roles in direct caregiving but also with evidence that mothers can act as gatekeepers who monitor and regulate the form, timing, and frequency of fathers' involvement (Allen & Hawkins, 1999). As Doucet and Hawkins discuss in this volume, mothers' oversight of child care is a product of a social reality in which mothers have been expected to do the majority of child care – a pattern that is almost universal, remains the norm in many cultures, and is difficult to change. Canadian family policy scholars Kershaw et al. (2008) draw on Fraser's (1994) interpretation of this kind of care specialization falling to women as one of several indicators of an androcentric model of citizenship. Fraser offers a universal caregiver model of citizenship that recognizes increased labour force participation by women and calls for social policies to induce greater numbers of men to undertake more care of children and other dependents, and generally to embrace an ethic of care that would reduce domestic violence as well. In Canada, fathers and community program practitioners are increasingly recognizing both the mother-centric bias of many health, education, and social programs, and the prescriptive messages fathers receive about what their involvement with their children should look like (Hodgins, 2007). At the same time, the question of what actions ought to follow this recognition, particularly at the policy level, remains open-ended. As Kershaw et al. (2008) note, social policy in Canada is so focused on labour-market involvement that it seems far from conceiving or contributing to men's roles in caregiving within the context of family life.

Ecological Embeddedness: Contextualizing Father Involvement

The Canadian social-research agenda acknowledges and takes as a primary value the need to understand father involvement as diverse, embedded in multi-faceted social contexts, and multiply determined. Father involvement investigators in Canada, as elsewhere, stress the need to characterize, conceptualize, and respond to the diversity of fathers' behaviours and experiences since these are embedded within numerous kinds of couple relationships; family structures; cultural and religious communities; socioeconomic circumstances; residential institutions, including hospitals, longterm care facilities, and prisons; and legislative frameworks, such as those governing paternity leave and custody decision making. Fathers' sociopolitical and personal histories are also diverse. They may include, for example, varied experiences of fatherhood within their families of origin, experiences in an "Indian" residential school, or, for political asylum seekers, armed conflict in their country of origin. Rather than search for a universal fatherhood experience or the "typical" Canadian father, scholars and practitioners are oriented toward understanding the diversity of fathers' experiences based on their ethnicity; their socio-economic status; their locale, whether rural, remote, or urban; the health and development of their children, whether typical or atypical; and other key sources of variability. While fathers may share many similar experiences in the process of becoming fathers, specific challenges, goals, and expectations are associated with their culture, religion, employment status, immigration history, sexual orientation, or relationship with their child's mother – to name just a few sources of variation.

Familial and Social Systems

The need to develop context-sensitive understandings has been salient throughout the short history of Canadian fatherhood studies. For example, an early study of Canadian families found that the largest contributor to the quality of fathers' and mothers' nurturance of their children was whether the partners, individually or together, had sustained employment to generate a stable family income (Maxwell, 1997). Another early study identified the bidirectionality of fathers' embeddedness within the family system, suggesting that when fathers are struggling, particularly when their relationship with their partner is unhappy, the well-being of the entire family is affected (Watson, Watson, Wetzel, Bader, & Talbot, 1995). This Canadian study and another by Bouchard and Lee (2000) found that the most frequent causes of marital conflict were low levels of fathers' participation in household chores, jealousy over mothers' preoccupation with a new baby, and difficulty adjusting to profound changes in the marital relationship. Bouchard and Lee found that the couple relationship was key to the father-child relationship: the more a man felt supported by his partner in his role as a father, the more he enjoyed fathering and the more involved he became.

Other Canadian investigators, such as Devault and her colleagues in French Canada (e.g., Devault et al., 2008), also conceive of father involvement as a multi-relational construct embedded within the broader family system. Lamb (1997, 2004), whose scholarship on fatherhood in the American context has been formative for the field, emphasizes a need to recognize the interdependent nature of fathering relationships within other relational contexts and particular cultures, religions, and economic circumstances, as well as within the context of a gender-segregated labour market and certain public policies affecting families (Lamb, 1997; Marsiglio & Cohan, 2000; Palkovitz, 2002). In Canada, an emphasis on a contextualizing approach is underpinned by Canadian social scholars' signature belief in a population health model that emphasizes multiple determinants of health and well-being, many of which are social in nature and based within the family and community. This model assumes that citizen engagement is a major contributor to promoting health and well-being (Kishchuk, 2001) and that fathers, mothers, and other family members are producers of support, growth, and learning for themselves and their children (Doherty, 2000).

Consistent with a population health model, some father involvement scholars in Canada draw on Bronfenbrenner's (1986) ecological model. This model conceptualizes the multiple systems that shape and are shaped by an individual's experiences. Thus, investigators have sought to characterize fathers' goals, strengths, challenges, and needs (what Bronfenbrenner referred to as the *ontosystem*) in relation to the co-parenting and parent-child dynamics in which fathers are engaged *(microsystem)*, community-level structures *(mesosystem)*, institutions, policies, and legislation *(exosystem)*, and cultural values and societal prescriptions *(macrosystem)*. Drawing on Bronfenbrenner's (1979) earlier notion of the *chronosystem,* some investigators are also interested in understanding how and why expectations, forms, and levels of father involvement have changed over time in Canada. The chronology concept weaves together many of the themes addressed in this book, such as fathers' roles in families before and after immigration to

Canada, the impacts of residential schools on Indigenous men's journeys to learn fatherhood, shifts in family law that have brought about more opportunities for fathers to remain in (or take up) caregiving roles with their children following separation and divorce, and the impacts of traditional and post-structural feminism on men's thinking about masculinity. The related concept of generativity, discussed in the chapter by Pratt, Lawford, and Allen in this volume, concerns the ways that experiences, stories, and recollections of fatherhood are communicated, adapted, resisted, and transformed across generations.

The More Things Change ...
To date, the chronology concept has been undertheorized and not well integrated into understandings of men, masculinity, and fatherhood. Yet theories, programs, and policies would be greatly informed by a more comprehensive socio-historical and intersectional analysis of how institutional policies and structures have constructed discourses of gender roles, men, masculinity, fatherhood, and families over time. For example, every generation conceives of itself as living in a time of rapid social change, and fatherhood researchers are not immune from thinking that the social constructs of masculinity and fatherhood are currently undergoing dramatic shifts. Yet family life has changed dramatically in every era, though the nature and degree of these shifts have varied within different segments of Canadian society. Imagine, for example, the absolute shift for Indigenous families when suddenly the government called for the removal of all school-aged children to government-run institutions and the equally profound and challenging shift as the right to raise one's children was restored to Indigenous families. Often, children and youth returned to communities no longer well equipped to care for them, and many First Nations are struggling today with the impacts of this history.

Other aspects of Canadian society have changed less than we might imagine. For example, evidence of significant shifts in fathers' direct involvement in child care is equivocal. While fathers have become more involved with their children over the past two decades, on average they still spend far less time in direct care of their children compared to mothers. Within dual-earner, heterosexual couples, for example, the convergence of paid work hours between men and women raises important questions about the division of labour within families. Women in these couples are still much more likely than men to modify their patterns of work to accommodate family responsibilities (Karambayya & Reilly, 1992; Stone, 1994). Women's workforce participation is often disrupted after the birth or adoption of a child. More than four in 10 women aged 25 to 44 who are working part-time (43%) do so because of the need to care for their children or for other family reasons; in comparison, fewer than one in 10 men (7%) work part-time to accommodate family demands (Statistics Canada, 2008). Whereas women still spend more time in unpaid household labour and caring for children, men have gradually increased their involvement in child care and, to a lesser degree, in housework. In 2006, Statistics Canada (2006b) showed that while the average time fathers spent on housework and child care had increased from 1986, fathers were still spending only about two thirds as much time as mothers in direct care for their children. Among fathers of children under five years old, the increase was slightly more, from 1.0 hour per day in 1986 to 1.6 hours per day in 2005. For mothers of children under five, it was 2.6 hours per day in 1986 and 3.4 hours per day in 2005 (Marshall, 2006).

One of the primary implications of the shift to more mother participation in the labour force and more father participation in child care is that decision making about parental responsibilities is becoming more complex, with increased role ambiguity, increased emphasis on negotiation of roles, and fluidity in the ways in which parents respond to the demands of everyday life. For example, Marshall (2009) reported that work-family balance is an important concern for dual-earner families in Canada, with 24% of men and 38% of women in families with two full-time jobs and preschool children reporting severe time stress. Another pattern that has endured is that fathers continue to spend more time each day engaged in paid work and commuting, while mothers spend, on average, less time in the paid workforce (Marshall, 2006). This pattern is sometimes seen as an aspect of the patriarchal dividends accruing to men, who are economically privileged in the labour market with better wages and opportunities for promotion than women. At the same time, this pattern means that some women have more time available to spend with their children. This gender gap, combined with the rapid increase in the number of lone-mother-headed households and accumulating evidence that a lack of positive father involvement can have negative consequences for children (see Allen, Daly, & Ball in this volume, and Flouri & Buchanan, 2003), forms the rationale for constructing father involvement as a public issue.

Diversity and Social Inclusion: A Canadian Approach to Father Involvement

Canada is both the original home of over 600 distinct First Nations, Métis, and Inuit populations and a nation of immigrants, with over 200 ethnic origins represented in the 2006 census. Indigenous peoples constitute nearly 4% of Canada's population. The 2006 census showed that 19.5% of individuals living in Canada today were born in another country, and that approximately 1.1 million immigrants came to Canada between 2001 and 2006 (Statistics Canada, 2006a). (The top three countries of origin were China, India, and the Philippines.) Such a culturally diverse population results in a wealth of approaches to fatherhood; no single image, role model, or standard characterizes "the Canadian father." Additionally, Canadians are spread across the largest national land mass in the world, and fathers span the country, living in areas that range from remote villages, where helping children to learn skills for living on the land or sea is often an important role for fathers, to cosmopolitan centres, where facilitating and regulating children's engagement with the risks and opportunities of urban life are some of the tasks of fatherhood.

To date, little research has explored the heterogeneity of fathers and the related diversity of forms of father involvement. Theory and research have primarily focused on the experience of middle-class men of European heritage living in urban families (Roopnarine, 2004; Tamis-LeMonda & Cabrera, 2002). Heterosexuality and Euro-Western normative ideals of fatherhood have been assumed, with little critique (Hearn, 2002). A goal of Canadian research on father involvement is to go beyond the dominant portrayals of fathers in "intact" heterosexual nuclear families and expand the focus of research to groups of fathers who remain outside the normative gaze and are often excluded from theoretical conceptualizations, policies, community outreach, and programs. These groups of fathers include Indigenous men, gay men, social fathers, immigrants and refugees, adolescents, and fathers of children with disabilities. Furthermore, little research to date recognizes the dynamic chronological dimension of fathering, whereby fathers today live in different contexts from their forebears, do not embody the same cultural predilections, and cannot automatically apply the lessons they may have learned about fatherhood from their own fathers (Daly, 1993).

While diversity has emerged as a primary focus of father involvement research in Canada, social inclusion is equally important. The concept of social inclusion became a priority for investigators and social policy and program developers in the mid-1990s as a way of encapsulating Canadian values such as multiculturalism, protection of minority rights, equity, bilingualism, and religious freedom (Richmond & Saloojee, 2005). Advocates and scholars are currently struggling to articulate theory, policy tools, and program models that encompass all fathers, especially those who have been disadvantaged historically, culturally, legally, and/or economically, and those in sexual minority groups. Crucial here is a critical assessment of community supports for fathers, with a view to ensuring that the needs of all fathers in Canada who are motivated to be positively involved with their children are addressed in policy, legislation, and health and social service programs.

Involving Fathers in Research and Policy Discussions

Today, most Canadian investigators, policy analysts, and practitioners are starting with the premise that Canada's diverse population calls for approaches that are clearly situated in culturally defined subpopulations of fathers. Most scholars of father involvement aim to avoid reproducing or prescribing hegemonic white, middle-class, heterosexual images of ideal fatherhood and are instead emphasizing the diversity of manifestations of fathers' involvement with their children. Reflecting this orientation, many father involvement scholars in Canada are choosing qualitative research methods wherein theoretical hypotheses and concepts are being derived inductively through, for example, grounded theory development, hermeneutics, and phenomenology. The common objective is to construct conceptual understandings and guidelines for policy and practice that resonate with diverse populations of fathers, mothers, children, and practitioners in the widely varying circumstances in which Canadian families live.

During this exploratory phase, Canadian researchers are tending to choose methodologies that involve fathers and families themselves through community-engaged research. Given the grassroots origins of the growing father involvement movement in Canada (Kishchuk, 2001), and in the absence of a robust and differentiated knowledge base about diverse conditions and experiences of father involvement, participatory action research has been found to be particularly well suited because of its theoretical flexibility and commitment to community building (Doherty, 2000). Underlying this approach is the conviction that fathers are producers of learning for and about themselves and of support, growth, and social changes within their families and communities. As a relational praxis of knowledge co-generation and a springboard for social action, participatory action research is a promising approach to engaging fathers in processes of personal and social transformation (Definney & Ball, in press).

Research questions are concerned with how to use policy tools and legislation to reduce barriers to positive father involvement and how to strengthen the capacity of community-based programs to reach out effectively to support men in becoming positively involved as fathers and in sustaining connections with their children over time and across changing circumstances. For example, in this volume, Strega and her colleagues present research findings pointing to the need to increase child welfare workers' awareness of fathers' rights to be included in child welfare decision making and to increase their readiness to assess fathers' potential to be resources for children who are subjects of child protection investigations. Also in this volume, McKay, Marshall, and Doucet examine the impacts of Canada's move to a father focus in parental leave policy on patterns of fathers' leave-taking and the duration of fathers' leave. And Beaton, Nicholas, McNeill, and Wenger discuss the potential of a family-centred model (McDaniel, Hepworth, & Doherty, 1992) and the Citizen Health Care Model (Mendenhall & Doherty, 2006) to support fathers of children with chronic health conditions, underscoring the need for policy reforms that can enable fathers to sustain involvement in caring for their ill children.

Understanding Similarities and Differences across Populations of Fathers

In 2003, a team of Canadian investigators and community partners joined together for the first nationally networked study of father involvement in Canada, with an explicit focus on diversity and social inclusion. Led by Daly and described by Daly, Ashbourne, and Brown (2009), the study investigated seven populations of fathers who had previously been underrepresented in theory, research, policy decisions, and father involvement promotion materials and programs: immigrant and refugee fathers; new fathers; young fathers; separated and divorced fathers; fathers of children with special needs; gay, bisexual, transgendered, and transsexual fathers; and Indigenous fathers. The findings indicate that fathers share some similar experiences when their child is at a particular stage in his or her development (e.g., infancy, school-aged, adolescence, and grown children) and when their relationship to their child's mother is in a similar state or stage (e.g., the transition to fatherhood, co-parenting in a co-residential union, co-parenting following union dissolution, lone parenting). These findings are discussed by co-investigators in this inaugural Canadian study (Ball, 2009; Daly et al., 2009; Devault, Dubeau, & Forget, 2009; Este & Tachble, 2009). However, the findings also underscore a need to conceptualize and respond programmatically to the unique needs, strengths, goals, and circumstances of fathers in specific subpopulations. Acknowledging the diversity of fathers is a first step toward a socially inclusive vision for father involvement initiatives that include the insights and perspectives of individuals, organizations, and communities outside of the cultural and structural mainstream (Long, 2007).

Visibility, Outreach, and Engagement: Father-Supportive Policies and Practices

While the characteristics of fathers and families in Canada are changing, the terrain of father involvement research and program outreach is also shifting to make fathers' experiences, needs, and goals more salient. Growing momentum among investigators, the legal community, and social service practitioners aims to reduce fathers' relative invisibility in family theory, family law, parent support initiatives, and programs for children, youth, and families. Efforts are being made to strengthen fathers' engagement, sense of empowerment, and resources so as to support them in making themselves and their contributions to caring for children more visible. The agenda includes an examination of men's reluctance to seek help and support. Some programs have emphasized the development of father-friendly resources. However, investigators and program developers have made little progress in understanding or breaking through men's apparent resistance to seeking help (Addis & Mahalik, 2003; Fagan & Palm, 2004; Statistics Canada, 2001) and their apparent tendency toward individualism compared to women's more collectivist or communal tendencies (Kaufman, 1993).

Pointing to shifting gender practices in parenting culture in Canada, Daly et al. (2009) emphasize the need to base programs of support for fathers on a recognition that the kinds of information and support men need and the kinds of programs to which they will respond are not likely to be the same as those for mothers. These investigators note that most fathering programs in Canada that are modelled after mothering programs usually have not been well attended. Furthermore, while many researchers focus on how fathers' involvement affects children, the investigators suggest that a more productive approach to understanding and reaching out to fathers might be turning the tables to look at how involvement with their children affects fathers. Based on a secondary analysis of data obtained from diverse populations of fathers in a national study, Daly et al. found that fathers of young children often talk about the importance of children for their own sense of growing maturity, responsibility, and engagement, and for learning about their emotions and how to deal with them in the contexts of their parenting activities. Fathers were also found to express regrets about a lack of time for their leisure and exercise. The findings of this study suggest that programs for fathers might be framed as ways for men to learn about their emotions and responses to parenting and to share their experiences with other fathers. Drawing on their own and others' research pointing to the positive effects of father involvement on fathers' mental health and self-concept, Daly et al. recommend that advocacy for Canadian government investment in fathering programs could effectively emphasize the salutary effects of positive father involvement on *fathers'* health, as much as on outcomes for children.

Developing policy and program supports for father involvement policy is the one means by which Canadian social values, norms, assumptions, laws, and institutional practices are propagated. Fathers are often overlooked as a specific population in demographic analysis, policy decision making, and child and family service programs. Fathers are nevertheless affected – directly or indirectly – by policies that govern, for example, their opportunities to engage with their newborn child, their access to information about their child, and the conditions of their engagement if their child is taken into protective custody or if their relationship with their child's mother dissolves. Exploratory studies, descriptive surveys, and policy analyses are beginning to examine how key contextual factors – such as family law, discussed by Whitehead and Bala in this volume, and provisions for parental leave, discussed by McKay, Marshall, and Doucet in this volume – affect fathers' involvement with their children from before birth and over time.

In 2006, a group of investigators undertook an inventory of policies in Canada that may shape fathers' rights, responsibilities, and opportunities for involvement with their children (Lero, Ashbourne, & Whitehead, 2006). The objectives were to explore how diverse populations of fathers in various social circumstances are affected by these policies and to stimulate public debate and scholarly analysis of how policies and practices might improve supports for Canadian fathers' involvement with their children. Recognizing the diversity of fathers in Canada with respect to economic, social, and familial circumstances, the policy analysts also examined how policies differentially affect particular subgroups of fathers. These authors concluded that fathers are all but invisible in government policies and programs in Canada, which tend to be oriented toward the well-being of mothers and children. The researchers found that policies and programs that do include fathers frequently make normative assumptions about the validity of cultural stereotypes of parenting, family life, sexuality, and children's needs that can hinder certain groups or populations of fathers from receiving the support they need to be positively involved in the lives of children (Lero et al., 2006).

Striking a similar chord, a survey of programs in Canada found that diverse populations of fathers remain in the outfield in terms of the reach of parent support and education programs (Devault, Gaudet, Bolté, & St-Denis, 2005). A study of parent education program curricula in British Columbia also found almost no specific mention of fathers or attribution of fathers' specific contributions to child care (Hodgins, 2007). When fathers are identified as co-caregivers with mothers, Hodgins found, they are often cast as helpers rather than primary caregivers.

Getting Beyond Mother-Centred Approaches to Fathers
The mother-centred lens through which families have been viewed throughout Euro-Western history has provided only a peripheral view of fathers (Broughton & Rogers, 2007; Lupton & Barclay, 1997; Pleck, 2004). Until recently, scant research has shed little light on how men in Canada approach fatherhood, on their experiences of becoming fathers, or on how they and their children are affected by the father-child relationship.

Critical resistance to mother-centrism in discourses, policies, and practices of parenting and father involvement dominates the work under way in Canada on fatherhood. The exclusive focus on maternal experience in the prenatal, antenatal, and postnatal periods, and on maternal contributions to infant and child development through mother-child health programs continually communicates to men that their role as father is negligible. The assumption that men need to learn the attitudes, skills, and forms of responsiveness thought to typify "the good mother" frames men's readiness for parenting – and their masculinity itself – as deficient with respect to fathers' positive contributions to their children's well-being. Among investigators in Canada who have taken up this issue, Bouchard and Lee (2000) and Doucet (2006) have addressed maternal influence on the father role (sometimes construed as maternal gatekeeping) and elucidated the tensions for fathers' involvement created by the interplay between hegemonic and subordinate masculinities. Expanding this critique to a deconstruction and unlearning of "the good mother" script may also be an important step toward getting beyond the constraining binary of mothering and fathering, and realizing new possibilities for positive parental involvement with children.

Reconceptualizing Masculinity: Gendered Constructions of Caring for Children

Expressions, meanings, and expectations associated with father involvement in Canada have shifted significantly away from sharply differentiated gender roles in which fathers are cast as breadwinners, protectors, and disciplinarians, and toward a less gender-specific set of expectations and encouragement of more direct involvement of fathers in practical caregiving and emotionally nurturing activities. Demographic trends – particularly rising rates of divorce and lone parenting and increased participation of mothers in the workforce – are transforming fathers' and mothers' understandings of fatherhood and placing new demands on fathers to become more involved in hands-on care of their children.

Within Canada's changing social contexts, many men are struggling to become involved fathers. Lacking identifiable and meaningful father role models (Daly, 1993), they must look for guidance to an array of sources, including past experiences of being fathered, family role models (including mothers and other women), media images, visions of family life co-created with their partners, and their own dreams, hesitations, and ability to respond to what their children bring into the father-child relationship. Doucet (2006) argues that a changing social discourse of involved fatherhood in Canada has not been mirrored by shifts in policy, and gender-differentiated roles therefore tend to be sustained even when parents aim for greater gender equity and non-traditional parenting styles.

Included in What?

An emphasis on social inclusion in Canadian father involvement research aims to reveal disparities between public and private experiences of fathering. However, when envisioning the broad ideal of social inclusion, we need to ask: "Included in what?" When relating this crucial question to father involvement, the concern is whether emerging concepts and programmatic approaches to encouraging father involvement reproduce prescriptive and outmoded images of fathers based on normative Euro-Western, heterosexual, gendered discourses of masculinity and parenting. Referring to US policy contexts, Coltrane (2007) warns that initiatives promoting father involvement may promulgate a particular narrow model of the family. A substantial amount of mass media in the US focuses attention on fatherhood and delivers a relatively homogeneous cultural message about what fatherhood means and how it is enacted, despite increasing evidence of the diversity of American fathers. Lupton and Barclay (1997) caution that most parenting interventions draw from a body of research that "provides a highly normative perspective on fatherhood by advocating appropriate behaviours in men and identifying those who fail to fit the ideal of the involved father" (51). Images of the good father who looks the part of a representative of the dominant culture, who is a steady wage earner, and who cheerfully takes his cues from his child's mother as to when, where, and how to be involved with his child prevail.

The experience of a First Nation man who participated in Ball's study of Aboriginal fathers described in Chapter 6 underscores this point. He said: "I hide my tattoos and take my biker clothes down a notch when I'm picking my son up from daycare and know I'll be seen on the street with him, or else people look at me as if they suspect I kidnapped someone else's kid." This self-disclosure, variously echoed in several chapters in this volume, conveys how much fatherhood – or at least "ordinary" heterosexual, dominant-culture fatherhood – is experienced by some men as a heavily prescribed performance. While Canadian society is opening to the fact that no universally valid way of "doing fatherhood" exists, this expansion of possibilities for how to father brings with it ambivalence and nostalgia for a seemingly simpler time when the concept of fatherhood admitted a narrower range of possibilities. Recognition of diversity and the right to social inclusion by a wide variety of fathers offers new opportunities for Canadian children and families, but it also raises new questions, controversies, and dilemmas such as those discussed by Doucet and Hawkins in this volume. For example, how does father involvement in care activities expand our traditional thinking about feminized care activities? What practices of care do fathers participate in? To what extent are fathers engaged in critically resisting normative gendered discourses of parenthood and hegemonic masculinity?

Gender Binaries and the (De)construction of the Essential Father
A question of acute importance to the father involvement field is raised by Hodgins (2011). In response to an assertion by Hearn (2002), she observes that "the importance of fathers' involvement is often couched in terms of fathers' essential and uniquely male role in parenting" (109). Citing several policy examples that rely on the construction of fathers as essential, Hodgins asks: "What form of masculinity is envisioned in this essential, uniquely

male parent? Are fathers who are gay, bisexual or transgendered, or those who do not like sports or rough and tumble play, part of this vision?" (109)

As Hodgins notes, deconstructing the essential father is not necessarily welcomed by the father involvement field. Nevertheless, while fathers unquestionably can be important contributors to child development, a dearth of evidence exists that they are essential to children's optimal growth and development (Silverstein & Auerbach, 1999). Arguably, mothers are not "essential" either; rather, it is the presence of caring adults in a child's life and the attributes of the primary caregiver(s), rather than their gender, that are critical to child outcomes. The instability of the constructed "ordinary father" and the realization that children can thrive in a variety of family constellations have the potential to disrupt many social policies and institutions in Canada.

Drawing on recommendations made by Richmond and Saloojee (2005) to develop a made-in-Canada approach to social inclusion that is policy relevant, Long (2007) suggests that a fundamentally new way to think about men in Canadian society is needed. This new way begins with listening to fathers' stories in research that reaches across cultures and involves "insiders" as well as "outsiders" of population groups in sharing a basic respect for the integrity, autonomy, and uniqueness of fathers and diverse communities. Research by Doucet (2006) involving 118 Canadian fathers in primary caregiving roles with their children illustrates this approach. According to Doucet, these fathers' accounts "are filled with visible and inchoate contradictions, which tell how fathers are both determined to distance themselves from the feminine but are also, in practice, radically revisioning masculine care and ultimately our understanding of masculinities" (237). These reconceptualizations of masculinity draw attention to a need for critical masculinity studies, for as Hodgins (2011) points out, "while multiple forms of masculinity exist, they are not all equal in their persuasion or dominance" (110). For example, despite Canadians' awareness of and relative sensitivity to diverse embodiments of masculinity and fatherhood, policy and program initiatives in Canada still tend to ignore or discount the diverse needs and circumstances of disadvantaged fathers, especially Indigenous, immigrant and refugee, and gay, bisexual, and transmasculine fathers.

Challenging Heteronormative Thinking

Some gay fathers and fathers who sometimes refer to themselves as "queer" vividly illustrate both the expanding possibilities for enacting masculinity in Canada and the power differentials that exist among varying forms of masculinity. The twenty-first century has brought unprecedented legal and social recognition to men living in same-sex family structures as common-law or married partners. In addition to the right to be legally married, most provinces have opened doors for men to adopt children. In Toronto, parent education courses called "Daddies and Papas 2B" and "Trans Fathers 2B" are consistently oversubscribed (Veldhoven & Vernon, 2009; Ware, 2009). At the same time, Prince Edward Island continues to limit adoption to heterosexual parents. In some school districts, such as Surrey, British Columbia, educators must fight for the right to have non-traditional family structures represented in school libraries (Smith, 2004). And Epstein (2009) and the other authors of *Who's Your Daddy* – a landmark collection of writings by Canadian gay, lesbian, bisexual, transgendered, and queer (GLBTQ) parents and their grown children – describe how GLBTQ parents and their children feel and respond to social and, in some cases, legal pressure to present a sanitized and essentially heteronormative portrait of their family life.

What insights can be gleaned from the experiences of queer fathers with respect to the ways in which they approach masculinity in the context of raising children? What can we learn from their children's experiences and developmental outcomes? While little research has focused on these questions, Stacey and Biblarz (2001; Biblarz & Stacey, 2010) report research findings suggesting that compared to children of heterosexual parents, children of lesbian and gay parents show higher self-esteem, better mental health, better communication with parents, more empathy toward social diversity, and less traditional gender stereotyping. Their research is provocative and can stimulate exploration of new frontiers in research, theory, policy, and family law. Similarly, *Who's Your Daddy?* provokes scholars and practitioners to push beyond the binaries and boundaries of heteronormative thinking about parenting. There is a need to focus research on gay and transgendered fathers and their children, given that most research about non-heterosexual parents has focused on lesbian mothers. Such research would enable an examination of the intersection and influence of gender identity and sexual identity on parenting and on children's own constructions of gender roles with respect to caring for children.

Father-Supporting Initiatives

Despite the growing momentum in father involvement research and advocacy, and some evidence of increasing father involvement, fathers remain a vastly untapped resource for promoting children's optimal health and development. Fathers continue to be portrayed in Canadian media in ways that ignore or denigrate them or that relegate them to the role of provider. Community services such as child health and early development programs tend to overlook them, focusing only on mothers. Fathers have little support for gaining the skills they need to be positively and effectively involved as their children grow and develop. Relatively little dedicated funding and few formal policies specifically address outreach and support for father involvement. In Canada, no controlled research studies have been conducted to assess the impacts of community-level or individually focused interventions designed to promote positive father involvement. As Pruett, Cowan, Cowan, and Pruett (2009) comment with reference to US research, in contrast with the research literature on father involvement, little investment has been made in outcome research on father involvement programs. Father-focused practice in community programs is just beginning to gain momentum; some provincial governments have allocated small amounts of funding for training and employment of father outreach and support workers in community-based family resource centres, child development centres, and community health promotion programs. Canadian practitioners working on family services and early childhood programs are currently seeking leadership and direction in discerning effective practices and informing policy supports.

Obstacles to providing socially inclusive services for fathers in Canada have included a lack of referral systems and information networks. Over ten years ago, Taylor, Brown, and Beauregard (1999) observed that fathers, practitioners, volunteers, and investigators craved opportunities to share information and actively support father involvement. However, they noted that "across Canada, people who do innovative work with fathers remain isolated from one another" (134). To counter that isolation, several key coalitions have formed in the past decade to raise fathers' visibility, share and mobilize knowledge, and lobby governments to create new policies, reform existing ones, and invest in father involvement initiatives. Key organizations and initiatives are described below.

ProsPère

A pioneering organization in Canada that combined research, advocacy, clearing house, and training for staff in community-based programs was ProsPère. This Québec-based network operated from 1993 to 2010 as a coalition of researchers focused on father involvement as a protection against child victimization. Their early research led to other studies, all conducted in partnerships with communities; to the development of a new tool to assess salient dimensions of father-child relationships; and to a series of training workshops for staff of community-based agencies that were well positioned to reach out to fathers.

Father Involvement Research Alliance (FIRA)

Much of the recent research on father involvement in Canada has been produced by investigators across the country working in a variety of disciplines and networked through the coalition Father Involvement Research Alliance (FIRA; www.fira.ca). Created in 2004, FIRA brings together an array of scholars, community-based practitioners, policy-makers, funders, and fathers who contribute unique and sometimes divergent perspectives, resources, practice experience, and research activity in support of FIRA's goals:

(a) to create a vital, sustainable network of people interested in enhancing father involvement; (b) to increase Canadian research and knowledge on father involvement; (c) to inform public decision making, community development, and policy development; and (d) to develop tools, resources, and training to be used in practice. The FIRA website functions as the main clearing house in Canada for resources and research reports on father involvement. FIRA has supported community capacity-building projects, the first national conference on father involvement (Hoffman, 2008), and a project to enhance post-secondary training in community engagement focused on fathers. It has been active in bringing forward policy recommendations through provincial and federal round tables, consultations, and expert advisory committees.

Dad Central Ontario (Formerly Father Involvement Initiative – Ontario Network)

Formed in 1997, the Father Involvement Initiative – Ontario Network (now Dad Central Ontario) (www.dadcentral.ca) was the first provincially based coalition of organizations and individuals that joined together to consolidate and mobilize knowledge about father involvement, with a focus on fathers of young children (0-6 years). The network takes a population health approach, emphasizing broad-based community engagement and diversity. Its goal is to be a catalyst for acknowledging and supporting fathers' involvement in the development of healthy and resilient children. To achieve this goal, FII-ON creates partnerships among various stakeholders, including fathers, mothers, service providers, policy and decision makers, employers and the business sector, labour organizations, professional associations, community-based coalitions, government, academic institutions, and the media. FII-ON recognizes that the individual and collective efforts of network partners are as diverse as the communities in which they are located. To create a sense of common purpose and approach across diverse stakeholders, FII-ON is guided by the following principles: child first, importance of both parents, responsible father involvement, social responsibility, diversity, empowerment, collaboration, and sustainability. Actions undertaken by FII-ON are decentralized and variously funded. They include community development, community capacity building, social marketing, creation of partnerships, knowledge development, and educational activities.

Father Involvement Network – British Columbia

Father Involvement Network – British Columbia (FIN-BC; www.bccf.ca/node/24) was formed within the BC Council for Families in 2006. It is the second province-based network of organizations and individuals supporting father involvement. It aims to replicate key functions of FII-ON, though on a smaller scale, reflecting the smaller constituency in British Columbia, a smaller budget, and a shorter history. There are promising signs that similar networking approaches may emerge in other provinces and territories.

Transforming the Landscape of Father Involvement in Canada

To what extent do current policies and community programs attempt to unsettle dominant European-heritage, heterosexist discourses of fatherhood and masculinity? Do new and competing discourses about fatherhood support fathers and practitioners who wish to critically resist dominant discourses of masculinity and parenting? How do the ways in which Canadian policy analysts and practitioners think about supports for fathers reproduce narrow visions of functional families, healthy parenting, and responsible father involvement? Do fathers' goals and needs even register in practitioner training or in health and social service planning for children and families? The chapters that follow explore some of these questions.

Canadian investigators are working to understand the myriad pathways that fathers in Canada are forging in pursuit of their personal goals for involvement with their children. One promise of the socially inclusive stance taken by Canadian investigators who are joining the movement to conceptualize fathers' experiences and enhance their visibility is the potential for a nuanced, contextualized, post-structural understanding that recognizes the intersectionality of gender and notions of caring for children with realities of ethnicity, immigration status, economic status, sexuality, and other factors. This differentiated and contextualized understanding, springing from research that engages fathers themselves, can help to disrupt some of the dominant theories that tend to portray father involvement as a normative and monolithic experience. At the same time, these new understandings should militate against the hegemonic exposition of "best practices" – as if practices with proven effectiveness with one population of fathers and families could be expected to have similar meanings and impact with other populations in different contexts. Ultimately, these contextualized understandings will contribute to a transformative approach to social inclusion that admits multiple forms of positive father involvement and numerous ways to support diverse fathers in Canada.

Notes

1 Statistics Canada surveys restrict the definition of a family member to those occupying the same dwelling, reflecting a notion of family as people living together over time. This definition fails to capture familial bonds of parents living apart from their children due to work, separation and divorce, incarceration, institutionalization, child welfare, homelessness, and other conditions. Changes in the ways Canada counts family members are recommended by Ravanera and Hoffman in this volume.

2 Limitations in the measurement of domestic violence are beyond the scope of the current discussion, but particularly likely sources of underestimation are reluctance to report domestic violence, emotional violence, and violence occurring to partners who are no longer co-resident.

References

Addis, M., & Mahalik, J. R. (2003). Men, masculinity, and the contexts of help seeking. *American Psychologist, 58*(1), 5-14.

Allen, S. M., & Hawkins, A. J. (1999). Maternal gatekeeping: Mothers' beliefs and behaviors that inhibit greater father involvement in family work. *Journal of Marriage and the Family, 61*(1), 199-212.

Amato, R. (1998). More than money? Men's contributions to their children's lives. In A. Booth & A. Crouter (Eds.), *Men in families: When do they get involved? What difference does it make?* (pp. 241-278). Mahwah, NJ: Lawrence Erlbaum.

Ball, J. (2009). Indigenous fathers' involvement in reconstituting "circles of care." *American Journal of Community Psychology, 45*(1-2), 124-138.

Biblarz, T. J., & Stacey, J. (2010). How does the gender of parents matter? *Journal of Marriage and Family, 72*, 3-22.

Bouchard, G., & Lee, C. M. (2000). The marital context for father involvement with their preschool children: The role of partner support. *Journal of Prevention and Intervention in the Community, 20*(1-2), 37-53.

Bronfenbrenner, U. (1979). *The ecology of human development: Experiments by nature and design.* Cambridge, MA: Harvard University Press.

Bronfenbrenner, U. (1986). Ecology of the family as a context for human development. *Developmental Psychology, 22*, 723-742.

Broughton, T. L., & Rogers, H. (2007). Introduction: The empire of the father. In T. L. Broughton & H. Rogers (Eds.), *Gender and fatherhood in the nineteenth century* (pp. 1-42). New York, NY: Palgrave Macmillan.

Cannon, E. A., Schoppe-Sullivan, S., Mangelsdorf, S. C., Brown, G. O., & Sokolowski, M. S. (2009). Parent characteristics as antecedents of maternal gatekeeping and fathering behavior. *Family Process, 47*(4), 501-519.

Coltrane, S. (2007). Fathering: Paradoxes, contradictions, and dilemmas. In M. Kimmel & M. Messner (Eds.), *Men's Lives* (7th ed., pp. 448-465). Boston, MA: Pearson.

Daly, K. (1993). Reshaping fatherhood: Finding the models. *Journal of Family Issues, 14*(4), 510-530.

Daly, K., Ashbourne, L., & Brown, J. L. (2009). Fathers' perceptions of children's influence: Implications for involvement. *The Annals of the American Academy of Political and Social Science, 624*, 61-77.

Day, R. D., & Lamb, M. E. (2004). Conceptualizing and measuring father involvement: Pathways, problems and progress. In R. D. Day & M. E. Lamb (Eds.), *Conceptualizing and measuring father involvement* (pp. 1-15). Mahwah, NJ: Lawrence Erlbaum.

Definney, S., & Ball, J. (in press). Participatory action research: Praxis for social change. In A. Devault, G. Forget, & D. Dubeau (Eds.), *Fathering: Building and sharing knowledge through participatory research.* Ottawa, ON: University of Ottawa Press.

Devault, A., Dubeau, D., & Forget, G. (2009). *La paternité au XXIe siècle* [Fatherhood in the twenty-first century]. Laval, QC: Les Presses de l'Université Laval.

Devault, A., Gaudet, J., Bolté, C., & St-Denis, M. (2005). A survey and description of projects that support and promote fathering in Canada: Still work to do to reach fathers in their real-life settings. *Canadian Journal of Community Mental Health, 24*(1), 5-17.

Devault, A., Milcent, M., Ouellet, F., Laurin, I., Jauron, M., & Lacharite, C. (2008). Life stories of young fathers in contexts of vulnerability. *Fathering, 6*(3), 226-248.

Doherty, W. J. (2000). Family science and family citizenship: Towards a model of community partnership with families. *Family Relations, 49*, 319-325.

Doucet, A. (2006). *Do men mother? Fathering, care and domestic responsibility.* Toronto, ON: University of Toronto Press.

Doucet, A. (2009). Dad and baby in the first year: Gendered responsibilities and embodiment. *The Annals of the American Academy of Political and Social Science, 624*, 78-98.

Dutton, D. G., & Nicholls, T. (2005). The gender paradigm in domestic violence research and theory: Part 1 – The conflict of theory and data. *Aggression and Violent Behavior, 10*(6), 680-714.

Epstein, R. (Ed.). (2009). *Who's your daddy? And other writings on queer parenting*. Toronto, ON: Sumach Press.

Este, D. C., & Tachble, A. A. (2009). The perceptions and experiences of Russian immigrant and Sudanese refugee men as fathers in an urban center in Canada. *The Annals of the American Academy of Political and Social Science, 624,* 139-155.

Fagan, J., & Palm, G. (2004). *Fathers and early childhood programs*. Clifton Park, NY: Delmar Learning.

Flouri, E., & Buchanan, A. (2003). The role of father involvement in children's later mental health. *Adolescence, 26*(1), 63-78.

Fraser, N. (1994). After the family wage: Gender equity and the welfare state. *Political Theory, 22*(4), 591-618.

Gaunt, R. (2008). Maternal gatekeeping: Antecedents and consequences. *Journal of Family Issues, 29*(3), 373-395.

Grandin, E., Lupri, E., & Brinkerhoff, M. B. (1998). Couple violence and psychological distress. *Canadian Journal of Public Health, 89*(1), 43-47.

Hearn, J. (2002). Men, fathers and the state: National and global relations. In B. Hobson (Ed.), *Making men into fathers: Men, masculinities and the social politics of fatherhood* (pp. 245-272). Cambridge, England: Cambridge University Press.

Hodgins, B. D. (2007). *Father involvement in parenting young children: A content analysis of parent education programs in British Columbia*. Unpublished master's project, University of Victoria, Victoria, BC. Retrieved from the Early Childhood Development Intercultural Partnerships website: http://www.ecdip.org/docs/pdf/B.D.%20Hodgins%20Masters%20Project%20Write-up.pdf.

Hodgins, B. D. (2011). Father involvement initiatives: Social inclusion or the (re)construction of hegemonic masculinity? In A. Pence & J. White (Eds.), *Critical perspectives in child and youth care* (pp. 95-117). Vancouver, BC: UBC Press.

Hoffman, J. (2008). *Father involvement research 2008: Diversity community visibility conference report*. Retrieved from the Father Involvement Research Alliance website: http://www.fira.ca/cms/documents/200/Father_Involvement_Research_2008_Conference_Report.pdf

Karambayya, R., & Reilly, A. (1992). Dual earner couples: Attitudes and actions in restricting work for family. *Journal of Organizational Behavior, 13*(1), 585-601.

Kaufman, M. (1993). *Cracking the armour: Power, pain, and the lives of men*. Toronto, ON: Penguin.

Kershaw, P., Pulkingham, J., & Fuller, S. (2008). Expanding the subject: Violence, care and (in)active male citizenship. *Social Politics International, 15*(2), 182-206.

Kishchuk, N. (2001). *Case studies of the regional mobilization of population health: Final report*. Ottawa, ON: Health Canada, Populations and Public Health Branch.

Lamb, M. E. (1997). Fathers and child development: An introductory overview and guide. In M. E. Lamb (Ed.), *The role of the father in child development* (3rd ed., pp. 1-18). New York, NY: John Wiley.

Lamb, M. E. (Ed.). (2004). *The role of the fathers in child development* (4th ed.). Hoboken, NJ: John Wiley.

Lero, D., Ashbourne, L., & Whitehead, D. (2006). *Inventory of policies and policy areas influencing father involvement*. Guelph, ON: Father Involvement Research Alliance.

Long, D. (2007). *All dads matter: Towards an inclusive vision of father involvement initiatives in Canada*. Guelph, ON: Father Involvement Research Alliance. Retrieved from http://www.fira.ca/cms/documents/176/April7.Long.PDF

Lupton, D., & Barclay, L. (1997). *Constructing fatherhood: Discourses and experiences*. London, England: Sage.

Marshall, K. (2006). Converging gender roles. *Perspectives on Labour and Income, 7*(7), 5-17. Statistics Canada – Catalogue no. 75-001-XPE.

Marshall, K. (2009). The family work week. *Perspectives on Labour and Income, 10*(4), 5-13. Statistics Canada – Catalogue no. 75-001-X.

Marsiglio, W., & Cohan, M. (2000). Contextualizing father involvement and paternal influence. *Marriage and Family Review, 29*(2-3), 75-95.

Maxwell, J. (1997). Parenting families in the 1990s: Parenting and the global economy. *Canada's Children: Child Welfare League of Canada*, (Autumn), 7-10.

McDaniel, S., Hepworth, J., & Doherty, W. J. (Eds.). (1992). *Medical family therapy: A biopsychosocial approach to families with health problems.* New York, NY: Basic Books.

Mendenhall, T. J., & Doherty, W. J. (2006). Citizen health care: A model for engaging patients, families, and communities as coproducers of health. *Families, Systems, and Health, 24*(3), 251-263.

Palkovitz, R. (1997). Reconstructing "involvement": Expanding conceptualizations of men's caring. In A. J. Hawkins & D. C. Dollahite (Eds.), *Generative fathering: Beyond deficit perspectives* (pp. 201-216). Thousand Oaks, CA: Sage.

Palkovitz, R. (2002). Involved fathering and child development: Advancing our understanding of good fathering. In C. S. Tamis-LeMonda and N. Cabrera (Eds.), *Handbook of father involvement: Multidisciplinary perspectives* (pp. 119-140). Mahwah, NJ: Lawrence Erlbaum.

Parke, R. D. (2004). Fathers, families and the future: A plethora of plausible predictions. *Merrill-Palmer Quarterly, 50*(4), 456-470.

Pleck, J. H. (1979, October). Men's family work: Three perspectives and some new data. *Family Coordinator, 28,* 481-488.

Pleck, J. H. (2004). Two dimensions of fatherhood: A history of the good dad–bad dad complex. In M. E. Lamb (Ed.), *The role of the father in child development* (4th ed., pp. 32-57). Hoboken, NJ: John Wiley.

Pruett, M. K., Cowan, C. P., Cowan, A., & Pruett, K. (2009). Lessons learned from the Supporting Father Involvement Study: A cross-cultural preventive intervention for low-income families with young children. *Journal of Social Service Research, 35*(2), 163-179.

Richmond, T., & Saloojee, A. (Eds.). (2005). *Social inclusion: Canadian perspectives.* Black Point, NS: Fernwood.

Roopnarine, J. L. (2004). African American and African Caribbean fathers: Levels, quality, and meaning of involvement. In M. E. Lamb (Ed.), *The role of the father in child development* (4th ed., pp. 58-97). Hoboken, NJ: John Wiley.

Schoppe-Sullivan, S. J., Brown, G. L., Cannon, E. A., Mangelsdorf, S. C., & Szewczyk Sokolowski, M. (2008). Maternal gatekeeping, coparenting quality, and fathering behavior in families with infants. *Journal of Family Psychology, 22*(3), 389-398.

Schoppe-Sullivan, S. J., McBride, B. A., & Ho, M. R. (2004). Unidimensional versus multidimensional perspectives on father involvement. *Fathering, 2*(2), 147-163.

Silverstein, L., & Auerbach, C. (1999). Deconstructing the essential father. *American Psychologist, 54*(6), 397–407.

Smith, M. (2004). Questioning heteronormativity: Lesbian and gay challenges to education practice in British Columbia, Canada. *Social Movement Studies, 3*(2), 131-145.

Stacey, J., & Biblarz, T. J. (2001). (How) does the sexual orientation of parents matter? *American Sociological Review, 66,* 159-183.

Statistics Canada. (2001). *Census of the population.* Ottawa, ON: Author.

Statistics Canada. (2005). *General Social Survey – Victimization.* Cycle 18: An overview of findings (Catalogue no. 85-565-XIE). Ottawa, ON: Author.

Statistics Canada. (2006a). *General Social Survey – Family.* Cycle 20. Ottawa, ON: Author.

Statistics Canada. (2006b). *The General Social Survey: Overview of the time use of Canadians.* Ottawa, ON: Author.

Statistics Canada. (2006c). *Persons in same-sex unions by broad age groups and sex for males, 2006 counts, for Canada, provinces and territories – 20% sample data.* Ottawa, ON: Author.

Statistics Canada. (2007). *Participation and activity limitation survey* (Catalogue no. 89-628-ZIE-No. 003) Ottawa, ON: Author.

Statistics Canada. (2008). *Labour force historical review* (Catalogue no. 71F0004XCB). Ottawa, ON: Author.

Statistics Canada. (2009). *Income trends in Canada 1976-2007* (Catalogue no. 13F0022XIE). Ottawa, ON: Author.

Stone, L. (1994). *Dimensions of the job-family tension.* Ottawa, ON: Statistics Canada.

Tamis-LeMonda, C. S., & Cabrera, N. (2002). Handbook of father involvement: Multi-disciplinary perspectives. Mahwah, NJ: Lawrence Erlbaum.

Taylor, A., Brown, F., & Beauregard, B. (1999). Engaging fathers in becoming involved with their children. In E. Lowe (Ed.), *Linking research to practice: Second Canadian forum* (pp. 130-135). Ottawa, ON: Canadian Child Care Federation.

Veldhoven, C., & Vernon, T. (2009). Daddies and Papa 2B: The evolution of possibilities. In R. Epstein (Ed.), *Who's your daddy? And other writings on queer parenting* (pp. 53-64). Toronto, ON: Sumach Press.

Ware, S. M. (2009). Boldly going where few men have gone before: One trans man's experience. In R. Epstein (Ed.), *Who's your daddy? And other writings on queer parenting* (pp. 65-72). Toronto, ON: Sumach Press.

Watson, W. J., Watson, L., Wetzel, W., Bader, E., & Talbot, Y. (1995). Transition to parenthood. Canadian Family Physician, *41*, 807-812.

2
Canadian Fathers: Demographic and Socio-Economic Profiles from Census and National Surveys

Zenaida R. Ravanera and John Hoffman

One hundred years ago, an appropriate and adequate definition of a father would have been "a biological male parent living with his children." However, recent changes in families precipitated by factors such as high rates of divorce and increased rates of child-bearing and parenting outside of marriage have broadened the realities of Canadian fatherhood considerably. In some family arrangements, biological and custodial roles of fathers are no longer filled by the same person (Cabrera, Tamis-LeMonda, Bradley, Hofferth, & Lamb, 2000; King, 1999; Marsiglio, Amato, Day, & Lamb, 2000).

Significant shifts in fathers' roles and working patterns have also been influenced by changes in the lives of women. Specifically, women are better educated, work outside the home more often, and earn much higher incomes than in the past. For example, in 2001, 58% of university graduates were female (Frenette & Zeman, 2007), a trend that has almost certainly contributed to the steady rise in the proportion of mothers who work outside the home. In 2005, 69% of husband/wife families with children under 16 had both parents in the workforce compared to 39% in 1976 (Marshall, 2006). Currently almost three out of ten women in dual-earner families out-earn their husbands, up from 11% in 1967 (Sussman & Bonnell, 2006). These changes in the earning and caring patterns of mothers have contributed to an evolution in men's activities at home, including the roles they take on as fathers. More fathers are doing unpaid child care and domestic work (Marshall, 2006), and increasing numbers of men are taking on the role of stay-at-home parent. In 1976, only 4% of Canada's stay-at-home parents were fathers. By 2008, this number had risen to 10% (Statistics Canada, 2009).

Thus far, changes in families have been studied primarily from the perspective of women's experiences. Parenting norms and domestic activities have also changed for men, yet Canada has produced very little in the way of demographic and other quantitative research on fathers. This chapter presents a demographic and socio-economic profile of Canadian fathers using the information that is available from the Canadian census and other national surveys. This profile includes data on the number of Canadian fathers, the age at which men become fathers, differences between fathers and non-fathers, fathers' time use, the social and economic advantages of fatherhood, and selected data on subpopulations of fathers for whom data are available. These subpopulations include Aboriginal fathers, lone fathers, immigrant fathers, divorced and separated fathers, and young fathers.

How Many Fathers Are There?

Perhaps the most salient piece of demographic information about Canadian fathers is that, given the way data are currently gathered through the Canadian census, no one can say for sure how many Canadian men are fathers. The census does not ask respondents if they have children; rather, it asks how many people live within the household, including dependent children (Statistics Canada, 2001).[1]

Until 1991, the decennial censuses in Canada asked women to report the number of children to whom they had given birth. However, this question was dropped from the 2001 Canadian census, and it was not asked in the 2011 census (Statistics Canada, 2008a, 14). No census has asked men a similar question on the number of children they have biologically fathered. This makes identifying and counting fathers a surprisingly challenging and complex task, which is further complicated by the diversity of fathering in the new millennium. Today's fathers are not just biological, adoptive, and stepfathers; they are also fathers in blended families, men who have children in common-law relationships, gay fathers with or without partners or co-parents, single fathers (in increasing numbers), men who have fathered children with multiple partners, and increasingly, divorced and separated fathers, some of whom live with their children part-time.

One consequence of these changes in families is that increasing numbers of fathers do not live with their children full-time, and, as noted earlier, men who live apart from their children are essentially invisible as fathers in census data. Under the current method of data collection, in which respondents are not asked whether they have children but rather if they live with children, a non-custodial, divorced, biological father would not be counted as a father in census terms. Meanwhile, an unmarried man who has never sired children automatically becomes a "census father" when he takes up residence with a woman with children.

These concerns notwithstanding, in terms of constructing a demographic profile of Canadian fathers with information from the most recent (2006) Canadian census, we are restricted to the de facto census definition of a father: a man living with his own or his partner's dependent children. Although the census includes men of all ages, the fathers we profile are men aged 15 to 64 living with children under the age of 25.

Table 2.1

Living arrangements of all men aged 15 to 64 and marital status of fathers, by age groups, 2006

	15-19		20-29		30-39		40-49		50-64		Total 15-64	
	Number[a]	%	Number	%	Number	%	Number	%	Number	%	Number	%
Living arrangements of men												
Living with children under 25	5,735	0.5	226,740	11.4	1,071,845	52.6	1,592,765	63.1	928,565	31.9	3,825,645	36.3
Not living with children under 25	1,082,720	99.5	1,764,380	88.6	964,965	47.4	929,860	36.9	1,984,240	68.1	6,726,170	63.7
Total	1,088,455	100.0	1,991,120	100.0	2,036,810	100.0	2,522,625	100.0	2,912,805	100.0	10,551,815	100.0
Marital arrangements of fathers												
Married	1,000	17.4	113,390	50.0	809,405	75.5	1,294,920	81.3	797,050	85.8	3,015,760	78.8
Common-law	2,000	34.8	98,590	43.5	220,820	20.6	200,140	12.6	73,510	7.9	595,060	15.6
Lone	2,740	47.7	14,760	6.5	41,620	3.9	97,705	6.1	58,005	6.2	214,830	5.6
Total	5,735	100.0	226,740	100.0	1,071,845	100.0	1,592,765	100.0	928,565	100.0	3,825,645	100.0

a To prevent the possibility of associating small figures with any identifiable individual, numbers are rounded to multiples of 5. Totals are independently rounded; thus, some totals do not necessarily equal the sum of individual rounded figures.

Source: From Statistics Canada, 2010, "Census of Population, 2006 [Canada]: Public Use Microdata File, Hierarchical File" [machine readable data file] (Ottawa, ON: Statistics Canada [producer(s)], Statistics Canada, Data Liberation Initiative [distributor(s)]).

According to the 2006 Canadian census (Statistics Canada, 2010) there are approximately 3.8 million fathers in Canada, or 36% of all men aged 15 to 64 (see Table 2.1). The highest proportion of fathers (at 63%) is in the 40 to 49 age group. Many men under 40 would not yet have fathered children, and most children of men 50 and older would have already left home to live independently. The majority of fathers (79%) are married; 16% are in a common-law relationship, and 6% are lone fathers. The increasing trend in cohabitation is reflected in the differences by age group in the proportion cohabiting: 44% of fathers aged 20 to 29 live common-law compared to only 8% of those aged 50 to 64. While young fathers in common-law relationships may eventually marry their partners, these increasing rates of cohabiting fathers are likely to manifest themselves in older age groups in the future.

At What Age Do Men Become Fathers?

Men become parents about three to four years later in life than women do. According to the Canadian 2001 General Social Survey (Statistics Canada, 2002) (see Table 2.2), men born between 1966 and 1970 became fathers, on average, at the age of 32.4, whereas women born in the same period had their first child at approximately 28 years of age. Over the past 30 years, the age at which men enter fatherhood has gradually increased. Men born between 1941 and 1945, for example, became fathers at an average age of 28.5 years, almost four years younger than men born in the late 1960s. This trend for more recent cohorts to enter parenthood at an older age follows from

Table 2.2

Median age at birth of first child, by five-year birth cohorts

Birth cohort	Men	Women
1926-30	28.4	25.2
1931-35	28.1	24.3
1936-40	27.7	23.6
1941-45	28.5	23.8
1946-50	28.7	25.1
1951-55	30.2	26.2
1956-60	30.5	26.7
1961-65	30.9	27.1
1966-70	32.4	27.8

Source: Adapted from "Young Canadians' Family Formation: Variations in Delayed Start and Complex Pathways," by Z. R. Ravanera, F. Rajulton, and T. K. Burch, 2005, *PSC Discussion Papers Series, 19*(1), Table 2, which is based on Statistics Canada, 2002, "General Social Survey, Cycle 15, 2001 [Canada]: Family History, Main File" [machine readable data file] (Ottawa, ON: Statistics Canada [producer(s)], Statistics Canada, Data Liberation Initiative [distributor(s)]).

the increasing age at which Canadians experience other significant life events. For example, compared to men born in the mid-twentieth century, men born in the 1960s and 1970s started regular employment, left their parental homes, and entered into cohabitation or marriage at later ages (Ravanera, Rajulton, & Burch, 2006).

However, as Table 2.2 shows, the increase in age of first paternity (and maternity) has not always been a steady one. Men born between 1936 and 1940 became fathers at an average age of 27.7, a little more than half a year younger than their counterparts born ten years earlier and almost a year younger than men born in the next half decade (1941-45). Still, the parents who were born between 1926 and 1945 had more children and had them at younger ages than their own children did, and the age of first parenthood continued to increase with each subsequent generation (Beaujot, 2000; Ravanera, Rajulton, & Burch, 2005b, 2006). Socio-economic factors are often cited as reasons for the later ages of transitions to adulthood, including the transition to parenthood. The need for higher education, and thus a longer period spent in school, and the difficulty in having a stable job are constraints to marrying and to having children at an early age (Beaujot, Ravanera, & Burch, 2007).

Employment, Education, and Socio-Economic Status of Fathers and Non-Fathers

As Table 2.3 shows, fathers tend to be better off socio-economically than their childless counterparts. Fathers have higher median incomes than non-fathers and are also more likely than non-fathers to have a university education (29% vs. 19%), work mainly full-time (90% vs. 63%), and own their home (82% vs. 70%).

However, a comparison of socio-economic status between fathers (defined as living with children less than 25 years of age) and non-fathers is best done for particular age groups, since both socio-economic factors and the likelihood of living with children are influenced by one's age. For example, Table 2.3 shows that fathers are more likely than non-fathers to have a university education (29% vs. 19%), but that gap is accounted for primarily by the education levels of older fathers. In the 20 to 29 age group, non-fathers are almost twice as likely as fathers to have a university education. In the 30 to 39 age group, rates of university education are about the same for fathers and non-fathers, while in subsequent age groups (40-49 and 50-64) fathers are increasingly more likely to have a university education than non-fathers. The age group with the highest proportion of men living with children (63% in Table 2.1) is 40-49. In this age group, fathers have higher incomes than non-fathers ($49,000 vs. $36,000) and are more likely to have a university education (28% vs. 20%), to work full-time (92% vs. 81%), and to own their homes (85% vs. 65%).

Table 2.3

Socio-economic characteristics of men, by age groups and fatherhood status, 2006

Socio-economic characteristics	15-19		20-29		30-39		40-49		50-64		All Ages	
	Non-fathers	Fathers	Non-fathers	Fathers	Non-fathers	Fathers	Non-fathers	Fathers	Non-fathers	Fathers	Non-fathers	Fathers
Education (%)[a]												
No diploma or degree	67.2	61.7	13.4	23.4	12.6	12.5	19.7	14.1	22.6	14.9	25.6	14.5
High school	28.6	24.0	37.1	30.1	23.8	21.7	24.8	21.8	22.3	21.2	27.8	22.1
Trade, apprenticeship, college	3.8	11.7	28.9	35.0	32.0	36.1	35.2	36.0	33.8	30.3	27.6	34.6
University or higher	0.4	2.6	20.6	11.6	31.5	29.7	20.2	28.1	21.3	33.6	19.1	28.8
Work status (%)												
Worked mainly full-time	15.4	41.9	67.9	87.8	83.1	92.0	80.5	91.5	66.0	84.1	62.8	89.5
Worked mainly part-time	40.5	20.6	20.3	5.1	6.9	3.4	6.3	3.4	8.9	5.6	16.3	4.1
Not employed	44.1	37.4	11.8	7.1	10.1	4.6	13.2	5.1	25.1	10.3	20.9	6.4
Housing tenure (%)												
Owned	78.0	43.1	61.3	57.3	58.8	77.6	65.0	85.1	79.5	87.8	69.5	81.9
Rented	22.0	56.9	38.7	42.7	41.2	22.4	35.0	14.9	20.5	12.2	30.5	18.1
Median total individual income ($)	1,000	7,000	18,000	32,000	34,000	45,000	36,000	49,000	38,000	48,000	23,000	46,000
Median wages & salaries ($)	1,000	1,000	15,000	29,000	31,000	42,000	32,000	45,000	20,000	40,000	14,000	42,000
Total number of men	1,082,720	5,735	1,764,380	226,740	964,965	1,071,845	929,860	1,592,765	1,984,240	928,565	6,726,170	3,825,645

a Due to rounding, some totals do not add up to exactly 100.0%.

Source: From Statistics Canada, 2010, "Census of Population, 2006 [Canada]: Public Use Microdata File, Hierarchical File" [machine readable data file] (Ottawa, ON: Statistics Canada [producer(s)], Statistics Canada, Data Liberation Initiative [distributor(s)]).

The interpretation of the socio-economic differences between fathers and non-fathers is complex. Could these differentials be attributed to fatherhood status? That is, does living with children result in better socio-economic conditions? Some empirical studies have shown that fatherhood benefits not only children and mothers but also fathers themselves (Hawkins & Dollahite, 1997; Snarey, 1993). Eggebeen and Knoester (2001), for example, found that men living with at least one minor child (under eighteen years old) have more attachment to the labour force and work more hours per week than non-fathers or men who do not live with children. They attribute this to the assumption of a "good provider" role. That is, living with children seems to engender a sense of responsibility that results in stronger attachment to the labour force.

However, another possible explanation is that men who become fathers possess characteristics that are conducive to having better socio-economic status. For example, most men tend to first enter the workforce or acquire a college or university education and secure paying jobs before becoming fathers (Ravanera et al., 2006). Men with higher education and with greater abilities to earn are more likely to get married (than to stay in a common-law relationship) and, subsequently, to have children (Ravanera & Rajulton, 2007). Married men with higher education levels are also less likely to separate from their partners and thus continue to live with their children (Raley & Bumpass, 2003; Ravanera, Rajulton, & Burch, 2005a).

Fathers' Time Spent on Paid and Unpaid Work
Periodically, Statistics Canada gathers information through a survey where respondents fill in a diary on how they spend their time over a 24-hour period. Data on time use are collected in such a way that each day of the week is represented. Estimates from the 2005 General Social Survey on time use (Statistics Canada, 2006a) show that the differences between mothers and fathers in the total amount of time spent on work vary by labour-force status (see Table 2.4).

If we look at the total of paid and unpaid work for Canadian parents working full-time, fathers and mothers work almost an equal total amount of time – fathers for 10.3 hours and mothers for 10.4 hours. However, fathers spend more time on paid work and mothers do more unpaid work. In 2005, full-time employed fathers spent an average of 7.6 hours a day on paid work compared to 6.1 hours for mothers, but fathers devoted 2.8 hours a day to unpaid work compared to mothers' 4.4 hours. For unemployed parents and those working part-time, mothers' combined paid and unpaid work hours are greater than those of fathers, with the difference mainly coming from time spent on unpaid work. For instance, unemployed mothers spent, on average, 7.3 hours on unpaid work, whereas unemployed fathers spent 4.9 hours.

Canadian Fathers 33

Table 2.4

Average hours per day of paid and unpaid work, men and women aged 25 to 54 with children under 19 years old

Labour-force status		Paid work	Unpaid work			Total paid and unpaid[a]
			Child care	Other unpaid	All unpaid[a]	
Men	Full-time	7.6	0.9	1.9	2.8	10.3
	Part-time	3.5	1.1	2.5	3.5	7.0
	Not employed	1.8	1.5	3.4	4.9	6.7
Women	Full-time	6.1	1.2	3.1	4.4	10.4
	Part-time	3.1	1.9	4.1	6.0	9.1
	Not employed	0.7	2.8	4.5	7.3	8.0

a Totals are independently rounded; thus, some totals do not necessarily equal the sum of individual rounded figures.

Source: From Statistics Canada, 2006, "General Social Survey, Cycle 19, 2005 [Canada]: Time Use, Main File" [machine readable data file] (Ottawa, ON: Statistics Canada [producer(s)], Statistics Canada, Data Liberation Initiative [distributor(s)]).

Table 2.5

Participation in and time spent on paid work, housework, and unpaid work, men aged 25 to 54 living with children under 19 years old

	1986	1992	1998	2005
	Participation (%)			
Total paid and unpaid	95	97	99	99
Paid work and related	70	64	68	70
Housework	53	69	77	71
Other unpaid	56	63	67	65
Child care	38	50	53	52
Shopping and services	31	33	36	29
	Average hours per day spent by participants			
Total paid and unpaid	9.3	9.4	9.8	10.0
Paid work and related	9.1	9.5	9.5	9.9
Housework	2.0	2.3	2.1	2.1
Other unpaid	2.4	2.3	2.4	2.3
Child care	1.6	1.6	1.8	1.8
Shopping and services	2.4	2.0	1.7	1.9

Source: From 1986, 1992, 1998, and 2005 General Social Surveys. Statistics Canada, 1990, "General Social Survey, Cycle 2, 1986 [Canada]: Time Use, Mobility, and Language Use, Time Use Summary File" [machine readable data file]; 1993, "General Social Survey, Cycle 7, 1992 [Canada]: Time Use, Time Use Summary File" [machine readable data file]; 1999, "General Social Survey, Cycle 12, 1998 [Canada]: Time Use, Episode File" [machine readable data file]; 2006, "General Social Survey, Cycle 19, 2005 [Canada]: Time Use, Main File" [machine readable data file] (Ottawa, ON: Statistics Canada [producer(s)], Statistics Canada, Data Liberation Initiative [distributor(s)]).

While fathers devoted fewer hours to unpaid work than mothers in 2005, fathers are, on average, doing more child care and housework than they were 25 years ago (see Table 2.5).

To understand what has changed, it is important to note that the General Social Survey on time use asks respondents to record their activities on a designated day. Those who report having done a certain activity on the day relevant to the survey – housework, child care, paid work, and so on – are referred to as participants. Time spent on a specific activity is averaged for a 24-hour day over a seven-day week, and estimates could be computed for both participants and non-participants or for participants only.[2] Hence, the average daily times spent on child care in Table 2.4, averaged over both participants and non-participants, are lower than the times noted in Table 2.5, which include participants only. Likewise, the average daily hours spent on various categories of paid and unpaid work by male participants cannot be totalled because not all men were participants in all categories.

As Table 2.5 shows, participant fathers (as defined in the previous paragraph) increased their time spent on child care and housework between 1986 and 2005: 0.2 hours (12 minutes) more per day for child care and 0.1 hours (six minutes) more per day for housework. Although these may seem like modest increases, two noteworthy changes have occurred. One is that substantially more fathers are doing child care and housework on a regular basis. As Table 2.5 shows, fathers' participation rate in housework increased from 53% in 1986 to 71% in 2005, and child care participation increased from 38% to 52% over the same period. By contrast, participation rates of mothers with preschool children in both activities have been 90% since the mid-1980s (Marshall, 2006). The other change is that participating fathers, particularly those with preschoolers, have increased their time spent caring for children since 1986. Marshall's (2006) comparison of fathers with at least one child under the age of five shows that in 2005, participating fathers were devoting 36 minutes more per day to child care than their counterparts in 1986. The increase in father involvement in child care is similar to what has been documented in other industrialized nations. Analysis of cross-national data shows that both fathers' participation rates and fathers' time spent on child care increased steadily between the 1960s and the 1990s (Gauthier, Smeeding, & Furstenberg, 2004). However, in the 1990s, Canadian and American fathers with children under the age of five were spending more time on child care than fathers in countries like Norway, Sweden, Germany, and Australia (Gauthier & Monna, 2004).

Advantages of Fatherhood

As has been shown with census data (discussed above), fathers tend to be better off socio-economically than non-fathers. Analysis of data on Canadians' social networks gathered through the General Social Survey on Social

Table 2.6

Informal network indicators by fatherhood status, Canadian men aged 30 to 64, 2003

	All men		Fathers		Non-fathers	
Indicators of social capital	N	Mean	N	Mean	N	Mean
Mean number of neighbours known	6,743	2.65	3,723	2.74	3,020	2.55
Trust in family[a]	6,630	4.74	3,662	4.78	2,968	4.69
Factor score – trust in neighbours[b]	5,433	0.00	3,222	0.05	2,211	-0.08
Factor score – social capital[b]	5,321	0.00	3,163	0.07	2,159	-0.10

a   Mean of score that ranges from 1 *(cannot be trusted)* to 5 *(can be trusted a lot)*.
b   Mean score from factor analysis of a number of indicators, with an overall mean of 0. A
    positive score indicates greater, and a negative score, lower social capital.
Source: Adapted from "Informal Networks Social Capital of Fathers: What Does the Social
Engagement Survey Tell Us?" by Z. Ravanera, 2007, *Social Indicators Research, 83*(2), Table 2, based
on Statistics Canada, 2004, "General Social Survey, Cycle 17, 2003 [Canada]: Social Engagement"
[machine readable data file] (Ottawa, ON: Statistics Canada [producer(s)], Statistics Canada, Data
Liberation Initiative [distributor(s)]).

Engagement conducted in 2003 (Statistics Canada, 2004) suggests that living with children also has a beneficial effect on men's social networks.[3]

As Table 2.6 shows, men living with children aged 24 or under had higher levels of social capital from informal networks than men not living with children. Social capital refers to the personal relationships and social networks that enhance the health, well-being, and productivity of individuals in society. On average, fathers report knowing more neighbours and having higher levels of trust in their family and neighbours than non-fathers. It is possible that the wider social network of fathers could be attributed to living with children; however, it is also likely that men who live with children are simply more sociable to begin with than those who don't.

Subpopulations of Fathers
While the census and survey data do point to benefits of fatherhood, these advantages do not apply equally to all fathers. Social and economic differences between fathers can arise from various life experiences such as disruption of family life by separation or divorce, or becoming a father at an age when schooling is not yet finished or a career has not been established. Socio-economic difficulties could also stem from belonging to a socio-economically disadvantaged group. The following section examines available demographic information on immigrant fathers, Aboriginal fathers, young fathers, lone (single) fathers, and divorced and adoptive fathers.

Immigrant Fathers
Immigrant fathers, one of the most significant subgroups of fathers, constitute just over one quarter of all men in Canada aged 15 to 64 who live with

dependent children (see Table 2.7). Our tabulation of the 2006 census data showed 1,041,100 immigrant fathers – that is, men born outside of Canada and living with children aged 24 years or younger (Statistics Canada, 2010). About 42% of these immigrant fathers arrived in Canada between 1991 and 2006.

Table 2.7

Socio-economic characteristics of fathers aged 15 to 64, by immigration status, 2006

Socio-economic characteristics	Non-immigrants	Immigrants			All immigrants
		Before 1991	1991-2000	2001-2006	
Marital arrangements of fathers (%)[a]					
Married father	73.9	88.9	94.9	96.8	91.7
Father in common-law relation	19.7	5.7	3.8	2.3	4.7
Lone father	6.4	5.4	1.3	1.0	3.7
Level of education (%)					
No diploma or degree	15.2	15.3	10.3	6.8	12.7
High school	23.1	20.8	20.8	12.4	19.6
Trade, apprenticeship, college	38.3	30.7	19.5	12.7	24.9
University or higher	23.3	33.2	49.3	68.1	42.8
Work status (%)					
Worked mainly full-time in 2005	91.4	87.5	85.1	75.8	85.1
Worked mainly part-time in 2005	3.5	5.1	5.4	7.8	5.5
Not employed in 2005	5.1	7.5	9.5	16.5	9.4
Housing tenure (%)					
Owned	84.9	84.2	72.8	45.6	75.4
Rented	15.1	15.8	27.2	54.4	24.6
Median total income ($)	50,000	43,000	33,000	22,000	36,000
Median wages and salaries ($)	45,000	38,000	30,000	16,000	32,000
Total number	2,756,910	605,750	280,050	155,305	1,041,100
% of total number of fathers	72.6	15.9	7.4	4.1	27.4
% of immigrants		58.2	26.9	14.9	100.0

a Due to rounding, some totals do not add up to exactly 100.0%.
Source: From Statistics Canada, 2010, "Census of Population, 2006 [Canada]: Public Use Microdata File, Hierarchical File" [machine readable data file] (Ottawa, ON: Statistics Canada [producer(s)], Statistics Canada, Data Liberation Initiative [distributor(s)]).

Compared to Canadian-born fathers, immigrant fathers are more likely to be married and less likely to be lone fathers. Over 90% of immigrant fathers are married compared to 74% of non-immigrant fathers. Likewise, less than 5% of immigrant fathers are in common-law relationships while 20% of non-immigrant fathers live common-law. The proportion of immigrant men who are lone fathers is also lower: 3.7% for immigrant fathers compared to 6.4% for non-immigrant fathers. This suggests that the rate of divorce or separation, the most common cause of lone parenthood in men, is lower among immigrant fathers as well.

Socio-economic data show that while immigrant fathers are more likely to be highly educated than Canadian-born fathers, they are also more likely to be in precarious economic situations, particularly those who have been in Canada for shorter periods of time. For example, 68% of fathers who immigrated to Canada between 2001 and 2006 are university graduates compared to 23% of non-immigrant fathers. Yet on the other three socio-economic indicators of economic well-being – working full-time, median total income, and house ownership – immigrant fathers, especially the most recent immigrants, are less well off than non-immigrant fathers. However, socio-economic conditions of immigrant fathers improve with a longer stay in Canada. Unlike fathers who arrived in Canada between 2001 and 2006, immigrant fathers who arrived before 1991 have median incomes and rates of full-time employment and home ownership similar to those of non-immigrant Canadian fathers.

Aboriginal Fathers
The Aboriginal population of Canada is younger and growing more rapidly than the general Canadian population (Steffler, 2008). Gathering demographic information on Aboriginal fathers is complicated by the fact that not all Indigenous peoples identify as Aboriginal in the Canadian census. Registered Indians constitute the largest proportion of Canada's Indigenous population. Other types of Indigenous peoples include Non-Status Indian, Métis, and Inuit. This section presents data on men who identified as Aboriginal in the 2006 Canadian census and lived with dependent children.

Aboriginal fathers, constituting 3% of all Canadian fathers, differ from their non-Aboriginal counterparts on numerous measures. They are less likely to be married and more likely to be living in common-law relationships. As Table 2.8 shows, 56% of Aboriginal fathers are married compared to 80% of non-Aboriginal fathers, and the proportion of Aboriginal fathers living in a common-law union (31%) is more than double that of non-Aboriginal men living with children (15%). Likewise, the proportion of lone fathers is more than twice as high for Aboriginal (13%) as for non-Aboriginal fathers (5%).

38   *Zenaida R. Ravanera and John Hoffman*

Table 2.8

Socio-economic characteristics of fathers aged 15 to 64, by Aboriginal status, 2006

Socio-economic characteristics	Aboriginal	Non-Aboriginal
Marital arrangements of fathers (%)		
Married father	56.2	79.6
Father in common-law relation	30.7	15.0
Lone father	13.1	5.4
Level of education (%)		
No diploma or degree	38.2	13.7
High school	19.2	22.2
Trade, apprenticeship, college	35.0	34.6
University or higher	7.6	29.5
Work status (%)		
Worked mainly full-time in 2005	75.5	90.0
Worked mainly part-time in 2005	7.1	4.0
Not employed in 2005	17.4	6.0
Housing tenure (%)		
Owned	51.8	83.0
Rented or band housing	48.2	17.0
Median total income ($)	29,000	47,000
Median wages and salaries ($)	23,000	42,000
Total number	126,335	3,699,310

Source: From Statistics Canada, 2010, "Census of Population, 2006 [Canada]: Public Use Microdata File, Hierarchical File" [machine readable data file] (Ottawa, ON: Statistics Canada [producer(s)], Statistics Canada, Data Liberation Initiative [distributor(s)]).

Aboriginal fathers also have a socio-economic profile that is much different from that of non-Aboriginal men living with children. For example, 43% of Aboriginal fathers have post-secondary education compared to 64% of non-Aboriginal fathers. Aboriginal fathers are also less likely to work mainly full-time or own their homes, and they earn less than non-Aboriginal fathers. The average wage or salary of Aboriginal fathers is just over half that of non-Aboriginal fathers (see Table 2.8).

Young Fathers
It is very difficult to determine the number of teenaged fathers in Canada because children born to teenaged parents most often live with the mother. As can be seen in Table 2.1, the 2006 census identified 5,735 Canadian men

Table 2.9

Full-time school attendance, men aged 15 to 29, by fatherhood status, 2006

	15-19		20-29		15-29	
	Non-fathers	Fathers	Non-fathers	Fathers	Non-fathers	Fathers
School attendance (%)						
Did not attend school	20.4	57.4	61.8	86.4	46.0	85.6
Attended school full-time	79.6	42.6	38.2	13.6	54.0	14.4
Total number	1,082,720	5,735	1,764,380	226,740	2,847,105	232,475

Source: From Statistics Canada, 2010, "Census of Population, 2006 [Canada]: Public Use Microdata File, Hierarchical File" [machine readable data file] (Ottawa, ON: Statistics Canada [producer(s)], Statistics Canada, Data Liberation Initiative [distributor(s)]).

aged 15 to 19 living with dependent children. This probably represents only a minority of the actual number of teenaged males who have fathered a child. Interestingly, of the teenaged fathers who do live with their children, almost half (48%) are lone fathers. Unlike in the past, when non-marital pregnancy often led to marriage, much of today's teenaged child-bearing occurs outside of marriage or within cohabiting unions that are subsequently dissolved. Therefore, only 17% of the teenaged fathers who live with their children are married, and 35% are in common-law unions.

Teenaged fathers differ from their childless peers and slightly older (aged 20-29) fathers on several measures. As can be seen in Table 2.9, compared to teenaged boys who are not parents, teenaged fathers are less likely to be attending school full-time (43% vs. 80%). Compared to childless 15- to 19-year-olds, teen fathers are more likely to be working full-time (42% vs. 15%) and more likely to live in rental housing (57% vs. 22%; see Table 2.3). Fathers aged 15 to 19 living with children are socio-economically disadvantaged compared to fathers aged 20 to 29: these two groups have median annual incomes of $7,000 and $32,000, respectively (Table 2.3).

Of the *older* young Canadian men (aged 20-29), about 11% (or some 227,000 in total) are living with dependent children (see Table 2.1). Half of these fathers are married, 44% are in cohabiting unions, and 7% are lone fathers. Similar to teenaged fathers, fathers in their 20s are less likely than non-fathers of the same age to be attending school full-time (14% vs. 38%, Table 2.9) and are more likely to be working full-time (88% vs. 68%, Table 2.3). These figures suggest that young fathers who live with their children must often sacrifice certain opportunities of youth, such as post-secondary education, or in the case of teen fathers, high school education, in order to earn the income their children depend on.

40 *Zenaida R. Ravanera and John Hoffman*

Table 2.10

Marital status of lone fathers aged 15 to 64, by age group, 2006

	15-19	20-29	30-39	40-49	50-64	Total
Marital status (%)[a]						
Never married – single	100.0	87.0	51.6	25.3	11.1	31.7
Married	0.0	2.5	3.1	2.3	3.6	2.8
Separated/divorced	0.0	10.0	42.5	67.9	73.5	59.6
Widowed	0.0	0.5	2.8	4.5	11.7	5.8
Total number	2,740	14,760	41,620	97,705	58,005	214,830
Percentage of all lone fathers	1.3	6.9	19.4	45.5	27.0	100.0

a Due to rounding, some totals do not add up to exactly 100.0%.
Source: From Statistics Canada, 2010, "Census of Population, 2006 [Canada]: Public Use Microdata File, Hierarchical File" [machine readable data file] (Ottawa, ON: Statistics Canada [producer(s)], Statistics Canada, Data Liberation Initiative [distributor(s)]).

Lone Fathers

A lone father is defined here as a man living with at least one child aged 24 years or younger but not living with a marital spouse or common-law partner. Approximately 215,000 men aged 15 to 64 were lone fathers in 2006. Most of these men (60%) became lone fathers through separation or divorce (see Table 2.10). About 32% of men living with children have never been married. Only 6% of lone fathers are widowers.

Lone fatherhood through divorce or separation is most likely at older ages. At age 50 to 64, for example, 74% of lone fathers are separated or divorced. Among younger men, lone fatherhood more commonly occurs due to child-bearing outside of marriage – at age 20 to 29, 87% of lone fathers are single. Surprisingly, about 3% of lone fathers report that they are married. It is possible that these men are no longer living with their spouse but still record themselves as married because they have not formally separated.

Socio-Economic Status of Lone Fathers

As Table 2.11 shows, lone fathers are socio-economically worse off than married fathers. They have lower median annual incomes than married fathers ($40,000 vs. $49,000) and are also less likely to have a university education (16% vs. 32%), work full-time (81% vs. 90%), or own their home (61% vs. 86%).

Lone fathers' socio-economic status is more similar to that of fathers in common-law unions. Lone and common-law fathers have similar educational attainment and similar levels of income. However, fathers in common-law unions are more likely to work full-time and to own their homes.

Canadian Fathers 41

Table 2.11

Socio-economic characteristics of fathers aged 15 to 64, by marital status, 2006

Socio-economic characteristics	Married	Common-law	Lone
Level of education (%) [a]			
No diploma or degree	12.4	22.0	22.8
High school	21.6	23.3	25.7
Trade, apprenticeship, college	33.7	38.8	35.3
University or higher	32.2	15.9	16.2
Work status (%)			
Worked mainly full-time in 2005	90.4	88.4	81.2
Worked mainly part-time in 2005	3.8	4.7	6.1
Not employed in 2005	5.8	6.9	12.7
Housing tenure (%)			
Owned	85.6	70.5	61.0
Rented	14.4	29.5	39.0
Median total income ($)	49,000	38,000	40,000
Median wages and salaries ($)	44,000	35,000	32,000
Total number of fathers	3,015,760	595,060	214,830

a Due to rounding, some totals do not add up to exactly 100.0%.
Source: From Statistics Canada, 2010, "Census of Population, 2006 [Canada]: Public Use Microdata File, Hierarchical File" [machine readable data file] (Ottawa, ON: Statistics Canada [producer(s)], Statistics Canada, Data Liberation Initiative [distributor(s)]).

Divorced Fathers and Custody of Children

Understanding and interpreting trends in lone fatherhood are complicated by the fact that living arrangements for children of divorced and separated parents have become more complex and varied in recent years, with some children living equal or close to equal time with both parents after divorce.

Information on custody arrangements is not available from the Canadian census. When a couple is divorced or separated, their child is reported by the parent with whom the child lives most of the time. In the case of joint custody with a child spending equal time with each parent, only the parent who happens to have the child in his or her household on the day of the census should report the child as part of the household: that parent would therefore be deemed by the census to be a lone parent. The other parent would be expected to not report the child as part of the household and would thus be considered childless for census purposes. However, it is possible that each parent would think of him- or herself as a single (lone) parent.

Table 2.12

Percentage of dependents involving custody orders, by party granted custody, 1995-2004

| | | Party granted custody (%) | | | |
Year	Total number of dependent children	Husband only	Wife only	Jointly to husband and wife	All others
1999	38,433	9.3	56.8	33.8	0.2
2004	31,764	8.1	45.0	46.5	0.4
2003	33,098	8.3	47.7	43.8	0.2
2002	35,153	8.5	49.5	41.8	0.2
2001	36,660	9.0	51.2	39.7	0.2
2000	37,096	9.1	53.5	37.2	0.2
1998	37,851	9.5	59.5	30.5	0.5
1997	39,204	11.0	61.3	27.6	0.1
1996	43,844	12.1	63.2	24.5	0.2
1995	47,118	10.9	67.6	21.4	0.2

a   Due to rounding, some totals do not add up to exactly 100.0%.
Source: Statistics Canada. (1995–). *Divorces.* (Catalogue no. 84F0213XPB). Ottawa, ON: Author.

Surveys provide some data on custody arrangements for children when parents separate. The administrative survey from the Central Registry of Divorce Proceedings at the Department Justice Canada accessed through CANSIM, Statistics Canada's socio-economic database, shows that court-ordered custody arrangements for dependent children, which constitute the minority of post-divorce and post-separation custody agreements, have changed significantly over the past decade (see Table 2.12). In 1995, custody of two thirds of the children (68%) was granted to the mother alone, but by 2004, this had decreased to less than half of the children (45%). In contrast, joint custody of children increased from 21% in 1995 to 46% in 2004. (These custody data do not include children whose parents did not go through the legal divorce procedure. This would mean that the administrative survey data also exclude children of couples of common-law unions who subsequently separated and children born to parents who never married or cohabited.)

However, while there is a trend toward more joint custody in court-ordered arrangements (most separating and divorcing parents reach custody and living arrangements for their children outside of court), it cannot be assumed that children live equal or approximately equal time with both parents after divorce and separation when joint custody is granted. In many joint custody cases, parents share responsibility for major decisions about the children, but the children reside primarily with one parent, as survey data show. Data from the National Longitudinal Survey of Children and Youth (Juby, Marcil-

Gratton, & Le Bourdais, 2004) show that in 1998/99, seven out of ten children whose parents had separated within the two previous years were living primarily with one parent (63% with the mother, 7% with the father). Only 12% of children were in shared living arrangements. Similarly, a more recent survey of parents with written or verbal arrangements for spending time with children showed that 14% reported shared living arrangements for their children (Robinson, 2009).

Fathers of Non-Biological Children

It is difficult to obtain information about adoptive fathers and stepfathers because the Canadian census does not collect information that allows researchers to distinguish adopted and stepchildren from biological children. Another challenge, specific to obtaining information about adoptive fathers, is that adoption statistics generally record the number of children adopted rather than the number of adoptive parents.

Stepfathers are not easily identified and counted due to the complex nature of stepfamilies, which include families where a father lives with his partner's children only, or with both his own and his partner's biological children (full- or part-time), and in some cases, with biological children from the new union as well. Similarly, adoptive families may include biological children or stepchildren as well as adopted children. Thus, if stepfathers or adoptive fathers reside with their stepchildren or adopted children, they are counted in the census as fathers but not as stepfathers or adoptive fathers.

However, the 2006 General Social Survey (Statistics Canada, 2008b) gathered information about the type of children reported by the respondents. This makes it possible to identify fathers of biological children only, stepchildren only, adopted children only, and a combination of biological, adopted, and stepchildren. Because there are few fathers in some of these categories, we combined certain ones to create three categories of fathers: (1) fathers of biological children only, (2) fathers with any stepchildren (including those with biological and stepchildren), and (3) fathers with any adopted children (including those with biological and/or stepchildren in addition to adopted children).

Table 2.13 contains estimates of the numbers and percentages of fathers in these three categories. However, due to the small sample size, especially of adopted fathers, we did not restrict estimates to men living with dependent children under the age of 25 as we did with other data in this chapter. The population totals (Total Number) in Table 2.13 refer to men who have children of any age, including independent children who do not live at home. Thus, the total number of fathers in Table 2.13, 8.1 million, differs from the total in Table 2.3, 3.8 million.

Almost 13% of men aged 15 to 64 with any children (including independent children who no longer live at home) are stepfathers, while 3.6% have

Table 2.13

Demographic characteristics of fathers with children of any age, by type of father, 2006

Demographic characteristics	Fathers of			
	Biological children[a] (%)[d]	Step-children[b] (%)	Adopted children[c] (%)	All children (%)
Age				
15-19	0.1	0.1	0.0	0.1
20-29	4.5	4.8	0.8	4.4
30-39	18.0	19.7	6.5	17.8
40-49	26.2	35.8	17.6	27.1
50-64	31.4	32.1	40.7	31.8
65 and older	19.9	7.4	34.4	18.8
Marital status (%)				
Married	77.7	51.9	81.1	74.5
Common-law	9.6	30.8	7.2	12.2
Lone	12.8	17.3	11.6	13.3
Total number[e]	6,758,100	1,015,400	289,000	8,062,500
Percent of total	83.8	12.6	3.6	100.0

a Biological only.
b Stepchildren only and stepchildren plus biological.
c Adopted only and adopted plus biological and/or stepchildren.
d Due to rounding, some totals do not add up to exactly 100.0%.
e Numbers have been rounded to multiples of 100.
Source: Adapted from Statistics Canada, 2008, "General Social Survey, 2006 [Canada]. Cycle 20: Family Transitions (main file)" [machine readable data file] (Ottawa, ON: Statistics Canada [producer(s)], Statistics Canada, Data Liberation Initiative [distributor(s)]).

adopted children. Fathers of adopted children tend to be older. Approximately 75% are age 50 or older, which may reflect the fact that adoption usually occurs later in life, often after years of attempts to have biological children. Stepfathers tend to be younger and less likely to be married than adoptive fathers and fathers with biological children only, which probably reflects the higher rates of divorce, repartnering, and common-law relationships in the younger generation of fathers. Almost one in three stepfathers lives with a common-law partner compared to less than 10% for other types of fathers.

Invisible Fathers

As noted earlier, fathers who do not reside with their children are invisible in the census. The most common reason for fathers not living with their children is divorce or separation, and it would appear that a considerable number of men fall into this category. Canada has a high rate of divorce in couples with children – an estimated 30% of children born in 1984 experienced their parents' divorce by age 15 (Juby et al., 2004). An undetermined number of fathers never resided with their child's mother, and these fathers would be invisible not only in the census but, quite likely, also in birth records since the identity of the father is sometimes unacknowledged in birth records (Lero, Ashbourne, & Whitehead, 2006).

However, Canada's 1995 and 2006 General Social Surveys did ask respondents whether they have biological, step-, or adopted children. A new analysis of data from men interviewed for these General Social Surveys (Beaupré, Dryburgh, & Wendt, 2010) revealed that 81% of the fathers (defined as men living with children aged 18 or younger) were living with their children full-time, that 11% were living with at least one of their children part-time, that 3.5% had at least one child who lived elsewhere, and that 4.5% were not residing with any of their children (down from 7.2% in 1995). Thus, 19% of Canadian fathers lived apart from at least some of their children, at least some of the time.

We also have very little demographic information about gay fathers. Only recently has the Canadian census begun asking about sexual orientation. What *is* known is that the 2006 census counted 46,895 men aged 15 to 64 in same-sex couple unions (Statistics Canada, 2006c). Furthermore, 3% of all male same-sex couples identified in the census reported having children aged 24 or under living in their home (Statistics Canada, 2007). This undoubtedly under-represents the number of Canadian gay fathers, since gay men become parents in varied circumstances, including through adoption or surrogacy, in the context of heterosexual marriage, and in co-parenting relationships with lesbian parents. Some gay fathers who become parents in heterosexual relationships continue to live with the child's mother after coming out, while others have yet to disclose their gay identity to their spouses (Epstein & Duggan, 2006). Some of these men would be counted as fathers in the census, but not necessarily as gay fathers.

Conclusion

As noted in the introduction to this chapter, the living and working patterns in Canadian families and the roles played by parents have evolved in the past few decades, yet these changes have been studied primarily in terms of how they affect the lives of women. Creating a demographic profile of Canadian fathers is one component of the broader study of father involvement. But given the current tools at our disposal, it is not possible to accurately determine the number of fathers in Canada, particularly fathers in certain subgroups. This situation is not likely to change until the Canadian census and other main instruments for tracking population are modified in ways that better reflect the evolving complexity and diversity of family arrangements in Canada.

Suggestions for the census include asking men (and women) a question on the number of children ever biologically fathered (and ever born) and modifying the instructions so that biological, adopted, and stepchildren are identifiable (Ravanera, 2008). It would also be helpful if non-resident parents would be able to record that they have children with whom they do not reside on a full-time basis. It would be productive to conduct father-focused analyses of existing data sets such as the General Social Survey, the National Longitudinal Survey of Children and Youth, and other national surveys. One reason why such analyses are not often done may be that researchers and policy-makers have tended to focus on maternal and child health, often ignoring the role that fathers may play in promoting child and family health and well-being. This father-oriented research will be increasingly useful as family-related policies such as parental leaves are formulated or reviewed to reflect the increasing involvement of fathers in their children's lives.

These changes and adjustments would greatly improve researchers' ability to gain insight into demographic factors that affect fathers' involvement with their children and families. For example, we have shown that although fatherhood status tends to be socially and materially advantageous for men, these benefits are not shared equally by all subpopulations of fathers. Teenaged fathers, Aboriginal fathers, lone fathers, and immigrant fathers are all socio-economically disadvantaged compared to the general population of men living with children. These social disadvantages may, at times, affect the ability of these men to engage in their parenting roles.

Moreover, as long as the census only allows the identification of a father as simply a man who resides with his own or his partner's children, it will be impossible to assess the number of fathers who do not live with their children, as well as those who live with their children on a part-time basis, particularly for the subgroups of disadvantaged fathers (teenaged, Aboriginal, and immigrant fathers) who are not generally well represented in national surveys. This hinders attempts to shed light on the concerns about the potential impacts of father absence on child development (East, Jackson, & O'Brien, 2006) and the impacts of divorce and separation on father-child relationships (Kruk, 2008).

Understanding the influence of fathers on children requires following up families over a relatively long period of time. This is being done in the United States, for example, in longitudinal studies such as the Fragile Families and Child Wellbeing Study, the Early Head Start National Evaluation father studies, and the Early Childhood Longitudinal Study (Cabrera et al., 2004). In Canada, the Survey of Labour and Income Dynamics and the National Population Health Surveys are longitudinal surveys that can provide only limited insights since they are not primarily aimed at understanding fatherhood. In the National Longitudinal Survey of Children and Youth, it would be worth exploring possibilities of drawing the fathers into the survey. Currently, except for the few fathers who are identified as persons most knowledgeable about their children, fathers are not part of the survey in the same way that mothers are or in the way that fathers are in the longitudinal surveys in the United States. In the Canadian Household Panel Survey, currently in the planning stage, research on fatherhood would be greatly benefited by including a module on father involvement in one panel of the survey, and periodically thereafter.

The uncertainties and gaps in our knowledge about Canadian fathers impede efforts to develop appropriate policies, programs, and other supports that could help more fathers, particularly vulnerable fathers, fully engage in their parenting role and build strong supportive relationships with their children. Improved understanding of the unique challenges and strengths of subpopulations of fathers and further research on the ways in which cultural experiences shape fatherhood could help governments and societal institutions to identify ways to support various groups of fathers and mitigate the disadvantages experienced by some subpopulations.

Acknowledgments
The authors gratefully acknowledge the help of Ching Du, PhD candidate, University of Western Ontario; Jianye Liu, Associate Professor, Lakehead University; and Rajulton Fernando, Professor Emeritus, University of Western Ontario, in the preparation of tables for this chapter.

Notes
1 In data based on the 1981, 1986, and 1991 censuses, Statistics Canada made available information on whether females aged 15 years and over were living with dependent children. Starting in 1996, this information was also provided for males 15 years and over.
2 The averaging for a 24-hour day over a seven-day week explains why, for example, the participation rate for paid work is seemingly low. The participation rate in paid work of, say, 70% is due to the many responses of no paid work activity reported on a Saturday or Sunday. (http://www.statcan.gc.ca/pub/12f0080x/2006001/4147817-eng.htm; see also Statistics Canada, 2006b).
3 The General Social Survey on Social Engagement gathered information on social networks such as the number of people the respondents felt close to, how many people they knew in their neighbourhood, and their level of trust in family and friends (Ravanera, 2007).

References
Beaujot, R. (2000). *Earning and caring in Canadian families*. Peterborough: Broadview Press.
Beaujot, R., Ravanera, Z., & Burch, T. K. (2007). Toward an HRSDC family research framework. *Population Studies Centre Discussion Papers Series, 21*(2). Retrieved from http://ir.lib.uwo.ca/pscpapers/vol21/iss2/1
Beaupré, P., Dryburgh, H., & Wendt, M. (2010). Making fathers "count." *Canadian Social Trends*. Ottawa, ON: Statistics Canada. Retrieved from http://www.statcan.gc.ca/pub/11-008-x/2010002/article/11165-eng.htm.
Cabrera, N., Tamis-LeMonda, C. S., Bradley, R. H., Hofferth, S., & Lamb, M. E. (2000). Fatherhood in the twenty-first century. *Child Development, 71*(1), 127-136.

Cabrera, N. J., Brooks-Gunn, K., Moore, J., Bronte-Tinkew, T., Hall, N., Reichman, J., ... Boller, K. (2004). The DADS initiative: Measuring father involvement in large-scale surveys. In R. D. Day & M. E. Lamb (Eds.), *Conceptualizing and measuring father involvement* (pp. 417-449). Mahwah, NJ: Lawrence Erlbaum.

East, L., Jackson, D., & O'Brien, L. (2006). Father absence and adolescent development: A review of the literature. *Journal of Child Health Care, 10*(4), 283-295.

Eggebeen, D. J., & Knoester, C. (2001). Does fatherhood matter for men? *Journal of Marriage and the Family, 63*(2), 381-393.

Epstein, R., & Duggan, S. (2006). Gay fathers cluster executive summary: Father involvement community research forum spring 2006. Retrieved from the Father Involvement Research Alliance website: http://fira.ca/cms/documents/44/Gay_Fathers.pdf

Frenette, M., & Zeman, K. (2007). *Why are most university students women? Evidence based on academic performance, study habits and parental influences.* Ottawa, ON: Statistics Canada. Retrieved from http://www.statcan.gc.ca/pub/11f0019m/11f0019m2007303-eng.pdf

Gauthier, A. H., & Monna, B. (2004). *Parent's time investment into children.* (Research Brief Series: Issue #3. Comparative Public Policy Research Laboratory.) Calgary, AB: University of Calgary.

Gauthier, A. H., Smeeding, T. M., & Furstenberg, F. F. (2004). Are parents investing less time in children? Trends in selected industrialized countries. *Population and Development Review, 30*(4), 647-671.

Hawkins, A. J., & Dollahite, D. C. (1997). *Generative fathering: Beyond deficit perspectives.* Thousand Oaks, CA: Sage.

Juby, H., Marcil-Gratton, N., & Le Bourdais, C. (2004). *When parents separate: Further findings from the National Longitudinal Survey of Children and Youth.* Ottawa, ON: Department of Justice Canada. Retrieved from http://www.justice.gc.ca/eng/pi/fcy-fea/lib-bib/rep-rap/2005/2004_6/p4.html

King, R. B. (1999). Time spent in parenthood status among adults in the United States. *Demography, 36*(3), 377-385.

Kruk, E. (2008). *Custody, access and parental responsibility: The search for a just and equitable standard.* Guelph, ON: Father Involvement Research Alliance. Retrieved from http://www.fira.ca/cms/documents/181/April7_Kruk.pdf.

Lero, D. S., Ashbourne, L. M., & Whitehead, D. L. (2006). *Inventory of policies and policy areas influencing father involvement.* Guelph, ON: Father Involvement Research Alliance. Retrieved from http://www.fira.ca/cms/documents/22/FIRA-Inventory_of_Policies.pdf

Marshall, K. (2006). Converging gender roles. *Perspectives on Labour and Income, 7*(7), 5-17. Statistics Canada – Catalogue no. 75-001-XPE.

Marsiglio, W., Amato, R., Day, D., & Lamb, M. E. (2000). Scholarship on fatherhood in the 1990s and beyond. *Journal of Marriage and the Family, 62*(4), 1173-1191.

Raley, R. K., & Bumpass, L. (2003). The topography of the divorce plateau: Levels and trends in union stability in the United States after 1980. *Demographic Research, 8*(8), 245-260.

Ravanera, Z. (2007). Informal networks social capital of fathers: What does the Social Engagement Survey tell us? *Social Indicators Research, 83*(2), 351-373.

Ravanera, Z. (2008). *Profiles of fathers in Canada.* Guelph, ON: Father Involvement Research Alliance. Retrieved from http://www.fira.ca/cms/documents/204/Profiles_of_Fathers_in_Canada.pdf.

Ravanera, Z. R., & Rajulton, F. (2007). Changes in economic status and timing of marriage of young Canadians. *Canadian Studies in Population, 34*(1), 49-67. Retrieved from http://www.doaj.org/doaj?func=openurl&issn=03801489&genre=journal.

Ravanera, Z. R., Rajulton, F., & Burch, T. K. (2005a). *Cohort and social status differentials in union dissolution: Analysis using the 2001 General Social Survey* (Discussion Paper No. 05-09). London, ON: University of Western Ontario. Retrieved from Population Studies Centre website http://ir.lib.uwo.ca/pscpapers/vol19/iss9/1/.

Ravanera, Z. R., Rajulton, F., and Burch, T. K. (2005b). Young Canadians' family formation: Variations in delayed start and complex pathways. *PSC Discussion Papers Series, 19*(11), Article 1. Retrieved from http://ir.lib.uwo.ca/pscpapers/vol19/iss11/1.

Ravanera, Z. R., Rajulton, F., & Burch, T. K. (2006). Men's life course trajectories: Exploring the differences by cohort and social class. *Social Biology, 53*(3-4), 120-139.

Robinson, P. (2009). Parenting after separation and divorce: A profile of arrangements for spending time with and making decisions for children. *Juristat, 29*(4). Statistics Canada – Catalogue no. 85-002-X. Retrieved from http://www.statcan.gc.ca/pub/85-002-x/2009004/article/10931-eng.htm#a1.

Snarey, J. (1993). *How fathers care for the next generation: A four-decade study.* Cambridge, MA: Harvard University Press.

Statistics Canada. (2001). *PUMF on Individuals: User Documentation* (Catalogue no. 95M0016XCB). Ottawa, ON: Author.

Statistics Canada. (2002). General Social Survey, Cycle 15, 2001 [Canada]: Family History, main file [machine readable data file]. Ottawa, ON: Statistics Canada [producer(s)], Statistics Canada, Data Liberation Initiative [distributor(s)].

Statistics Canada. (2004). General Social Survey, Cycle 17, 2003 [Canada]: Social Engagement [machine readable data file]. Ottawa, ON: Statistics Canada [producer(s)], Statistics Canada, Data Liberation Initiative [distributor(s)].

Statistics Canada. (2006a). General Social Survey, Cycle 19, 2005 [Canada]: Time use, main file [machine readable data file]. Ottawa, ON: Statistics Canada [producer(s)], Statistics Canada, Data Liberation Initiative [distributor(s)].

Statistics Canada. (2006b). *The General Social Survey: Overview of the time use of Canadians.* Ottawa, ON: Author. Retrieved from http://www.statcan.gc.ca/pub/12f0080x/12f0080x2006001-eng.pdf

Statistics Canada. (2006c). *Persons in same-sex unions by broad age groups and sex for males, 2006 counts, for Canada, provinces and territories – 20% sample data.* Ottawa, ON: Author.

Statistics Canada. (2007). *2006 census – Family portrait: Continuity and change in Canadian families and households in 2006, Findings* (Catalogue no. 97-553-XWE2006001). 2006 Analysis Series. Ottawa, ON: Author.

Statistics Canada. (2008a). *2011 census content consultation report: Census year 2011* (Catalogue no. 92-137-X). Retrieved from http://www.statcan.gc.ca/pub/92-137-x/92-137-x2008001-eng.pdf.

Statistics Canada. (2008b). General Social Survey, 2006 [Canada]. Cycle 20: Family transitions (main file) [machine readable data file]. Ottawa, ON: Statistics Canada [producer(s)], Statistics Canada, Data Liberation Initiative [distributor(s)].

Statistics Canada. (2009). Unpublished data from the Labour Force Survey. Retrieved via e-mail on September 11, 2009.

Statistics Canada. (2010). Census of Population, 2006 [Canada]: Public Use Microdata File, Hierarchical File [machine readable data file]. Ottawa, ON: Statistics Canada [producer(s)], Statistics Canada, Data Liberation Initiative [distributor(s)].

Steffler, J. (2008). Aboriginal Peoples: A young population for years to come. *Horizons, 10*(1), 13-20.

Sussman, D., & Bonnell, S. (2006). Wives as primary breadwinners. *Perspectives on Labour and Income, 7*(8), 10-17. Statistics Canada – Catalogue no. 75-001-XIE.

3
Fathers Make a Difference in Their Children's Lives: A Review of the Research Evidence

Sarah Allen, Kerry Daly, and Jessica Ball

How does a father make a difference in his child's life? Scholars from diverse disciplinary perspectives have grappled with this question using various theoretical frameworks, methodological and measurement approaches, levels of analysis, and sampling strategies. Although research has mapped some common pathways of influence between fathers and children, many questions remain to be explored. Before we can make a general claim that fathers make a difference to child outcomes, we need to carefully interpret the accumulated research evidence, with close attention to its complexity. It is important to identify within this research the kinds of fathers, the diverse circumstances, and the people, groups, and institutions that influence child development outcomes for a variety of children. Using this approach, we recognize not only the diversity within fathers, families, children, and society, but also the embeddedness of child development outcomes in social contexts and varying conditions over time. Thus, although fathers can make a difference in child development outcomes in certain ways, times, and contexts, their impact on these outcomes remains one factor among many potentially contributing factors (Palkovitz, 2002).

Theoretical Orientation: Systemic Ecological Framework
Research demonstrating links between father involvement and child development outcomes often points to the specific ways in which fathers influence those outcomes in a variety of domains through direct pathways (e.g., how spending time with children raises their social competence). A broader conceptualization of child development, however, views fathering as a multilateral process that is strongly contextualized and influenced by factors that move beyond individual characteristics of the father and include child factors (including the quality of the relationship with the child), mother factors (including the quality of the relationship with the mother), co-parental factors (parenting style, presence of conflict, nature of the parenting relationship such as living together or apart), and factors associated with the

larger context within which the father and child are embedded: factors related to culture, institutional practices, economic opportunities, social support, socio-economic status, and cultural and ethnic resources (Doherty, Kouneski, & Erickson, 1998; Hewlett, 2000). This framework recognizes that a father's influence occurs within a complex environment of other influences and not only allows one to see the contributions of fathers but also improves the visibility of the many ways in which fathers matter to children.

Accordingly, in this chapter, we use a theoretical approach focusing on fathers' influence within the context of systemic and ecological determinants of child development and well-being. Specifically, we are interested in the theories advanced by Bronfenbrenner (1979), Schor and Menaghan (1995), Doherty et al. (1998), and Earls and Carson (2001), all of whom argue that child development outcomes are affected by multiple systems comprising the mother and father, the family, and the community, institutions, and culture within which the child lives; all of these, in turn, affect each other in reciprocal, bidirectional ways within a holistic system.

Adopting a systemic ecological model allows researchers to reconceptualize father involvement beyond direct effects and maternal standards of care to highlight the many ways in which fathers indirectly influence child development outcomes on many levels through a multiply determined process. This is congruent both with the conceptual shift over the past 30 years within fathering scholarship toward placing more value on indirect effects and with seeing these indirect effects as potentially more important than direct effects (Lamb, 2010). Within this theoretical model, fathers represent an integral component of the child's microsystem (i.e., the child's immediate relationships with parents), but they can also indirectly affect child development outcomes through the influence the father has on larger macro- and exosystems (e.g., schools, health care providers, parenting practices). For example, Canadian researchers Ball and Moselle (2007) argue that fathers indirectly influence child development outcomes through their direct influence on family income; adequacy of food and housing; access to high-quality early childhood education and care, post-secondary educational opportunities, and leisure opportunities; and availability of social support. These less direct effects of father involvement often flow through the mediating variable of family resources; however, other variables such as the quality of the relationship the father has with the child's mother (regardless of marital status) also indirectly impact child development outcomes through the variables of family cohesion and child-rearing strength (Ball & Moselle, 2007; Doherty et al., 1998). This attentiveness to indirect effects is evidenced in Pleck's (2010b) revised version of the original father involvement conceptualization presented in 1985 by Lamb, Pleck, Charnov, and Levine. In his later work, Pleck moves beyond engagement, accessibility, and responsibility to include the domains of indirect care and process responsibility. These additions to the model highlight the many ways in which fathers care indirectly for their children through providing for and making arrangements for goods and services to benefit the child, being an advocate for the child within various social institutions, and providing a source of emotional and instrumental support for other people (primarily mothers) who provide direct care for their children (Pleck, 2010b).

To balance the preoccupation in the literature with the unidirectional influence of fathers on children, it is important to explore how children influence fathers. An integral component of the systemic ecological model is the attention it gives to bidirectional effects. Research suggests that children can and do influence the adult development of the father in terms of shifts in his values, expectations, use of time, relationships with the co-parent, and orientation toward the self (Daly, Ashbourne, & Brown, 2009). Likewise, many theoretical developments have highlighted the ways in which children influence not only their father's individual adult development (Hawkins, Christiansen, Sargent, & Hill, 1993; Palkovitz, 2002) but also his other relationships, including those with the child's mother or with his employer (Doherty et al., 1998). Research has also demonstrated that a mother's actions, behaviours, and beliefs can influence father involvement levels (Allen & Hawkins, 1999), indicating yet another potential source of bidirectionality within a systemic family model. Although an integral component of any systemic, ecological, and bidirectional model involves an examination of these bidirectional effects on the father from multiple sources, providing a review of the research in these domains is beyond the scope of this chapter. Also beyond its scope is an examination of the ways in which the child's inherent genetic, biochemical, and neurological makeup impacts child development outcomes. It is possible, for example, that a child's IQ level could have more explanatory power with respect to measurable cognitive development than some socio-cultural factors within the systemic ecological model (such as levels of father involvement). Overall, the primary focus of this chapter is to explore the direct and indirect ways in which fathers influence their children's development. To this end, we first address the primary ways in which the term *father involvement* has been operationalized in the research literature and some of the limitations inherent in this conceptualization.

What Is Father Involvement?

How Father Involvement Is Operationalized
The dominant way in which father involvement has been measured is by examining the time a father and child spend together. This includes frequency of contact, amount of time spent together, and perceived accessibility and availability of the father. It can also include the amount of time fathers

spend performing routine physical child care such as bathing and preparing meals and clothing, in addition to the amount of time fathers spend playing with their child and how effective, mutual, and reciprocal the play is. Many of the measures within this conceptualization utilize variations of the constructs of engagement, accessibility, and responsibility emphasized by Lamb et al. (1985).

The quality of the father-child relationship is another common way in which father involvement has been operationalized. In research studies using this measure, a father is defined as involved if his relationship with his child can be described as sensitive, warm, close, friendly, supportive, intimate, nurturing, affectionate, encouraging, comforting, and accepting (Day & Lamb, 2004; Lamb, 2000; Palkovitz, 1997; Pleck, 1997; Pleck & Masciadrelli, 2004; Schoppe-Sullivan, McBride, & Ho, 2004). Fathers have also been classified as being involved if their child has developed a strong, secure attachment to them. Investment in the paternal role, another measure of father involvement, concentrates on assessing the father's level of investment in child rearing, including his ability to be an authoritative parent and the degree to which he facilitates and attends to his child's needs.

Finally, some research has equated father involvement with father presence and family structure (Day & Lamb, 2004; Lamb, 2000; Palkovitz, 1997; Pleck, 1997; Pleck & Masciadrelli, 2004; Schoppe-Sullivan et al., 2004). This method of measurement dominates the father absence literature and often relies on correlational studies that demonstrate the importance of father presence by comparing children who do not live with their fathers with those who do. Overall, tremendous variation in the conceptualization and measurement of father involvement exists due to different scenarios, different methods of assessment, and different populations (Day & Lamb, 2004).

Limitations of the Father Involvement Construct

Several limitations exist regarding the ways in which father involvement has been conceptualized and measured, and the ways in which its impacts have been understood and assessed. These limitations present a variety of challenges and qualifications to the interpretation of the research findings presented in this chapter. From a methodological point of view, one significant limitation of father involvement research to date is that most studies are correlational and often cross-sectional. This makes it problematic to infer the direction of causality and impossible to account for selection effects or pre-existing conditions inherent in the child or other contexts that may be indirectly impacting child development outcomes (Pleck & Masciadrelli, 2004). Population sampling and representative issues are also important considerations. For example, many of the studies of children who live without their fathers utilize African-American samples. This has led some scholars to question whether the detrimental child development outcomes associated with father absence may be due in part to the disadvantaged, disenfranchised, and de-privileged experience of systemic and institutionalized racism that flows through the experience of poverty, low parent education, and teen motherhood (C. C. Harper & McLanahan, 2004). Moreover, much of the research focusing on the impact of father involvement on child development is based on studies conducted in the United States and results in samples with different ethnic characteristics and family demographics from those of Canada. To the extent that research is available, we include findings from research about Canadian fathers and families.

Perhaps the largest conceptual limitation to the father involvement research is that father involvement is often cast as a unidimensional construct. Direct engagement with children (e.g., playing, reading), as articulated by Lamb, Pleck, and Levine (1987), has tended to dominate assessments of father involvement. In particular, the emphasis has been on the way in which fathers engage with young children (predominantly in preschool years). Although this research has provided important insights into fathers' direct impact on their children through various types of play and caregiving activities, many of the developmental and contextual pathways of influence have been overlooked. Adopting a systemic ecological model shifts the focus from an analysis of micro environments and unidimensional assumptions toward more innovative approaches.

Some scholars have begun to explore father involvement as a multidimensional construct (Hawkins et al., 2002; Palkovitz, 1997; Schoppe-Sullivan et al., 2004) that changes over time as a function of the child's stages of development and fathers' developmental challenges (Palkovitz & Palm, 2005). For example, researchers have highlighted the importance of exploring other dimensions beyond direct engagement, including financial support, responsibility for care arrangements, warmth or closeness of the relationship, and emotional responsiveness (Cabrera, Tamis-LeMonda, Bradley, Hofferth, & Lamb, 2000). However, efforts to construct a pragmatic yet valid and reliable measure of father involvement have had to face the challenge of balancing the need to capture the complex dimensions of father involvement with the practical need for a user-friendly format (Schoppe-Sullivan et al., 2004). Thus, significant measurement challenges lie ahead in the effort to capture the multi-dimensional nature of father involvement (Day & Lamb, 2004).

Summary of the Literature

Direct Effects of Father Involvement
Before exploring the many indirect and contextual pathways through which fathers influence their children, it is important to briefly highlight the wealth

of father involvement scholarship that focuses primarily on direct effects. The discussion of these effects will focus on the substantive areas of four child development outcomes – cognitive, emotional, social, and physical health – and will reference a much more extensive and detailed table of research findings and sources found in the appendix to this chapter. As such, only large trends found in numerous studies will be reported here as general themes in the research. Readers are encouraged to refer to the appendix for more specific citations. When reviewing this research, it is important to keep in mind that many of the findings are nuanced and qualified in ways that space constraints do not allow us to explicate. Presenting data in a table format has its limitations. For example, it is easy to gloss over important differences among the studies. In addition, not all the studies cited are equally credible, nor is it easy to compare results fairly due to the diverse ranges in ages of children and fathers studied, sample sizes, sampling strategies, measures of father involvement and outcome variables, definitions of fathers, robustness of findings, and differences in outcomes based on the gender of the child. Given the scope and vision for this chapter, these differences will not be addressed specifically. The key idea in citing these data is to demonstrate that the research reports statistically significant effects of positive father involvement on various domains of child development. It is important to summarize the literature on direct effects before exploring the role played by indirect pathways, the aim of this latter exploration being understanding of the more systemic ecological determinants of father involvement and children's well-being.

Cognitive Development
Research indicates that having an involved father can benefit children not only in the forms of higher intellectual competence, problem solving, and cognitive abilities, but also in the forms of higher school grades, higher educational attainment, increased academic motivation, positive attitudes toward school, and enjoyment and value of education. Conversely, the absence of father involvement has been linked to detrimental outcomes such as lower academic performance and achievement, lower intellectual ability, lower educational attainment, and increased likelihood of experiencing behavioural problems at school such as having difficulty paying attention, being expelled or suspended, or being non-compliant.

Emotional Development and Well-Being
Research indicates that children of involved fathers tend to be more likely to have high self-esteem, manage their emotions and impulses in an appropriate manner, demonstrate a high tolerance for stress and frustration, be happy, and feel securely attached to their fathers. This research also

indicates a relationship between positive father involvement and a lower frequency of internalizing symptoms (such as depression, sadness, and anxiety) and externalizing symptoms (including delinquent, violent, or disruptive behaviour). In contrast, research suggests that children who live without their fathers tend to be more likely to demonstrate negative internalizing and externalizing behaviours and are more likely to be unhappy, sad, or hyperactive.

Social Development
Research suggests that children of involved fathers tend to demonstrate social competence, social initiative, social maturity, and pro-social development. In addition, they tend to be more likely to have friends, be well liked by their peers, and experience positive friendship qualities such as generosity and reciprocity. Their social relationships are less likely to be aggressive, conflictual, and negative. Children of involved fathers also tend to be more likely to have long-term, close friendships embedded in social networks, have close intimate relationships with romantic partners as adults, and be less likely to divorce. In contrast, research suggests that children who live without their fathers are more likely to choose deviant peers, have trouble getting along with other children, and be more aggressive.

Physical Health
A number of physical health outcomes for children are directly influenced by their father's own health choices, characteristics, and behaviours. For example, father obesity, BMI score, percentage body fat, diet, activity levels, and enjoyment of physical activity are all positively correlated with obesity levels, BMI scores, and percentage of body fat in their children. Children who live without their fathers are more likely to experience health-related problems such as higher infant mortality rates; higher incidence of burns, bad falls or accidents, obesity, and asthma; poorer health if diabetic; and greater risk of physical abuse or harm due to physical neglect. Regarding the latter, Sedlak and Broadhurst (1996) argue that although parents may not be the perpetrators of the maltreatment, the stressors of single parenting combined with the context of inadequate social and practical support may help explain the empirical link between parent structure and child maltreatment. Children who live without their fathers are also more likely to use and abuse drugs and alcohol, and to engage in earlier and risky sexual activity.

These research results on direct effects yield insight into the ways in which specific behaviours and activities of fathers can influence children's well-being. Regardless of measurement approach, the overall pattern of research findings supports a positive link between greater involvement and positive child development outcomes. There is, however, a danger in construing father involvement as causal. As Palkovitz (2002) notes, the contributions of father involvement must be assessed within a broader context of possible direct and indirect contributors to developmental outcomes.

Indirect Pathways and Contextual Factors in Father Involvement

In keeping with our theoretical orientation and its emphasis on indirect, multiply determined processes, it is important to identify broad categories of factors that have emerged in the father involvement literature as being important mechanisms by which fathers make a difference in their children's lives through indirect pathways. To this end, this section will explore the impact on fathers and children of socio-economic status (SES), the co-parental relationship, ethnic and cultural contexts, and institutional and ideological practices, with attention given to non-residential fathering when research is available.

Socio-Economic Status

We conceptualize the term *socio-economic status* broadly to include not only a father's access to social capital and economic resources in the form of employment opportunities, job characteristics, education levels, and income, but also how these variables influence his own attitudes, beliefs, and behaviours in relationship to fathering. We also explore the impact of poverty, or lack of adequate socio-economic resources, on child development outcomes.

Research suggests that perhaps the most influential way in which fathers indirectly impact their children is through their socio-economic status. In fact, Cabrera et al. (2000) argue that the often negative impact of father absence on child development outcomes flows through many paths, an important one being economic loss and disadvantage. It is possible, therefore, that many of the negative consequences outlined above relating to children who do not reside with their father are flowing, in part, through the loss of social capital and economic resources associated with marital dissolution. For example, Kesner and McKenry's (2001) research suggests that contrary to popular belief, single-parent family structure is not by itself a risk factor for children's social development outcomes. They argue that because SES also influences these outcomes, controlling for it would reveal that no differences exist between children from single- and two-parent homes on measures of social skills and conflict management. Likewise, Battle (2002) argues that when socio-economic status was accounted for, family configuration (father presence or absence) was not statistically significant in predicting educational achievement.

There is growing evidence that many of the negative effects associated with father absence are related to poverty. Children who live without their fathers are, on average, more likely to be poor (Horn & Sylvester, 2002); the US Census Bureau (2003) reported that children in single-mother-headed homes are five times more likely to be poor. In Canada, 13% of all children live in a low-income family (average income after taxes below $21,400), and children from single-parent-headed households are much more vulnerable to poverty than children from two-parent families (Fleury, 2008). Research suggests that the intersecting effects of poverty and racial/ethnic background (due to the often inequitable and minoritizing macro-level contexts within which these are experienced) can have a stronger impact on child development outcomes than a father's child-rearing practices (Mosley & Thompson, 1995; Pleck, 1997). This suggests that the indirect benefits a child receives from a father's income may be more important than the more direct effects that his parenting style may have on certain child development outcomes. Indeed, Averett, Gennetian, and Peters (1997) found that levels of father care were less influential on cognitive development than were the child care centres their children were placed in, suggesting a possible interaction among fathers' income levels, access to high-quality child care providers, and cognitive development. In fact, some scholars argue that father presence may not be as important as the money that fathers contribute to the family's resources (Battle, 2002; Kesner & McKenry, 2001).

This is further borne out in research on poverty, which suggests that a father's ability to provide economic resources protects the child from the documented ill effects of poverty on physical health in the form of poor nutrition and health problems (Finnie & Bernard, 2004; Klerman, 1991; Kornberger, Fast, & Williamson 2001). The literature on poverty also consistently documents that inadequate economic resources put children at a greater risk of developmental delay (Finnie and Bernard, 2004; Kornberger et al., 2001), low school grades, dropping out of school (Levin, 1986), and emotional and behavioural problems such as depression, low self-esteem, conflict with peers, and a variety of behavioural disorders including conduct disorder (Brooks-Gunn, Britto, & Brady, 1999; Duncan & Brooks-Gunn, 1997; Finnie & Bernard, 2004; Klerman, 1991; Kornberger et al., 2001; Marsiglio, Amato, Day, & Lamb, 2000; Mayer, 1997; McLoyd & Wilson, 1991). Many of these effects of poverty mirror those discussed in the father absence literature and could easily be conflated with the detrimental effects of father absence on children. Disentangling the relative contributions of these direct and indirect effects is complex.

Outside of the circumstances of poverty, a father's earnings remain influential on child outcomes. Fathers' earnings have been positively associated with the psychological well-being of sons and daughters (Amato, 1998). For example, in Mexican-American families, fathers' income was negatively associated with depressive symptoms in adolescent children (Crouter, Davis, Updegraff, Delgado, & Fortner, 2006). Indeed, some scholars have found that fathers' earnings are positively associated with the educational attainment of young adult sons and daughters even when mothers' earnings are controlled for (Kaplan, Lancaster, & Anderson, 1998; Yeung, Duncan, & Hill, 2000).

Tightly bound to the impact of fathers' earnings on child development outcomes are the ways in which mothers' and fathers' employment characteristics and opportunities interact to shape the amount of time fathers have available to be engaged in their children's lives. Lamb (2000) reports that in two-parent families where mothers are employed, fathers are more involved with their children when compared with families with non-employed mothers. When mothers earn more money than fathers, fathers are also likely to spend more time caring for their children (Casper & O'Connell, 1998). Additionally, when parents work non-standard work schedules, fathers are more likely to be involved in providing care to children (Presser, 1995). Gerson (1993) also found that fathers in middle- to high-level management positions, self-employed fathers, and blue-collar working fathers were less engaged in daily child care tasks than were lower-level white-collar workers; this was due to variance in job characteristics associated with different types of employment such as flexibility in work schedules, total work hours, non-standard hours, and hours worked from home. Interestingly, some researchers have found that fathers who have higher incomes spend less time with their children than do low-income fathers but that the time they do spend is more positive (Levy-Schiff & Israelashvili, 1988). Some research also suggests that when fathers are required to take on fathering responsibilities due to unemployment, they have a tendency to parent more harshly, and children may suffer as a result (Russell, 1983, as cited in Cabrera et al., 2000). This suggests that more opportunities for father involvement may not always benefit children, depending on the reason for that increased amount of available time. This research indicates the need to explore more carefully the many and varied ways in which job characteristics operating within the broader macro-level system of the work-family context can have indirect implications for child development outcomes.

Although our discussion of socio-economic status has focused primarily on fathers' earnings and employment characteristics, paternal education levels also have indirect effects. Research indicates that a father's level of education is positively associated with children's cognitive and achievement test scores (Blau & Grossberg, 1992; Parcel & Menaghan, 1994), school attendance (Brown & Rife, 1991), and occupational status and earnings later in life (Amato, 1998). Similarly, Sayer, Gauthier, and Furstenberg (2004) documented a negative effect of a father's low education level on the time a father spends with his child. They hypothesized that this was probably flowing through the impact of low education on job characteristics such as having multiple jobs or jobs with inflexible or non-standard hours.

Understanding these employment circumstances may help explain why some studies report that fathers with higher levels of education are more accessible to and engaged with their school-aged children (Blair, Wenk, & Hardesty, 1994; Goldscheider & Waite, 1991), which has implications for child outcomes.

As a final caveat, it is important to explore how being able to provide for one's child impacts the father and his orientation toward fathering. Danziger and Radin (1990) found that young fathers who were able to provide economically for their children were also more likely to be engaged with and nurturing of them, even if they lived apart, due in part to their belief that being a "good father" equated with being a "good provider." Their research suggests that enhanced job opportunities and earning power encourage young fathers to take on parental obligations. Likewise, Peters and Ehrenberg (2008) found that among divorce group participants, structural factors – including a father's higher socio-economic status – were predictors of higher assessment scores on combined nurturant fathering and involvement measures. This suggests that a father's ability to find, provide, and secure economic resources for his child helps him to remain involved in his child's life regardless of his marital status. This commitment to fathering found within the characteristics of the father is likely to positively impact his child's development in the form of increased direct positive father involvement. Other characteristics inherent in the father, such as his level of education, also influence child development outcomes but through indirect pathways by increasing the child's access to opportunities.

Although non-resident fathers may have fewer opportunities to be involved in face-to-face contact with their children, their involvement in their children's lives through the payment of child support has been found to impact a wide variety of positive child cognitive development outcomes. For example, the payment of child support has been found to be a factor in improved cognitive test scores; higher reading, verbal, and math ability (Argys, Peters, Brooks-Gunn, & Smith, 1998; King, 1994); better educational achievement, success, and competence, including higher grades and attained education level (Amato & Gilbreth, 1999; Graham, Beller, & Hernandez, 1994; King, 1994; Knox & Bane, 1994; Marsiglio et al., 2000; McLanahan, Seltzer, Hanson, & Thomson, 1994), and increased probability of graduating from high school and attending university or college (Menning, 2006). In fact, Graham et al. (1994) found that payment of child support helps children overcome about two thirds of the disadvantage in years of school completed and reduces high school drop-out rates as well as the percentage of students who fall behind their age cohorts in high school. In addition, child support payments have been found to improve children's access to educational resources and increase the amount of cognitive stimulation in the home (Graham et al., 1994; Knox & Bane, 1994).

Payment of child support has also been linked to higher levels of social and emotional adjustment, fewer behavioural problems, better ratings on the personal maturity scale, positive behavioural adjustment and adaptation after divorce, and general well-being in children (Amato & Gilbreth, 1999; Furstenberg, Morgan, & Allison, 1987; Greene & Moore, 2000; King, 1994; Lamb, Sternberg, & Thompson, 1997; McLanahan et al., 1994). Likewise, the payment of child support has been linked to positive physical health outcomes for children, including the decreased likelihood of a low-birth-weight baby (Graham & Beller, 2002; Padilla & Reichman, 2001), and improved children's standards of living, health, and nutrition (McLanahan et al., 1994). These findings have led some scholars to argue that the amount of child support received from non-resident fathers has more of an impact on child development outcomes than income from any other source (Argys et al., 1998; Beller & Chung, 1988; Knox, 1996).

The Co-Parental Relationship
Another way in which fathers indirectly impact their child's well-being is through the relationship they have with the child's mother. When fathers are supportive and encouraging, mothers tend to be more competent parents. They tend to be more patient, flexible, emotionally responsive, sensitive, and available to their infants and young children (Snarey, 1993). This tends to enhance the quality of the mother-child relationship and thus facilitates positive developmental outcomes for the children (Lamb, 1997) such as popularity with their peers (Boyum & Parke, 1995), increased self-control (Brody et al., 1994), and positive relationships with peers and intimate partners (Amato, 1998). Other positive indirect benefits of a supportive co-parental relationship have been documented for infants. For example, fathers can indirectly influence the physical health and well-being of their infants through facilitating optimal health outcomes for mothers. When fathers are emotionally supportive of their parenting partner, mothers are more likely to enjoy a greater sense of well-being and good postpartum mental health (Gjerdingen, Froberg, & Fontaine, 1991); have a relatively problem-free pregnancy, delivery process, and nursing experience (Biller, 1993); and maintain or adopt healthy pregnancy behaviours (Teitler, 2001). For example, Wolfberg et al. (2004) found that 75% of women whose partners attended a breastfeeding-promotion class initiated breastfeeding. Research indicates that single mothers are twice as likely as married mothers to experience a bout of depression and experience higher levels of stress (Cairney, Boyle, Offord, & Racine, 2003), suggesting that fathers can have a positive indirect impact on mothers' health and children's well-being.

When the co-parental relationship is not supportive, however, children tend to suffer. Fathers who show little warmth or are abusive toward their parenting partners have partners who are more likely to feel emotionally drained, irritable, and distracted. This increases the likelihood that these mothers will employ non-effective parenting strategies (such as harsher and less consistent discipline) when interacting with their children and will respond to them in an impatient, non-nurturing manner (Amato, 1998), which has implications for child outcomes.

Indirect co-parental effects can also flow through the pathway of marital quality. Happily married parents tend to interact more positively with their infants (Levy-Schiff, 1994), preschool children (Lindahl, Clements, & Markman, 1997), and school-aged children (Simons, Beaman, Conger, & Chao, 1993), which suggests possible linkages to observable child development outcomes. Schoppe, Mangelsdorf, and Frosch (2001) found that high levels of supportive co-parenting have been associated with fewer externalizing behaviour problems in preschoolers. Likewise, frequent positive conversations between husbands and wives were found to be a significant indirect factor affecting children's sociability (Kato, Ishii-Kuntz, Makino, & Tsuchiya, 2002). It is likely that a positive co-parental relationship models many important relationship skills that children can use in their own relationships, such as providing emotional support, resolving conflict effectively, showing respect, and having positive, open communication. In contrast, marital dissatisfaction and marital arguments when children are young have been associated with adverse effects on paternal synchrony, which negatively impacted the security of the infant-father attachment (Lundy, 2002). In turn, these attachment difficulties are associated with children's behaviour problems when they are older (Aldous & Mulligan, 2002). In addition, research consistently documents a negative association between marital conflict and a variety of child development outcomes, including academic success, behavioural conduct, emotional adjustment, self-esteem, well-being, and social competence (Amato, 1998; Cummings & O'Reilly, 1997; Davies & Cummings, 1994; Emery, 1988; Grych & Fincham, 1990; S. E. Harper & Fine, 2006; Kandel, 1990).

When examining the co-parental relationship, emphasis is often placed on relationship quality and the ways in which the father is supportive of the mother. However, the reverse trend of mothers being supportive of fathers is also an important co-parental relationship dynamic that has implications for children. Mothers may act as gatekeepers and unduly monitor or restrict the ways in which fathers are involved in their children's lives (Allen & Hawkins, 1999). This behaviour may be perceived by the father as unsupportive, which impacts his level of father involvement. For example, Bouchard, Lee, Asgary, and Pelletier (2007) found that a father's perception that his partner has confidence in his parenting ability was related not only to his own feelings of competency and motivation as a father but also to an increased level of involvement with his child. In more serious cases, mothers who intentionally alienate their former partners (referred to as parental alienation syndrome) during divorce transition can indirectly and adversely affect child outcomes, with children reporting feelings of diminished self-esteem, self-hatred, and depression, and increased use of drugs and alcohol (Baker, 2005; Weigel & Donovan, 2006).

Further insight into the importance of the co-parental relationship emerges from the research on non-residential fathers. Davis and Friel (2001) argue that family context, family process, patterns of interaction, and quality of family relationships tend to have more explanatory power with regard to child development outcomes than does the presence or absence of fathers as measured by family structure. Specifically, a father's frequency of contact with his child and his child's feelings about him have proven to be inconsistent predictors of child development outcomes or adjustment (Amato, 1998; Marsiglio et al., 2000). By contrast, the most crucial mediating variable for children with non-residential fathers on child development outcomes is the quality (not quantity) of the father's relationship with the mother and the child (Amato, 1998; Kelly, 2000; Marsiglio et al., 2000).

This suggests not only that the quality of the father-child relationship tends to be related to the quality of the mother/non-resident father relationship and the mother-child relationship (Devault et al., 2008; Dunn, Cheng, O'Connor, & Bridges, 2004) but also that some of the most influential pathways of influence on children of divorce are indirect. Fathers' perceptions of support received from their former spouse contribute to their levels of co-operative co-parental interaction after divorce (Madden-Derdich & Leonard, 2000), which predicts more frequent father-child contact (Sobolewski & King, 2005; Whiteside & Becker, 2000), which in turn predicts higher relationship quality, more responsive fathering, stronger ties between non-resident fathers and their children, and positive child development outcomes (Sobolewski & King, 2005). Non-resident father involvement is related positively to mother's involvement and negatively to interparental conflict (Flouri, 2006), which suggests indirect yet positive implications for child development outcomes (S. E. Harper & Fine, 2006).

With the exception of situations where levels of interparental conflict are particularly high, children generally do better in many domains of child development after marital dissolution when they are able to maintain meaningful relationships with both parents (Amato, 1993; Heath & MacKinnon, 1988; Lamb, 1997). However, many factors come into play in determining the amount of father-child contact that occurs, such as the father's income, future partnerships and stepchildren, and level of satisfaction with the existing arrangements (Swiss & Bourdais, 2009). Non-residential fathers often experience tension between the desire to spend time with their child and the time available to them, which is sometimes constrained by the structural barriers of custody arrangements and employment (Hallman, Deinhart, & Beaton, 2007). The indirect pathways of influence rooted in the quality of the parental alliance combined with more direct pathways of influence through parental warmth, sensitivity, and discipline style can make the difference between a well-adjusted child after divorce and one who experiences negative child development outcomes (Whiteside & Becker, 2000).

Research on co-parental relationships is critical for understanding the indirect ways in which fathers influence their children, whether or not they reside with their children. Rohner and Veneziano (2001) conclude that we may be better off studying father involvement from a triadic (mother-father-child) or systemic perspective rather than focusing on the dyadic (father-child) relationship. When assessing the impact of father involvement on child outcomes, researchers often neglect to control for the quality of the mother-child relationship, which could account for a portion of the observable effects. For example, Amato (1994) observed that the extent of a mother's child care and the quality of the relationship with the child may account for the supposed positive effect of the father's child care. This highlights the need to consider systemic, bidirectional, and indirect pathways when assessing child outcomes.

Ethnicity and Cultural Contexts

The resources and challenges for different ethnic groups provide another social backdrop for exploring the indirect pathways by which fathers influence their children. In Canada, many cultural, subcultural, and cross-cultural variations of fathering exist. Este and Tachble (2009) explored the experience of fatherhood for Sudanese refugee men living in Canada and found that they were operating within a unique system of stressors, including underemployment, language barriers, cultural loss, racism, and mental health issues. In a similar vein, Shimoni, Este, and Clark (2003) studied immigrant fathers from the former Yugoslavia, South America, South Asia, and China within a Canadian context and found that the stressors of underemployment and immigrant status were impacting the father's ability to effectively fill the role of provider in the family. These cultural challenges may have indirect effects on child development outcomes, particularly if they begin to flow through the variables of economic loss and disadvantage. Economic loss, however, is not the only potential indirect effect. Qin (2009) found that Chinese fathers, in addition to dealing with loss of employment status when they immigrated to the United States, were struggling psychologically with the transition to a new culture and experiencing elevated levels of stress and alienation. These feelings acted as a psychological barrier to father involvement, and adolescent children reported experiencing an associated sense of emotional disconnect from their fathers.

Although the challenges associated with newcomer and minority status have the potential to indirectly and negatively impact child development outcomes, these experiences can also be positive. For example, Este and Tachble (2009) found that newcomer fathers saw themselves as important holders of cultural knowledge, values, customs, heritage, and traditions. Although these fathers may have been economically disadvantaged, they were also important role models for their children in providing strategies for how to navigate the structural and cultural stressors unique to their immigrant status. Unique cultural contexts often provide opportunities for fathers to reconstruct fathering in ways that work for them. A study of Native American fathering in the United States found that fathers saw themselves more as protectors and disciplinarians of their children than as economic providers due in part to the high levels of unemployment in their community, which allowed men to seek other ways to define themselves as involved fathers (Keltner, 1996). This suggests that although minority status may present economic challenges to fathers that indirectly and negatively impact child outcomes, this situation can also present fathers with unique opportunities to reconstruct the meaning and experience of fathering, which can positively influence their children's development.

Institutional and Ideological Practices
Some scholars argue that despite the emergence of the "new fatherhood" (LaRossa, 1997), ideologically rooted assumptions relating to mothers and fathers still seem to relegate fathers to less important parental roles. For example, Wall and Arnold (2007) performed an analysis of a year-long Canadian newspaper series dedicated to family issues and found that support for father involvement operated within the assumptions of fathers as part-time, secondary parents whose relationship with children was less important than that of mothers. These public commentaries on the roles of fathers reflect a set of attitudes and practices that may continue to limit the commitment of fathers to be primary parents in their children's lives. At the same time, national time-use studies indicate that men are increasing their overall commitment to parenting activities, which is slowly transforming the image of fathers as "helpers" to mothers toward a model of co-parenting where roles and responsibilities are shared equally (Cabrera et al., 2000).

The need to make institutional practices and policies more father friendly can be seen within a variety of institutional contexts. Children's education programs and services, community parenting resources and classes, hospital labour and delivery units, family-friendly work policy initiatives, and other social service delivery agencies have attempted to incorporate more father-friendly policies, practices, and service delivery in efforts to support and strengthen men's involvement in their children's lives. How shifts in these public policies and practices directly and indirectly impact child development outcomes needs to be carefully explored in the literature (see also

Chapter 10 in this volume). Many organizations that provide father-friendly parenting classes report improvements on measures of father involvement. For example, Benzies, Magill-Evans, Harrison, MacPhail, and Kimak (2008) found that fathers' completion of their early intervention program designed to strengthen new fathers' skills with their infants improved father-infant interaction. Likewise, McAllister, Wilson, and Burton (2004) were able to identify approaches and strategies that were the most effective in encouraging fathers' engagement in their children's early education. In addition, hospitals have been able to demonstrate how shifts in their service delivery have enabled fathers to be more involved in their children's well-being, which resulted in optimal outcomes for the children (Tessier et al., 2009).

Brown, Callahan, Strega, Walmsley, and Domenelli (2009) argue that policies, practices, and discourses within the child welfare system in Canada have made many fathers invisible regardless of whether or not they are deemed a risk or an asset to the family. Unfortunately, invisibility is not the only challenge fathers face within institutional contexts. When seen, fathers are often viewed through a deficit lens (Hawkins & Dollahite, 1997) and are represented as deviant, irresponsible, irrelevant, or even dangerous. Brown et al. (2009) further argue that the gendered institutional practices of the welfare workers themselves – in conjunction with larger cultural discourses on gender, ethnicity, class, and culture – systematically reproduce biases and stereotypes of "deadbeat dads" within the child welfare system. Within this larger cultural context, macro-level ideologies in the form of institutional paradigms and practices can present unique challenges to the micro-level relationships between fathers and children. This has led some scholars to advocate for a reframing of child welfare practices, policy, and discourse in Canada that is more inclusive of fathers (Strega et al., 2008; see also this volume, Chapter 11).

Conclusion
Within the systemic ecological model, many factors are interconnected and act simultaneously in multiple direct, indirect, and mutually causal ways. With this understanding, it is imperative to make distinctions among the significant and non-significant pathways of influence and their ensuing direct and indirect effects. Identifying multiple pathways of influence on child development outcomes flowing through the varying circumstances of mothers, fathers, and broader macro-level influences adds complexity to our understanding of child development outcomes but does not always tell us which factors, when considered within the larger matrix of interacting influences, are the most important or statistically significant. In our effort to sort out this complexity, it is important to recognize that direct and measurable effects on children may exist independent of the father or be influenced by the father indirectly in such an insignificant manner that the connection

becomes statistically and conceptually meaningless. The reverse of this scenario is also possible, where fathers can independently and uniquely impact child outcomes independent of significant indirect influences of mothers, teachers, or child care providers. The task of future research will be to determine not only which pathways of influence (direct, indirect, multiple), when compared simultaneously with other pathways of influence, are the most significant for understanding child development outcomes but also which ones open up viable options for facilitating and supporting change. This, however, cannot be determined until researchers begin assessing multiple, direct, and indirect factors of influence on child development outcomes as embedded within mesosystems ranging from the micro- to macro-levels of analysis.

Required within this more nuanced empirical examination of father involvement is an equally sophisticated theoretical analysis of the "essential father" question. Some fathering advocates argue that fathers are essential to positive child development outcomes because they provide a uniquely male contribution to child development that cannot be met adequately within other parenting contexts. Research suggests, however, that the assumptions on which this hypothesis rest are problematic. Pleck (2010a) argues that in order for the hypothesis to be verified, research must demonstrate that father presence and positive child outcomes are specifically mediated by father involvement *and* by his unique maleness as operating within the context of gender differences in parenting. The research, however, indicates that these assumptions receive only modest and highly qualified support. Consequently, Pleck (2010a) argues against the "essential father" hypothesis in favour of the "important father" hypothesis, which rests on the assumption that good fathering is one of many factors that contribute to positive child development outcomes, and that although it can operate independently of good mothering, it is not necessarily tied to the father's "maleness."

This "important father" hypothesis is congruent with years of parenting research that consistently indicates that "parental warmth, nurturance, and closeness are associated with positive child outcomes regardless of whether the parent involved is a mother or a father" (Lamb, 2010, 11). This suggests that the gendered characteristics and differences of the parent (their inherent "maleness" or "femaleness") central to the "essential father" hypothesis are much less important in mediating child development outcomes than the quality of the relationship parents have with the child (Lamb, 2010).

Extant research on the effects of father involvement has many limitations. First, much of the literature reviewed focuses on the dynamics of nuclear families, including the impact of divorce; considerably less attention is paid to other, potentially important macro-level influences on child outcomes, including child care providers, early childhood educators, extended family, grandparents, peers, siblings, involved friends, and neighbours. Furthermore, little research has been conducted on the multiple pathways that exist in families with gay, lesbian, bisexual, and transgendered fathers (Epstein, 2009) or in adoptive families. A third limitation concerns the fact that child development outcomes are typically assessed on very specific dimensions in a highly compartmentalized fashion (e.g., cognitive, social, and physical health). The influences of fathers on children are complex, and child developmental outcomes are equally complex in that many connections exist among the cognitive, social, emotional, and physical dimensions of children's well-being. Failing to recognize this complexity may limit our conceptualization of child well-being to the easily measured and readily quantifiable outcomes endemic in the literature while we gloss over the more elusive, yet potentially crucial development of characteristics such as love, morality, character, awareness, and compassion within the child.

Perhaps the most challenging task of future father involvement research will be to track how specific beliefs, actions, and behaviours of fathers ripple out in unforeseen and undetermined ways into the larger mesosystems in which they are embedded. For example, a father who sits down to help his son with his homework (a very direct, face-to-face form of father engagement) may, in addition to directly enhancing the child's academic achievements, support the child's mother, who does not have time that evening to help with homework because of a work deadline. This evidence of support for the mother may help the mother to be more available to the child later, may strengthen the marriage, or may increase child-rearing strength or family cohesion, all of which may effect positive child outcomes indirectly, simultaneously, holistically, and indeterminately at a later time. This highlights the need for future research both to engage with previously overlooked dimensions of father involvement and to explore how they interact within larger systemic and temporal frameworks.

The focus of this chapter has been on how fathers influence the developmental outcomes of their children. There is ample research evidence pointing to some very specific and direct ways in which fathers can shape these outcomes for their children. A review of the research literature, such as that found in the appendix to this chapter, readily leads one to the conclusion that positively involved fathers make a salutary difference to developmental outcomes for children. However, central to our thesis is the need to exercise caution in taking an overly simplistic view of these relationships. We argue for the merits of a systemic ecological framework that includes multiple pathways for understanding the influences of fathers and how these effects operate. Our response to the question of how fathers matter is that the answers are complex and partial, encouraging a differentiated mapping in order to track the diverse pathways of how fathers influence their children's lives.

Appendix 3.1

Impact of positive father involvement on child development outcomes

Research finding	Source
POSITIVE FATHER INVOLVEMENT AND ITS EFFECTS ON CHILDREN'S COGNITIVE DEVELOPMENT	
Infants of involved fathers tend to demonstrate higher cognitive functioning.	Nugent, 1991
Toddlers of involved fathers tend to demonstrate higher IQs by age three.	Yogman, Kindlon, & Earls, 1995
Children of involved fathers tend to demonstrate superior problem-solving and adaptive skills.	Biller, 1993
Children of involved fathers tend to be more playful, resourceful, skillful, and attentive when presented with a problem.	Mischel, Shoda, & Peake, 1988
Children of involved fathers tend to have higher grade point averages and better achievement test scores, and demonstrate more cognitive competence on standardized intellectual assessments.	Astone & McLanahan, 1991; Cooksey & Fondell, 1996; Feldman & Wentzel, 1990; Gadsden & Ray, 2003; Howard, Lefever, Borkowski, & Whitman, 2006; McBride, Schoppe-Sullivan, & Ho, 2005; National Center for Education Statistics, 1997; Nord & West, 2001; Radin, 1994; Snarey, 1993; Wentzel & Feldman, 1993
Children of involved fathers tend to be more likely to enjoy school and have positive attitudes toward school.	Flouri, 2006; Flouri, Buchanan, & Bream, 2002; National Center for Education Statistics, 1997
Children of involved fathers tend to be more likely to graduate and participate in extracurricular activities. They also tend to be less likely to fail a grade, have poor attendance, be suspended or expelled, or have behaviour problems at school.	Astone & McLanahan, 1991; Brown & Rife, 1991; Mosley & Thompson, 1995; National Center for Education Statistics, 1997; Nord & West, 2001; William, 1997; Zimmerman, Salem, and Notaro, 2000
Adolescent boys whose fathers demonstrated academic support were more likely to demonstrate academic motivation to try hard in school, feel their grades were important, and place a high value on education.	Alfaro, Umana-Taylor, & Bamaca, 2006

▶

◄ *Appendix 3.1*

Research finding	Source
Children whose fathers were interested, helpful, and available tended to be invested in school achievement and worked on their potential at school because their fathers were more apt to recognize and approve of their efforts.	Doyle, Markiewicz, Brendgen, Lieberman, & Voss, 2000
Higher non-resident father involvement tends to predict lower probabilities of school failure among adolescents, fewer externalizing and internalizing problems for adolescents at school, and overall better academic outcomes.	Kelly, 2000; King & Sobolewski, 2006; Menning, 2006; Whiteside & Becker, 2000
Children of single adolescent mothers strated better socio-emotional and academic functioning in school-related areas than children who did not.	Howard et al., 2006

POSITIVE FATHER INVOLVEMENT AND ITS EFFECTS ON CHILDREN'S EMOTIONAL DEVELOPMENT AND WELL-BEING

A father may not become actively involved in his child's school performance until after the child has begun to evidence problems in that area. This explains the potentially counter-intuitive inverse relationship found in this study between father involvement and children's school achievement.	McBride, Dyer, Liu, Brown, & Hong, 2009
Infants of involved fathers tend to be securely attached to them. The long-term effects of a secure father-child attachment have been associated uniquely with general self-esteem for adolescent children.	Cox, Owen, Henderson, & Margand, 1992; Doyle et al., 2000
Infants of involved fathers tend to be more curious and eager to explore the environment, relate more maturely to strangers, react more competently to complex and novel stimuli, and be more trusting in branching out in their explorations.	Biller, 1993; Pruett, 1997
Children of involved fathers tend to be more likely to demonstrate a greater tolerance for stress and frustration.	Mischel et al., 1988

►

◄ *Appendix 3.1*

Research finding	Source
Children of involved fathers tend to be better able to manage their emotions and impulses in an appropriate manner, report positive psychological adjustment, and demonstrate a greater internal locus of control.	Biller, 1993; Mosley & Thompson, 1995; Radin, 1994; Ross & Broh, 2000; Veneziano, 2000; Williams & Radin, 1999
Daughters of involved fathers tend to be happier, busier, and more willing to try new things.	Mosley & Thompson, 1995
Father involvement has been found to contribute significantly and independently to adolescent happiness.	Flouri & Buchanan, 2003a
High father involvement tends to be associated with children's increased feelings of paternal acceptance, which is a factor that plays a role in the development of self-concept and self-esteem.	Culp, Schadle, Robinson, & Culp, 2000
Children of involved fathers tend to have high self-esteem.	Deutsch, Servis, & Payne, 2001; Ross & Broh, 2000
Children of involved fathers tend to demonstrate a lower frequency of externalizing symptoms such as delinquent, violent, disruptive, and anti-social behaviour; lying; and behavioural problems such as conduct disorder and hyperactivity.	Aldous & Mulligan, 2002; Amato & Rivera, 1999; Flouri, 2006; Flouri & Buchanan, 2002a; Formoso, Gonzales, Barrera, & Dumka, 2007; Harris, Furstenberg, & Marmer, 1998; Howard et al., 2006; King & Sobolewski, 2006; Mosley & Thompson, 1995; Zimmerman, Salem, & Maton, 1995; Zimmerman, Salem, & Notaro, 2000
Higher non-resident father involvement tends to predict decreases in adolescent delinquency, fewer externalizing and internalizing problems for adolescents, and less emotional distress.	Coley & Medeiros, 2007; King & Sobolewski, 2006; Stewart, 2003
Positive father involvement tends to be associated with a lower frequency of internalizing symptoms in children such as depression, emotional distress, sadness, fear, guilt, psychological distress, and anxiety.	Dubowitz et al., 2001; Easterbrooks & Goldberg, 1990; Field, Lang, Yando, & Bendell, 1995; Flouri, 2006; Formoso et al., 2007; Furstenberg & Harris, 1993; Harris et al., 1998; Jorm, Dear, Rodgers, & Christensen, 2003; Zimmerman et al., 1995

►

◄ *Appendix 3.1*

Research finding	Source
Non-residential fathers who engage in authoritative parenting are less likely to have adolescents who experience symptoms of depression or various externalizing problems.	Barber, 1994; Furstenberg & Cherlin, 1991; Simons, Whitbek, Beaman, & Conger, 1994
Early father involvement has been found to protect against psychological maladjustments in adolescents from non-intact families.	Flouri & Buchanan, 2003b
Non-residential fathers who demonstrate paternal warmth increase positive measures of child well-being.	S. E. Harper & Fine, 2006
A close, non-conflictual stepfather-stepchild relationship improves adolescent well-being and close relationships with both stepfathers and non-resident fathers, and is associated with better adolescent outcomes with regard to grades, self-efficacy, internalizing and externalizing behaviours, and acting out in school.	King, 2006; White & Gilbreth, 2001; Yuan & Hamilton, 2006
In adoptive families, young adults' ratings of paternal nurturance and involvement were strongly and positively correlated with their reports of current psycho-social functioning.	Schwartz & Finley, 2006

POSITIVE FATHER INVOLVEMENT AND ITS EFFECTS ON CHILDREN'S SOCIAL DEVELOPMENT

Father involvement has been correlated with children's positively overall social competence, social initiative, social maturity, pro-social development, and capacity for relatedness with others.	Forehand & Nousiainen, 1993; Kato et al., 2002; Krampe & Fairweather, 1993; Parke, 1996; Snarey, 1993; Stolz, Barber, & Olsen, 2005
Children of involved fathers tend to be more likely to have positive peer relations and be popular and well liked. Their peer relations are typified by less negativity, less aggression, less conflict, more reciprocity, more generosity, and more positive friend ship qualities.	Ducharme, Doyle, & Markiewicz, 2002; Hooven, Gottman, & Katz, 1995; Lieberman, Doyle, & Markiewicz, 1999; Lindsey, Moffett, Clawson, & Mize, 1994; Updegraff, McHale, Crouter, & Kupanoff, 2001; Youngblade & Belsky, 1992

►

Fathers Make a Difference in Their Children's Lives 73

◄ *Appendix 3.1*

Research finding	Source
Children of involved fathers tend to show fewer negative emotional reactions during play with peers, experience less tension in their interactions with other children, solve conflicts by themselves rather than seeking the teacher's assistance, and demonstrate a greater sense of social competence.	Dubowitz et al., 2001; Suess, Grossman & Sroufe, 1992
Positive father involvement tends to protect children from extreme victimization and is negatively associated with bullying behaviour.	Flouri, 2006
Pro-social experiences with fathers tend to play a key role in dissuading daughters from anti-social behaviour.	Kosterman, Haggerty, Spoth, & Redmond, 2004
Children of involved fathers are more likely to have pro-social sibling interactions.	Volling & Belsky, 1992
Children who feel close to their fathers tend to be more likely to have long-term, successful marriages; be satisfied with their romantic partners in mid-life; have more successful intimate relationships; and be less likely to divorce. Likewise, young adults whose fathers were more sensitive in their early play interactions had more secure, healthy partnership representations of their current romantic relationship.	Flouri & Buchanan, 2002b; Franz, McClelland, & Weinberger, 1991; Grossmann, Grossmann, Winter, & Zimmermann, 2002; Moller & Stattin, 2001; Risch, Jodl, & Eccles, 2004
Children of involved fathers tend to be more likely to have supportive social networks consisting of long-term close friendships.	Franz et al., 1991
The strongest predictor of empathic concern in children and adults is high levels of paternal involvement with a child.	Bernadette-Shapiro, Ehrensaft, & Shapiro, 1996; Koestner, Franz, & Weinberger, 1990; Radin, 1994
Fathers' warmth and nurturance significantly predicts children's moral maturity and is associated with more pro-social and positive moral behaviour in boys and girls.	Mosley & Thompson, 1995

►

◄ *Appendix 3.1*

Research finding	Source

POSITIVE FATHER INVOLVEMENT AND ITS EFFECTS ON CHILDREN'S PHYSICAL HEALTH

Father involvement tends to be associated with less substance abuse, less drug use, and less drinking among adolescents	Coombs & Landsverk, 1988; Harris et al., 1998; Zimmerman, Salem, & Notaro, 2000
Father closeness was correlated with children's use of alcohol, cigarettes, and hard drugs, and was connected to family structure, with two-parent families ranking higher on father closeness than single-parent families. Father closeness was also negatively correlated with the number of a child's friends who smoke, drink, and smoke marijuana.	Dorius, Bahr, Hoffmann, & Harmon, 2004; National Fatherhood Initiative, 2004
Obesity of the father is associated with a four-fold increase in the risk of obesity of sons and daughters at age 18. A father's BMI (body mass index) predicts sons' and daughters' BMIs independent of the off-spring's alcohol intake, smoking, and physical fitness, and the father's education.	Burke, Beilin, & Dunbar, 2001; Davison & Birch, 2001
The father's (not the mother's) total nd and percentage body fat was the best predictor of changes in the daughter's total and percentage body fat as well as the father's diet and enjoyment of physical activity. As his BMI rose, so did his daughter's.	Davison & Birch, 2001; Figueroa-Colon, Arani, Goran, & Weinsier, 2000
Fathers' physical inactivity was a strong predictor of children's inactivity.	Finn, Johannsen, & Specker, 2002; Fogelholm, Nuutinen, Pasanen, Myohanen, & Saatela, 1999; Trost, Kerr, Ward, & Pate, 2001
Living in a married household tends to reduce the risk of early sexual activity and pregnancy.	Moore & Chase-Lansdale, 2001

►

Fathers Make a Difference in Their Children's Lives 75

◄ *Appendix 3.1*

Research finding	Source

EFFECTS OF CHILDREN NOT RESIDING WITH THEIR FATHER ON CHILDREN'S COGNITIVE DEVELOPMENT

Children who do not reside with their fathers tend to be:

• More likely to have lower scores on achievement tests and academic performance, lower scores on intellectual ability and intelligence tests, and lower grade point averages, and to spend an average of 3.5 hours less per week studying	Duncan, Brooks-Gunn, & Klebanov, 1994; Hetherington & Stanley-Hagan, 1997; Horn & Sylvester, 2002; Kelly, 2000; Luster & McAdoo, 1994; McLanahan & Sandefur, 1994; Painter & Levine, 2000; Pong & Ju, 2000; Snarey, 1993; US Department of Health and Human Services, 1995; Zick & Allen, 1996
• More likely to drop out of school, repeat a grade, and complete fewer years of schooling, and less likely to graduate or enroll in college	Krein & Beller, 1988; McLanahan & Sandefur, 1994; Nord & West, 2001; Painter & Levine, 2000
• More likely to experience behaviour problems at school such as having difficulty paying attention, disobedience, and being expelled or suspended	Dawson, 1991; Hetherington & Stanley-Hagan, 1997; Horn & Sylvester, 2002; Mott, Kowaleski-Jones, & Mehaghan, 1997

EFFECTS OF CHILDREN NOT RESIDING WITH THEIR FATHER ON CHILDREN'S EMOTIONAL DEVELOPMENT AND WELL-BEING

Children who do not reside with their fathers tend to be:

• More likely to exhibit a variety of negative internalizing and externalizing behaviours, including disruptive or anxiety disorders, affective disorders, psychological disorders, behavioural problems, conduct problems, and difficulty in emotional and psychosocial adjustment	Anderson, 2002; Brent, Perper, Moritz, & Liotus, 1995; Bush, Mullis, & Mullis, 2000; Carlson, 2006; Cuffe, McKeown, Addy, & Garrison, 2005; Demuth & Brown, 2004; Griffin, Botvin, Scheier, Diaz, & Miller, 2000; C. C. Harper & McLanahan, 2004; Hetherington & Stanley-Hagan, 1997; Jenkins, 1995; Kandel, Rosenbaum, & Chen, 1994; Kasen, Cohen, Brook, & Hartmark, 1996; Kelly, 2000; Kemppainen, Jokelainen, Isohanni, Järvelin, & Räsänen, 2002; Horn & Sylvester, 2002; Painter & Levine, 2000
• More likely to engage in criminal or delinquent behaviour, score higher on delinquency and aggression tests, commit a school crime, or experience elevated incarceration risks	

►

◄ *Appendix 3.1*

Research finding	Source
• More likely to report feelings of being depressed, dependent, and hyperactive (male children)	Mott et al., 1997
• More likely to experience internalizing problems such as anxiety and depression (female children)	Coley, 2003; Kandel et al., 1994
Although adolescents in single-mother or single-father families are significantly more delinquent than their counterparts residing with two biological, married parents, these differences are reduced once various family processes such as supervision, monitoring, involvement, and closeness are accounted for.	Brannigan, Gemmell, Pevalin, & Wade, 2002; Demuth & Brown, 2004
Father involvement reduced both the size and significance of nearly all the statistically significant family structure effects on adolescent behaviour.	Carlson, 2006

EFFECTS OF CHILDREN NOT RESIDING WITH THEIR FATHER ON CHILDREN'S SOCIAL DEVELOPMENT

Children who do not reside with their fathers tend to be more likely to choose deviant peers, have trouble getting along with other children, be at higher risk for peer problems, and be more aggressive.	Horn & Sylvester, 2002; Mott et al., 1997

EFFECTS OF CHILDREN NOT RESIDING WITH THEIR FATHER ON CHILDREN'S PHYSICAL HEALTH

Children who do not reside with their fathers tend to be:

• More likely to experience health-related problems	Ellis et al., 2003; Harknett, 2005; McLanahan & Sandefur, 1994; Metzler, Noell, Biglan, & Ary, 1994; Miller & Moore, 1990; Horn & Sylvester, 2002; Painter & Levine, 2000; Quinlan, 2003; Sedlak & Broadhurst, 1996; Teachman, 2004; Thompson, Auslander, & White, 2001; US Department of Health and Human Services, 1988
• More likely to be diagnosed with asthma and experience an asthma-related emergency even after taking into account demographic and socio-economic conditions	
• At greater risk of being physically abused or harmed by physical neglect	

►

Fathers Make a Difference in Their Children's Lives 77

◄ *Appendix 3.1*

Research finding	Source
• More likely to engage in greater and earlier sexual activity, to become pregnant as a teenager, or to have a child outside of marriage.	
• More likely to experience poorer health if they were diabetic even when statistically controlling for race, child's age, and family socio-economic status	
Infant mortality rates are 1.8 times higher for for infants of unmarried mothers than married mothers, in part because unmarried mothers are less likely to obtain prenatal care, more likely to have a low-birthweight baby, and more likely to report cigarette use during their pregnancy.	Matthews, Curtin, & MacDorman, 2000; McLanahan, 2003; Padilla & Reichman, 2001; US Department of Health and Human Services, 1995
Compared to children of married cohabiting parents, children of unmarried, cohabiting parents and unmarried parents living apart are 1.76 and 2.61 times, respectively, more likely to be diagnosed with asthma.	Harknett, 2005
Marital disruption after birth is associated with a six-fold increase in the likelihood a child will require an emergency room visit and a five-fold increase of an asthma-related emergency.	Harknett, 2005
When compared to children living with both biological parents, toddlers living in stepfamilies and single-parent families are more likely to suffer a burn, have a bad fall, or be scarred from an accident.	O'Connor, Davies, Dunn, & Golding, 2000
Compared to obese children, non-obese children are more likely to reside with their father.	Strauss & Knight, 1999
Children who live with a single parent or in stepfamilies tend to be more likely to use and abuse illegal drugs, alcohol, or tobacco compared to children who live with both biological or adoptive parents; also report higher rates of drinking and smoking.	Bronte-Tinkew, Moore, Capps, & Zaff, 2006; Griffin et al., 2000; Johnson, Haffmann, & Gerstein, 1996; Kelly, 2000; Mandara & Murray, 2006;they Painter & Levine, 2000

References

Aldous, J., & Mulligan, G. M. (2002). Fathers' child care and children's behavior problems: A longitudinal study. *Journal of Family Issues, 23*(5), 624-647.

Alfaro, E. C., Umana-Taylor, A. J., & Bamaca, M. Y. (2006). The influence of academic support on Latino adolescents' academic motivation. *Family Relations, 55*(3), 279-291.

Allen, S. M., & Hawkins, A. J. (1999). Maternal gatekeeping: Mothers' beliefs and behaviors that inhibit greater father involvement in family work. *Journal of Marriage and the Family, 61*(1), 199-212.

Amato, R. (1993). Children's adjustment to divorce: Theories, hypotheses, and empirical support. *Journal of Marriage and the Family, 55*(1), 23-38.

Amato, R. (1994). Father-child relationships, mother-child relations, and offspring psychological well-being in early adulthood. *Journal of Marriage and the Family, 56,* 1031-1042.

Amato, R. (1998). More than money? Men's contributions to their children's lives. In A. Booth & A. Crouter (Eds.), *Men in families: When do they get involved? What difference does it make?* (pp. 241-178). Mahwah, NJ: Lawrence Erlbaum.

Amato, R., & Gilbreth, J. G. (1999). Nonresident fathers and children's well being: A meta-analysis. *Journal of Marriage and the Family, 61,* 557-573.

Amato, R., & Rivera, F. (1999). Paternal involvement and children's behavior problems. *Journal of Marriage and the Family, 61*(2), 375-384.

Anderson, A. L. (2002). Individual and contextual influences on delinquency: The role of the single-parent family. *Journal of Criminal Justice, 30*(6), 575-587.

Argys, L. M., Peters, H. E., Brooks-Gunn, J., & Smith, J. R. (1998). The impact of child support on cognitive outcomes of young children. *Demography, 35*(2), 159-173.

Astone, N. M., & McLanahan, S. S. (1991). Family structure, parental practices, and high school completion. *American Sociological Review, 56,* 309-320.

Averett, S. L., Gennetian, L. A., & Peters, E. H. (1997, October). *Paternal child care and children's cognitive development.* Paper presented at Conference on Father Involvement, Fatherhood Initiative, Bethesda, MD.

Baker, A. J. L. (2005). Parent alienation strategies: A qualitative study of adults who experienced parental alienation as a child. *American Journal of Forensic Psychology, 23*(4), 1-23.

Ball, J., & Moselle, K. (2007). Fathers' contributions to children's well-being. Research reviewed for *Father Involvement for Healthy Child Outcomes: Partners Supporting Knowledge Development and Transfer* (Population Health Fund Project, Public Health Agency of Canada).

Barber, B. L. (1994). Support and advice from married and divorced fathers: Linkages to adolescent adjustment. *Family Relations, 43,* 433-438.

Battle, J. (2002). Longitudinal analysis of academic achievement among a nationwide sample of Hispanic students in one- versus dual-parent households. *Hispanic Journal of Behavioral Sciences, 24*(4), 430-447.

Beller, A. H., & Chung, S. S. (1988). The impact of child-support on the educational attainment of children. *Population Index, 54,* 438.

Benzies, K., Magill-Evans, J. M., Harrison, M. J., MacPhail, S., & Kimak, C. (2008). Strengthening new fathers' skills in interaction with their five-month-old infants: Who benefits from a brief intervention? *Public Health Nursing, 25*(5), 431-439.

Bernadette-Shapiro, S., Ehrensaft, D., & Shapiro, J. L. (1996). Father participation in childcare and the development of empathy in sons: An empirical study. *Family Therapy, 23*(2), 77-93.

Biller, H. B. (1993). *Fathers and families: Paternal factors in child development.* Westport, CT: Auburn House.

Blair, S. L., Wenk, D., & Hardesty, C. (1994). Marital quality and paternal involvement: Interconnections of men's spousal and parental roles. *Journal of Men's Studies, 2,* 221-237.

Blau, F. D., & Grossberg, A. J. (1992). Maternal labor supply and children's cognitive development. *Review of Economic and Statistics, 74,* 474-481.

Bouchard, G., Lee, C. M., Asgary, V., & Pelletier, L. (2007). Fathers' motivation for involvement with their children: A self-determination theory perspective. *Fathering, 5*(1), 25-41.

Boyum, L. A., & Parke, R. D. (1995). The role of family emotional expressiveness in the development of children's social competence. *Journal of Marriage and the Family, 57,* 593-608.

Brannigan, A., Gemmell, W., Pevalin, D. J., & Wade, T. J. (2002). Self-control and social control in childhood misconduct and aggression: The role of family structure, hyperactivity, and hostile parenting. *Canadian Journal of Criminology, 44*(2), 119-142.

Brent, D. A., Perper, J. A., Moritz, G., & Liotus, L. (1995). Post-traumatic stress disorder in peers of adolescent suicide victims: Predisposing factors and phenomenology. *Journal of the Academic Academy of Child and Adolescent Psychiatry, 34*(2), 209-215.

Brody, G., Stoneman, Z., Flor, D., McCrary, C., Hastings, L., & Conyers, O. (1994). Financial resources, parental psychological functioning, parent co-caregiving, and early adolescent competence in rural two-parent African-American families. *Child Development, 65,* 590-605.

Bronfenbrenner, U. (1979). *The ecology of human development: Experiments by nature and design.* Cambridge, MA: Harvard University Press.

Bronte-Tinkew, J., Moore, K. A., Capps, R. C., & Zaff, J. (2006). The influence of father involvement on youth risk behaviors among adolescents: A comparison of native born and immigrant families. *Social Science Research, 35*(1), 181-209.

Brooks-Gunn, J., Britto, R., & Brady, C. (1999). Struggling to make ends meet: Poverty and child development. In M. E. Lamb (Ed.), *Parenting and child development in "nontraditional" families* (pp. 279-304). Mahwah, NJ: Lawrence Erlbaum.

Brown, C. S., & Rife, J. C. (1991). Social, personality, and gender differences in at-risk and not-at-risk sixth grade students. *Journal of Early Adolescence, 11,* 482-495.

Brown, L., Callahan, M., Strega, S., Walmsley, C., & Domenelli, L. (2009). Manufacturing ghost fathers: The paradox of father presence and absence in child welfare. *Child and Family Social Work, 14*(1), 25-34.

Burke, V., Beilin, L. J., & Dunbar, D. (2001). Family lifestyle and parental body mass index as predictors of body mass index in Australian children: A longitudinal study. *Journal of Obesity, 25*(2), 147-157.

Bush, C. A., Mullis, R. L., & Mullis, A. K. (2000). Differences in empathy between offender and nonoffender youth. *Journal of Youth and Adolescence, 29*(4), 467-478.

Cabrera, N., Tamis-LeMonda, C., Bradley, R., Hofferth, S., & Lamb, M. (2000). Fatherhood in the twenty-first century. *Child Development, 71,* 127-136.

Cairney, J., Boyle, M., Offord, D. R., & Racine, Y. (2003). Stress, social support and depression in single and married mothers. *Social Psychiatry and Psychiatric Epidemiology, 38,* 442-449.

Carlson, M. J. (2006). Family structure, father involvement, and adolescent behavioral outcomes. *Journal of Marriage and Family, 68,* 137-154.

Casper, L. M., & O'Connell, M. (1998). Work, income, the economy and married fathers as childcare providers. *Demography, 35,* 243-250.

Coley, R. L. (2003). Daughter-father relationships and adolescent psychosocial functioning in low-income African American families. *Journal of Marriage and Family, 65,* 867-875.

Coley, R. L., & Medeiros, B. L. (2007). Reciprocal longitudinal relationships between nonresident father involvement and adolescent delinquency. *Child Development, 78*(1), 132-147.

Cooksey, E. C., & Fondell, M. M. (1996). Spending time with his kids: Effects of family structure on fathers' and children's lives. *Journal of Marriage and the Family, 58,* 693-707.

Coombs, R. H., & Landsverk, J. (1988). Parenting styles and substance abuse during childhood and adolescence. *Journal of Marriage and the Family, 50,* 473-482.

Cox, M. J., Owen, M. T., Henderson, V. K., & Margand, N. (1992). The prediction of infant-father and infant-mother attachment. *Developmental Psychology, 28,* 474-483.

Crouter, A. C., Davis, K. D., Updegraff, K., Delgado, M., & Fortner, M. (2006). Mexican American fathers' occupational conditions: Links to family members' psychological adjustment. *Journal of Marriage and Family, 68,* 843-858.

Cuffe, S. P., McKeown, R. E., Addy, C. L., & Garrison, C. Z. (2005). Family psychosocial risk factors in a longitudinal epidemiological study of adolescents. *Journal of American Academic Child Adolescent Psychiatry, 44,* 121-129.

Culp, R. E., Schadle, S., Robinson, L., & Culp, A. M. (2000). Relationships among paternal involvement and young children's perceived self-competence and behavioral problems. *Journal of Child and Family Studies, 9*(1), 27-38.

Cummings, E. M., & O'Reilly, A. W. (1997). Fathers in family context: Effects of marital quality on child adjustment. In M. E. Lamb (Ed.), *The role of the father in child development* (3rd ed., pp. 49-65). New York, NY: Wiley.

Daly, K. J., Ashbourne, L., & Brown, J. (2009). Fathers' perceptions of children's influence: Implications for involvement. *The Annals of the American Academy of Political and Social Science, 624,* 61-77.

Danziger, S. K., & Radin, N. (1990). Absent does not equal uninvolved: Predictors of fathering in teen mother families. *Journal of Marriage and the Family, 52*(3), 636-642.

Davies, T., & Cummings, E. M. (1994). Marital conflict and child adjustment: An emotional security hypothesis. *Psychological Bulletin, 116,* 387-411.

Davis, E. C., & Friel, L. V. (2001). Adolescent sexuality: Disentangling the effects of family structure and family context. *Journal of Marriage and Family, 63,* 669-681.

Davison, K. K., & Birch, L. L. (2001). Child and parent characteristics as predictors of change in girls' body mass index. *International Journal of Obesity, 25*(12), 1834-1842.

Dawson, D. A. (1991). Family structure and children's well-being: Data from the 1988 National Health Interview Survey. *Journal of Marriage and the Family, 53*(3), 573-585.

Day, R., & Lamb, M. (2004). *Conceptualizing and measuring father involvement.* Mahwah, NJ: Lawrence Erlbaum.

Demuth, S., & Brown, S. L. (2004). Family structure, family process, and adolescent delinquency: The significance of parental absence versus parental gender. *Journal of Research in Crime and Delinquency, 41*(1), 58-81.

Deutsch, F. M., Servis, L. J., & Payne, J. D. (2001). Paternal participation in child care and its effects on children's self-esteem and attitudes toward gendered roles. *Journal of Family Issues, 22,* 1000-1024.

Devault, A., Milcent, M., Ouellet, F., Laurin, I., Jauron, M., & Lacharite, C. (2008). Life stories of young fathers in contexts of vulnerability. *Fathering, 6*(3), 226-248.

Doherty, W. J., Kouneski, E. F., & Erickson, M. F. (1998). Responsible fathering: An overview and conceptual framework. *Journal of Marriage and the Family, 60,* 277-292.

Dorius, C. J., Bahr, S. J., Hoffmann, J. P., & Harmon, E. L. (2004). Parenting practices as moderators of the relationship between peers and adolescent marijuana use. *Journal of Marriage and Family, 66,* 163-178.

Doyle, A. B., Markiewicz, D., Brendgen, M. Lieberman, M., & Voss, K. (2000). Child attachment security and self-concept: Associations with mother and father attachment style and marital quality. *Merrill-Palmer Quarterly, 46*(3), 514-539.

Dubowitz, H., Black, M. M., Cox, C. E., Kerr, M. A., Litrownik, A. J., Radhakrishna, A., ... Runyan, D. K. (2001). Father involvement and children's functioning at age six years: A multisite study. *Child Maltreatment, 6,* 300-309.

Ducharme, J., Doyle, A. B., & Markiewicz, D. (2002). Attachment security with mother and father: Association with adolescents' reports of interpersonal behavior with parents and peers. *Journal of Social and Personal Relationships, 19,* 203-231.

Duncan, G. J., & Brooks-Gunn, J. (1997). *Consequences of growing up poor.* New York, NY: Russell Sage Foundation Press.

Duncan, G. J., Brooks-Gunn, J., & Klebanov, K. (1994). Economic deprivation and early childhood development. *Child Development, 65,* 296-318.

Dunn, J., Cheng, H., O'Connor, T. G., & Bridges, L. (2004). Children's perspectives on their relationships with their non-resident fathers: Influences, outcomes, and implications. *Journal of Child Psychology and Psychiatry, 45,* 553-566.

Earls, F., & Carson, M. (2001). The social ecology of child health and well-being. *Annual Reviews of Public Health, 22,* 143-166.

Easterbrooks, M. A., & Goldberg, W. A. (1990). Security of toddler-parent attachment: Relation to children's sociopersonality functioning during kindergarten. In M. T. Greenberg, D. Cicchetti, & E. M. Cummings (Eds.), *Attachment in the preschool years: Theory, research and intervention* (pp. 221-244). Chicago, IL: University of Chicago Press.

Ellis, B. J., Bates, J. E., Dodge, K. A., Fergusson, D. M., Horwood, J., Pettit, G. S., & Woodward, L. (2003). Does father absence place daughters at special risk for early sexual activity and teenage pregnancy? *Child Development, 74*(3), 801-821.

Emery, R. E. (1988). *Marriage, divorce, and children's adjustment.* Newbury Park, CA: Sage.

Epstein, R. (Ed.). (2009). *Who's your daddy? And other writings on queer parenting.* Toronto, ON: Sumach Press.

Este, D. C., & Tachble, A. (2009). Fatherhood in the Canadian context: Perceptions and experience of Sudanese refugee men. *Sex Roles, 60,* 456-466.

Feldman, S. S., & Wentzel, K. R. (1990). Relations among family interaction patterns, classroom self-restraint and academic achievement in preadolescent boys. *Journal of Educational Psychology, 82,* 813-819.

Field, T., Lang, C., Yando, R., & Bendell, R. (1995). Adolescents' intimacy with parents and friends. *Adolescence, 30*(117), 133-140.

Figueroa-Colon, R., Arani, R. B., Goran, M. I., & Weinsier, R. L. (2000). Paternal body fat is a longitudinal predictor of changes in body fat in premenarcheal girls. *American Journal of Clinical Nutrition, 71*(3), 829-834.

Finn, K., Johannsen, N., & Specker, B. (2002). Factors associated with physical activity in preschool children. *Journal of Pediatrics, 140,* 81-85.

Finnie, R., & Bernard, A. (2004, June). *The intergenerational transmission of lone mother and low-income status: Family and neighbourhood effects.* Paper presented at Canadian Employment Research Forum Conference on Low Income, Ryerson University, Toronto, ON. Retrieved from http://www.cerforum.org/conferences/200406/papers/Finnie -Bernard.pdf

Fleury, D. (2008). Low-income children. *Perspectives on Labour and Income, 9*(5), 14-23. Statistics Canada – Catalogue no. 75-001-X.

Flouri, E. (2006). Non-resident fathers' relationships with their secondary school age children: Determinants and children's mental health outcomes. *Journal of Adolescence, 29*(4), 525-538.

Flouri, E., & Buchanan, A. (2002a). Life satisfaction in teenage boys: The moderating role of father involvement and bullying. *Aggressive Behavior, 28,* 126-133.

Flouri, E., & Buchanan, A. (2002b). What predicts good relationships with parents in adolescence and partners in adult life: Findings from the 1958 British birth cohort. *Journal of Family Psychology, 16,* 186-198.

Flouri, E., & Buchanan, A. (2003a). The role of father involvement and mother involvement in adolescents' psychological well-being. *British Journal of Social Work, 33*(3), 399-406.

Flouri, E., & Buchanan, A. (2003b). The role of father involvement in children's later mental health. *Journal of Adolescence, 26*(1), 63-78.

Flouri, E., Buchanan, A., & Bream, V. (2002). Adolescents' perceptions of their fathers' involvement: Significance to school attitudes. *Pyschology in the Schools, 39*(5), 575-582.

Fogelholm, M., Nuutinen, O., Pasanen, M., Myohanen, E., & Saatela, T. (1999). Parent-child relationship of physical activity patterns and obesity. *International Journal of Obesity, 23*(12), 1262-1268.

Forehand, R., & Nousiainen, S. (1993). Maternal and paternal parenting: Critical dimensions in adolescent functioning. *Journal of Family Psychology, 7,* 213-221.

Formoso, D., Gonzales, N. A., Barrera, M., & Dumka, L. E. (2007). Interparental relations, maternal employment, and fathering in Mexican American families. *Journal of Marriage and Family, 69,* 26-39.

Franz, C. E., McClelland, D. C., & Weinberger, J. (1991). Childhood antecedents of conventional social accomplishments in midlife adults: A thirty-five-year prospective study. *Journal of Personality and Social Psychology, 60,* 586-595.

Furstenberg, F. F., & Cherlin, A. J. (1991). *Divided families.* Cambridge, MA: Harvard University Press.

Furstenberg, F. F., & Harris, K. M. (1993). When and why fathers matter: Impacts of father involvement on the children of adolescent mothers. In R. I. Lerman & T. J. Ooms (Eds.), *Young unwed fathers: Changing roles and emerging policies* (pp. 117-138). Philadelphia, PA: Temple University Press.

Furstenberg, F. F., Morgan, S. P., & Allison, D. (1987). Paternal participation and childrens' well-being after marital dissolution. *American Sociological Review, 52,* 695-701.

Gadsden, V., & Ray, A. (2003, November). Fathers' role in children's academic achievement and early literacy. *ERIC Digest.*

Gerson, K. (1993). *No man's land: Men's changing commitments to family and work.* New York, NY: Basic Books.

Gjerdingen, D. K., Froberg, D. G., & Fontaine, P. (1991). The effects of social support on women's health during pregnancy, labor, and delivery, and the postpartum period. *Family Medicine, 23,* 370-375.

Goldscheider, F. K., & Waite, L. J. (1991). *New families, no families: The transformation of the American home.* Berkeley: University of California Press.

Graham J. W., & Beller, A. H. (2002). Nonresident fathers and their children: Child support and visitation from an economic perspective. In C. S. Tamis-LeMonda & N. Cabrera (Eds.), *Handbook of father involvement: Multidisciplinary perspectives* (pp. 431-453). Mahwah, NJ: Lawrence Erlbaum.

Graham, J. W., Beller, A. H., & Hernandez, M. (1994). The effects of child support on educational attainment. In I. Garfinkel, S. S. McLanahan, & K. Robins (Eds.), *Child support and child well-being* (pp. 317-354). Washington, DC: Urban Institute.

Greene, A. D., & Moore, K. A. (2000). Nonresident father involvement and child well-being among young children in families on welfare. *Marriage and Family Review, 29*(2-3), 159-180.

Griffin, K. W., Botvin, G. J., Scheier, L. M., Diaz, T., & Miller, N. L. (2000). Parenting practices as predictors of substance use, delinquency, and aggression among urban minority youth: Moderating effects of family structure and gender. *Psychology of Addictive Behaviors, 14*(2), 174-184.

Grossmann, K. E., Grossmann, K., Winter, M., & Zimmermann, P. (2002). Attachment relationships and appraisal of partnership: From early experience of sensitive support to later relationship representation. In L. Pulkkinen and A. Caspi (Eds.), *Paths to successful development: Personality in the life course* (pp. 73-105). New York, NY: Cambridge University Press.

Grych, J. H., & Fincham, F. D. (1990). Marital conflict and children's adjustment: A cognitive-conceptual framework. *Psychological Bulletin, 108,* 267-290.

Hallman, M., Deinhart, A., & Beaton, J. (2007). A qualitative analysis of fathers' experience of parental time after separation and divorce. *Fathering, 5*(1), 4-24.

Harknett, K. (2005). *Children's elevated risk of asthma in unmarried families: Underlying structural and behavioral mechanisms* (Working Paper #2005-01-FF). Princeton, NJ: Center for Research on Child Wellbeing.

Harper, C. C., & McLanahan, S. S. (2004). Father absence and youth incarceration. *Journal of Research on Adolescence, 14*(3), 369-397.

Harper, S. E., & Fine, M. A. (2006). The effects of involved nonresidential fathers' distress, parenting behaviors, inter-parental conflict, and the quality of father-child relationships on children's well-being. *Fathering, 4*(3), 286-311.

Harris, K. M., Furstenberg, F. F., & Marmer, J. K. (1998). Paternal involvement with adolescents in intact families: The influence of fathers over the life course. *Demography, 35*(2), 201-216.

Hawkins, A. J., Bradford, K. P., Palkovitz, R., Christiansen, S. L., Day, R. D., & Call, V. R. A. (2002). The inventory of father involvement: A pilot study of a new measure of father involvement. *Journal of Men's Studies, 10,* 183-196.

Hawkins, A. J., Christiansen, S. L., Sargent, K. P., & Hill, J. E. (1993). Rethinking fathers' involvement in child care: A developmental perspective. *Journal of Family Issues, 14,* 531-550.

Hawkins, A. J., & Dollahite, D. C. (1997). *Generative Fathering*. Thousand Oaks, CA: Sage.

Heath, D. H., & MacKinnon, C. (1988). Factors related to the social competence of children in single-parent families. *Journal of Divorce, 11*, 49-66.

Hetherington, E. M., & Stanley-Hagan, M. M. (1997). The effects of divorce on fathers and their children. In M. E. Lamb (Ed.), *The role of the father in child development* (3rd ed., pp. 191-211). New York, NY: John Wiley.

Hewlett, B. S. (2000). Culture, history and sex: Anthropological contributions to conceptualizing father involvement. *Marriage and Family Review, 29*, 59-73.

Hooven, C., Gottman, J. M., & Katz, L. F. (1995). Parental meta-emotion structure predicts family and child outcomes. *Cognition and Emotion, 9*(2-3), 229-264.

Horn, W. F., & Sylvester, T. (2002). *Father Facts* (4th ed.). Gaithersburg, MD: National Fatherhood Initiative.

Howard, K. S., Lefever, J. E., Borkowski, J. G., & Whitman, T. L. (2006). Fathers' influence in the lives of children with adolescent mothers. *Journal of Family Psychology, 20*(3), 468-476.

Jenkins, H. (1995). School delinquency and school commitment. *Sociology of Education, 68*, 221-239.

Johnson, R. A., Haffmann, J. P., & Gerstein, D. R. (1996). *The relationship between family structure and adolescent substance abuse*. Washington, DC: National Opinion Research Center for the United States Department of Health and Human Services.

Jorm, A. F., Dear, K. B. G., Rodgers, B., & Christensen, H. (2003). Interaction between mother's and father's affection as a risk factor for anxiety and depression symptoms: Evidence for increased risk in adults who rate their father as having been more affectionate than their mother. *Social Psychiatry and Psychiatric Epidemiology, 38*(4), 173-179.

Kandel, D. B. (1990). Parenting styles, drug use, and children's adjustment in families of young adults. *Journal of Marriage and the Family, 52*, 183-196.

Kandel, D. B, Rosenbaum, E., & Chen, K. (1994). Impact of maternal drug use and life experiences on preadolescent children born to teenage mothers. *Journal of Marriage and the Family, 56*, 325-340.

Kaplan, H. S., Lancaster, J. B., & Anderson, K. G. (1998). Human parental investment and fertility: The life histories of men in Albuquerque. In A. Booth & A. C. Crouter (Eds.), *Men in families* (pp. 55-109). Mahwah, NJ: Erlbaum.

Kasen, S., Cohen, P., Brook, J. S., & Hartmark, C. (1996). A multiple-risk interaction model: Effects of temperament and divorce on psychiatric disorders in children. *Journal of Abnormal Child Psychology, 24*(2), 121-150.

Kato, K., Ishii-Kuntz, M., Makino, K., & Tsuchiya, M. (2002). The impact of paternal involvement and maternal childcare anxiety on sociability of three-year-olds: Two cohort comparisons. *Japanese Journal of Developmental Psychology, 13*(1), 30-41.

Kelly, J. B. (2000). Children's adjustment in conflicted marriage and divorce: A decade review of research. *Journal of the American Academy of Child and Adolescent Psychiatry, 39*, 963-973.

Keltner, B. (1996). *American Indian parenting practices*. Paper presented at the Conference on Developmental, Ethnographic, and Demographic Perspectives on Fatherhood, Bethesda, MD.

Kemppainen, L., Jokelainen, J., Isohanni, M., Järvelin, M., & Räsänen, P. (2002). Predictors of female criminality: Findings from the northern Finland 1966 birth cohort. *Journal of the American Academy of Child and Adolescent Psychiatry, 41*(7), 854-859.

Kesner, J. E., & McKenry, C. (2001). Single parenthood and social competence in children of color. *Families in Society, 82*(2), 136-143.

King, V. (1994). Variation in the consequences of nonresident father involvement for children's well-being. *Journal of Marriage and the Family, 56*(4), 963-972.

King, V. (2006). The antecedents and consequences of adolescents' relationships with stepfathers and nonresident fathers. *Journal of Marriage and Family, 68*(4), 910-928.

King, V., & Sobolewski, J. M. (2006). Nonresident fathers' contributions to adolescent well-being. *Journal of Marriage and Family, 68*(3), 537-557.

Klerman, L. V. (1991). The health status of poor children: Problems and programs. In A. C. Huston (Ed.), *Children in poverty: Child development and public policy* (pp. 136-157). Cambridge, MA: Cambridge University Press.

Knox, V. W. (1996). The effects of child support payments on developmental outcomes for elementary school-age children. *Journal of Human Resources, 31*(4), 816-840.

Knox, V. W., & Bane, M. J. (1994). Child support and schooling. In I. Garfinkel, S. S. McLanahan, & K. Robins (Eds.), *Child support and child well-being* (pp. 285-316). Washington, DC: Urban Institute.

Koestner, R., Franz, C., & Weinberger, J. (1990). The family origins of empathic concern: A twenty-six-year longitudinal study. *Journal of Personality and Social Psychology, 58,* 709-717.

Kornberger, R., Fast, J., & Williamson, D. L. (2001). Welfare or work: Which is better for Canadian children? *Canadian Public Policy, 27*(4), 407-421.

Kosterman, R., Haggerty, K. P., Spoth, R., & Redmond, C. (2004). Unique influence of mothers and fathers on their children's antisocial behavior. *Journal of Marriage and Family, 66*(3), 762-778.

Krampe, E. M., & Fairweather, D. (1993). Father presence and family formations: A theoretical reformulation. *Family Issues, 14*(4), 572-591.

Krein, S. F., & Beller, A. H. (1988). Educational attainment of children from single-parent exposure, gender, and race. *Demography, 25*(2), 221-234.

Lamb, M. E. (1997). Fathers and child development: An introductory overview and guide. In M. E. Lamb (Ed.), *The role of the father in child development* (3rd ed., pp. 1-18). New York, NY: John Wiley.

Lamb, M. E. (2000). The history of research on father involvement: An overview. *Marriage and Family Review, 29,* 23-42.

Lamb, M. E. (2010). How do fathers influence children's development? Let me count the ways. In M. E. Lamb (Ed.), *The role of the father in child development* (5th ed., pp. 1-26). Hoboken, NJ: Wiley.

Lamb, M. E., Pleck, J. H., Charnov, E. L., & Levine, J. A. (1985). Paternal behavior in humans. *American Zoologist, 25,* 883-894.

Lamb, M. E., Pleck, J. H., & Levine, J. A. (1987). Effects of increased paternal involvement on fathers and mothers. In C. Lewis & M. O'Brien (Eds.), *Reassessing fatherhood: New observations on fathers and the modern family* (pp. 109-125). London, England: Sage.

Lamb, M. E., Sternberg, K. J., & Thompson, R. A. (1997). The effects of divorce and custody arrangements on children's behavior, development and adjustment. *Family and Conciliation Courts Review, 35*(4), 393-404.

LaRossa, R. (1997). *The Modernization of Fatherhood.* Chicago, IL: University of Chicago Press.

Levin, H. M. (1986). *Educational reform for disadvantaged students: An emerging crisis.* West Haven, CT: National Education Association Professional Library.

Levy-Schiff, R. (1994). Individual and contextual correlates of marital change across the transition to parenthood. *Developmental Psychology, 30,* 591-601.

Levy-Schiff, R., & Israelashvili, R. (1988). Antecedents of fathering: Some further exploration. *Developmental Psychology, 24,* 434-440.

Lieberman, M., Doyle, A., & Markiewicz, D. (1999). Developmental patterns in security of attachment to mother and father in late childhood and early adolescence: Associations with peer relations. *Child Development, 70*(1), 202-213.

Lindahl, K. M., Clements, M., & Markman, H. (1997). Predicting marital and parent functioning in dyads and triads: A longitudinal investigation of marital processes. *Journal of Family Psychology, 11,* 139-151.

Lindsey, E. W., Moffett, D., Clawson, M., & Mize, J. (1994, April). *Father-child play and children's competence.* Paper presented at the biennial meeting of the Southwestern Society for Research in Human Development, Austin, TX.

Lundy, B. L. (2002). Paternal socio-psychological factors and infant attachment: The mediating role of synchrony in father-infant interactions. *Infant Behavior and Development, 25*(2), 221-236.

Luster, T., & McAdoo, H. (1994). Factors related to the achievement and adjustment of young African American children. *Child Development, 65,* 1080-1094.

Madden-Derdich, D. A., & Leonard, S. A. (2000). Parental role identity and fathers' involvement in coparental interaction after divorce: Fathers' perspectives. *Family Relations, 49*(3), 311-318.

Mandara, J., & Murray, C. B. (2006). Father's absence and African American adolescent drug use. *Journal of Divorce and Remarriage, 46*(1-2), 1-12.

Marsiglio, W., Amato, P., Day, R. D., and Lamb, M. E. (2000). Scholarship on fatherhood in the 1990s and beyond. *Journal of Marriage and the Family, 62,* 1173-1191.

Matthews, T. J., Curtin, S. C., & MacDorman, M. F. (2000). Infant mortality statistics from the 1998 period linked birth/infant death data set. *National Vital Statistics Reports, 48*(12), 1-25. Hyattsville, MD: National Center for Health Statistics.

Mayer, S. E. (1997). *What money can't buy: Family income and children's life chances.* Cambridge, MA: Harvard University Press.

McAllister, C. L., Wilson, C., & Burton, J. (2004). From sports fans to nurturers: An early Head Start program's evolution toward father involvement. *Fathering, 2*(1), 31-59.

McBride, B. A., Dyer, W. J., Liu, Y., Brown, G. L., & Hong, S. (2009). The differential impact of early father and mother involvement on later student achievement. *Journal of Educational Psychology, 101*(2), 498-508.

McBride, B. A., Schoppe-Sullivan, S. J., & Ho, M. (2005). The mediating role of fathers' school involvement on student achievement. *Journal of Applied Development Psychology, 26*(2), 201-216.

McLanahan, S. (2003). *The fragile families and child well-being study: Baseline national report.* Princeton, NJ: Center for Research on Child Wellbeing.

McLanahan, S., & Sandefur, G. D. (1994). *Growing up with a single parent: What hurts, what helps.* Cambridge, MA: Harvard University Press.

McLanahan, S. S., Seltzer, J. A., Hanson, T. L., & Thomson, E. (1994). Child support enforcement and child well-being: Greater security or greater conflict? In I. Garfinkel, S. S. McLanahan, & K. Robins (Eds.), *Child support and child well-being* (pp. 285-316). Washington, DC: Urban Institute.

McLoyd, V. C., & Wilson, L. (1991). The strain of living poor: Parenting, social support, and child mental health. In A. C. Huston (Ed.), *Children in poverty: Child development and public policy* (pp. 105-135). Cambridge, MA: Cambridge University Press.

Menning, C. L. (2006). Nonresident fathering and school failure. *Journal of Family Issues, 27*(10), 1356-1382.

Metzler, C. W., Noell, J., Biglan, A., & Ary, D. (1994). The social context for risky sexual behavior among adolescents. *Journal of Behavioral Medicine, 17*(4), 419-438.

Miller, B. C., & Moore, K. A. (1990). Adolescent sexual behavior, pregnancy, and parenting: Research through the 1980s. *Journal of Marriage and the Family, 52*(4), 1025-1044.

Mischel, W., Shoda, Y., & Peake, K. (1988). The nature of adolescent competencies predicted by preschool delay of gratification. *Journal of Personality and Social Psychology, 54,* 687-696.

Moller, K., & Stattin, H. (2001). Are close relationships in adolescence linked with partner relationship in midlife? A longitudinal, prospective study. *International Journal of Behavioral Development, 25,* 69-77.

Moore, M. R., & Chase-Lansdale, L. (2001). Sexual intercourse and pregnancy among African American girls in high-poverty neighborhoods: The role of family and perceived community environment. *Journal of Marriage and Family, 63,* 1146-1157.

Mosley, J., & Thompson, E. (1995). Fathering behavior and child outcomes: The role of race and poverty. In W. Marsiglio (Ed.), *Fatherhood: Contemporary theory, research, and social policy* (pp. 148-165). Thousand Oaks, CA: Sage.

Mott, F. L., Kowaleski-Jones, L., & Mehaghan, E. G. (1997). Paternal absence and child behaviors: Does gender make a difference? *Journal of Marriage and the Family, 59*(1), 103-118.

National Center for Education Statistics. (1997). *Fathers' involvement in their children's schools.* Washington, DC: Government Printing Office.

National Fatherhood Initiative. (2004). *Family structure, father closeness, and drug abuse.* Gaithersburg, MD: National Fatherhood Initiative.

Nord, C. W., & West, J. (2001). *Fathers' and mothers' involvement in their children's schools by family type and resident status* (NCES 2001-032). Washington, DC: US Department of Education, National Center for Education Statistics.

Nugent, S. (1991). Cultural and psychological influences on the father's role in infant development. *Journal of Marriage and the Family, 53,* 475-485.

O'Connor, T., Davies, L., Dunn, J., & Golding, J. (2000). Differential distribution of children's accidents, injuries, and illnesses across family type. *Pediatrics, 106,* 68.

Padilla, Y. C., & Reichman, N. E. (2001). Low birthweight: Do unwed fathers help? *Children and Youth Services Review, 23*(4-5), 427-452.

Painter, G., & Levine, D. I. (2000). Family structure and youths' outcomes: Which correlations are causal? *Journal of Human Resources, 35*(3), 524-549.

Palkovitz, R. (1997). Reconstructing "involvement": Expanding conceptualizations of men's caring in contemporary families. In A. J. Hawkins & D. C. Dollahite (Eds.), *Generative fathering: Beyond a deficit perspective* (pp. 200-216). Thousand Oaks, CA: Sage.

Palkovitz, R. (2002). Involved fathering and child development: Advancing our understanding of good fathering. In C. S. Tamis-LeMonda & N. Cabrera (Eds.), *Handbook of father involvement: Multidisciplinary perspectives* (pp. 119-140). Mahwah, NJ: Lawrence Erlbaum.

Palkovitz, R., & Palm, G. (2005, November). *Transitions within fathering.* Paper presented at the Theory Construction and Research Methodology Workshop, National Council on Family Relations, Phoenix, AZ.

Parcel, T. L., & Menaghan, E. G. (1994). *Parents' jobs and children's lives.* New York, NY: Walter de Gruyter.

Parke, R. D. (1996). *Fatherhood.* Cambridge, MA: Harvard University Press.

Peters, B., & Ehrenberg, M. F. (2008). The influence of parental separation and divorce on father-child relationships. *Journal of Divorce and Remarriage, 49,* 78-109.

Pleck, J. H. (1997). Paternal involvement: Levels, sources, and consequences. In M. E. Lamb (Ed.), *The role of the father in child development* (3rd ed., pp. 66-103). New York, NY: John Wiley.

Pleck, J. H. (2010a). Fatherhood and masculinity. In M. E. Lamb (Ed.), *The role of the father in child development* (5th ed., pp. 27-57). Hoboken, NJ: Wiley.

Pleck, J. H. (2010b). Paternal involvement: Revised conceptualization and theoretical linkages with child outcomes. In M. E. Lamb (Ed.), *The role of the father in child development* (5th ed., pp. 58-93). Hoboken, NJ: Wiley.

Pleck, J. H., & Masciadrelli, B. (2004). Paternal involvement by U.S. residential fathers. In M. E. Lamb (Ed.), *The role of the father in child development* (4th ed., pp. 222-271). New York, NY: John Wiley.

Pong, S., & Ju, D. (2000). The effects of change in family structure and income on dropping out of middle and high school. *Journal of Family Issues, 21*(2), 147-169.

Presser, H. (1995). Job, family and gender: Determinants of non-standard work schedules among employed Americans in 1991. *Demography, 32,* 577-598.

Pruett, K. D. (1997). How men and children affect each other's development. *Zero to Three, 18*(1), 3-11.

Qin, D. B. (2009). Gendered processes of adaptation: Understanding parent-child relations in Chinese immigrant families. *Sex Roles, 60*(7-8), 467-481.

Quinlan, R. J. (2003). Father absence, parental care, and female reproductive development. *Evolution and Human Behavior, 24,* 376-390.

Radin, N. (1994). Primary caregiving fathers in intact families. In A. E. Gottfried & A. W. Gottfried (Eds.), *Redefining families: Implications for children's development* (pp. 55-97). New York, NY: Plenum.

Risch, S. C., Jodl, K. M., & Eccles, J. S. (2004). Role of the father-adolescent relationship in shaping adolescents' attitudes toward divorce. *Journal of Marriage and Family, 66,* 46-58.

Rohner, R. P., & Veneziano, R. A. (2001). The importance of father love: History and contemporary evidence. *Review of General Psychology, 5*(4), 382-405.

Ross, C. E., & Broh, B. A. (2000). The role of self-esteem and the sense of personal control in the academic achievement process. *Sociology of Education, 73,* 270-284.

Sayer, L. C., Gauthier, A. H., & Furstenberg, F. F. (2004). Educational differences in parents' time with children: Cross-national variations. *Journal of Marriage and Family, 66,* 1152-1169.

Schoppe, S. J., Mangelsdorf, S. C., & Frosch, C. A. (2001). Coparenting, family process, and family structure: Implications for preschoolers' externalizing behavior problems. *Journal of Family Psychology, 15*(3), 526-545.

Schoppe-Sullivan, S. J., McBride, B. A., & Ho, M. R. (2004). Unidimensional versus multidimensional perspectives on father involvement. *Fathering, 2*(2), 147-163.

Schor, E. L., & Menaghan, E. G. (1995). Family pathways to child health. In B. Amick, S. Levine, A. R. Tarlov, & D. C. Walsh (Eds.), *Society and Health* (pp. 18-45). New York, NY: Oxford University Press.

Schwartz, S. J., & Finley, G. E. (2006). Father involvement, nurturant fathering, and young adult psychosocial functioning: Differences among adoptive, adoptive stepfather, and nonadoptive stepfamilies. *Journal of Family Issues, 27*(5), 712-731.

Sedlak, A. J., & Broadhurst, D. D. (1996, September). *The third national incidence study of child abuse and neglect: Final report.* Washington, DC: US Department of Health and Human Services, National Center on Child Abuse and Neglect.

Shimoni, R., Este, D., & Clark, D. E. (2003). Paternal engagement in immigrant and refugee families. *Journal of Comparative Family Studies, 34,* 555-568.

Simons, R. L., Beaman, J., Conger, R. D., & Chao, W. (1993). Childhood experience, conceptions of parenting, and attitudes of spouse as determinants of parental behavior. *Journal of Marriage and the Family, 55,* 91-106.

Simons, R., Whitbek, L., Beaman, J., & Conger, R. D. (1994). The impact of mothers' parenting, involvement by nonresidential fathers, and parental conflict on the adjustment of adolescent children. *Journal of Marriage and the Family, 56,* 356-374.

Snarey, J. (1993). *How fathers care for the next generation: A four-decade study.* Cambridge, MA: Harvard University Press.

Sobolewski, J. M., & King, V. (2005). The importance of the coparental relationship for nonresident fathers' ties to children. *Journal of Marriage and Family, 67,* 1196-1212.

Stewart, S. D. (2003). Nonresident parenting and adolescent adjustment. *Journal of Family Issues, 24*(2), 217-244.

Stolz, H. E., Barber, B. K., & Olsen, J. A. (2005). Toward disentangling fathering and mothering: An assessment of relative importance. *Journal of Marriage and Family, 67,* 1076-1092.

Strauss, R. S., & Knight, J. (1999). Influence of the home environment on the development of obesity in children. *Pediatrics, 103*(6), e85.

Strega, S., Fleet, C., Brown, L., Dominelli, L., Callahan, M., & Walmsley, C. (2008). Connecting father absence and mother blame in child welfare policies and practice. *Children and Youth Services Review, 30,* 705-716.

Suess, G. J., Grossmann, K. E., & Sroufe, L. A. (1992). Effects of infant attachment to mother and father on quality of adaptation in preschool: From dyadic to individual organization of self. *International Journal of Behavioral Development, 15,* 43-65.

Swiss, L., & Bourdais, C. (2009). Father-child contact after separation: The influence of living arrangements. *Journal of Family Issues, 30*(5), 623-652.

Teachman, J. D. (2004). The childhood living arrangements of children and the characteristics of their marriages. *Journal of Family Issues, 25*(1), 86-111.

Teitler, J. O. (2001). Father involvement, child health, and maternal health behavior. *Children and Youth Services Review, 23*(4-5), 403-425.

Tessier, R., Charpak, N., Giron, M., Cristo, M., Dalume, Z. F., and Ruiz-Pelaez, J. G. (2009). Kangaroo mother care, home environment and father involvement in the first year of life: A randomized controlled study. *Acta Paediatrica, 98,* 1444-1450.

Thompson, S. J., Auslander, W. F., & White, N. H. (2001). Influence of family structure on health among youths with diabetes. *Health and Social Work, 26*(1), 7-14.

Trost, S. G., Kerr, L. M., Ward, D. S., & Pate, R. R. (2001). Physical activity and determinants of physical activity in obese and non-obese children. *International Journal of Obesity, 25*(6), 822-829.

Updegraff, K. A., McHale, S. M., Crouter, A. C., & Kupanoff, K. (2001). Parents' involvement in adolescents' peer relationships: A comparison of mothers' and fathers' roles. *Journal of Marriage and Family, 63,* 655-668.

US Census Bureau. (2003). *Children's living arrangements and characteristics: March 2002* (P20-547). Washington, DC: Government Printing Office.

US Department of Health and Human Services. (1988). *National Health Interview Survey.* Hyattsville, MD: National Center for Health Statistics.

US Department of Health and Human Services. (1995, September). *Report to Congress on out-of-wedlock childbearing.* Hyattsville, MD: Public Health Service, Centers for Disease Control and Prevention, National Center for Health Statistics.

Veneziano, R. A. (2000). Perceived paternal and maternal acceptance and rural African American and European American youths' psychological adjustment. *Journal of Marriage and Family, 62*(1), 123-132.

Volling, B. L., & Belsky, J. (1992). The contribution of mother-child and father-child relationships to the quality of sibling interaction: A longitudinal study. *Child Development, 63,* 1209-1222.

Wall, G., & Arnold, S. (2007). How involved is involved fathering? An exploration of the contemporary culture of fatherhood. *Gender and Society, 21*(4), 508-527.

Weigel, D. J., & Donovan, K. A. (2006). Parental alienation syndrome: Diagnostic and triadic perspectives. *Family Journal, 14*(3), 274-282.

Wentzel, K. R., & Feldman, S. S. (1993). Parental predictors of boys' self restraint and motivation to achieve at school: A longitudinal study. *Journal of Early Adolescence, 13,* 183-203.

White, L., & Gilbreth, J. G. (2001). When children have two fathers: Effects of relationships with stepfathers and noncustodial fathers on adolescent outcomes. *Journal of Marriage and Family, 63,* 155-167.

Whiteside, M. F., & Becker, B. J. (2000). Parental factors and the young child's postdivorce adjustment: A meta-analysis with implications for parenting arrangements. *Journal of Family Psychology, 14*(1), 5-26.

William, M. V. (1997). *Reconceptualizing father involvement.* Unpublished master's thesis, Georgetown University, Washington, DC.

Williams, E., & Radin, N. (1999). Effects of father participation in child rearing: Twenty-year follow-up. *American Journal of Orthopsychiatry, 69*(3), 328-336.

Wolfberg, A. J., Michels, K., Shields, W., O'Campo, P., Bronner, Y., & Bienstock, J. (2004, September). Dads as breastfeeding advocates: Results from a randomized controlled trial of an educational intervention. *American Journal of Obstetrics and Gynecology, 191,* 708-712.

Yeung, W. J., Duncan, G. J., & Hill, M. S. (2000). Putting fathers back in the picture: Parental activities and children's adult outcomes. *Marriage and Family Review, 29*(2-3), 97-113.

Yogman, M. W., Kindlon, D., & Earls, F. (1995). Father involvement and cognitive/behavioral outcomes of preterm infants. *Journal of the American Academy of Child and Adolescent Psychiatry, 34,* 58-66.

Youngblade, L. M., & Belsky, J. (1992). Parent-child antecedents of five-year-olds' close friendships: A longitudinal analysis. *Developmental Psychology, 28,* 700-713.

Yuan, A. S. V., & Hamilton, H. A. (2006). Stepfather involvement and adolescent well-being. *Journal of Family Issues, 27*(9), 1191-1213.

Zick, C. D., & Allen, C. R. (1996). The impact of parents' marital status on the time adolescents spend in productive activities. *Family Relations, 45,* 65-71.

Zimmerman, M. A., Salem, D. A., & Maton, K. I. (1995). Family structure and psychosocial correlates among urban African-American adolescent males. *Child Development, 66,* 1598-1613.

Zimmerman, M. A., Salem, D. A., & Notaro, C. (2000). Make room for daddy II: The positive effects of fathers' role in adolescent development. In R. D. Taylor & M. C. Wang (Eds.), *Resilience across contexts: Family, work, culture, and community* (pp. 233-253). Mahwah, NJ: Lawrence Erlbaum.

4
Feminist Mothers Researching Fathering: Advocates, Contributors, and Dissenters

Andrea Doucet and Linda Hawkins

Over the past decade, we have each worked – separately and together – with and alongside men in academic and activist projects that have focused on men's lives and on fathering. This chapter draws specifically on our involvement since 2003 with the Father Involvement Research Alliance, which is funded by the Community-University Research Alliances (CURA) program of the Social Sciences and Humanities Research Council of Canada (SSHRC). Through this research program, we cultivated a shared interest in reflecting on the complex and evolving intersections between fathering and feminism. We conversed over the years on how our respective, deeply held commitments to both feminist ideals and active fathering could lead to areas of potential conflict for us and for our participation in the program of research. Our thinking was expanded when we co-presented a session on some of the tensions between fathering and feminism at the 25th annual Association for Research on Mothering conference (a feminist venue); at the final formal project meeting of the FIRA-CURA group (March 2008), we co-facilitated a session devoted to this topic with our father research colleagues. Those presentations were our first attempt to work through some of the pressures that we felt around feminism and fathering, pressures that were a weighty presence for us throughout the FIRA-CURA program.

In this chapter, we seek to make visible the "elephant in the room" and to reflect on the theoretical tensions that arise when complementary and potentially conflicting approaches work alongside one another. Given that feminist research on mothering and multidisciplinary research on fathering are two burgeoning areas of research in Canada and internationally, it is important that these fields of scholarship, and the people who work within and across them, find meaningful ways to contribute to overall theoretical and practical understandings of research on care work. In addition to this goal, our chapter takes up two of this book's purposes: identifying directions for future research and reducing barriers that impede community-based supports for active fathering. We thus point to practical challenges and opportunities that face collaborators working with researchers who hold a strong commitment to father involvement but from diverse theoretical and ideological positions. Our overall argument is that a broader continuing dialogue is required between feminist scholars and fathering scholars, particularly because research focused on families and personal relationships will continue to draw on and serve these and other constituencies.

This chapter is built on our shared experiences as feminists and as mothers, on interactions with other fatherhood researchers and fathers, and on conversations with other feminists and pro-feminists in the research group and beyond. As qualitative researchers informed by broad principles of reflexivity (Mauthner & Doucet, 2003), we offer this story as one interpretation of an unfolding narrative where theoretical and political approaches operate in what we perceive as complementary as well as conflicting ways.

Our reflections are part of a longer and wider conversation on the tensions that can arise when social groups with both shared *and* competing identities and political commitments join together in supporting a common cause or goal. Other conversations have resonance with the one we describe in this chapter: for instance, there are long-standing reflections by feminists on the challenges of working across diverse groups of women and on how commitments to multiple identities and conflicting politics regarding gender, ethnicity, class, sexuality, age, and culture can cause irreconcilable conflicts (hooks 1989, 1990; Ward, 2004). We also join other dialogues that have explored the difficulties of bringing feminism and men's issues together; these include conversations about feminism and fathering (Gardiner, 1998, 2002; Silverstein, 1996), feminists linking with fathers' rights movements (Crowley, 2009; Gavanas, 2004), women attempting to bring men more generally into feminist agendas (Erturk, 2004), tensions that arise when women interview men on issues of importance to women (Presser, 2004), and men attempting to reconcile being male feminists (Digby, 1998).

In this chapter, we begin by outlining some of the broad principles and subjective experiences we share with regard to our feminist positionality and describing how and why we became advocates for active fathering within the features and dynamics of the FIRA project. Second, we point to contributions from feminist understandings of gender and care that have been brought to the research table on men's active involvement in parenting. Third, we highlight how, as the project unfolded, we shifted between participating as contributors and as dissenters in this fathering alliance, and how the latter role was especially encouraged by points of tension between particular viewpoints on fathering experiences and feminist research. Overall, this chapter focuses on how we continually navigated our positioning in the complex relations between feminism and research on active fathering.

Our Backgrounds: Feminists and Fathering Advocates

We have two distinct research and activist backgrounds. Our understanding of what a father might be is informed by our experiences as mothers, feminists, women in academia, and researchers on fathering. As birth mothers, we share physical and emotional understandings of bearing children and providing care. We are shaped by the continuing negotiations of division of care and of waged work with engaged male co-parents and others in our care networks.

Defining ourselves as feminist researchers translates, in brief, as being sensitive to issues of gendered power relations in society and in research practice more widely. We are also informed by our respective activism experiences with diverse women, which demand that we cultivate an awareness of our own assumptions and how they matter when we consider how to engage in social change for women. As feminists, we are part of a community that supports critical action intended to better women's lives; as academic feminists, we are supported but continually challenged to bring a critical perspective to our work. At the same time, when we consider how women may benefit from the results of our research, we are aware of the constant need to ask "Which women?" and "How will we speak for them?" (Code & Burt, 1995). Both activist and academic feminist circles are communities that we greatly value. Thus, we bring to our work on fathering a deep valuing of care work, a commitment to diversity that requires new learning and personal reflection, assurance that new ways are possible but that gains are over the long term, and responsibility to our feminist communities to contribute to change. We joined the FIRA-CURA project with an interest in contributing to the cutting edge of intellectual, policy, and public conversations about active fathering across diverse Canadian populations. Specifically, Andrea served as co-lead of the New Fathers cluster, a role she shared with one of Canada's veteran fathering researchers and activists, Ed Bader; Linda worked as a collaborator examining themes across clusters and as the coordinator for the alliance.

We decided to participate in the FIRA project for five reasons. First, as feminist scholars well versed in debates on gendered inequities in care work, we knew that the ongoing prescribed roles for men as financial providers and their limited roles as caregivers constituted a continuing imbalance in contemporary society that required greater attention and alteration. Importantly, as feminists working on issues of gender equality in workplace and domestic relations, we held firmly to the view that the research and public conversation on active fathering both benefits from and requires the participation of women. With Silverstein (1996), we saw our work as "an effort to inject a feminist voice into the redefinition of fathering, which [we both saw] ... as essential both to the achievement of equality for women, and to the reconstruction of the masculine gender role" (4).

Second, we both held the view that men doing more care work could potentially translate into women having increased access to more choices and support in relations of employment and care, while also possibly contributing to an undoing of traditional family structures and ideologies. From our vantage, the public valuing of men *at home* could radically undermine the prescriptive roles that contribute to the double and triple day for women and could alter the myriad assumptions that devalue women's paid labour and unpaid care. For example, we imagine that men's participation in care work would recast the need for quality child care as a support for men's labour-force participation.

Third, from both a research and community perspective, we were interested in being part of a collaborative process that used participatory methodologies to seek, hear, and understand narratives from men of diverse social backgrounds in Canada (including young fathers, Aboriginal fathers, fathers of children with disabilities, immigrant fathers, new fathers, separated fathers, and LGBTQ families). This work had great promise of widening the script on fathering to include voices not often heard and to illuminate a broader experience of families and fathering. Methodologically, the work included a community-based approach that shifts the power, of owning and asking about what is important, from academic researchers to a shared relationship with community organizations and individual fathers.

Our fourth reason for joining the FIRA project was our awareness of the fact that the bulk of research and advocacy on changing family ideologies has been done on women and by feminist scholars. That is, while attention to fathers' perspectives has been increasing, most of the research conducted on family lives has still centred on understandings gleaned from women. Although this research was initially focused on white, middle-class women (see Saffilios-Rothschild, 1969), increasing attention has been given to stories about the lives of teen mothers (Edin & Kefalas, 2005), low-income mothers (Hays, 2003; Lareau, 2003), lesbian mothers (Epstein, 2009; Goldberg & Allen, 2007), immigrant mothers (Ornelas, Perreira, Beeber, & Maxwell, 2009; Segura, 1994), and mothers of children with disabilities (Malacrida, 2009). We wanted to be part of this movement toward a broader scholarship attending to families and intersectionality, and we saw the importance of involving men in this dialogue and discussion. Moreover, knowing that a cohort of male Canadian scholars and service providers was working on issues related to active fathering highlighted the need to recognize that men do engage and educate other men about the importance of care work and the need to move beyond seeing education about care as a responsibility of women.

Finally, from a policy and community-impact perspective, we were aware that understanding how the role of men in care work and fathering is conceptualized is critical in policy and programming contexts. There is an increasingly "gender neutral" approach to government and private research and program funding whereby gendered social and economic realities are rendered invisible. For example, programs funded broadly to serve "families" are assumed to serve both fathers and mothers, and may negatively affect women and organizations that serve women; arguably, this "gender neutral" approach may also negatively affect men and programming for men.

While we joined the FIRA project as advocates of active father involvement, our commitment to overall, common goals was not always straightforward. Specifically, tensions in the coalition were exacerbated when individual scholars and community advocates were challenged to think through the possible losses and gains for their particular constituencies when a specific methodology, policy proposal, or research finding threatened those constituencies. For women, the gains from active and involved fathering include potential for more egalitarian partnerships, a reduction in the double day, and greater access to employment opportunities. Potential losses were notable for particular groups of women for whom male involvement in their families was viewed as detrimental rather than beneficial; such groups include women who have experienced family violence and women who were facing custody battles with men (Boyd, 2003; Kershaw, Pulkingham, & Fuller, 2008).

In the next two sections, we highlight how we alternated among and straddled the tensions and relations between being contributors and dissenters in the FIRA-CURA project.

Contributors

Our role as feminist contributors to FIRA had a threefold focus. First, we were concerned with bringing attention to differences and diversity among men. Second, we focused on highlighting diverse family forms and the importance of inclusive terminology. Finally, we feel we assisted in the difficult task of sifting through and assessing multiple, often competing, voices speaking about fathering and the claims they made about which needs – for attention, representation, research, and advocacy – were greatest. Each of these focuses is explored below.

Attention to Differences and Diversity

As feminist researchers and advocates, we saw several junctures in the project where we believe years of experience and attention to gender, diversity, and disadvantages made a contribution in this particular fathering alliance. First, we were able to draw from scholarship on feminism(s) and pro-feminist masculinities to underline the need to attend to diversity within and between fathering experiences and identities. Although the FIRA-CURA project was set up to reflect the multiplicity of fathering experiences in Canada, there were both subtle attempts and explicit requests by several around the table to have the alliance speak in one voice. Key players in the project felt that a clear and strong message was essential to effect policy change, and because of the wide scope and long gestation period leading up to the alliance, the project was viewed as a crucial platform from which to provide this public voice for father involvement. For these players, capitalizing on this opportunity to influence government policies affecting fathers required a singular unified message regardless of the exceptionally large-scale alliance; they worried that speaking of subtleties, such as differing recommendations or experiential nuances, could lead to a perception of fractured or splintered opinion and ultimately dilute the effects of the alliance.

Where we understood the desire for and perceived need of a united voice as informed by our own experiences as advocates in other arenas, we worked to try to find common ground among diverse clusters working across a wide range of fathering needs and interests. Our consistent contribution was to remind our collaborators that while the desire to advocate for one position/ one voice was understandable, it was highly unlikely. Our position in this regard drew on well-established debates on the theory and practice of intersectionality (McCall, 2005) or interlocking systems of domination (Razack, 1998) as ways of understanding and theorizing the diversity of gender experiences and the structures that enable and constrain change. We also saw these broad theoretical lenses as reminders of the barriers to achieving a common voice across men's needs, as they explained how the axes of identity and structure constantly create points of connection and disconnection between women's and men's interests and relevant policy responses (Siltanen & Doucet, 2008). Feminist contributions to thinking on intersectionality were relevant to understanding the barriers to achieving a common voice across men's needs. Nevertheless, several participants remained convinced that supporting a range of voices did not work to men's advantage; this was especially the case for those seeking policy change with respect to custody and access in cases of separation and divorce, and for those who wanted to use the project to set up a larger and more sustainable alliance following the research activities. While a strong case could potentially be made by the alliance for increased funding for community programming for fathers, since this was a shared issue across cluster identities and politics, a lack of clarity remained regarding advocating for policy change.

Diversity in Family Forms and Inclusive Terminology
The FIRA-CURA project was set up to encompass a variety of family forms. The seven research clusters were established in recognition of the fact that Canadian families and the fathers within them are diverse. At the same time, a strong viewpoint underpinning the project tended, from our perspectives, to underplay the gendered differences and inequities that remain a central part of family life and to "fall back" on traditional conceptualizations of heterosexual nuclear families as neutral territory. Long-standing feminist work on families and care work makes visible the deeply gendered processes

that continue to be part of care work and parenting, including the persistent connection between women and the responsibility for care for dependent others across the life course, and the associated "costs of caring" that many women may face as result of an imbalance in care work (Crittenden, 2001; Folbre, 1994). This spotlight on gendered processes was critical to counter a tendency among some participants to presume that men would be included in care work or programming by substituting the category or label "father" for "mother" rather than to attend to differences of lived experiences of men and women.

Contributions from feminists and others in the coalition drew attention to the importance of inclusive language and terminology. Feminist scholars, for example, have often highlighted that words obscure the relations of power underpinning those words; one oft-repeated example is how referring only to "child poverty" ignores the wider context, where the situation is actually about "women's poverty" and its dire consequences for children (Lister, 2006; Little, 2003).

One of the most vocal and ongoing conflicts that occurred at the FIRA-CURA project concerned the use of the term *father* or *parent*. While the decision to be flexible in language use rather than adhere to one or the other was eventually made, the debate required a gender analysis. For many members of the FIRA-CURA project, the very intentional use of the word *father* is critical as it identifies what was previously invisible: namely, that men as well as women are participants in caring work in families. These researchers and advocates had worked for years to have the term *father* used explicitly and strategically in their work. The use of the term *parent* was to be avoided, as it was seen to exclude fathers because organizations and programs using the term *parent* often mean *mother*. For example, the FIRA-CURA cluster on new fathers demonstrated that programs and media directed at new parents claimed to provide services and information for "family-centred care" but were modelled on "mother-centred care." Likewise, the FIRA-CURA cluster on fathers of children with special needs found the same "mother-centred care" focus when looking at activities set up for caregivers of ill children. On the other hand, feminist-inspired thinking also saw a rationale for reclaiming the term *parent* rather than *father* by the research cluster that was focused on gay dads and lesbian, gay, bisexual, transgendered, queer (LGBTQ) families. From this perspective, it was clear that the word *father* often inadvertently refers only to heterosexual men, couples, and nuclear families with the normative prescription of a mother-father dyad (see also Ruddick, 1997), which renders invisible families with more than two parents and those with two or more mothers.

Many other project discussions highlighted the importance of terminology, and changing terminology in particular: clarity in these discussions was contributed by feminist work on language and power (see Cameron, 1998;

Kerber, 1988; Spender, 1995). For example, during the project, one cluster changed its name from the Gay Dads research cluster (as formulated in the original proposal in 2002) to the LGBTQ research cluster. Over the course of our work together, a shared commitment grew among several alliance members to challenge a number of assumptions that continued to arise, such as those related to fathers' employment and socio-economic status. This commitment included revealing and challenging the heterosexist bias in analysis and policy, the ongoing impacts of colonization, misunderstandings of the continued disruption of Indigenous men's fathering on and off reserves, and the marginalization of men more generally as carers through exclusionary language.

Multiple Voices and the Politics of Need

Parallel to the gradual softening of the call for "one voice for fathers" was a tendency to posit the social exclusion of different kinds of fathers as almost a "hierarchy of needs" among some FIRA-CURA project members. Debates ensued about whose issues were more pressing and in need of attention on policy and public agendas. At one point, a conversation unfolded about whether the term *victim* or *marginalized* should be used to describe many groups and individual fathers in Canada; the discussion gradually moved away from viewing fathers as victims, as this implied that someone or something was *oppressing* men in their fathering practices and identities, and was not appreciative of fathers as agents in their worlds. Concurrently, the use of the word *invisible* increased with the acknowledgment that for many years, fathers were – and still are – largely invisible in policy and public discussions on parents and children, albeit in different ways for different kind of fathers: young/teen fathers, for example, in contrast to fathers of children with special needs engaging with the health care system.

The replacement of the potential term *victim* with the word *invisible* then led to ongoing positioning of groups as the *most* invisible. In this vein, each cluster was able to describe instances of how their population was rendered deeply invisible by structure and historical circumstance – young, gay or LGBTQ, immigrant, Indigenous, new fathers, or fathers of children with special needs. While differences among these groups remain, several common threads were identified, such as understandings that arise from experiences of racism, migration, and poverty reported by Indigenous and immigrant fathers. In our view, this is reminiscent of the evolution of thinking and acting beyond liberal feminism, which focuses mainly on access to employment or other resources, toward a wider feminist analysis that critically examines the more complex social realities of women's and men's lives.

Although all of the research clusters claimed to be representing the most invisible group, the separated and divorced father cluster was certainly the most vocal, persistent, and aggressive in asserting its claim. The predominant focus of that cluster was on non-custodial single fathers who were living with court-mandated outcomes and were often in high conflict with mothers. While we, as mothers, recognized the extreme difficulty and pain that these fathers experienced in relation to forced separation from their children, what was missing, or invisible, in the "divorced fathers as victims" argument was a wider exploration of the multitude of fathers who live in mediated or other non-court-mandated outcomes such as active fathers in blended families and single fathers in sole or shared-custody arrangements. As explored below, this claim of "most injured" and the rhetoric surrounding it led us to sometimes shift our position from contributors to dissenters within the alliance.

Dissenters

Our positioning as occasional dissenters from the mainstream of discussion in the FIRA-CURA project was a stance that was sometimes shared by others in the group who were explicitly cognizant of the challenges engendered by the project's ideological complexities, including feminist concerns and active fatherhood (e.g., Ball, 2009; Epstein, 2009; Whitehead & Bala, this volume). Most often, we expressed dissent in conversation with other members of the alliance. At one point, we even went so far as to consider leaving the project after strongly expressing dissent in a broader public gathering where arguments that seemed more aligned with fathers' rights agendas than with research or policy analysis were presented as a product of the FIRA-CURA project. This brought up issues of what membership in the project meant to us. As we both gained from and contributed to the credibility of the project, we also questioned our accountability for the products of other project members.

More generally, two tensions ignited concern and drew together disparate feminist and pro-feminist male voices into a concerted response. The first tension was related to the issue of how to value and "give voice" to fathers' perspectives where structural conditions continue to favour them: that is, to recognize patriarchal privilege and still honour the context of men's experience as fathers. The second concerned the contested question of whether there is anything "essential" about fathers' contributions to children's lives.

Fathers and the Patriarchal Dividend

As discussed above, the view of fathers as marginalized, as disenfranchised, and even as victims within family discourse often surfaced at meetings. At such times, we found ourselves having to develop clarity about our own approach to fathering. We have come to see that combining our feminist principles with the promotion of active fathering involves a double vision. Metaphorically speaking, this is like having two pairs of eyeglasses: one pair for short-term insights and a second for long-range consequences. Quite simply, sitting at the table with fathering advocates and researchers, we had to keep switching our glasses.

To take a short-range view is to focus on the stories being told, some of which were indeed quite painful to hear, such as stories of fathers struggling with courts and public discourses that may view them as secondary or second-best caregivers. The stories of teen dads who had little access to their children and who were often given a cold and judgmental shoulder from community and health care professionals were received as heartbreaking narratives. Similarly, the anguish that was articulated in the narratives of divorced and separated fathers who had limited or no access to their children were also heard sympathetically across the diverse clusters of the FIRA-CURA project group.

Nevertheless, taking a wider perspective means also attending to the structural conditions within which women and men parent and enact their everyday lives and recognizing that continuing gender inequities remain systemic. In Canada and globally, those inequities include women's dispro-portionate investment in care work and men's access to greater earnings and social privileges. As argued in Chapter 10 of this book, fathers' participation in caregiving is increasing in Canada, whether they do it as active fathers living in diverse family forms, as stay-at-home dads, or as fathers on parental leave (see McKay, Marshall, & Doucet, this volume).

It is also the case that fathers face difficulty in accessing workplace policies that are intended to support parental leaves; much research on work and family neglects the relationship between work and care by men (Daly, Ashbourne, & Hawkins, 2008). Nevertheless, while individual fathers may lose power and authority in the workplace when they trade "cash for care" (Hobson, 2002), as a gendered group, men still benefit from the ever-present "patriarchal dividend" (Connell, 1995) that accrues to males in society. The same is not true for women. While men may come to appreciate the personal and social benefits of being involved fathers, it is still women who over-whelmingly pay the social and economic price for care (see Crittenden, 2001).

Taking a wider view on fathering means remaining aware of some key challenges for feminists researching single fathering; this is an area of study and activism where fathers' rights groups can use particular research results to justify political aims that deeply counteract central feminist principles. That is, arguments for active fathering may be picked up by particular fathers' rights groups whose overall political objectives are antithetical to many feminist groups and women's interests. Two examples are mandated shared parenting agreements that do not take violence into account and joint custody when fathers were rarely present before the divorce (see Kershaw et al., 2008).

Also of concern are movements from the political and religious conservative right that insist on innate differences between women and men, mothering and fathering. These include international chapters of the Promise Keepers and the "Fatherhood Responsibility Movement," which emphasize and promote ideals of fathers as family breadwinners and heads of the household and mothers as natural primary caregivers and supplementary or non-earners (Coltrane, 1997, 2001; Gavanas, 2002, 2004; Messner, 1997). Moreover, as discussed below, support for men's involvement in the family can unwittingly turn into completely different sets of arguments about essential differences between women and men or about the moral superiority of particular family forms.

Are Fathers Essential?

Working alongside academics and practitioners who had a particular stake in increasing public understandings of involved fathering, the conversation could, intentionally or inadvertently, head into territory where claims of the essential contributions of fathers were promoted. Such well-rehearsed narratives on the critical importance of fathers occupy a central place in much of the fathering scholarship and indeed are part of the FIRA resource list. We are in general agreement that children benefit from having two (or more) loving parents. We also hold to the view that the involvement of fathers can indeed be beneficial for children as well as for fathers and mothers (see Allen & Daly, 2002; Daly, Ashbourne, & Brown, 2009). Yet for several reasons, we do not subscribe to the "essential father" argument that posits that fathers' roles in children's lives are essential for child development.

First, claims that fathers are essential to children's lives may sometimes inadvertently undermine the position of single mothers who parent without men (see Kershaw et al., 2008). Here we draw on feminist scholarship on care, families, and fathering (Boyd, 2003; Featherstone, 2009; Hollway, 2006; Sevenhuijsen, 1998, 2000) as well as on work by fathering scholars (Coltrane, 2001; Pleck, 2008) who argue, in different ways, for the possibility and potential for men to care without making arguments for the *necessity* of male or men's involvement in care. As pioneering fathering scholar Pleck (2008) put it in his FIRA conference keynote address, "Essential father theory is widely accepted by the lay public and even among professionals, but empirical support for fathers making an essential ... contribution to development is at present quite weak" (see also Auerbach and Silverstein, 1999; Silverstein, 1996).

Of course, this issue of the "essential father" also raises the issue of whether there is anything "essential" about motherhood, and we come to the same position, which constitutes the second reason for arguing that fathers are not "essential" to children's lives. We argue that it is important to recognize variability in mothering practices and ideologies (Ruddick, 1995; Scheper-Hughes, 1992), and we would apply this understanding to our research on fathering as well. Nevertheless, the issue of particular or structural visioning remains critical in the underlying approach that we have taken. That is, while in some particular cases, fathers may be the more appropriate or involved parent, at the wider level of social positioning – including within the ideological, discursive, social, economic, and cultural landscapes – it is mainly women and female networks of care who take on the overall responsibility for care work. This partly explains the mother-centric focus of research, policy, and programming discussed in Chapter 1. That is, women continue to carry the burden of "social reproduction," and as feminists, we hold strongly to continuing to recognize this underlying foundation.

Taking this broad position also means recognizing the rich social networks of care that many women build around children, including "other-mothers" (Hill Collins, 2000), people doing "kin work" (Stack, 1974), those undertaking "community responsibility" (Doucet, 2006), and any carers within larger networks of care that extend beyond the nuclear family (Hansen, 2005). While men contribute to networks of care in ways that are underexplored (Hansen, 2005), the building and maintaining of the networks around care remain women's work. Within the FIRA-CURA project, it was feminists – and even more so the Indigenous Fathers cluster led by Jessica Ball (see Ball, 2009) – who repeatedly brought this perspective into view.

In relation to the issue of the "essential father," we have held to a twofold position that has meant recognizing the possibilities and potential for fathers to be fully involved in caregiving but only if it *does not* take away from the larger social understandings of women's predominant role in terms of both gains and losses – both the pleasures and burdens, the power and oppression – that are tied to caregiving. That is, we tried to be aware of and sensitive to men's desires to be engaged fathers and to the losses that are incurred when social and legal forces pull them away from their children, while at the same time acknowledging the wider networks of mainly *female* care, investment, and, sometimes, loss of social privileges that accompany heavy investments of time and energy in care work. This position is, in turn, rooted in wider debates on "strategic essentialism" wherein feminist theorists have argued that while it is important to recognize gender differences in some contexts, this move should be a "strategic" one that does not translate into "absolutist categorizations of difference" but rather is a recognition that "meanings are always relative to particular constructions in specified contexts" (Scott, 1988, 175). Fuss (1989) articulated this brilliantly over two decades ago when she wrote that "essentially speaking we need to theorize essentialist spaces from which to speak and, simultaneously, to deconstruct those spaces and keep them from solidifying" (118; see also Doucet, 2004, 2006).

Conclusion

This chapter reflects on lessons and challenges of integrating our shared interests in feminism, research, and active fathering. While maintaining an overall position as advocates for engaged fathering, we have vacillated between being contributors and dissenters in this ongoing national fathering dialogue. As contributors, we supported the FIRA research and ongoing dialogue on differences and diversity among men, the rich variability of well-functioning family forms, and the need for inclusive terminology, while also issuing a cautionary note about how to mediate between competing voices for recognition on the national fathering agenda in addition to our own research contributions.

Alternatively, we found ourselves dissenting from the group when particular groups of fathers, or those advocating for them, whose interests might compete at the policy and programming level with those of mothers dominated the discussion table. As dissenters, we were vocal in arguing against a view that promulgated the "essential" need for fathers in families, once again pointing to the richness of the variety of family forms in Canada.

Looking back over our seven years as active contributors to this important Canadian conversation on changing fatherhood, we have identified several key challenges, learning points, and opportunities for scholars examining fathering with a feminist lens. A first challenge is that of pulling together varied political, intellectual, and community agendas surrounding fathering as a set of experiences, practices, and identities. It is now widely acknowledged in feminist scholarship that at least one version of a fathering agenda (the fathers' rights agenda) works against women's interests. As feminists working on the FIRA-CURA project, perhaps our greatest challenge was when we unexpectedly found ourselves close neighbours to this agenda within the FIRA alliance and had to find a way to navigate through the conversation without walking away from it altogether. A second, related challenge is how or whether scholars working from feminist perspectives can contribute as part of a research group in which ideas that seem to threaten our fundamental feminist principles are being articulated, albeit with other voices dissenting in addition to our own. Indeed, in the FIRA-CURA project, there were some moments when we wondered whether remaining at the table posed risks that could endanger our reputations in our feminist communities. We found (and find) ourselves clarifying our work to those colleagues who did not readily see how research related to men and care intersected in a relevant way with feminist concerns.

The lessons that can be taken away from the experiences we have recounted in this chapter are threefold, with implications for research, practice, and policy. First, working closely with these tensions can sharpen one's awareness of taken-for-granted aspects of feminist work. What was perhaps unique about working with the issue of fathering is that we had to more intentionally and vocally attend to the intersections among language, power, and caregiving in a way that has become regular and often unquestioned practice in feminist circles. What was also unique was that our own awareness of men's perspectives and experiences greatly added to our own understanding of gender – our attitudes toward how gender works and what men and women do in caring were expanded and enriched.

Second, widening the gender analysis of caregiving work to include men's perspectives is not an easy task. While women have largely contributed to and controlled this conversation, it is also a recurring feminist goal to have men more involved in care work. To achieve this, however, means including men's diverse perspectives at the discussion table. Finally, our initial enthusiasm for encouraging increased fathering involvement has been tempered with the view that the stakes can be high for feminists who work with men to explore men's participation in an area of social life that is of such central importance to many women's lives. As participants deeply engaged in Canada's most extensive coalition of fathering researchers and community practitioners, we argue that greater attention must be given by both feminists and fathering advocates to these tensions involved in actually achieving the goal of increasing active fathering involvement.

Note
This chapter is equally co-authored.

References
Allen, S. M., & Daly, K. (2002). *The effects of father involvement: A summary of the research evidence.* Carleton Place, ON: Father Involvement Initiative, Ontario Network.
Auerbach, C., & Silverstein, L. B. (1999). Deconstructing the essential father. *American Psychologist, 54*(6), 397-407.
Ball, J. (2009). Fathering in the shadows: Indigenous fathers and Canada's colonial legacies. *The Annals of the American Academy of Political and Social Science, 624*(1), 29-48.
Boyd, S. B. (2003). *Child custody, law and women's work.* Don Mills, ON: Oxford University Press.
Cameron, D. (1998). *The feminist critique of language: A reader.* London, England: Routledge.
Code, L., & Burt, S. D. (1995). *Changing methods: Feminists transforming practice.* Peterborough, ON: Broadview Press.
Coltrane, S. (1997). Scientific half-truths and postmodern parody in the family values debate. *Contemporary Sociology, 28*(1), 7-10.
Coltrane, S. (2001). Marketing the marriage solution: Misplaced simplicity in the politics of fatherhood: 2001 presidential address to the Pacific Sociological Association. *Sociological Perspectives, 44*(4), 387-418.
Connell, R. W. (1995). *Masculinities.* London, England: Polity Press.
Crittenden, A. (2001). *The price of motherhood: Why the most important job in the world is still the least valued.* New York, NY: Henry Holt.
Crowley, J. E. (2009). Conflicted membership: Women in fathers' rights groups. *Sociological Inquiry, 79*(3), 328-350.
Daly, K. J., Ashbourne, L., & Brown, J. L. (2009). Fathers' perceptions of children's influence: Implications for involvement. *The Annals of the American Academy of Political and Social Science, 624*(1), 61-77.

Daly, K., Ashbourne, L., & Hawkins, L. (2008). Work-life issues for fathers. In K. Korabik, D. S. Lero, & D. L. Whitehead (Eds.), *Handbook of work-family integration: Research, theory, and best practices* (pp. 249-264). Burlington, MA: Academic Press.

Digby, T. (Ed.). (1998). *Men doing feminism.* London, England: Routledge.

Doucet, A. (2004). Fathers and the responsibility for children: A puzzle and a tension. *Atlantis, 28*(2), 103-114.

Doucet, A. (2006). *Do men mother? Fathering, care, and domestic responsibility.* Toronto, ON: University of Toronto Press.

Edin, K., & Kefalas, M. (2005). *Promises I can keep: Why poor women put motherhood before marriage.* Berkeley: University of California Press.

Epstein, R. (2009). *Who's your daddy? And other writings on queer parenting.* Toronto, ON: Sumach Press.

Erturk, Y. (2004). Considering the role of men in gender agenda setting: Conceptual and policy issues. *Feminist Review, 78,* 3-21.

Featherstone, B. (2009). *Contemporary fathering: Theory, policy and practice.* Bristol, England: Polity Press.

Folbre, N. (1994). *Who pays for the kids? Gender and the structures of constraint.* London, England: Routledge, Chapman & Hall.

Fuss, D. (1989). *Essentially speaking: Feminism, nature and difference.* London, England: Routledge.

Gardiner, J. K. (1998). Feminism and the future of fathering. In T. Digby (Ed.), *Men doing feminism* (pp. 255-291). London, England: Routledge.

Gardiner, J. K. (2002). *Masculinity studies and feminist theory: New directions.* New York, NY: Colombia University Press.

Gavanas, A. (2002). The Fatherhood Responsibility Movement: The centrality of marriage, work and male sexuality in reconstructions of masculinity and fatherhood. In B. Hobson (Ed.), *Making men into fathers: Men, masculinities and the social politics of fatherhood* (pp. 213-242). Cambridge, England: Cambridge University Press.

Gavanas, A. (2004). *Fatherhood politics in the United States: Masculinity, sexuality, race, and marriage.* Chicago: University of Illinois Press.

Goldberg, A. E., & Allen, K. R. (2007). Imagining men: Lesbian mothers' perceptions of male involvement during the transition to parenthood. *Journal of Marriage and Family, 69*(2), 352-365.

Hansen, K. V. (2005). *Not-so-nuclear families: Class, gender and networks of care.* Piscataway, NJ: Rutgers University Press.

Hays, S. (2003). *Flat broke with children: Women in the age of welfare reform.* New York, NY: Oxford University Press.

Hill Collins, P. (2000). *Black feminist thought: Knowledge, consciousness, and the politics of empowerment.* Boston, MA: Unwin Hyman.

Hobson, B. (2002). *Making men into fathers: Men, masculinities and the social politics of fatherhood.* Cambridge, England: Cambridge University Press.

Hollway, W. (2006). Family figures in twentieth-century British "psy" discourses. *Theory Psychology, 16*(4), 443-464.

hooks, b. (1989). *Talking back: Thinking feminist, thinking black.* Boston, MA: South End Press.

hooks, b. (1990). *Yearning: Race, gender and cultural politics.* Boston, MA: South End Press.

Kerber, L. (1988). Separate spheres, female worlds, women's place: The rhetoric of women's history. *Journal of American History 75*(1), 9-39.

Kershaw, P., Pulkingham, J., & Fuller, S. (2008). Expanding the subject: Violence, care, and (in)active male citizenship. *Social Politics, 15,* 182-206.

Lareau, A. (2003). *Unequal childhood: Class, race and family life* Berkeley: University of California Press.

Lister, R. (2006). Children (but not women) first: New Labour, child welfare and gender. *Critical Social Policy, 26*(2), 315-335.

Little, M. (2003). The leaner, meaner welfare machine: The Harris government's ideological and material attack on single mothers. In D. Brock (Ed.), *Making normal: Social regulation in Canada* (pp. 235-258). Toronto, ON: University of Toronto Press.

Malacrida, C. (2009). Performing motherhood in a disablist world: Dilemmas of motherhood, femininity and disability. *International Journal of Qualitative Studies in Education, 22,* 99-117.

Mauthner, N. S., & Doucet, A. (2003). Reflexive accounts and accounts of reflexivity in qualitative data analysis. *Sociology, 37,* 413-431.

McCall, L. (2005). The complexity of intersectionality. *Signs: Journal of Women in Culture and Society, 30*(3), 1771-1800.

Messner, M. A. (1997). *Politics of masculinities: Men in movements.* Thousand Oaks, CA: Sage.

Ornelas, I. J., Perreira, K. M., Beeber, L., & Maxwell, L. (2009). Challenges and strategies to maintaining emotional health: Qualitative perspectives of Mexican immigrant mothers. *Journal of Family Issues, 30*(11), 1556-1575.

Pleck, J. (2008, October). *Why does father involvement promote child and adolescent development: Addressing an under-theorized issue.* Keynote address presented at the Father Involvement Research Alliance Conference 2008: Diversity, Visibility, Community, Toronto, ON.

Presser, L. (2004). Violent offenders, moral selves: Constructing identities and accounts in the research interview. *Social Problems, 51*(1), 82-101.

Razack, S. H. (1998). *Looking white people in the eye: Gender, race, and culture in courtrooms and classrooms.* Toronto, ON: University of Toronto Press.

Ruddick, S. (1995). *Maternal thinking: Towards a politics of peace.* Boston, MA: Beacon.

Ruddick, S. (1997). The idea of fatherhood. In H. L. Nelson (Ed.), *Feminism and families* (pp. 205-220). New York, NY: Routledge.

Saffilios-Rothschild, C. (1969). Family sociology or "wives" family sociology? A cross-cultural examination of decision making. *Journal of Marriage and the Family, 31,* 290-301.

Scheper-Hughes, N. (1992). *Death without weeping: The violence of everyday life in Brazil.* Berkeley: University of California Press.

Scott, J. W. (1988). *Gender and the politics of history.* New York, NY: Columbia University Press.

Segura, D. A. (1994). Working at motherhood: Chicana and Mexican immigrant mothers and employment. In E. N. Glenn, G. Chang, & L. R. Forcey (Eds.), *Mothering: Ideology, experience and agency* (pp. 211-233). London, England: Routledge.

Sevenhuijsen, S. (1998). *Citizenship and the ethics of care: Feminist considerations on justice, morality and politics.* London, England: Routledge.

Sevenhuijsen, S. (2000). Caring in the Third Way: The relation between obligation, responsibility and care in Third Way discourse. *Critical Social Policy, 25*(1), 5-38.

Siltanen, J., & Doucet, A. (2008) Gender relations in Canada: Intersectionality and beyond. Toronto, ON: Oxford University Press.

Silverstein, L. B. (1996). Fathering is a feminist issue. *Psychology of Women Quarterly, 20*(1), 3-37.

Spender, D. (1995). *Nattering on the Net: Women, power, and cyberspace.* Melbourne, Australia: Spinifex Press.

Stack, C. (1974). *All our kin: Strategies for survival in a black community.* New York, NY: Harper & Row.

Ward, J. (2004). "Not all differences are created equal": Multiple jeopardy in a gendered organization. *Gender and Society, 18*(1), 82-102.

Part 2
The Diversity of Fathering
Experiences: Contested Terrain

5
Young Fatherhood, Generativity, and Men's Development: Travelling a Two-Way Street to Maturity

Michael W. Pratt, Heather L. Lawford, and James W. Allen

> I broke the pattern when it comes to the fathers before ... I want to be there for my child. My father never took the time to listen to me ... I want [my son] to do whatever he wants because I can't really do that now.
>
> — 19-year-old father, on his hopes for his one-year-old son

Erikson's (1950) stage model of personality development provides us with a broad framework for understanding and representing growth and change in human lives, linking them with culture and biology. The mid-life period of the human life cycle, the seventh of eight stages in Erikson's model, is characterized by generativity, which entails a primary injunction to care for the next generation. This injunction shapes the lives of men and women, their families, and their wider societies. Parenting is perhaps the core context for this mid-life generativity, yet parenthood and the generative concern it often inspires may begin much earlier than mid-life, as the voice of the young father above conveys. In this chapter, we explore the relationship between fathering and generativity, and examine how it unfolds across adulthood.

We consider the concept of generative fathering from two directions: how the experience of fatherhood can affect the course of generative development in men, on the one hand, and how generative variations in men's personalities can shape fatherhood experiences, on the other. Most research on the impact of fatherhood on generativity has taken a broad view of how the transition to fathering might prepare the way for a general adult developmental progression to caring for the welfare of future generations in maturity (Snarey, 1993). Research on the possible influences of variations in generativity on the fathering experience has focused more on individual personality variations among men and on predictions of how the father role is enacted and experienced depending on those variations (Christiansen & Palkovitz,

1998). Yet it seems plausible that both of these directions of influence, from fatherhood to generativity and the reverse, operate across men's adult life course. Drawing on the research literature as well as on our own studies, we explore this duality here, paying particular attention to evidence on the early period of this developmental process.

We begin with a description of Erikson's construct of generativity and its implications for fathering. Next, we describe theory and research on fathering and men's identity development, particularly the development of a generative sense of self. This is followed by a review of how fatherhood can impact men's generativity and by some research of our own on generative fathering in a sample of young men from the Fatherhood Involvement Research Alliance (FIRA). We go on to review research on how generativity can shape the experience and anticipation of fathering in men. The chapter ends with a summary and commentary on future research and on the themes and policy implications relevant to this book.

Erikson's Concept of Generativity

Erikson (1950) saw generativity as the positive pole of the seventh (of eight) stage of development; he suggested that generativity characterized the long period of middle adulthood in the human life course. For Erikson, generativity represented an investment in the care of future generations, primarily as a way of leaving a legacy of the self after death. All of Erikson's stages have a contrasting pole of unsuccessful adaptation, and he called the problematic pole during stage seven "stagnation," an inability to invest in the care and guidance of future generations; stagnation was often characterized by a preoccupation with the self. As with each of his stages, Erikson (1968) saw successful adaptation during this stage as following from the attainment of adaptation in the previous stage (in this case, the sixth stage of "intimacy" in young adulthood) and as laying the groundwork for the final stage of "ego integrity" in old age. While Erikson represented these stages as complex and intertwined across the life course, he suggested that issues of generativity typically come to the fore during the period of mid-life and that the early prototype for generative caring is in the rearing of one's children (though one might be generative in many other ways as well). Erikson's framework thus implies that fathering should be a key experience in the ongoing development and expression of generativity for many men.

Indeed, one important contemporary perspective draws on Erikson's ideas to focus broadly on the positive potential that fathers in our culture have for engaging in generative caring within the family itself (Hawkins & Dollahite, 1997). Generative fathering responds to children's needs as they develop and change, and is oriented around principles of commitment, caring, connection, and communication (Dollahite & Hawkins, 1998). Hawkins and Dollahite (1997) argue that their framework provides a way to counter both the "relative deficit" position that has been a focal point of research and theorizing on fatherhood (as compared with motherhood) and the stereotype of men as "incompetent" parents in much social science research (e.g., Blankenhorn, 1995), a stereotype that is even stronger with respect to young fathers (Rhoden & Robinson, 1997). Hawkins and Dollahite argue that high levels of generative engagement with the fathering role are important for both men and children. Broadly, then, this stance focuses on the generic importance of fathering in the human life cycle, as fathers contribute to the lives of children, to families and society, and to their own personal development.

Recent Research on Generativity

Over the past two decades, McAdams and his associates (e.g., McAdams & de St. Aubin, 1992) have pursued a program of research on generativity of personality. They have expanded Erikson's framework into a more detailed model of seven elements of generativity and have sought to develop measures for assessing the presence and level of generativity characterizing each of these seven components. The most widely studied of these have been the four elements of generative concern or motivation, generative plans or strivings, generative action, and generative narration or "storying" of these qualities in one's life. For example, generative concern is measured by the Loyola Generativity Scale (LGS), a 20-item questionnaire assessing both caring and the self's legacy (one item, for example, states "I think I will be remembered for a long time after I die"). By developing this framework and its associated measurement tools, McAdams and colleagues have provided a model of individual variability in generativity, treating generativity not just as a hallmark issue of a particular period in the life course, but as a quality that may vary systematically between individuals. Furthermore, McAdams (2001) suggests that generativity may not be confined to the mid-life period but may extend over a wider range of the life course. This idea is at least implicit in Erikson's (1950) general epigenetic framework but is more explicit in McAdams's formulation and suggests that patterns of generative fathering may unfold across adulthood.

Based on the McAdams model, certain elements of the generativity framework may be more salient at different points in the life cycle. Stewart and Vandewater (1998) suggest that generative motivation or concern may be especially salient earlier in the adult life course, whereas generative plans and actions may be more likely in mid-life, given the opportunities provided for such activities in the social context of adult responsibility. Pratt, Norris, Arnold, and Filyer (1999) observed that generative narration was more common in mid- and later adulthood.

As well, Kotre (1984) describes several different types of generative expression unfolding over the life course, including biological, parental, technical, and societal forms. Procreation (biological) and parental care (parenting) may be followed by and contribute to technical forms of teaching important social values and skills; a broader focus on value preservation and transmission is the hallmark of societal forms of generativity in mid-life and later adulthood in the fathering role (Snarey, 1993; Vaillant, 2002).

Finally, McAdams and colleagues have also explored how individual variations in generativity may be expressed in the "life story" or identity narratives of adulthood (McAdams, 2006; McAdams, Diamond, de St. Aubin, & Mansfield, 1997). Highly generative adults in this research were found to tell a distinctive sort of commitment story about their lives that focused on several characteristic features, including a sense of early advantage, a concern for the needs of others, a commitment to pro-social goals for the future, and the capacity to see the self as transforming negative events and changes into positive outcomes (which McAdams, 2006, labels a "redemption" theme). McAdams's research shows that redemption is in fact an especially characteristic theme of the generative life story. Such transformations of bad events into good outcomes, while only one element of a generative narrative style, may play a particularly key role in supporting positive identity growth and change. In this chapter, we suggest that fatherhood can provide men with an opportunity for the expression of a new, more generative identity that is focused on caring for youth, which transforms the sense of self and potentially supports generative growth and action into the future. Such a change in the life story and its implications provide one mechanism linking fatherhood and generative development across adulthood.

Impact of Fatherhood on Men's Development

In this discussion, we focus on the meaning of fatherhood for men's own development, recognizing that a father's role in child development and the family is both important and distinctive (Parke, 1998). Over the past 20 years, there has been an effort to explore the potential impact that fatherhood might have on men's development. A. Cowan (1988) discusses men's transition to parenthood as a time of challenge and opportunity, and recognizes the mixed effects that fatherhood may have on some men. Some aspects of life satisfaction may decline during this period for most couples, and fathers, just like mothers, often express an increased sense of stress in integrating this new role for the self into their lives (A. Cowan, 1988). However, new fathers can also experience a sense of possibility with regard to identity change and growth. A. Cowan suggests three potential areas of change in fathers' view of themselves: sense of identity, locus of control, and self-esteem. C. P. Cowan and Cowan (1992) found that men, as they became first-time parents, tended to show patterns of differentiation and integration across new roles, as well as new conflicts between these roles, and changes ensued in each of these three areas of the self – sometimes positive, sometimes more negative.

Contextual Factors in Fathers' Experiences

In a discussion on parenthood as a generator of adult development, Palkovitz (1996) suggests that a key factor in understanding the relations between the parent role and adult development is a coherent model for understanding levels of parent engagement. Palkovitz argues that becoming a parent is experienced differently by different individuals and that the level of parent involvement will mediate the scope of identity change and growth. Those who are more involved will generally be more likely to show such transformations in the self. Palkovitz also points out that parents may take on many forms of involvement, including caregiving, providing, planning, and teaching, to name a few.

Variability in the fathering experience is also influenced by societal and historical factors (an example of "modifying" factors, according to Palkovitz, 1996). As many argue (see LaRossa, 1988; Pleck, 1998), there has been something of a cohort change in Euro-Canadian culture's ideological sense of the appropriate or expected level of father involvement with infants and children, though perhaps one that is more modest than is sometimes depicted. From the nineteenth through the mid-twentieth century, fathers in many North American cultures were dominantly portrayed as "distant breadwinners" (Pleck, 1998). Families today, often with both the mother and father as earners, do expect more father involvement with their children, and men often contrast themselves with their own fathers on this dimension, seeing themselves as "doing better" on engagement (Pleck, 1998). Thus, these cultural transformations shape the ways in which fathers measure their sense of self against social norms. Dienhart and Daly (1997) argue that contemporary Canadian culture's ideology of shared family parenting is often not well supported by the "on the ground" situations of work pressures, time demands, and practices that couples must negotiate to enable fathers' greater involvement. While expectations are changing, social conditions do not always keep pace.

An additional class of factors that influences father involvement and self-evaluation, according to Palkovitz (1996), comprises individual and personal factors. Of particular interest to the current discussion is the age of fathers. As we will see, young fathers provide an especially interesting case for study because they highlight an early transition to fatherhood that is off-time and separated from other, usually accompanying, life changes. Also, as noted above, these young men are not typically viewed as having much potential for generative fathering (Rhoden & Robinson, 1997), so careful study of their experience of this transition will prove rewarding.

Our focus here is on changes in how men view themselves – the identity component noted by A. Cowan (1988). Several recent studies have addressed what men themselves have to say about changes in the sense of identity that fatherhood brings. Palkovitz (2002), for example, asked a sample of 40 fathers (average age = 26 years) to discuss what the transition to fatherhood had meant to them. In a qualitative analysis of these data, Palkovitz found that several broad themes were expressed in men's comments, including settling down (45% mentioned) and becoming more giving (35%), more responsible (32%), and more generative (29%; e.g., seeing their child do better than them, leaving a legacy). Young men in the sample (aged 20-25) were also more likely to mention something Palkovitz labelled "jolt": fatherhood as a shock to their life course and focus.

Roy and Lucas (2006), based on qualitative analyses of interviews with 77 men aged 17 to 40 years, reported that these men experienced fatherhood as a transformational change to the self. Furthermore, the men often experienced generative investment in the father role as a way to make up for difficult or troubled pasts in their own lives and also as a way to sustain a positive sense of self under the stresses of contemporary troubled lives. For some of these men, generative care for children was seen as a way to rework one's own past failures, to repair "damage" or failures in the life course, or to establish a stronger sense of purpose. Devault et al. (2008) reported similar findings with a sample of young fathers from Québec. As we describe below, our own research with young fathers (Lawford, Dienhart, Devault, & Pratt, 2008) also highlights many of these themes, showing how generative engagement with children may matter to men's sense of personal identity in restorative ways.

In summary, interest in the transition to fatherhood and its role in identity change during men's adult development has increased recently. The studies referred to above shed light on the diversity of the fatherhood experience and how that experience relates to the transformation of the self and the development of a sense of generativity in the identity of the adult caretaker (e.g., Roy & Lucas, 2006). As Snarey (1993) also argues, based on his own longitudinal research, generative concern and involvement with one's children may serve as a stepping stone toward a later, broader generative involvement with youth and the wider society. We now go on to explore how transitions in fathers' sense of identity may potentially serve to mediate this growth.

Fatherhood as an Opportunity to Become Generative

Fatherhood as a Predictor of Men's Generativity
Several studies have provided evidence on the potential role of fatherhood in enhancing men's generative concern for youth. McAdams and de St.

Aubin (1992) observed that young adult men in their sample who were not fathers were significantly less likely to show such generative concern compared with women (either mothers or not) or with men who had become fathers. Generative concern as measured on the Loyola Generative Scale (LGS) is a broad index that focuses primarily on social acts outside the family milieu. Although it did not measure men's development over time, this study did suggest that the experience of parenting might be important for the growth of men's generative motivations. Similar sex differences were reported by Peterson, Smirles, and Wentworth (1997): young women showed an advantage over young men on the LGS but no gender differences on the LGS were found between their parents at mid-life.

McKerring and Pakenham (2000) also examined the question of gender differences in parenthood and generative concern. These authors found that for men (mean age = 41 years), involvement in parenting activities with children was a positive predictor of their level of generative concern on the LGS. However, this study showed no such relation for women. A study by Rothrauff and Cooney (2008) showed, in contrast, that by mid-life (mean age = 49), childless men and women did not differ from those with children in terms of generative concern. This result may suggest that avenues other than parenthood (e.g., mentoring, teaching) can provide opportunities for the growth of generative concern in men by mid-life, as noted by Erikson (1950).

Christiansen and Palkovitz (1998) studied several possible predictive factors in fathers' experiences that were correlated with generativity (as measured on an Erikson personality inventory that included both parental and societal generativity). They found that fathers' levels of actual behavioural involvement with their preschoolers were not strongly related to their generativity, whereas their attitudes about role identity as a father (how capable they felt as a father and to what extent fathers were important and should be engaged in parenting) were substantially positively related. This suggests that a general sense of identity and role may be more important than actual day-to-day behaviours in predicting generative development.

All of the studies mentioned so far were cross-sectional in nature: that is, they studied parenthood status and/or activities and generativity at the same point in time. Snarey (1993), however, used an existing longitudinal data set involving 240 men from the Boston area to assess fathering and generativity at several points in time. Snarey rated interview and observational records of parenting involvement from a sample of men in their early 30s and then rated the men's societal involvement and care for youth and the wider society in mid-life (age 47). This research showed clearly that previous involvement in the socio-emotional development of one's own children in childhood and adolescence correlated positively with a wider radius of generative societal care in mid-life men. The mechanisms for this link to generative action are not clearly indicated from these findings, but their longitudinal nature allows us to see both continuities and variations in the same men over time and tells a plausible story of the expansion from engagement with one's own children to engagement with youth in the wider society in mid-life.

One explanation for this pattern might be that most men experience some degree of transformation in terms of identity through experiences of fatherhood (Palkovitz, 2002). Such a transformation through fatherhood may have many components linked to generativity, including redemptive elements (McAdams, 2006). We next describe findings from a Canadian study, the Father Involvement Research Alliance (FIRA) interview study, on the potential importance of the fatherhood experience for young men's generative identity development.

The FIRA Study – Transforming the Self Through Fatherhood

In this large qualitative study on the experience of fatherhood, over 230 men were interviewed from seven different "clusters," or community-university alliances, across Canada. These clusters comprised new fathers, immigrant fathers, Indigenous fathers, divorced and separated fathers, gay fathers, fathers of special needs children, and young fathers. For the most part, men recruited for participation through these clusters were likely to be committed to their fathering roles, given their willingness to serve as research participants. All were asked similar open-ended questions about their experience of fatherhood: their involvement with children, what they got out of being a father, positive and negative experiences with children, and so on. Here we focus on findings from 35 young fathers (average age 22 at the time of interview), most of whom had become parents before the age of 21. This sample was collected by Annie Devault, team leader for the FIRA Young Fathers cluster. About half of the men completed individual interviews and the rest were part of small focus group sessions. While many of these men described troubled earlier life histories, this was not always the case. The transcripts were read independently by a team of three investigators and coded for recurring themes by each member using a qualitative coding procedure that was initially guided by the "sensitizing concepts" (Patton, 2002) of generativity and the life story framework of McAdams (2001). Life change themes in the transcripts were identified; subsequently, the interviews were discussed among the group and consensus on coding category was reached (Lawford et al., 2008).

The experience of fatherhood was described by the young dads in the FIRA sample in a way that commonly emphasized its transformational or redemptive nature as a life change, as previously reported by others (Devault et al., 2008; Palkovitz, 2002; Roy & Lucas, 2006). McAdams (2006) highlights the way in which such a redemptive theme of "transforming bad into good" is deeply embedded in the mainstream media stories of Hollywood and the United States generally. Not surprisingly, this dominant European heritage "master narrative" of one's life as self-transformation and improvement is likely to be widely appropriated by men (including many young Canadian men) as a way to craft their own individual life stories. Our findings suggest that such a life story had been adopted by the young dads in the FIRA cluster in their accounts of experiences of fatherhood. Such a transformational narrative may be important for sustaining a sense of commitment during challenging life experiences generally. For example, Maruna (1997), studying the autobiographies of people released from prison, reported that such redemption themes patterned the life stories of those individuals who succeeded in avoiding reincarceration by "going straight." It seems plausible to us that the FIRA sample of relatively motivated young fathers might describe a similar commitment script that could help to sustain their continuing efforts at engagement with their children, often under challenging circumstances (see, for example, McAdams et al., 1997).

Indeed, most of the 35 men in the young fathers sample had experienced social and economic hardship. Many of them did not have custody, and some did not have regular contact with their children. The common pattern of transformative life story observed in these young fathers was characterized by their description of an earlier problem, challenge, or difficulty. This difficulty might be of several types, as described below. The experience of fatherhood responsibility was then characteristically described as leading the individual to overcome this earlier problem and attain a greater sense of wholeness in one of several ways. This new-found sense of wholeness in turn helped the father to sustain generative care for the child on an ongoing basis and to bring a generative commitment to the long-term future of the child, a theme that was often elaborated in some detail as well.

In the interviews with these young fathers in the FIRA study, a generative theme was especially clear. Almost all the young fathers expressed the need to help their children become something better than what they had become and/or to offer their children more than they had been offered ("I want to be there for her in hard times when she's older"). Many young fathers also discussed their experiences of overcoming a difficult past before arriving at their current generative aspirations ("I try to live for my kids, not for myself"). We found that these discussions by young dads could be represented by three distinct themes, which sometimes co-occurred in the same transcript. All of these themes culminated in a redemptive experience of fatherhood bringing some sort of resolution to a challenging or difficult past (Lawford et al., 2008).

Finding Purpose

One common theme among many of the young fathers was a lack of purpose prior to having children. "I did not have any directions at all," said one young father. "I was pretty lost." Many reported a lack of motivation to find meaningful employment or to work toward independent living situations. Here is how one 22-year-old man, now separated from his partner but sharing custody of his two-year-old son, described it:

[Before my child was born] I wasn't a very ambitious person. I didn't have a job and I was living with friends who were on welfare. I didn't really have a life. And then my girlfriend got pregnant. That's when I smartened up, as they say, and I got a hold of myself. I found an apartment, I found a job – no, actually, it was my mother who found a job at the hospital for me [laughs]. I found an apartment, and then I had [the child] ... She was six months pregnant when she told me. So I had three months to think about it – having a child, finding a job, getting my life back on track. Making a life for myself, because I didn't have one. Not at all!

Settling Down and Turning Over a New Leaf

A second prominent theme among young fathers was overcoming a previously troubled past. Fatherhood inspired them to "straighten up" and consider their choices. Many described achieving great strides with respect to quitting alcohol or drugs, reconciling key relationships, or ending dangerous or unhealthy associations. A 21-year-old man who had a first child at 14 and a second with a different partner at 20 said:

Well, at first, when I found out that my girlfriend at that time was pregnant, I did not really think much of it because that night that we did have intercourse, I think I was really drunk and really high on drugs. But then, later on, it kind of just hit me – hey, I'm 14, she's 13 and pregnant, I am going to be a dad. That hit me like a ton of bricks and it got me ... well, I have to stop doing this stuff. Maybe once in a while going out to a bar, having a drink or two, that is okay, but not to what I am doing now, drinking every day, every night. I stopped.

Repairing Hurt

The third theme presented in the transcripts was overcoming pain from past childhood experiences. A number of young men in the sample had experienced foster care or abuse or neglect from a parent. In these situations, the typical focus was to prevent the next generation from having to repeat that experience. A 22-year-old man whose 2-year-old daughter was conceived while he was living on the street said:

It has changed my life. In a way, it has given me motivation. I grew up without a father and I created this little girl, and I would never want her to go through what I went through emotionally. And it has just given me a reason to change my life, to become someone more important, responsible, and successful for her benefit.

Each of these transformative themes involves a dramatic turn toward a generative identity. Most of the young fathers' narratives mentioned finding a new purpose beyond the self or current needs toward something better for their children and their children's future. Similar themes were noted by Palkovitz (2002) and Roy and Lucas (2006) in their interviews with fathers across a range of ages, as well as in Devault et al.'s (2008) life stories of younger dads.

These youth, through their experiences of fatherhood and their life stories, appear to have found a way to organize their memories from earlier life into a meaningful framework that can encourage positive choices in the future. Of course, these men's life patterns will not be transformed overnight. Relationship problems, limited knowledge and skill, and troublesome behaviours will likely continue. But according to McAdams et al. (1997), this generative life script has potential to feed back to inform future intentions, concerns, and actions. Fatherhood, among these young, committed men, may have conveyed a transformation to a new identity; this idea provides support for a hypothesized link between this new role and a more generative self.

Generativity as an Enhancer of Fathering and the Fatherhood Experience

In this section, we turn the tables by discussing how generativity can influence men's experiences of fatherhood, including their sense of self, engagement with children and family, and anticipation of future fatherhood.

Impact of Generativity on Men's Experiences of Fatherhood and Mentoring

How do generative fathers differ from others in their experience of the fathering role? Hart, McAdams, Hirsch, and Bauer (2001) reported that for a sample of mid-life mothers and fathers, higher generativity scores on the LGS were predictive of a more positive sense of self as a good role model and teacher of values to their own children. King and Pratt (2007) have shown that differences in generativity among parents were reflected in variations in how adults narrated their family lives. For example, in a study focused on parents' stories about teaching their 8-year-old children, King and Pratt found that both mothers and fathers in a sample of 35 Canadian families narrated stories about children's learning of important family values (like kindness or hard work) and their school problems in more optimistic ways if the parent was more generative on the LGS. Generative parents' stories were also more attentive to and expressive of the child's perspective in the episode recounted than were the stories of less generative parents, and this was true for both mothers and fathers (King & Pratt, 2007). Generative parents thus appeared to see themselves as more optimistic and caring in their efforts with children.

Impact of Generative Fathering on Children

Studies of parental generativity and parenting practices and styles to date show that mothers who are more generative on the LGS are generally more positive and effective in their parenting styles with adolescents (Peterson et al., 1997; Van Heil, Mervielde, and de Fruyt, 2006); these patterns of associations may be somewhat less clear for fathers (Pratt, Danso, Arnold, Norris, & Filyer, 2001). Snarey's (1993) longitudinal research shows that variations in fathers' levels of involvement in children's early lives, especially for daughters during adolescence, were substantial predictors of adult daughters' educational and occupational mobility in comparison to their parents. There were also similar, though weaker, effects for sons. These results suggest that children's adult achievements are predictable from fathers' earlier generative activities. Peterson's (2006) follow-up study of young adults also shows that psychological adjustment and life satisfaction were positively related to variations in their parents' generativity as measured by the LGS during the child's late adolescence. These longitudinal findings were relatively parallel for both mothers and fathers in this study (B. E. Peterson, personal communication, November 5, 2009). Thus, generative fathering may provide both achievement and adaptation benefits for children's later outcomes.

Pratt, Norris, Hebblethwaite, and Arnold (2008) examined the stories told by adolescent children about the experiences of being taught by more, or less, generative parents. The stories about their parents' teaching of values that were recalled by children of more generative mothers and fathers were rated by independent coders as more specific, more positive, more engaged, and more caring compared to similar stories told by children of less generative parents. The pattern of these findings suggests that children's recollections of fathers' role in family socialization vary in terms of their impact, with stories about generative fathers (as well as mothers) appearing to be more compelling events for the child overall. These findings align with the evidence reviewed above that generative parents may be more successful than others in some aspects of socialization. We have replicated this pattern of findings in the stories of even younger children (8-year-olds) about more and less generative mothers and fathers (Pratt, Norris, Cressman, & Lawford, 2008). These findings suggest that being more generative may be linked to different patterns of parenting and thence to differential impacts on children's development and their memories of family life. While other potential factors might explain these findings, the results for youngsters' memories of their fathers as parents are compatible with a dynamic interplay between generativity level and the pattern of enactment and implications of the fathering role.

Venturing more widely beyond work on fatherhood, Marsiglio (2008) describes qualitative results based on over 50 interviews with men across the adult life course from ages 19 to 65 who were engaged in youth work of various types. Marsiglio illustrates from the interviews the extent to which generativity (the idea of "passing it on" from one generation to the next) seemed to be an underlying motivator for many of these men in initiating and sustaining this work with young people. Marsiglio also notes, as we have above, that "[Erikson] recognized that different forms of generativity may occur simultaneously, and that aspects of generativity may be expressed at an earlier age" (94), suggesting that this construct is clearly quite relevant to the experiences of mentoring and care of children by men across adulthood. Generativity in its wider societal forms seems to have clear benefits for youth.

Implications of Generativity for Men's Anticipation of Fatherhood

Do more generative men see themselves differently in the fathering role than others even prior to having children? A study by Allen, Lawford, and Pratt (2010) examines this question of views of future parenting among young adult men and women. In this study, the LGS was administered to 75 participants (mean age = 26) who were not yet parents. The participants were also engaged in interviews about how they were anticipating parenthood. The interview section included two questions about the participants' futures. The first question was based on the "possible selves" research of Markus and Nurius (1986), who suggest that the self that one envisions in one's future serves as an important cognitive and motivational guide for the future. The second interview question was about what participants anticipated it would be like to become a parent (adapted from Delmore-Ko, Pancer, Hunsberger, & Pratt, 2000).

The "possible selves" portion of Allen et al.'s (2010) study asked participants to describe three "hoped-for" future selves as well as three "feared" future selves. Both of the responses were then coded for whether they included a self that described becoming a parent in the future. The question adapted from Delmore-Ko et al. (2000) was coded for the number of hopes and the number of fears expressed about parenthood. On the "possible selves" question, more generative men on the LGS were more likely to describe a hoped-for parenting self than were less generative men, though no differences related to generativity levels emerged for women. In addition, more generative men described significantly more parenting hopes and significantly fewer parenting concerns than did less generative men. Again, there were no differences for women in the number of hopes and concerns described based on their level of generativity.

This study is important because it suggests that in addition to the role that actual fatherhood may play in men's generative development, as reviewed above, different levels of generative concern were also related to variations in how young men anticipated the fathering experience and how important it was to their future identities. As suggested, this complex developmental story of the relations between generativity and parenting may be particularly evident for men. As Stewart and Vandewater (1998) and others (e.g., Lawford, Pratt, Hunsberger, & Pancer, 2005) suggest, generative concern may be especially important at earlier points in the life course. In order to better understand men's experiences of being and becoming a father, it is important to study how this early care and concern for the next generation comes about and how it influences parenting experiences, both after men have children and perhaps even before.

Interestingly, Snarey (1993; Snarey, Son, Kuehne, Hauser, & Vaillant, 1987), in the longitudinal sample described above, examined the experience of "generativity chill" in men who were unable to have children in their relationships. Those men who were more likely to engage in "substitute" parenting actions involving the children of others were subsequently more likely to adopt children of their own rather than remaining childless. Other childless men who engaged in "self-centred" substitute activities such as personal health preoccupations or body building when the couple remained childless were unlikely to eventually adopt if they did not have a biological child. Snarey (1993) also showed that those men who actively sought out a role in caring for the children of others were more likely to achieve broader societal generativity at mid-life compared to those who did not. Thus, individual differences in generative qualities may shape men's biological or adoptive parenting (Kotre, 1984). Furthermore, Snarey's longitudinal study suggested that patterns of early "substitute" fathering may have implications for the longer-term adaptation of men to societal roles at mid-life.

Variations in early generativity thus seem to be important in the sense of self constructed by young men, even before becoming a father. Why should this be so? It appears that men's early generativity may lead them to construct a more inclusive sense of future self that entails a pro-social investment in offspring and a future family life. Such a self can provide motivational representations that guide goals for the future, as in the findings described by Snarey (1993) that childless men more engaged with youth were more likely to become adoptive fathers later.

Discussion and Conclusions

What have we learned from research on the relations between fatherhood and generativity in men's development? First, studies support the view that the experience of fatherhood can and commonly does shape a more generative self-identity in men (see, for example, Palkovitz, 2002). Becoming a father – and even more compellingly, engagement in the fathering role over time – can transform men's sense of self, commonly in the direction of providing more of a sense of purpose and an opportunity to repair or rework previous selves (Devault et al., 2008; Lawford et al., 2008; Roy & Lucas, 2006). It can also, over time, extend the compass of caring in men's lives toward mature generativity and concern for the future of the wider society (Snarey, 1993).

Second, a more generative self may foster a distinctive pattern of engagement in the fathering role. Young men who are more generative incorporate fatherhood as an important component of the future self and consider fathering in more hopeful and enthusiastic ways (Allen et al., 2010). Generative men also narrate their parenting experiences in more optimistic and thoughtful ways, and are described by their children as more effective and memorable teachers (King & Pratt, 2007; Pratt, Norris, Cressman, & Lawford, 2008).

Third, these interactive relations between fatherhood and generativity surely unfold across adulthood in complex ways. It has been argued that generativity itself develops across the adult period, moving from biological to parental to societal forms (e.g., Snarey, 1993), and thus across contexts of expression, from the family to societal and civic domains. Integrating these two directions of influence, early generativity may shape greater involvement in fathering and socialization in the family for men (Pratt et al., 2008), which in turn may predict more civic engagement and greater societal generativity later in mid-life (Snarey, 1993). While this is a plausible trajectory, direct longitudinal evidence for this longer-term pattern is needed. Perhaps, as suggested in the narrative research on generativity reviewed above (e.g., McAdams et al., 1997), one mechanism for these positive cycles is the construction of a more generative identity commitment for the self in fathers, which eventually supports an expansion and consolidation of men's generative action and goals across the wider societal context beyond the family.

While the general story of fathering and generativity may be partly an account of dynamic interactive growth over time, it may also be a story of individual trajectory differences. The young fathers of the FIRA sample whom we quoted above don't sound much like the more generative young men from the Allen et al. (2010) study, who contemplated the joys of their future family life. Fatherhood hit many of the unprepared young dads in the FIRA sample like "a ton of bricks," and generativity for them was a sudden discovery after that jolt. Perhaps we are seeing distinctive alternative beginnings to the fathering and generativity saga – and variability in how one finally gets to generativity may be quite important for the longer term. Only longitudinal research over the whole transition period could illuminate this.

Future Research and Themes

In this chapter, we have focused on early fatherhood, as in the FIRA young dads sample, and on the early beginnings of generativity development in the Erikson personality model because this time period has often been neglected in generativity research. Intriguingly, both early fatherhood and early variations in levels of generativity provide key windows on this question of generativity and fathering because they are off-time and outside the prototypical life sequence for the parenting transition, and they therefore serve to isolate these interactive effects more clearly from other factors that would more typically accompany them. Older off-time fathers and men's development during the later mid-life period would also be interesting to study in an effort to describe the relation of fatherhood and generativity across adulthood. Grandfathering is another interesting context for the study of generativity (see Pratt, Norris, Lawford, & Arnold, 2010). It is noteworthy that the present findings support the argument that aspects of generativity can be meaningful even quite early in development, well before the period of mid-life (Frensch, Pratt, & Norris, 2007; Lawford et al., 2005).

A further question touched on in the foregoing review is that of gender similarities and differences in the relationship of parenting and generativity. Fatherhood may be linked to the development of men's generativity, but how does this compare with motherhood and generativity development? Some studies reviewed above showed sex differences in these associations (e.g., Allen et al., 2010). More research is needed on the topic of sex role similarities and differences in generativity and its expression in parenting across adulthood.

What can be said about the themes of this book based on this chapter? Surely, this review suggests that there is much diversity in the fatherhood experience and its longer-term impacts. For example, fathers' levels of generativity predict important patterns of differences in their experiences and functioning, as do variations in how they construct a sense of self and the meaning of this transformation based on diverse earlier life courses in the FIRA sample (Lawford et al., 2008). "Repairing hurt" or "settling down" are parallel stories in their transformative nature, but they are also distinctive in focus and detail, and in their life implications. And there may be clear individual variations in the shape of early trajectories for more and less generative young men and their experiences of the jolt of fatherhood.

Fatherhood and fathering are evidently embedded in the individual life course and in broad patterns of personality development, as well as in changing families, subcultures, and cultural-historical contexts. All of these factors shape important variations. Generativity as a personality quality must be set in context as well and may be understood at broader levels than simply the individual personality – for example, as varying in expression across families, work lives, and cultures. More research is needed on these important contextual issues.

Policy Implications

In the course of the human life cycle, fatherhood is a role that most men will experience. For many, as we argue, it can be an opportunity for growth and development in generativity. But the extent to which fathering actually becomes a generative experience is variable. The evidence reviewed here supports the idea that more generative fathering has benefits for children, for the fathers themselves, and ultimately, for the wider society. It also appears that the potential for generative fathering is substantial across the life course, even in those often viewed as unable or unlikely to demonstrate this capacity (Rhoden & Robinson, 1997), such as the young fathers in the FIRA sample described above (Lawford et al., 2008). It is therefore critical to explore how generativity in fathering may be encouraged. To the extent that becoming a more generative parent involves a new, transformed way of thinking about the self, as argued here, developing ways of encouraging self-reflection and discussion of these experiences with other men in similar situations will be valuable. While societal expectations have moved in the direction of greater father engagement in recent years, concrete support for fathers' involvement with their children in Canadian society is not as high (e.g., Dienhart & Daly, 1997). Programs that support father involvement are key and would likely benefit from including such opportunities for reflection on the experience of parenting.

Across adulthood, fatherhood transforms and connects men's sense of self with their roles and functions in the family and the wider society and culture. It embeds men in the ongoing cycle of the generations and in profound injunctions to care for the future while preserving the past in ways that provide a sense of generative meaning and legacy for the maturing self.

References

Allen, J. W., Lawford, H. L., & Pratt, M. W. (2010). *Future parenting selves in young adult men and women: Eriksonian generativity, and attachment styles as predictors.* Unpublished manuscript, Wilfrid Laurier University, Waterloo, ON.

Blankenhorn, D. (1995). *Fatherless America.* New York, NY: Basic Books.

Christiansen, S. L., & Palkovitz, R. (1998). Exploring Erikson's psychosocial theory of development: Generativity and its relationship to paternal identity, intimacy, and involvement in childcare. *Journal of Men's Studies, 7,* 133-156.

Cowan, A. (1988). Becoming a father: A time of change, an opportunity for development. In P. Bronstein and C. Cowan (Eds.), *Fatherhood today* (pp. 13-35). New York, NY: Wiley.

Cowan, C. P., & Cowan, A. (1992). *When partners become parents: The big life change for couples.* New York, NY: Basic Books.

Delmore-Ko, P., Pancer, S. M., Hunsberger, B., & Pratt, M. W. (2000). The process of becoming a parent: How expectations influence the transition to parenthood. *Journal of Family Psychology, 14,* 625-640.

Devault, A., Milcent, M.-P., Ouellet, F., Laurin, J., Jauron, M., & Lacharite, C. (2008). Life stories of young fathers in contexts of vulnerability. *Fathering, 6,* 226-248.

Dienhart, A., & Daly, K. (1997). Men and women co-creating father involvement in a nongenerative culture. In A. Hawkins & D. Dollahite (Eds.), *Generative fathering: Beyond a deficit perspective* (pp. 147-164). Thousand Oaks, CA: Sage.

Dollahite, D. C., & Hawkins, A. J. (1998). A conceptual ethic of generative fathering. *Journal of Men's Studies, 7,* 109-132.

Erikson, E. H. (1950). *Childhood and society.* New York, NY: Norton.

Erikson, E. H. (1968). *Identity, youth and crisis.* New York, NY: Norton.

Frensch, K. M., Pratt, M. W., & Norris, J. E. (2007). Foundations of generativity: Personal and family correlates of adolescents' generative life story themes. *Journal of Research in Personality, 41,* 45-62.

Hart, H., McAdams, D. P., Hirsch, B., & Bauer, J. (2001). Generativity and social involvement among African-American and white adults. *Journal of Research in Personality, 35,* 208-230.

Hawkins, A. J., & Dollahite, D. (1997). Beyond the role-inadequacy perspective of fathering. In A. Hawkins & D. Dollahite (Eds.), *Generative fathering: Beyond a deficit perspective* (pp. 3-16). Thousand Oaks, CA: Sage.

King, M., & Pratt, M. W. (2007). *Teaching and learning in the family: The importance of generativity in parents' stories of socialization.* Unpublished senior honours thesis, Wilfrid Laurier University, Waterloo, ON.

Kotre, J. (1984). *Outliving the self: Generativity and the interpretation of lives.* Baltimore, MD: Johns Hopkins University Press.

LaRossa, R. (1988). Fatherhood and social change. *Family Relations, 37,* 451-457.

Lawford, H., Dienhart, A., Devault, A., & Pratt, M. W. (2008). *Fatherhood as a transformative experience in the life course: Comparing young and mature fathers on themes of generativity and identity change.* Paper presented at the Fathering 2008 Conference, Toronto, ON.

Lawford, H., Pratt, M. W., Hunsberger, B., & Pancer, S. M. (2005). Adolescent generativity: A longitudinal study of two possible contexts for learning concern for future generations. *Journal of Research on Adolescence, 15,* 261-273.

Markus, H., & Nurius, P. (1986). Possible selves. *American Psychologist, 41,* 954–969.

Marsiglio, W. (2008). *Men on a mission: Valuing youth work in our communities.* Baltimore, MD: Johns Hopkins University Press.

Maruna, S. (1997). Going straight: Desistance from crime and life narratives of reform. In R. E. Josselson & A. Lieblich (Eds.), *The narrative study of lives* (Vol. 5, pp. 59-93). Thousand Oaks, CA: Sage.

McAdams, D. (2001). Generativity in midlife. In M. E. Lachman (Ed.), *Handbook of midlife development* (pp. 395-443). Toronto, ON: John Wiley.

McAdams D. (2006). *The redemptive self: Stories Americans live by.* New York, NY: Oxford University Press.

McAdams, D. P., & de St. Aubin, E. (1992). A theory of generativity and its assessment through self-report, behavioural acts, and narrative themes in autobiography. *Journal of Personality and Social Psychology, 62,* 1003-1015.

McAdams, D. P., Diamond, A., de St. Aubin, E., & Mansfield, E. (1997). Stories of commitment: The psychosocial construction of generative lives. *Journal of Personality and Social Psychology, 72,* 678-694.

McKerring, H., & Pakenham, K. I. (2000). Gender and generativity issues in parenting: Do fathers benefit more than mothers from involvement in child care activities? *Sex Roles, 43,* 459-480.

Palkovitz, R. (1996). Parenting as a generator of adult development: Conceptual issues and implications. *Journal of Social and Personal Relationships, 13,* 571-592.

Palkovitz, R. (2002). *Involved fathering and men's adult development: Provisional balances.* Mahwah, NJ: Lawrence Erlbaum.

Parke, R. (1998). *Fatherhood.* Cambridge, MA: Harvard University Press.

Patton, M. Q. (2002). *Qualitative research and evaluation methods* (3rd ed.). Thousand Oaks, CA: Sage.

Peterson, B. E. (2006). Generativity and successful parenting: An analysis of young adult outcomes. *Journal of Personality, 74,* 847-869.

Peterson, B. E., Smirles, K. A., & Wentworth, A. (1997). Generativity and authoritarianism: Implications for personality, political involvement and parenting. *Journal of Personality and Social Psychology, 72,* 1202-1216.

Pleck, J. H. (1998). American fathering in historical perspective. In K. Hansen and A. Garey (Eds.), *Families in the U.S.: Kinship and domestic politics* (pp. 351-362). Philadelphia, PA: Temple University Press.

Pratt, M. W., Danso, H., Arnold, M. L., Norris, J., & Filyer, R. (2001). Adult generativity and the socialization of adolescents: Relations to mothers' and fathers' parenting beliefs, styles and practices. *Journal of Personality, 69,* 89-120.

Pratt, M. W., Norris, J., Arnold, M. L., & Filyer, R. (1999). Generativity and moral development as predictors of value socialization narratives for young persons across the adult lifespan: From lessons learned to stories shared. *Psychology and Aging, 14,* 414-426.

Pratt, M. W., Norris, J., Cressman, K., & Lawford, H. L. (2008, July). Generative parents and children's socialization memories: Stories of family teaching moments by young children and adolescents. Poster presented at the International Congress of Psychology, Berlin.

Pratt, M. W., Norris, J. E., Hebblethwaite, S., & Arnold, M. L. (2008). Intergenerational transmission of values: Family generativity and adolescents' narratives of parent and grandparent value teaching. *Journal of Personality, 76*(2), 171-198.

Pratt, M. W., Norris, J. E., Lawford, H. L., & Arnold, M. L. (2010). "What he said to me stuck": Adolescents' narrative representations of their grandparents as teachers. In K. C. McLean & M. Pasupathi (Eds.), *Narrative development in adolescence* (pp. 83-112). New York, NY: Springer.

Rhoden, J. L., & Robinson, B. (1997). Teen dads: A generative fathering perspective versus the deficit myth. In A. Hawkins & D. Dollahite (Eds.), *Generative fathering: Beyond a deficit perspective* (pp. 105-117). Thousand Oaks, CA: Sage.

Rothrauff, T., & Cooney, T. M. (2008). The role of generativity in psychological well-being: Does it differ for childless adults and parents? *Journal of Adult Development, 15,* 148-159.

Roy, K., & Lucas, K. (2006). Generativity as second chance: Low-income fathers and transformation of the difficult past. *Research in Human Development, 3,* 139-159.

Snarey, J. (1993). *How fathers care for the next generation: A four-decade study.* Cambridge, MA: Harvard University Press.

Snarey, J., Son, L., Kuehne, L., Hauser, S., & Vaillant, G. (1987). The role of parenting in men's psychosocial development. *Developmental Psychology, 23,* 593-603.

Stewart, A. J., & Vandewater, E. A. (1998). The course of generativity. In D. McAdams & E. de St. Aubin (Eds.), *Generativity and adult development: How and why we care for the next generation* (pp. 75-100). Washington, DC: American Psychological Association.

Vaillant, G. (2002). *Aging well.* Boston: Little, Brown.

Van Heil, A., Mervielde, I., & de Fruyt, F. (2006). Stagnation and generativity: Structure, validity and differential relationships with adaptive and maladaptive personality. *Journal of Personality, 74,* 543-573.

6

Aboriginal Fathers in Canada through Time

Jessica Ball

This chapter offers a general overview of the past, present, and promise for the future of Aboriginal fathers in Canada.[1] Emphasis is placed on bringing a temporal perspective to Aboriginal fathers' experiences, taking full account of socio-historical antecedents of their current journeys as a population and as individuals. To begin, a profile is offered of Aboriginal fathers in the context of First Nation and Métis family trends. The second section gives a brief account of how colonization shattered Aboriginal kinship-based societies, resulting in a current state of crisis for many Aboriginal men and their families. Next, the findings of a research study conducted by the author with 80 First Nation and Métis fathers are discussed, followed by implications for policy and program support, including recommended steps to support Aboriginal Peoples' recovery and the reconstruction of men's roles in circles of care for children. The final section calls for an expansion of research methods, scope, and assumptions to build our understandings of Aboriginal fathers and fathers in other, often marginalized, non-European-heritage populations.

It is important to note that Canada's First Peoples include hundreds of distinct cultural groupings, with considerable variations in quality of life among them. Because I had an opportunity to work with 80 First Nation and Métis fathers in a community-engagement research study, my focus in this chapter is on First Nation and Métis fathers in British Columbia. It should also be acknowledged that while some Aboriginal families are thriving and some Aboriginal fathers have had positive role models and connections with their children, in this chapter I focus on the challenges Aboriginal fathers encounter due to the difficult historical and current social conditions that shape their fatherhood journeys.

Aboriginal Fathering in Context

First Nation and Métis Family Trends
Census data indicate that a higher proportion of Aboriginal children (35%) than non-Aboriginal children (17%) live in lone-parent households (Statistics

Canada, 2006). Lone parenting is even more common among Aboriginal families living in urban areas, where over 50% of First Nation and Métis children live in lone-parent homes, compared to 17% of non-Aboriginal children. Most lone-parent households are headed by mothers although there are also more single-father-headed households among Aboriginal lone-parent households (6%) compared to non-Aboriginal lone-parent households (3%). Lone-father-headed households are twice as common for First Nation children living on reserves than for Canadian children as a whole (Health Canada, 2005).

The number of Aboriginal lone parents may be overestimated due to a number of unique trends in First Nation and Métis communities. For example, households may include a varying array of relatives and friends, and compared to non-Aboriginal couples, Aboriginal co-parents are less likely to be legally married. Individuals who are identified as lone parents may, in fact, be supported substantially in their parenting role by various family members. Nonetheless, the high incidence of lone parenthood is a concern because of the potential impacts on the social and economic well-being of all family members. Lone parenting is associated with a greater probability of living in poverty (Weitzman, 2003). Lone parenting in poverty is particularly likely for adolescent parents, and the number of children born to adolescent women living on reserves is high – about 100 births per 1,000 women, a rate seven times higher than for other Canadian adolescents (Guimond & Robitaille, 2008).

Census and other data sources suggest that many First Nation and Métis mothers and fathers are struggling to hold their families together and to secure an adequate quality of life for their children's healthy development. Aboriginal children and youth have by far the highest rates of hospitalizations due to illness, injury, and suicide attempts; the highest rates of early school leaving; and the highest rates of addiction, arrests, and juvenile detention compared to non-Aboriginal Canadian children and youth (Adelson, 2005; Canadian Institute for Child Health, 2000; Canadian Institute for Health Information, 2004; First Nations Centre, 2005). Related to the challenges of poverty, parental neglect is the most frequent justification given by child protection agencies for removal of First Nation children from family to government care (Trocmé et al., 2006).

There is growing recognition of the important contributions that fathers can and often do make to children's survival, health, and development. However, compared to non-Aboriginal men, First Nation and Métis men have a higher prevalence of unemployment, homelessness, and living in poverty (Statistics Canada, 2003); nine times more incarceration (Department of Public Safety, 2008); and higher rates of injuries resulting in hospital admissions, suicide, and mental and physical health problems (Health Canada, 2005). Combined with overwhelming social stigma, negative media stories, and negative expectations for their roles as fathers, these obstacles to positive involvement as fathers faced by First Nation and Métis men are formidable.

Understanding the dire predicament of so many Aboriginal families and gaining insights into Aboriginal men's experiences of fatherhood require a temporal perspective. In order to account for the troubling social conditions and personal difficulties experienced by Aboriginal Peoples in Canada and elsewhere, several scholars have explored the explanatory potential of the concept of intergenerational trauma (Kirmayer, Brass, & Tait, 2000; Menzies, 2006; Mussell, 1999; Robertson, 2006; Waldram, 2004; Wesley-Esquimaux & Smolewski, 2003; Yellow Horse Brave Heart & DeBruyn, 1998). Rather than viewing overall low levels of positive father involvement among Aboriginal men in terms of individual deficits, a grasp of socio-historical antecedents of the current, vulnerable situation for Aboriginal Peoples as a whole can put into context the challenges and potential for Aboriginal fathers today.

Historical Conditions and Current Challenges for Aboriginal Fathers
Historically, the family was the primary unit of production and the foundation of economics, governance, and law within First Nation and Métis societies (Dickason, 2009; Volo & Volo, 2007). Child-rearing was typically shared in family groups. Although children knew their immediate family, other members of the extended family – including cousins, aunts, uncles, great-grandparents, and other relatives – could equally be considered a sibling, parent, or grandparent. Responsibilities for caregiving, providing for the family group, and ensuring the health and well-being of present and future generations were organized according to gender and age; collectively, these interconnecting responsibilities created a web of relationships. Family meant life itself, as Nuu-chah-nulth Tribal Council Hereditary Chief Atleo (2004) expresses: "In the Nuu-chah-nulth worldview it is unnatural, and equivalent to death and destruction, for any person to be isolated from family or community" (27).

Disruption of traditional Aboriginal family systems began soon after European settlers arrived (Miller, 1996; Stremlau, 2005). Through various land reallocation systems and other federal policies, the patriarchal nuclear family structure was forced on Aboriginal Peoples across North America. The most damaging federal government interventions were the Indian residential schools and the child welfare system.[2] In the late nineteenth century, colonial government authorities concluded – as the Jesuits had centuries earlier – that the most expedient way to deal with "the Indian problem" and gain access to their land was to take control of Indian children, thereby ripping the heart and centre out of Aboriginal communities (Miller, 1996). Beginning in 1879 and operating until 1996, Indian residential schools took over the role of raising First Nation and Métis children. Although they resisted, many communities lost whole generations of children; by 1930, almost 75% of First Nation school-aged children were forcibly interned in residential schools (Fournier & Crey, 1997). Many children were abused physically, sexually, emotionally, and spiritually. The few who returned to their communities often found themselves alienated from their families, lands, and cultures (Dion Stout & Kipling, 2003). As historians and sociologists have documented, once the children were taken, the roles of adults in the family began to dissolve. Grandparents had no one to teach, women had no one to care for, and men had no home or family to protect and provide for (Dion Stout & Kipling, 2003).

When residential school survivors became fathers and mothers, most struggled because they had not experienced positive parental role modelling and most had no means of making a living for reasons that include government policies restricting their rights to tertiary education and to generate income on reserves (Wesley-Esquimaux & Smolewksi, 2003). In what has come to be known as the "Sixties Scoop," child welfare authorities removed First Nation and Métis children from their homes in record numbers from the 1960s into the late 1980s (Miller, 1996). By the early 1980s, First Nation and Métis children represented less than 4% of the population but made up 50%, 60%, and 70% of the child welfare caseloads in Alberta, Manitoba, and Saskatchewan, respectively (Bennett & Blackstock, 1992). This legacy continues. In some provinces, First Nation and Métis children outnumber non-Aboriginal children in government care by a ratio of 8:1 (Blackstock, Loxlely, Prakash, & Wien, 2005). Children who are removed from their homes and communities often suffer a crippling loss of identity. In addition to the losses sustained due to the residential school experience and the child welfare system, First Nation and Métis families have been further weakened by dispossession and degradation of their land, forced relocations of villages, dispersions of clans, and urbanization (Salee, 2006).

Aboriginal leaders and scholars assert that the crisis facing First Nation and Métis family life today is a direct consequence of colonization (Dion Stout & Kipling, 2003; Mussell, 2005; Royal Commission on Aboriginal Peoples, 1996) and not a consequence of inherent characteristics of individuals or cultural traditions. Many men and women who become fathers and mothers have lost confidence in their capacity to engage in the kinds of nurturing social interactions with young children that promote attachment and intimate social interaction (Wesley-Esquimaux & Smolewski, 2003).

Based on a study of historical trauma, First Nation scholars Wesley-Esquimaux and Smolewski (2003) assert that First Nation and Métis men have difficulty sustaining intimate relationships, meeting family obligations, and connecting with their children, and that these negative impacts are felt by their children and youth. According to Sto:lo First Nation Chief Mussell (2005), sequelae for First Nation and Métis men include emotional abandonment, loss of cultural identity and personal pride, substance abuse, and physical and mental health problems. Research involving non-Aboriginal fathers (e.g., Roopnarine, Brown, Snell-White, & Riegraf, 1995) has shown that poor living conditions, high mobility, extensive health problems, and social stigma exacerbate the challenges of developing positive father-child connections.

Statistical data and anecdotal reports from First Nation and Métis communities and family-serving agencies indicate that many First Nation and Métis fathers are elusive when it comes to family life. Several Aboriginal community leaders have spoken about the risks for Aboriginal children of having little exposure to positively and consistently involved fathers. For example, Grand Chief Edward John (2003) of the BC First Nations Summit has expressed that "Aboriginal fathers may well be the greatest untapped resource in the lives of Aboriginal children and youth." Research about non-Aboriginal fathers, reviewed by Allen, Daly, and Ball in this volume, shows significant correlations between father involvement and developmental outcomes for children, mothers, and fathers. Father absence, on the other hand, is associated with negative developmental and health outcomes for children and for fathers (Ball & Moselle, 2007).

A Research Study With Aboriginal Fathers

Increasing alarm about the patterns noted above motivated a study with 80 First Nation and Métis fathers of young children living in British Columbia (Ball, 2010). The study was intended, in part, to clarify whether theoretical questions and concepts that currently dominate scholarship on fathers' involvement and that guide parenting programs (e.g., gendered divisions of labour in families, impacts of parental leave provisions on fathers' involvement, and multi-generational transmission of fathering) are relevant and useful for understanding the experiences of Aboriginal fathers. Another objective was to identify what kinds of new understandings, policies, and community initiatives may be needed to represent and support Aboriginal fathers' positive involvement. As a community engagement study, emphasis was placed on engaging fathers in five partner communities in identifying goals, needs, and strategies for change.

Methods

Memoranda of Agreement to be involved in the study were developed for each of the five community partners in the study. An Aboriginal father in each community was recruited by community leaders to become part of the research team and to help recruit fathers with at least one child under seven years old. Each father completed the following: (a) a questionnaire focused on his family composition, household characteristics, work-family arrange-ments, and patterns of caring for children; (b) a questionnaire focused on programs and services that the father had used or would use if available; and (c) a 90-minute semi-structured, conversational interview conducted by an Aboriginal research team member. The interview questions aimed to help the father to tell his story of becoming a father; describe his experiences as a father in relation to his children, other family and community members, and community and government programs; and give his own account of factors affecting his journey as a father.

The interviews were audiotaped and transcribed, and the content analyzed by Indigenous and non-Indigenous team members. Data collection and analysis followed the grounded theory approach originated by Glaser and Strauss (1965; Glaser, 1978) and demonstrated in family interaction research by the author (Ball, Cowan, & Cowan, 1995). Over the course of interviews with the first 40 participants, interview questions underwent four successive iterations. The final 40 interviews used the same interview schedule. Data collection was stopped after 80 interviews had been analyzed, and saturation was achieved in that core themes predictably recurred during the interviews, and the themes could be substantiated with many examples from the fathers' accounts. Several months after the interviews, fathers were invited to gather in each community partner site to hear, comment on, and suggest revisions to the research team's interpretation of the data and to make recommenda-tions for action based on the findings.

The findings are summarized in this section using excerpts from the questionnaires and interviews. These are followed in subsequent sections by implications that the findings hold for policy and program support, including fathers' recommendations for specific steps they feel would sup-port their positive involvement with their children and for research and theory.

Participant Characteristics

Participants comprised 72 First Nation fathers, 7 Métis fathers, and one non-Aboriginal father of an Aboriginal child. All fathers resided in the prov-ince of British Columbia and were representative of the geographic distribu-tion of Aboriginal people in Canada: 45% lived on reserves and 55% lived off reserves in medium-sized towns. The number of children they reported being the father of ranged from 1 to 11 children ($M = 3.29$). The median annual household income among fathers who responded to the question about income ranged from (Can.) $20,000 to $39,000. (Nearly one quarter of the fathers declined to give information about their household income.) Over one quarter of the fathers reported having some kind of physical or mental disability. One third of the fathers were living with the mother of at least one of their children at the time they were interviewed.

The research most strikingly brought to light the complexity of Aboriginal fathers' family relationships, which seemed to indicate both the vestiges of the extended family system that was culturally normative before the residential schools and the significantly attenuating effects of colonial interventions on that system. When asked to identify the children in their family, most of the men's responses portrayed a complicated network of young people who lived in the household for varying amounts of time each week, or seasonally, or based on school holiday schedules. Children were variously related to the men: biologically, socially, legally, by marriage, via ex-partners, and so on. It was not uncommon, for example, for a father to be raising one or two of his own children along with his current partner's children, and also to be involved part-time in raising one or more other children – often a niece, nephew, or grandchild.

Many fathers did not live with any of their children. About one quarter did not have access to one or more of their children for various reasons: for example, the ending of a relationship and the moving away of an ex-partner and her child. Four fathers had no contact with their children as a condition of their parole. A few fathers acknowledged that they did not know how many children they had. As well, many fathers were living with partners who were not their children's biological mother and who had varying amounts of involvement with their children (e.g., on the days they had custody). At the same time, other family members, such as the father's mother or aunt, were sometimes highly involved in caring for a father's children, even to the extent that the children lived with the relative and the father visited and often stayed with them at the relative's home. This was especially common on reserves.

Some of the fathers were struggling to generate a living wage and to secure adequate housing, while a few had resigned themselves – for now – to being "couchsurfers" or to living in a shelter for homeless people. Although they were not specifically asked about residential school, adoption, or foster care, one fifth of the fathers stated that they had attended a residential school. Several fathers volunteered that they had spent all or part of their childhood in non-Aboriginal foster and adoptive homes. Nearly all who had not attended a residential school had been raised by one or both parents who had survived the schools.

It is worth noting that, unlike most experiences of doing research with Aboriginal people, the current study received so many calls from fathers wanting to participate that demand to participate exceeded the supply of funds, staff, and time available for the study. The first 80 fathers to come forward were interviewed, and most asked to be identified by their first name and community if they were quoted in any reports or presentations, a request we have honoured here. They saw the study as opening up new hope to be seen and heard by community-based program staff and by government agencies as a population that is yearning for support to learn fatherhood and connect or reconnect to family life.

Findings

This study was the first to focus on Aboriginal fatherhood in Canada, and the resulting picture is painted only in broad strokes. Nevertheless, there was remarkable agreement among the First Nation and Métis fathers about the impacts of colonial history on the extended family system and about their lack of opportunities to learn what it means to be a father, to love a child, to play, and to sustain a connection with their children through changes in their relationship with their children's mother or other changes in their lives. Nearly all the fathers' accounts spoke to personal difficulties in becoming positively involved fathers and placed these in a temporal perspective with reference to painful experiences in their own childhood and in the lives of Aboriginal men and women in Canada as a whole.

Fathers who were successfully involved with their children traced a personal journey of healing and coming to terms with their negative experiences in residential school or as secondary survivors of residential-school effects. They saw healing from these experiences as a first step on their journey to becoming involved fathers. Most fathers' narratives described a long and difficult road to accepting fatherhood, learning what it means to be a father, learning how to communicate and to play, and stepping up gradually to the responsibilities of fatherhood, often years after the birth of their first child:

> When my son was born, back then I didn't have any communication skills like normal fathers had. The affection of a loving father-child relationship, like normal fathers have, like kissing your younger children. I only learned that, years later, that was what it takes to love a child. There was nothing like that when I was growing up in residential school. (Tom, Comox)

Many – though not all – fathers described their own father as being unable to love, care for, and protect them, or said they had missed out on having a father altogether, leaving them with little personal experience in positive fathering to draw from when they became fathers themselves. The vast majority reported problems at some point in their lives with substance abuse, psychological distress, and difficulties in relationships with partners and relatives. For some, these issues persisted and prevented them from being as involved with their children as they would like to be. Four fathers described feeling so "low" about themselves that they felt they had nothing positive to offer their children. Three fathers said they did not think they were "worthy" of a relationship with their child:

Believe me, I would be there with my son if I felt I had anything to give him. I want to be involved and I intend to be involved, but that has to wait till I'm more sober, have some stability, maybe have some finances to provide a little ... until I am more together and he won't be ashamed to know who his father is. (Redmond, Prince George)

While their journey to learning fatherhood almost invariably took a hesitant and often interrupted course, all but four of the fathers who volunteered for the study currently had contact with at least some of their children. Most reported that they had sustained some degree of positive involvement over time, especially with children born after the father had matured and recovered from substance abuse or other personal challenges.

One quarter of the fathers described learning about caring for children from their mothers, their female partners, and other women in their community:

Overall, it has been Elders and women that I have learned from. I have learned most of my life from women. I remember this one time when we were sitting in church, this old lady was way up ahead and I watched her. It was just the way she rubbed her child's hair ... I wanted to do that. I wanted to be able to do that, so I have always asked women questions. (Dionne, Prince George)

Fathers who were involved with their children often credited their partner's receptivity, patience, and guidance in helping them to learn how to care for children.

Shifting constructions of masculinity in some Aboriginal communities were also identified by some fathers as a factor that had enabled them to assume caregiving roles with their children. For example, some participants described that a common outcome of residential school experience was learning how to "find a victim and abuse them" and "putting on a show about how macho you are." Countering these effects is a primary goal of the contemporary Aboriginal healing movement of which some fathers felt themselves to be a part. Healing often involves men in returning to traditional Aboriginal cultures, wherein men were positioned as providers, teachers, and supporters of women's roles. Traditionally, men would often take children out on long trips to teach them how to hunt, fish, and live on the land. Also, historically, the colonial government imposed on First Nations the requirement of installing men as leaders, whereas traditionally many First Nations were matriarchal, and men were not invested with power over women and children. Many fathers explained that the healing movement, including specific healing lodges and community programs, has opened up new opportunities for them to reconstruct their roles as gentle caregivers, teachers, and storytellers. Some fathers emphasized the reinforcing effects of watching a child learn and grow while feeling important in that child's life and experiencing a child's love:

> One thing I never felt before from anybody else ... how much they love me, how much they want me around. That's one thing that makes me happy, and it makes me want to be the best I can be for them. (Jacob, Terrace)

Fathers, especially those living in rural towns and settlements, pointed to a lack of support from programs and institutions, such as primary health clinics and schools. They all described incidents where they felt that programs, policies, and society as a whole were set up by women to welcome and meet the needs of women. A father who was raising his daughter on his own expressed this:

> I've had our daughter for nearly two years and no one has even tried to talk to us; they haven't made the effort. For years it has been all about the single mother, so the people that are trained to deal with parenting and children are so focused on women. I just want them to understand what I have had to do to bring this child up. (Brian, Lheidli T'enneh First Nation)

It is noteworthy that none of the fathers expressed blame toward women for their challenges. Andrew, from Prince George, explained: "We all went through the same history together, and we all face the same obstacles and have the same goal to rebuild ourselves back up and rebuild our communities back up to where they were." But some fathers expressed the view that certain colonial interventions had resulted in a greater loss of traditional family roles and dignity for Aboriginal men – especially policies that stripped Aboriginal Peoples of their land and their rights to make a livelihood, even on reserve lands.

Several fathers stressed that it will take time for Aboriginal families and communities to reconstruct cultural, social, and personal meanings and forms of fatherhood. They emphasized the need for family members, community programs, and Canadian society more broadly to show fathers patience and support as they build their confidence, courage, and capacity to connect with their children and play a fathering role in their lives. A few fathers reflected on the healing movement among Aboriginal Peoples in Canada as a positive social force within their communities that is helping to foster a renewed understanding of the roles, responsibilities, and joys of parenting, including fatherhood. Other fathers expressed grave concern about the future of fatherhood within Aboriginal cultures. They reflected on the high birth rate of Aboriginal children but the relatively low rate of Aboriginal children who live with their fathers. They pointed to high rates of substance abuse, suicide, incarceration, and poverty among Aboriginal young men. Through stories from their own lives and those of other men in their communities, they described how being raised without sustained, positive contact with a father compounds the socio-historical, economic, and emotional challenges for the next generation of young men who will face the birth of a child.

The Study's Implications for Research and Theory
Mainstream models of fatherhood reflected in policy, parent education, and media are rooted in European-heritage, middle-class perspectives. The presumption that these cultural and class-based models are relevant to all fathers can contribute significantly to the marginalization of fathers who are not of European-heritage descent and/or are poor, and can obscure both the struggles and the strengths of fathers belonging to a different demographic, including Aboriginal fathers. Lero, Ashbourne, and Whitehead (2006) conclude that father involvement policies and programs in Canada are informed by normative assumptions and gender-role stereotypes – including a mother-centred perspective – about parenting, family life, sexuality, and children's needs that can hinder certain groups of fathers and parents from receiving the support they need to be positively involved in the lives of children. The fathers in the current study also shed light on the Euro-Western bias in assumptions about the nature, challenges, and goals of men's journeys to become positively involved fathers. The current findings also indicate the need to cast acknowledged personal difficulties of many First Nation and Métis men within a broader temporal lens that extends both backward and forward in time, and in the context of the ongoing, generally inequitable quality of life and opportunities for Aboriginal people in Canada.

Some father involvement investigators in Canada are stressing the need to characterize, conceptualize, and respond to the diversity of fathers' behaviours and experiences as these are embedded within different family structures, ethnic identities, age, sexual orientations, and socio-economic circumstances (Ali, 2008; Epstein, 2009; Este & Tachble, 2009; www.fira.org). While fathers share many common experiences, they also may have specific challenges, goals, and expectations associated with their particular culture, religion, socio-economic circumstances, age, immigration or refugee status, sexual orientation, or relationship with their child's mother – to name a few sources of diversity. While scholarship on father involvement in Canada has grown and advocacy efforts have gained momentum over the past decade, almost no attention has focused on First Nation, Inuit, and Métis fathers. A review of the literature yields no published research studies except the community engagement study summarized here.

Research about father involvement needs to recognize the historical dimension of fathering, whereby Aboriginal fathers today are not in the same contexts, do not embody the same cultural predilections, and cannot automatically apply the lessons they may have learned about fatherhood from their forebears. The generative fathering theory, discussed by Pratt, Lawford, and Allen in this volume, has emphasized the multi-generational nature of fathering as a kind of forward-looking motivational idea for fathers (Hawkins & Dollahite, 1997; McAdams & de St. Aubin, 1998). But a backward look at socio-historical changes in fathers' motivations, behaviour patterns, and contexts within cultures and other population groups has not received much attention. Theoretical conceptualizations of father involvement could draw more on Bronfenbrenner's (1979) early concept of the *chronosystem,* examining how and why expectations, forms, levels, and accepted indicators of father involvement change over time within diverse populations. Recognition of the many levels of reciprocal influence between fathers and the changing social systems in which they participate provides a promising platform for scholars and advocates to advance recognition of fathers' involvement as a matter of public interest and a focus for public dialogue, policy reform, and program investments.

Canadian Aboriginal scholar Menzies (2006) has proposed an Intergenerational Trauma Model to understand Aboriginal men's experiences within the conceptual framework of traditional teachings of the First Nation medicine wheel. According to Aboriginal scholars Morrisseau (1998) and Nabigon and Mawhiney (1996), the medicine wheel teachings emphasize that there must be harmony among elements of the wheel – including oneself and one's family, community, and natural surroundings – in order to achieve and sustain wellness. The Intergenerational Trauma Model is predicated on the assumption that public policies in Canada have disrupted relations among these four spheres, pushing them further apart instead of holding them in a mutually supportive balance. The resulting disruption to Aboriginal ways of living in balance with nature and humanity has incubated negative social conditions for Aboriginal Peoples, making them significantly more vulnerable to a number of negative outcomes, including family dysfunction, social exclusion, and homelessness. Although the impact of intergenerational trauma may be most visible at the level of the individual, a holistic approach – as presented in Menzies's model – suggests that trauma affects all four spheres, as many of the fathers who participated in the current study described. Healing and positive growth depend on a restoration of harmony among individual, family, community, and national systems (including the First Nation or Métis nation and the nation of Canada), and this requires a holistic response ranging from individual counselling and social programs to housing, health, and employment programs (Menzies, 2006).

Conceptually, the interests of many investigators and public agencies funding research are not particularly relevant to Aboriginal fathers at this point in time. For example, a number of investigators are focused on parental

138   *Jessica Ball*

leave policies and the impact of various paternity leave allowances. These policies are not a priority for most Aboriginal men, who have the highest rate of unemployment among men in Canada. Also, many employed Aboriginal men work part-time or seasonally, are self-employed, or work in small businesses or in other work settings that do not provide paternity leave. Most fathers interviewed in the current study directed attention away from these areas of concerns and toward the challenges of regaining personal wellness, learning how to connect with and care for their children, sustaining or regaining relationships with other family members who can share in caring for children, and reconnecting with their cultural roots for their own identity development and to pass something of value on to their children.

The level of complexity of child care patterns and household composition found in the study of First Nation and Métis fathers described in this chapter is not readily grasped using mainstream survey questionnaires: for example, surveys asking questions about work-family balance, domestic division of labour, or parental problem solving. Questions such as how fathers share domestic and child care responsibilities with their partners, who takes time away from work to care for a sick child, and so on are not the most relevant questions to explore at this time. Rather, future studies could more fruitfully focus on personal and interpersonal conditions, social programs that may determine whether an Aboriginal father develops an identity as a father and becomes positively involved in learning fatherhood and participating in child care, and determinants of sustained positive connections with children as fathers' living arrangements and other circumstances change.

Many fathers in the current study based their approaches to fatherhood on direct teachings from their female partners, mothers, and aunts. Mothers' roles in facilitating father involvement have been well documented (Allen & Daly, 2007; Daly, 1993; Pleck & Mascaidrelli, 2004). However, our understandings of how female partners effectively model and teach fathers how to be positively involved in child care is not well developed, and this would also be a useful area for future research.

The Study's Implications for Policy and Program Support

Gatherings of fathers in the study were held in partnering communities after the data were analyzed and interpreted. About one third of the fathers who had participated in the study reviewed the findings and offered their confirmation that the interpretations generally represented their own perceptions of current patterns of Aboriginal fathers' experiences. The fathers were asked to identify specific steps they felt would support their positive involvement with their children. The following list of recommendations was developed from their responses:

1 Commit federal and provincial funds to programs across sectors including housing, health, education, correctional services, human resources, and social development in order to bring tangible improvements to the living conditions and life opportunities of Aboriginal people.
2 Improve the "father friendly" atmosphere in programs for children and families so that fathers feel welcome and comfortable.
3 Acknowledge and include Aboriginal fathers more in children's programs and in decision making about children: for example, in schools, hospitals, and child welfare.
4 Make information more accessible about how to have one's name registered on a child's birth record and about the possible legal, financial, and social ramifications of registering paternity on a birth record.
5 Implement "kith and kin" policies in child welfare practice so that if a child is taken into protective custody by the government, she or he is kept in a safe environment close to home so that visitation with the father can be sustained.
6 Provide legal representation, mediation, and counselling for fathers during custody decision making.
7 Produce and distribute easy-to-read print material and documentaries for the Aboriginal Peoples Television Network telling Aboriginal fathers' stories and conveying a message of encouragement and hope for Aboriginal fathers.
8 Engage Aboriginal fathers – in middle and secondary schools, for example – to promote awareness among adolescents about how fathers can be important in children's lives.

Several of these recommendations will require sustained, macrosystem, policy-driven efforts to reduce barriers and enable fathers to initiate and sustain positive engagement with children. These efforts will need to take a multi-sectoral approach, move beyond mother-centred policies and programs, and reach out to men in gender-specific and culturally grounded ways, as discussed below.

Using a Multi-Sectoral Approach
Most policies and programs to promote positive parenting and father involvement – from parental leave provisions to parenting support, education, and behaviour change programs – are targeted at individuals. Yet Aboriginal fathers' accounts in the current study pointed to a number of structural barriers that require policy and program reforms to strengthen Aboriginal families and improve their overall quality of life. Funding is needed for a multi-pronged approach involving programs that are prioritized, designed, and delivered by Aboriginal people to improve housing, education,

employment, quality child care, family services, legal aid, cultural programs, and community development (Ball, 2008). On the whole, federal, provincial, and territorial governments have failed to mobilize a thoughtful and co-ordinated response to improve the quality of life of First Nation and Métis families, despite the apology proffered by the Canadian government on June 11, 2008, for the multi-generational impacts of years of colonial inter-ventions (Office of the Prime Minister of Canada, 2008). Although Canada has an Aboriginal Action Plan (Minister of Indian Affairs and Northern Development, 1997), there is no legal framework for implementing it and no mechanism to monitor the extent to which it is implemented (Assembly of First Nations, 2006).

With a young and rapidly growing Aboriginal population, it is imperative to find ways to support First Nation, Métis, and Inuit fathers and their fam-ilies to regain their strengths in caring for children and youth. Programs are needed to provide expectant and new fathers and mothers with culturally relevant social support, mental health and addictions services, early child-hood care and development programs, and parenting education. Funding is also needed for outreach and services to fathers and mothers with special needs to provide ongoing support and respite for these parents and to keep vulnerable children close to home when families need to strengthen their parenting capacities or material resources. Investments are urgently needed for strategies to reduce adolescent fertility and to meet some of the unique needs of adolescent fathers and mothers. Investing in father involvement is not typically seen as falling within the scope of health, education, child welfare, or social development. Yet fathers' needs and potential contributions are evident across all of these sectors.

As fathers interviewed in the study stressed, it takes time and resources to strengthen individuals, families, and communities. Federal government investments in the Aboriginal Healing Foundation (AHF, 2006) have enabled the creation of resource materials and programs tailored to local community groups, including residential school healing programs, family reunification, and mental health. One example is an AHF resource guide for practitioners called *Warrior-Caregivers: Understanding the Challenges and Healing of First Nation's Men* (Mussell, 2005). However, given the time needed to reconstitute strong cultural communities and family structures, federal government con-tributions to healing programs need to be recommitted for some time to come. Aboriginal people often assert that it took seven generations to erode Aboriginal families, cultures, communities, and territories, and it will take seven generations to rebuild the strength of Aboriginal identities and societies (Brant Castellano, 2002).

Regarding First Nation families living on reserves, whose well-being is the fiduciary responsibility of the federal government, the First Nations Child and Family Caring Society and the Assembly of First Nations have called for funding for family support, quality child care, and prevention and early intervention programs at par with provincial services for children living off reserves and settlements (Blackstock et al., 2005). For First Nation and Métis children living off reserves, primarily in urban centres, the National Association of Friendship Centres, the Congress of Aboriginal People, and the Métis National Council have called for implementation of policies to expand access to child and family services delivered in culturally appropriate ways.

Moving Beyond Mother-Centred Policies and Programs

The idea that promoting fathers' involvement can contribute to the health and development of all family members has not yet taken hold in health policy discourse (Ball & Moselle, 2007). The focus remains almost exclusively on mothers' roles and needs, as well-baby clinics, child care, and family support programs communicate the belief that mothers are the critical link to child health and development. These approaches exacerbate fathers' sense of being peripheral. Furthermore, many agencies privilege the identity of mothers over fathers on children's records, including birth, health, child care, school, and child welfare records. A first step in securing a father's identification with fatherhood and involvement with his baby is to secure paternity designation on the child's birth certificate. More information directed to expectant and new Aboriginal fathers is needed since Aboriginal children have a much lower rate of paternity designation on their birth certificates and other records compared to non-Aboriginal children (Clatworthy, 2004; Mann, 2005).

Programs targeting Aboriginal youth and families need to evaluate their effectiveness in welcoming the participation of Aboriginal fathers and to ensure their relevance to Aboriginal youth who are preparing for fatherhood. As much as possible, programs need to offer (a) male outreach workers and Aboriginal staff; (b) materials about fathers' roles with children and youth, especially materials written specifically for First Nation and Métis men and featuring real-life circumstances and stories about how such men have learned fatherhood; (c) activities that will interest both men and women; and (d) policies that require accountability to fathers as well as mothers in communications between staff and parents about routine events and critical incidents involving their child (Ball & Roberge, 2007).

Until recently, there were no known programs specifically intended to help First Nation and Métis men effectively support their children's health and development (Ball & George, 2006; Manahan & Ball, 2008). However, father-focused practice in community-based programs is beginning to gain some momentum. Reports of activities such as "Dad's Nights," Father's Day events, and men's groups can now be found periodically in newsletters of community-based programs offered in First Nation and Métis community centre, and Friendship Centres. Indicative of an interest in understanding more about Aboriginal fathers, several hundred agencies serving First Nation and Métis families have ordered resource kits produced as a result of the research study highlighted in this chapter. Many of these agencies have reported on how they are using these resources to enhance staff awareness and increase the "father friendliness" of their program environments, scheduling, and activities. Some provincial governments have recently allocated funding for training and employment of part-time father outreach and support workers associated with, for example, community-based family resources centres, child development centres, and community health-promotion programs.

Recruiting men to work in community service programs is always difficult, and recruiting First Nation and Métis men is even more challenging. Practitioner training workshops and post-secondary education programs could do much more to recruit and retain Aboriginal trainees and students, and to ensure that coursework and practicum experiences prepare graduates to work effectively with Aboriginal families – including a specific focus on engaging with fathers. A recent review of post-secondary courses in professional education programs across Canada yielded only one course with the word "father" in the course title and few course outlines mentioning a focus on fathers (Hodgins, 2009). Similarly, a content analysis of 25 parent-education programs revealed that only four included any specific focus on fathers (Hodgins, 2007). Practitioner training programs are more likely to recruit and retain culturally diverse men, including Aboriginal men, if they highlight the distinctive nature and potential roles that fathers can play, as well as the distinctive needs and goals of First Nation, Métis, and Inuit fathers.

On a positive note, anecdotal reports indicate that support for fathers is being provided in a wide variety of ways through programs that do not ostensibly target father involvement. One such portal is Aboriginal Head Start (AHS), an early-learning and holistic-wellness program aimed at ensuring conditions for optimal development, health, and educational outcomes for Aboriginal preschoolers. One of the six mandated program components is parent involvement. AHS programs have the flexibility to develop in ways that are family centred and family preserving, and are delivered within a culturally based community development framework. In some regions of Canada, a priority of AHS has been to seek out fathers who could become involved on parent advisory committees, in outreach to other fathers, and in provincial and national events to ensure that fathers' needs, goals, and contributions are represented. While integration of father support within broader community supports for children and families has many advantages in terms of a delivery approach, its feasibility and sustainability depend on government commitment to funding the father involvement component.

Based on an analysis of data from the Father Involvement Research Alliance project (including data provided by the study discussed in this chapter), Daly, Ashbourne, and Brown (2009) found that fathers of young children often talk about the importance of children for their own sense of growing maturity, responsibility, and engagement, and for learning about their emotions and how to deal with them in the contexts of their parenting activities. They propose that one approach for programs to promote fathers' involvement might be to explore with fathers how their involvement with their children helps the father to develop emotionally and grow as a person. This approach seems promising for Aboriginal fathers, given their reports of needing to grow up as their children grow up and needing to develop more self-confidence, patience, and ability to play, display affection, and manage their anger.

Reaching Out to Men in Gender-Specific and Culturally Grounded Ways

The desire among Aboriginal Peoples to bring traditional teachings into contemporary life may help to focus attention on men's roles, including those related to caring for children (Manahan & Ball, 2008). Also, the Aboriginal women's movement in Canada is focusing some attention on men's roles, helping to create an environment that is conducive to social change among Aboriginal men.

Supporting "Families of the Heart"

Because Aboriginal families tend to be larger than non-Aboriginal families, many children – especially those living on reserves – still have opportunities to be raised among extended kin networks as they would have in the past. But Aboriginal scholar Brant Castellano (2002) has also described the creation among some Aboriginal people, especially those living in urban areas, of "families of the heart" (1), whereby children and adults who are variously related (or not) live together according to a kind of "open door" policy. This may be an emerging expression of how extended family systems are being readapted to suit contemporary contexts.

Analysis of Aboriginal Children's Survey data obtained by Statistics Canada (2009) found that many First Nation and Métis children may enjoy the benefits that can come from having extended family members involved in their care and often living in the same household rather than being raised within the nuclear and patriarchal family model that was imposed by colonial authorities. A changeable household composition and having multiple caregivers have tended to be cast in a negative light in mainstream, European-heritage models of the nuclear family and child development. However, as Brant Castellano (2002) points out, families of the heart can afford opportunities for Aboriginal children to develop varied relationships with a larger community of caregivers and for fathers and mothers to share the process of learning parenting and ensuring good care for their children with other adults. Thus, there is the promising potential for First Nation and Métis fathers to become part of "circles of care," an idea that has been elaborated elsewhere (Ball, 2010).

Changing Media Images of Aboriginal Fathers
Images of Aboriginal young men as subsisting on the edges of society and as chronically in trouble at school and with the law are prevalent in Canadian media. These images promulgate negative social expectations for Aboriginal boys as they begin to imagine possibilities for themselves as future fathers. Based on available research evidence involving non-Aboriginal young men, the prospects for Aboriginal boys and young men to become positively involved as young fathers are not good (Furstenberg & Weiss, 2001). To inspire Aboriginal youth to construct positive expectations for themselves in caring relationships as adults, media must show Aboriginal men assuming the role of positively involved father, including fathers who take on primary caregiving roles after a mother's departure for the day (stay-at-home dads) or for good (lone fathers). One example is a Health Canada video by and for Aboriginal youth featuring popular Aboriginal musician/actor George Leach talking about his experience of becoming a responsible young father (Goodchild, 1997).

Sustaining Connections Across Changing Circumstances
More effort needs to be made to identify, locate, and involve fathers of children who are taken into government care. Reforms are also needed to increase the transparency of laws and accessibility of legal aid for fathers implicated by decisions about child custody, visitation, and guardianship. In addition, given the high rate of incarceration of First Nation and Métis men, combined with the likelihood that most of them are fathers, it is important to include discussion of fatherhood and, when appropriate, to explore ways for fathers to communicate with their children and their guardians during the father's absence from home.

Conclusion
The frequent lack of involvement of First Nation and Métis fathers in their children's lives tends to be widely interpreted within the helping professions and Canadian society as a whole as reflecting these fathers' indifference toward their children (Claes & Clifton, 1998; Mussell, 2005). Generally, little acknowledgment is made of the complex challenges many of these men face. Most Aboriginal men in Canada have a distinctively painful personal and socio-cultural history and must deal with fallout from Indian residential schools, involvement in the child welfare system, and other continuing effects of colonization that present formidable obstacles to their well-being

and their ability to care for their children. Fortunately, First Nation and Métis peoples share a cultural heritage grounded in extended kinship systems that may provide the foundation and inspiration to revitalize Aboriginal fathers' involvement in caring for their children now and in the generations yet to come.

Acknowledgments
This chapter draws on findings of a research study conducted by the author as part of the Fathers Involvement Research Alliance and funded by the Social Sciences and Humanities Research Council of Canada, Community-University Research Alliances program (File No. 833-2003-1002), as well as by the BC Ministry of Children and Family Development through the Human Early Learning Partnership. The author thanks the five community partners and 80 fathers who participated in the research reported here, and the Aboriginal project team, including Candice Manahan, Ron Tsaskiy George, and Leroy Joe.

Notes
1 The terms *Indigenous* and *Aboriginal* are used almost synonymously in Canada to refer to the population of peoples who identify themselves as descendants of original inhabitants of the land now called Canada. The Canadian Constitution, Section 35, recognizes First Nation, Inuit, and Métis Peoples as Canada's First Peoples. The colonial government coined the term *Aboriginal* in the 1800s as a catch-all label. Some people refrain from using *Aboriginal* because of its colonial derivation. Some prefer the term *Indigenous* because it connects to a global advocacy movement of Indigenous peoples who use the term. *Aboriginal* is used in this chapter because it is still most widely used in Canada.
2 Bibliographies of information on the impact of residential schools can be found on the website of the Aboriginal Healing Foundation at http://www.ahf.ca.

References
Aboriginal Healing Foundation. (2006). *Final report of the Aboriginal Healing Foundation, Vol. 3: Promising healing practices in Aboriginal communities.* Ottawa, ON: Author.

Adelson, N. (2005, March-April). The embodiment of inequity: Health disparities in Aboriginal Canada. *Canadian Journal of Public Health, 96*(Suppl 2), S45-61.

Ali, M. (2008). Loss of parenting self-efficacy among immigrant parents. *Contemporary Issues in Early Childhood, 9*(2), 148-160.

Allen, S., & Daly, K. J. (2007). *The effects of father involvement: A summary of the research evidence* (2nd ed.). Guelph, ON: Health Canada.

Assembly of First Nations. (2006). *Royal Commission on Aboriginal people at ten years: A report card.* Ottawa, ON: Author.

Atleo, E. R. (2004). *Tsawalk: A Nuu-chah-nulth worldview.* Vancouver, BC: UBC Press.

Ball, J. (2008). Promoting equity and dignity for young Aboriginal children in Canada. *IRPP Choices, 14*(7), 1-30. Retrieved from http://www.irpp.org/choices/archive/vol14no7.pdf

Ball, J. (2010). Indigenous fathers reconstituting circles of care. *American Journal of Community Psychology, 45*(1-2), 124-138. doi:10.1007/s10464-009-9293-1

Ball, J., Cowan, P., & Cowan, C. (1995). Who's got the power? Gender differences in experiences of marital problem solving. *Family Process, 34*(3), 303-322.

Ball, J., & George, R. (2006). Policies and practices affecting Aboriginal fathers' involvement with their young children. In J. P. White, P. Maxim, & D. Beavon (Eds.), *Aboriginal policy research in Canada* (Vol. 3, pp. 123-144). Toronto, ON: Thompson Educational Press.

Ball, J., & Moselle, K. (2007, March). *Fathers' contributions to children's well-being: Systematic review of research for the Public Health Agency of Canada.* Population Health Fund Project presented at the Inaugural Canadian Men's Health Conference, Victoria, BC.

Ball, J., & Roberge, C. (2007). *Aboriginal fathers: A guide for community programs.* Victoria, BC: University of Victoria, Early Childhood Development Intercultural Partnerships Program.

Bennett, M., & Blackstock, C. (1992). *A literature review and annotated bibliography focusing on aspects of Aboriginal child welfare in Canada*. Winnipeg, MB: First Nations Child and Family Caring Society.

Blackstock, C., Loxlely, J., Prakash, T., & Wien, F. (2005). *Wen'de: We are coming to the light of day*. Ottawa, ON: First Nations Child and Family Caring Society of Canada.

Brant Castellano, M. (2002). *Aboriginal family trends: Extended families, nuclear families, families of the heart* [Contemporary Family Trends series]. Ottawa, ON: Vanier Institute of the Family.

Bronfenbrenner, U. (1979). *The ecology of human development: Experiments by nature and design*. Cambridge: MA: Harvard University Press.

Canadian Institute for Child Health (CICH). (2000). *The health of Canada's children* (3rd ed.). Ottawa, ON: Author.

Canadian Institute for Health Information (CIHI). (2004). Aboriginal Peoples' health. In *Improving the health of Canadians* (pp. 73-102). Ottawa, ON: Author.

Claes, R., & Clifton, D. (1998). *Needs and expectations for redress of victims of abuse at residential schools*. Ottawa, ON: Law Commission of Canada.

Clatworthy, S. (2004). Unstated paternity: Estimates and contributing factors. In J. P. White, P. Maxim, & D. Beavon (Eds.), *Aboriginal policy research: Setting the agenda for change* (Vol. 2, pp. 225-244). Toronto, ON: Thompson Educational Publishing.

Daly, K. (1993). Reshaping fatherhood: Finding the models. *Journal of Family Issues, 14*, 510-530.

Daly, K., Ashbourne, L., & Brown, J. L. (2009). Fathers' perceptions of children's influence: Implications for involvement. *The Annals of the American Academy of Political and Social Science, 624*, 61-77.

Department of Public Safety, Corrections Research Branch, Office of the Correctional Investigator (2008). *Aboriginal Inmates*. Ottawa, ON: Author.

Dickason, O. P. (2009). *Canada's First Nations: A history of founding peoples*. Oxford, England: Oxford University Press.

Dion Stout, M., & Kipling, G. (2003). *Aboriginal people, resilience and the residential school legacy*. Ottawa, ON: Aboriginal Healing Foundation.

Epstein, R. (Ed.). (2009). *Who's your daddy? And other writings on queer parenting*. Toronto, ON: Sumach Press.

Este, D., & Tachble, A. (2009). Fatherhood and the Canadian context: Perceptions and experiences of Sudanese refugee men. *Sex Roles, 60*(7-8), 456-466.

First Nations Centre. (2005). *First Nations Regional Longitudinal Health Survey 2002/03: Results for adults, youth and children living in First Nations communities*. Ottawa, ON: Assembly of First Nations and First Nations Information Governance Committee.

Fournier, S., & Crey, E. (1997). *Stolen from our embrace: The abduction of Aboriginal children and the restoration of Aboriginal communities*. Vancouver, BC: Douglas & McIntyre.

Furstenberg, F. F., & Weiss, C. C. (2001). Intergenerational transmission of fathering roles in at-risk families. *Marriage and Family Review, 29*(2-3), 181-201.

Glaser, B. (1978). *Theoretical sensitivity*. Mill Valley, CA: Sociology Press.

Glaser, B., & Strauss, A. (1965). *Awareness of dying*. Hawthorne, NY: Aldine Press.

Goodchild, M. (Writer/Director). (2005). *Balance: Healing through helping* [Video]. Ottawa, ON: Health Canada.

Guimond, E., & Robitaille, N. (2008). When teenage girls have children: Trends and consequences. *Horizons, 10*(1), 49-51.

Hawkins, A., & Dollahite, D. (1997). *Generative fathering: Beyond deficit perspectives*. Thousand Oaks, CA: Sage.

Health Canada. (2005). *First Nations comparable health indicators*. Ottawa, ON: Author. Retrieved from http://www.hc-sc.gc.ca/fniah-spnia/diseases-maladies/2005-01_health -sante_indicat-eng.php.

Hodgins, D. (2007). *Parent education curricula: Where are fathers represented?* Unpublished master's thesis, University of Victoria, Victoria, BC.

Hodgins, D. (2009). *Search of Canadian college and university courses for father themed courses*. Unpublished review, School of Child and Youth Care, University of Victoria, Victoria, BC.

John, E. (2003, March). *Presentation to the Aboriginal Leadership Forum on Early Childhood Development,* Vancouver, University of British Columbia.

Kirmayer, L., Brass, G., & Tait, C. (2000). The mental health of Aboriginal Peoples: Transformations of identity and community. *Canadian Journal of Psychiatry, 45*(7), 607-616.

Lero, D., Ashbourne, L., & Whitehead, D. (2006). *Inventory of policies and policy areas influencing father involvement.* Guelph, ON: Father Involvement Research Alliance.

Manahan, C., & Ball, J. (2008). Aboriginal fathers' support groups: Bridging the gap between displacement and family balance. *First Nations Child and Family Services Review, 3*(4), 42-49.

Mann, M. (2005). *Indian registration: Unrecognized and unstated paternity.* Ottawa, ON: Status of Women Canada.

McAdams, D. P., & de St. Aubin, E. (1998). *Generativity and adult development: How and why we care for the next generation.* Washington, DC: American Psychological Association.

Menzies, P. (2006). Intergenerational trauma and homeless Aboriginal men. *Canadian Review of Social Policy, 58,* 1-24.

Miller, J. R. (1996). *Shingwauk's vision: A history of Native residential schools.* Toronto, ON: University of Toronto Press.

Minister of Indian Affairs and Northern Development. (1997). *Gathering strength: Canada's Aboriginal action plan* (Catalogue no. R32-189-1997E). Ottawa, ON: Minister of Public Works and Government Services Canada. Retrieved from http://www.ahf.ca/downloads/gathering-strength.pdf.

Morrisseau, C. (1998). *Into the daylight: A wholistic approach to healing.* Toronto, ON: University of Toronto Press.

Mussell, W. J. (Ed.). (1999). *Journey towards wellness: From trauma and loss to cultural healing and restoration.* Saskatoon, SK: Native Mental Health Association of Canada.

Mussell, W. J. (2005). *Warrior-caregivers: Understanding the challenges and healing of First Nations men.* Ottawa, ON: Aboriginal Healing Foundation.

Nabigon, H., & Mawhiney, A. M. (1996). Aboriginal theory: A Cree medicine wheel guide for healing First Nations. In F. Turner (Ed.), *Social work treatment* (pp. 18-38). New York, NY: The Free Press.

Office of the Prime Minister of Canada. (2008, June 11). *Prime minister offers full apology on behalf of Canadians for the Indian residential schools* [Press release].

Pleck, J. H., & Mascaidrelli, B. P. (2004). Parental involvement: Levels, sources and consequences. In M. E. Lamb (Ed.), *The role of the father in child development* (pp. 222-271). New York, NY: Wiley.

Robertson, L. H. (2006). The residential school experience: Syndrome or historic trauma. *Pimatisiwin: A Journal of Aboriginal and Indigenous Community Health, 4*(4), 1-28.

Roopnarine, J. L., Brown, J., Snell-White, P., & Riegraf, N. B. (1995). Father involvement in child care and household work in common-law dual-earner and single-earner Jamaican families. *Journal of Applied Developmental Psychology, 16*(1), 35-52.

Royal Commission on Aboriginal Peoples. (1996). *Report of the Royal Commission on Aboriginal Peoples.* Ottawa, ON: Canada Communication Group.

Salee, D. (with Newhouse, D., & Levesque, C.). (2006). Quality of life of Aboriginal people in Canada: An analysis of current research. *IRPP Choices, 12*(6), 1-40.

Statistics Canada. (2003). *Aboriginal Peoples of Canada: Highlight tables, 2001 census.* Ottawa, ON: Author.

Statistics Canada. (2006). *Census of the population 2006.* Ottawa, ON: Author.

Statistics Canada. (2009). Selected findings from 2006 Aboriginal Children's Survey: First Nations people, Métis in Canada, Inuit in Canada. *Canadian Social Trends, Special Edition* (Catalogue no. 11-008). Ottawa, ON: Author.

Stremlau, R. (2005). To domesticate and civilize wild Indians: Allotment and the campaign to reform Indian families, 1875-1887. *Journal of Family History, 30*(3), 265-286.

Trocmé, N., MacLaurin, B., Fallon, B., Knoke, D., Pitman, L., & McCormack, M. (2006). *Mesnmimk Wasatek – Catching a drop of light. Understanding the over-representation of First Nations children in Canada's child welfare system: An analysis of the Canadian Incidence Study of Reported Child Abuse and Neglect.* Toronto, ON: Centre of Excellence for Child Welfare and First Nations Child and Family Caring Society.

Volo, J. M., & Volo, D. D. (2007). *Family life in Native America.* Westport, CT: Greenwood.

Waldram, J. B. (2004). *Revenge of the Windigo: The construction of the mind and mental health of North American Aboriginal Peoples.* Toronto, ON: University of Toronto Press.

Weitzman, M. (2003). Low income and its impact on psychosocial child development. In R. E. Tremblay, R. G. Barr, & R. DeV. Peters (Eds.), *Encyclopedia on early childhood development* (pp. 1-8). Montreal, QC: Centre of Excellence for Early Childhood Development. Retrieved from http://www.enfant-encyclopedie.com/Pages/PDF/WeitzmanANGxp.pdf.

Wesley-Esquimaux, C. C., & Smolewski, M. (2003). *Historic trauma and Aboriginal healing.* Ottawa, ON: Aboriginal Healing Foundation Research Series.

Yellow Horse Brave Heart, M., & DeBruyn, L. M. (1998). The American Indian holocaust: Healing historical unresolved grief. *American Indian and Alaska Native Mental Health, 8*(2), 56-79.

7

The Short End of the Stick? Fatherhood in the Wake of Separation and Divorce

Denise L. Whitehead and Nicholas Bala

Popular culture is filled with unflattering images of the post-separation father: "deadbeat dads," "disappearing dads," and the "abusive former husband" are common phrases that paint uncomplimentary portraits, to say the least. These images, however, are slowly giving way to a new dynamic of post-separation fatherhood. There is a growing acknowledgment that legal and structural barriers influence the opportunities and choices of fathers following separation (Whitehead, 2006). It is time to recognize more fully that fathers have at times been left holding the short end of the stick.

This chapter is about men who are separated or divorced from the mother of their children, or who never cohabited with the mother, and the effects of separation and living apart from their children on these fathers, their children, and society. It is also about how fathers have changed, how mothers have changed, and how, albeit slowly, the legal regime has changed. Understanding the changes in the roles and rights of separated or divorced fathers requires consideration of wider social developments in the past three decades in Canada (and in most developed countries) regarding the attitudes and behaviours relating to fathering. Although even in two-parent families, mothers still, on average, do more child care than fathers (often at the sacrifice of paid work), the number of fathers now engaged in regular child care in two-parent families has increased (Marshall, 2006). In a growing number of families, the father will at some point be the primary caregiver for the children (see McKay, Marshall, & Doucet, this volume). Most fathers understand the importance of their role in their children's lives and the rewards and pleasures of having a relationship with their children both within and outside a partnered relationship.

This chapter considers the role of fathers and their relationships with their children after separation, as well as the evolving legal regime that governs their rights and obligations. The chapter concludes by offering some suggestions about further legal and social reforms that are needed to address more effectively the needs of fathers, mothers, and children who are facing life-changing transitions.

Fathers and Their Children: Who Needs Whom?

The Social and Emotional Needs of Children

It is well established that fathers have an important role to play in developing and meeting the social-emotional needs of children, especially when fathers undertake active, developmentally appropriate, authoritative parenting (S. Allen & Daly, 2007). The good modern father is considered to be one who undertakes the appropriate fathering roles of breadwinner, supportive partner, nurturer, carer, and moral and ethical role model (Lamb, 2000). Father advocacy in the context of separation and divorce has largely endorsed the view that father involvement is an essential precursor to good child outcomes and that it serves the best interests of children and promotes the well-being of fathers themselves.

The view that father involvement is related to positive outcomes seems to strike deeply resonant social chords. The "good father" in the post-separation family is sometimes contrasted to the "selfish mother," who is seen to limit or terminate contact between fathers and their children (Rhoades, 2002, 74). As Rhoades (2002) argues, "A new rule is operating in the practice of family law, namely, that contact with fathers is almost always good for children (or lack of contact harms children)" (83). The reality is far more nuanced as parents deal with issues around parenting competencies, pre-separation roles, substance abuse, alienation, mental health concerns, and domestic and child abuse.

The impact of separation and divorce on children is complicated since it varies according to income, parenting capacity, and child age (Ambert, 2009; Lamb, Sternberg, & Thompson, 1997). On the positive side, research suggests that most children who experience parental separation and divorce fare quite well, particularly when financial resources are sufficient, conflict between their parents is minimal, their parents are psychologically healthy and engage in positive parenting, and the child is able to maintain a relationship with both parents (Lamb et al., 1997). Generally, father presence in children's post-separation lives has been associated with many positive outcomes, particularly when quality over quantity of contact time is measured. Those positive outcomes associated with father involvement include the provision of child support and increased child well-being as measured by greater high school completion, fewer mental health issues, and less youth crime (Amato & Gilbreth, 1999).

For some children, however, the effects of being raised in a single-parent family are associated with negative outcomes. Research has shown that – particularly if the parents are young, lack education, and are poor – children of separated and divorced parents are more likely to experience more negative outcomes relative to their peers who live with two parents, including behavioural problems, poor school performance, and becoming a young offender (Ambert, 2009). These risks can persist into adulthood: the effects of poverty and lack of financial resources can diminish high school completion and post-secondary prospects, and ongoing conflict among parents not only has negative effects on child well-being (Amato & Afifi, 2006; Amato & Sobolewski, 2001) but can also result in poorer relations between adult children and their fathers (Amato & Booth, 1996).

One of the challenges in discussing the separated or divorced father is the sheer diversity within that group. Fathering starts from many different family structures: children are born to very young fathers who never lived with the child's mother, to more tenuous early cohabiting relationships where the couple may not have firmly established themselves or their future, or to common-law or married couples who have viewed their relationship as permanent when the children were born but later found themselves moving in new directions. Young fathers are often struggling with poverty, a lack of education and job training, and a minimal or no permanent relationship with the mother; they therefore face very different issues with regard to remaining connected to their children compared to more established fathers who have lived with their children and have strong ties to work, community, and family (Ashbourne, 2006).

Research suggests that children born to parents who never lived together have less frequent contact with their fathers than children whose parents cohabited or were married and then separated (Le Bourdais, Juby, & Marcil-Gratton, 2001). Swiss and Le Bourdais's (2009) recent analysis of data from the Canadian General Social Survey, however, suggests that the parents' type of union (marital or cohabitating) may have very little influence on the amount of post-separation father-child contact, particularly as non-marital cohabitation becomes more common. Overall, as Juby, Marcil-Gratton, and Le Bourdais (2005) have emphasized, "the context into which the child is born is closely associated with the number and type of family transitions that occur later on during childhood" (5). Many children and their parents will experience a significant number of major life changes, such as repartnering (step-parents), children changing residential parents, new siblings, step-siblings, and so on. Fathers are not merely passive players in the changes that take place since they make decisions about their old and new families.

On one hand, research has highlighted that a father may be excluded from his child's life when the mother acts as a gatekeeper to a child's contact with the father (Marsiglio, Day, & Lamb, 2000). On the other hand, it is also well documented that mothers can serve as active facilitators and promoters of post-separation father-child relationships (Dienhart, 2001). Father-child relations are also affected by pre-existing marital discord and the actual divorce; the latter tends to decrease children's emotional bonds with their fathers as compared to their mothers, whose bond with their children is most affected by marital discord rather than the divorce itself (Amato and Sobolewski, 2001). Furthermore, as Lewis and Welsh (2005) describe, many fathers in two-parent families still tend toward a desire "to be there" for their children, but their care tends to be passive or oriented toward play or recreation compared to the day-to-day responsibilities shouldered by mothers, a care dynamic that may not translate well after divorce.

The Psycho-Social Needs of Separated and Divorced Fathers
While much of the divorce research and literature has focused on the needs of mothers and on the outcomes that separation and divorce have on child well-being (Amato, 1993; Amato & Cheadle, 2005), the needs of fathers are starting to garner more attention, both in research and in programs and policies. A 2007 report from Statistics Canada analyzing rates of depression for men and women following marital dissolution (including both legally married and common-law relationships) revealed that depression rates were higher for men than for women, even when other factors such as loss of contact with children, loss of social support, work status, and income were controlled (Rotermann, 2007). The loss of social support and loss of contact with children have been identified as potentially the most salient contributors to this finding. Men tend to mourn the loss of their children and family life more than they mourn the loss of their ex-spouse. In contrast, women, who often still have the primary care of the children after separation, tend to mourn the loss of the marital relationship more than men do (Baum, 2003; Kruk, 1994). Baum (2006) suggests that some fathers are unable to psychologically separate their role as husband from their role as father, which inhibits their mourning process and hinders their ability to move forward with a distinct identity as a father. In turn, some fathers may disengage from their children as the behavioural means to cope with their inability to be a father when they are no longer a husband.

In Canada, fathers and their needs are starting to gain attention and resources. Social service agencies across the country are now beginning to offer programs and services specifically oriented to the needs of divorced fathers. These efforts have brought attention to the idea that fathers may have specific needs that are distinct from mothers. Once the distinct social, emotional, and legal needs of fathers have been identified, supports and services can be tailored to achieve effective outcomes for fathers and, by extension, their children and former partners (Ashbourne, Whitehead & Hawkins, 2012).

When it comes to father-child relations, the question of who needs whom is not as straightforward as one might expect. Certainly, many children without an active father presence do well, although children raised in two-parent families, on average, have moderately better outcomes than children raised by single parents (Amato, 2003). The reality may be that it is the quality of the father in the child's life that makes the biggest difference. Parents' mental health issues, young parenting, conflict and poor parenting, and parental drug or alcohol abuse impact child outcomes more than father absence does. Children raised by competent and co-operative separated parents derive many of the same benefits as those raised in a family with two parents. From a social perspective, providing support for fathers who are willing and able to play an active and vital role in their children's lives is important, especially for those children who have parents facing challenges that may act as impediments to a good parent-child relationship.

Post-Separation Fatherhood in Canada

Historical and Life Course Transitions

Father involvement after separation can be understood as following two distinct but intersecting trajectories: (a) the overall historical socio-cultural movement toward more father involvement generally, and (b) the experience of changes within an individual's life, sometimes called a *life course perspective*. In 1998, Juby and Le Bourdais raised issues about "paternal role adjustment," citing concerns that fathers lacked clear and identifiable expectations about what forms father involvement should take, particularly for the non-resident father (164). From a socio-cultural perspective, this is changing as fathers assume a greater role in parenting and as the everyday care of children in intact families is translating into greater comfort and involvement in post-separation parenting. The life course perspective is necessary to understanding the individual movement to involved fatherhood after separation, as well as the changes that men experience as they undergo familial changes and assume multiple family roles (e.g., father with a partner, lone parent, stepfather).

An ongoing challenge in the study of separation and divorce is that the information and statistics we gather often do a poor job of reflecting what families actually do (e.g., settlements, private negotiations, litigation, or some combination of these, such as settlements that occur just before trial). There is often confusion in the research and literature between families in which there is joint legal custody (i.e., an agreement or court order for joint decision-making responsibility) versus those in which there is joint physical custody (i.e., roughly equal sharing of care and time with the children). Furthermore, many families are missed in some data sets and research where the focus is on divorce outcomes only, ignoring the separations of common-law or never-married couples. While data sets such as Canada's National Longitudinal Survey of Children and Youth (NLSCY) have shed light on what families do outside of the divorce courts, we do not have comprehensive numbers on how families deal with separation and divorce in Canada. Furthermore, much of the data used in research often reflects a lag in time so that the data may not completely square with what parents are doing today. This can significantly skew the picture presented of what fathers (and mothers) are doing. Therefore, it may be best to view the extant data as suggestive. The following discussion includes some of the best data we have, but further analysis of new waves of data will continue to update the picture of what is happening in families.

Father-Child Contact

As researchers have documented, separation and divorce is often just one of many transitions that parents and their children experience as they move into lone parenthood, stepfamilies, or custody changes (Juby, Le Bourdais, & Marcil-Gratton, 2003). In Canada, the 2006 census data reveal that there are 1.4 million one-parent families, representing 16% of all Canadian families that have dependent children (Milan, Vezina, & Wells, 2007). Overall, mothers continue to head the majority of lone-parent families (80.1%), while father-led lone-parent families constitute 19.9%. However, the proportion of lone-father families is increasing faster than that of lone-mother families: between 2001 and 2006, father-led lone-parent families increased by 14.6% while mother-led lone-parent families increased by 6.3%. Changes in how custody is arranged (usually via settlements as opposed to court orders) are largely responsible for this trend; in 2003, only 47.7% of custody arrangements for divorcing couples provided for sole custody to the mother (down from 78.2% in 1980), and there was an increase in joint legal custody arrangements, which accounted for 43.8% of custody arrangements in 2003 (Milan et al., 2007), up from 5% in 1980 (Juby et al., 2005). Analysis by Juby and colleagues (2003) found that father-only custody arrangements, like mother-only custody, tend to be fairly stable over time. On average, lone-parent fathers are economically better off than lone-parent mothers, but even single fathers are often supporting their children on a low income (Juby et al., 2003).

The topic of father-child contact has often been approached with concern over the tendency of fathers to diminish or lose contact with their children over time. US researchers found that between 1976 and 2002, non-resident fathers have, overall, increased their time with their children (Amato, Meyers, & Emery, 2009), a trend that has also ocurred in Canada (Juby, Billette, Laplante, & Le Bourdais, 2007). This trend for increased contact between fathers and their children is probably even more pronounced for separated and divorced fathers over the last 10 to 15 years, given the increased cultural focus on involved fathering. But this increase in post-separation father involvement has not been uniform. Although some fathers now have very significant involvement with their children, a significant number of fathers still have limited or no contact with their children, or their contact diminishes considerably as the time after separation increases. In 2003, Juby et al. reported that as time after separation increased, some two fifths of children had more contact with their fathers (including some children who moved to live with their fathers), while three fifths had less contact. This raises the question, why do father-child relationships deteriorate in some cases and why are they maintained or strengthened in others?

The Impact of Separation on Relations With Fathers
Overall, longitudinal data have demonstrated that living and parental contact arrangements tend to be quite transitory as children and parents experience various life changes and as children age (Juby et al., 2003). Scott, Booth, King, and Johnson (2007) showed that adolescence, in particular, can prove to be a challenging time for parent-child closeness, regardless of marital stability, as children seek greater independence from their parents, turn more to peers, and become more involved with school, work, and extracurricular activities. Father-child closeness and the prevention of post-divorce deterioration of that relationship and related to pre-divorce mother-child relationship quality and the child's overall general well-being. Hawkins, Amato, and King's (2007) research involving interviews with adolescents suggests that children who are generally well behaved and do not cause much trouble are more likely to remain closer to their non-resident fathers than are children who have behavioural or academic difficulties.

Yet research has also shown that some father-child relationships become closer after separation and divorce. Swiss and Le Bourdais (2009) have identified numerous factors that impact the amount of father-child contact following separation:

- gender of the child, with boys more likely to spend more time with their fathers;
- the age of the child at the time of separation, with older children spending more time with their fathers;
- income, with higher-income fathers spending more time with their children;
- the father's new partner, with fathers being less likely to see their own children when the new partner does not have children; and
- satisfaction with the type of custody agreement, with greater satisfaction resulting in more father-child contact (how the agreement is reached, whether by judicial order or not, is not related to satisfaction with the type of custody arrangement).

Repartnering: A Life Course Transition
Transitions in the form of family are significant events for almost all children who have experienced their parents' separation. Juby, Le Bourdais, and

Marcil-Gratton's (2005a) analysis of NLSCY data indicates that repartnering is the norm: after two years of separation, one third of children had at least one parent repartner; after five years this rises to two thirds, and after 10 years, close to 90%.

Fathers experience repartnering from two vantage points – their own relationship and the relationship of their ex-spouse. The timing of fathers' repartnering has been identified as a critical event in terms of their relationship with their children from prior relationships. Men tend to repartner more quickly than women (Juby et al., 2007). Furthermore, the birth of a child to the father's new union is more likely to decrease non-resident father-child contact than the father living with stepchildren (Manning, Stewart, & Smock, 2003). Canadian researchers have detected a more nuanced understanding: when they removed fathers who had never lived with their children from the analysis, the birth of a child to a new union did not decrease non-resident father-child contact (Juby et al., 2007).

Overall, the research shows that men tend to be most actively engaged in fathering the children with whom they live. Men are more likely to spend time with the children of their current partner, often decreasing contact with their own child (Schmeeckle, 2007). Juby et al. (2007) report, however, that timing is everything – Canadian fathers who repartner very soon after separation were far more likely to reduce contact with their children. Fathers and their children need time to establish a pattern and rhythm for their time together (Kruk, 1994), and delaying repartnering may allow them time to strengthen their relationship.

The addition of a stepfather – the point at which a father's ex-partner chooses to repartner, thus adding a new male person to the equation – is also significant. There is a general trend toward less father involvement between non-resident fathers and their children when a stepfather is introduced (Juby et al., 2007). Children, however, tend to retain a much higher opinion of their biological father than they do of their stepfather, reporting greater closeness and fairness (Juby et al., 2005a). Although some stepfathers may have a rivalry with fathers and may be viewed as "intruders" or "gatekeepers" to the father-child relationship, research demonstrates the positive role that some stepfathers play as a father ally, helping to protect and nurture the relationships among family members, including both ex-spouses and children (Marsiglio & Hinojosa, 2007).

Shared Parenting: A Socio-Cultural Shift
One of the most significant shifts over the last quarter century has been the movement toward the concept of both parents actively sharing parenting responsibilities after separation and divorce. While any level of post-separation parenting can be regarded as shared, there are important legal

distinctions in the types of arrangements regarded as shared post-separation parenting.

When joint *legal* custody is agreed to or granted by a court, parents are expected to engage jointly in the decision making regarding important aspects of the child's life such as education, medical care, or religious upbringing. By 2003, 44% of Canadian children were in shared legal custody (Milan et al., 2007). Joint legal custody, however, is quite distinct from the living arrangement that the child will have. The parents may have joint legal custody of a child, but the child may have a primary residence (or live in the physical care or custody) of one parent. The parents may also have an arrangement of joint legal *and* physical custody, with the parents sharing decision making and the child spending roughly equal time with each parent.

There is no legal definition of shared or joint physical custody, but most parents in Canada seem to have the idea that it involves roughly equal sharing of time, with many assuming that each parent has responsibility for the child at least 40% of the time (the threshold in the Federal Child Support Guidelines for varying child support to take account of shared parenting; see Kruk, 2008; Moyer, 2004). According to data from the 2006 General Social Survey, approximately 14% of parents had a shared custodial living arrangement (Robinson, 2009).

Parents are more likely to have shared physical custody arrangement in the following situations: it has been agreed to privately between parents, as opposed to a court order (Juby et al., 2005); the parents exhibit flexible, co-operative, and child-focused parenting (Gill, 2004; Moyer, 2004); the mother is employed outside of the home (Juby, Le Bourdais, & Marcil-Gratton, 2005b); the father's work hours coincide with the times when children are at school or daycare (Juby et al., 2005b); the mother has completed post-secondary education or (somewhat unexpectedly) the mother hasn't completed high school (Juby et al., 2005b); the father has previously been the primary caregiver (Juby et al., 2005b); the family has a relatively high income (Juby et al., 2005b; Moyer, 2004); and the parents live in close proximity (most less than 10 kilometres) (Gill, 2004).

While shared physical custody is often touted as best for the child, long-term data has revealed it to be the custodial arrangement most likely to change (into either mother or father sole custody) (Juby et al., 2003). Analysis of NLSCY data confirms the transitory nature of shared physical custody: 85% of families who started in this type of arrangement were still in some kind of shared custody arrangement two years after separation, but this dropped to only 8% six years later (Juby et al., 2005). Children who have been in shared physical custody are also more likely to segue into sole father custody if the children are young at the time of separation, perhaps reflecting previous caregiving patterns, but girls are significantly less likely than boys to move from shared physical custody into father-only custody (Juby et al., 2005). The message for fathers may be that regardless of the way in which a shared physical custody arrangement eventually evolves, the opportunity to share custody is associated with a greater degree of involvement by both parents, even after the child ceases to be in a shared living arrangement (Juby et al., 2005b; Juby et al., 2005).

Custody and Law Reform

There have been enormous changes in attitudes, practices, and law with regard to the role of fathers in the lives of their children after separation or divorce. Historically, the common law gave married fathers an absolute right to custody of their children. Then, in the nineteenth century, legislation was enacted that gave mothers the right to seek custody of their children. Throughout much of the twentieth century, Canadian courts operated on the presumption that if parents separated, children, especially those of "tender years" (i.e., under the age of seven years) should be placed in the custody of their mothers (see, for example, *Talsky v. Talsky,* 1976, for "rule of common sense" per Spence J.). By the early 1980s, Canadian appeal courts accepted that all matters related to the care of children should be based on an assessment of the best interests of the individual child. The "tender years" presumption was rejected as based on conventional thinking and was replaced by a primary caregiver presumption that was, in theory, gender neutral but that in fact usually favoured the application of a mother for custody (see, for example, *R. v. R.,* 1983). Fathers' rights groups, however, frequently claim that many judges still operate on the basis of an unarticulated presumption in favour of mothers in custody cases.

Historically, for "illegitimate children" – those born "out of wedlock" – there was a presumption against the father having any rights or obligations, and children raised by "unwed mothers" were the subject of social prejudice and legal disadvantage. Although most Canadian statutes that govern parental rights were reformed in the 1970s and 1980s to give equal status to mothers and fathers, some laws continued to give mothers greater rights, in particular concerning children born out of wedlock. In 2003, the Supreme Court of Canada ruled unconstitutional a BC statute that denied fathers of children born out of wedlock the opportunity to register their paternity on the children's birth certificates and to share in naming their children without maternal consent (see *Trociuk v. British Columbia [Attorney General],* 2003). While the Supreme Court recognized that some fathers might forfeit their rights by not exercising them or that they could be denied these rights if the birth were the product of a rape, the Court held that it was discriminatory to presumptively treat all fathers of children born out of wedlock as unequal to mothers.

A Movement for Change

Fathers were traditionally relegated to the margins of their children's lives after separation with custody arrangements that tended to endorse the children living primarily with their mother. Fathers have become very vocal in no longer wishing to serve only in the role of visitor or "Disneyland Dad" in the lives of their children (Hallman, Dienhart, & Beaton, 2007).

Of current concern to organized father advocacy groups is the charge that the justice system discriminates against fathers, as well as the claim that children's rights and interests have suffered as a consequence (Boyd, 2006; Erera & Baum, 2009; Geldhof, 2003). The portrayal of fathers as victims of an unjust legal system that fails to provide true equality and opportunity to fathers has been a cornerstone of fathers' groups seeking a legal presumption of equal-time shared parenting in the event of separation (Geldhof, 2003; Kruk, 2008). This has resulted in a polarization, characterized as a "gender war zone" (Bala, 1999), with some of the advocacy groups for both fathers and mothers adopting entrenched positions to advance their claims. While often invoking a rhetoric that is couched in terms of the best interests of children, these advocacy efforts can often be seen as efforts to advance parental rights. Formulating how best to describe and address the changing roles of parenting can, at times, result in simplistic portrayals that fail to illuminate how complex these interactions are for fathers, mothers, and children. Collier and Sheldon (2006) articulate this complex reality:

> It is clear that describing the rise of the FRM [fathers' rights movement] in terms of a "backlash" to increased female power is, at best, a caricature which fails to capture the multifaceted, fast changing, complex realities of men's and women's experiences of family breakdown and shifting gender roles. The greater prominence of the FRM might be better understood as one aspect of a complex renegotiation of understandings of men's role as parent in the light of shifting gender relations, household forms, discourses of parenting and childhood, legal norms and modes of governance. (14)

The growing emphasis on fathers, and particularly fathers versus mothers, has been part of a wider trend since the mid-1990s, as fathers have increasingly demanded that the law and courts respond to their needs (Boyd, 2003, 2006). The call to treat fathers and mothers equally by allowing both parents to share the care of children equally often overpowers discussions about children's true rights and needs, past parenting practices, and the importance of men's labour-force attachment (Boyd, 2006).

Canada's 1998 Parliamentary Special Joint Committee on Child Custody and Access and its final report, *For the Sake of the Children,* sympathized with the plight of fathers and advocated a legislative presumption of "shared parenting," although exactly what this would entail was somewhat ambiguous. Successive federal governments, however, have resisted making changes to the Divorce Act or sanctioning presumptions for shared post-separation parenting (Bala, 1999; Boyd, 2000; Department of Justice Canada, 2002). The Province of Alberta is noteworthy for having enacted legislation changes in the form of the Family Law Act (2003), changes that have created a presumption that parents have joint guardianship, though this is not a presumption of equal shared care of children.

Some changes have been made, including the clear recognition of the option for parents to share custody. Furthermore, since 1986, the law has directed courts to be guided by the principle that a "child should have as much contact" with each parent as is "consistent with the best interests of the child"; in making custody orders, therefore, the courts are to take into consideration the willingness of each parent to "facilitate contact" with the other parent – dubbed the "friendly parent rule" per Subsection 16(10) of the federal Divorce Act. That both parents ought to be involved in their children's lives (except in cases of abuse or neglect) is now a well-established principle in Canadian courts (Cossman, 2001). It has been suggested that changing terms such as "custody" and "access" to a more inclusive focus on shared parenting and responsibility would alter the winner-versus-loser mentality associated with post-separation parenting (Department of Justice Canada, 2002). Ultimately, Canada's federal government decided not to change terminology, believing that such a change would not improve parental relationships (Cossman, 2001; Department of Justice Canada, 2002), though such changes in terminology have been made in the United Kingdom and in some American states.

Some of the discourse about the family justice system seems premised on the belief that legal processes offer parents the opportunity for truth seeking and that the end result of litigation will be an "unequivocally satisfying" determination of the child's best interests (Moloney, 2008, 44). Moloney (2008) suggests the impossibility of this outcome and advocates that a more realistic focus is establishing "good-enough decisions ... linked with appropriate and good-quality dispute resolution processes" (46). Even in the absence of formal legislative reform, the reality for an increasing number of separated parents has been a gradual trend toward a voluntary arrangement that recognizes a significantly greater role for fathers than occurred a quarter century ago and – for a growing number, but still a minority – some form of shared parenting or even father custody.

Despite these changes in practice, there continue to be efforts to change Canadian law to mandate presumptions for shared custody, such as the introduction of the Private Member's Bill C-422 in June 2009. While such a bill, without the endorsement of the government, is unlikely to be enacted, the persistence of such efforts speaks to the depth of ongoing efforts to seek changes in the attitudes and laws governing post-separation parenting.

High-Conflict Parents and Parental Alienation

One of the most challenging issues facing the family justice system is parents who are in high conflict with each other or engaged in behaviours that have been labelled "parental alienation." These parents are prone to anger, distrust, and an inability to focus on their children's needs as separate from their own; one or both parents engage in repeated litigation and uncooperative parenting to the detriment of their children (Lamb et al., 1997, 396). Over the last 20 years, the growing number of allegations of parental alienation, where one parent (usually the father) claims that the other parent has deliberately waged a campaign to turn their children against him, has garnered considerable attention and debate (Bala, Hunt, & McCarney, 2010). In some of these cases, a child may become alienated from a parent, rejecting that parent and resisting visitation not because of the child's own experiences but as a reflection of the hostile feelings and attitudes of an alienating parent (Fidler & Bala, 2010; Fidler, Bala, & Saini, 2012).

Fewer than 10% of separating families experience high conflict and bitter tug-of-wars over their children that are characterized by high levels of hostility, attempts to undermine the child's relationship to other parent, and repeated court applications. These cases, however, use a disproportionately large amount of court time and resources (Brownstone, 2009; Cossman, 2001). Mothers and fathers are equally likely to engage in this type of behaviour. Higher rates of mother-initiated parental alienation reflect the fact that mothers are much more likely to have primary care of children and hence to be able to influence their children, while fathers are more likely to make unsubstantiated allegations of parental alienation against custodial mothers. In many cases, children resisting visits with a non-custodial parent have been found to be "justifiably estranged" due to poor parental conduct, abuse, or inappropriate parenting (Bala et al., 2010).

Most families are able to make their own post-separation parenting arrangements with minimal or no professional assistance. Some families require significant legal or mediation services to arrive at a negotiated settlement. A minority of separated couples are highly engaged in conflict for a long period of time and may require intensive mediation, counselling, or legal services. Ultimately, even in the context of higher conflict, most parents come to a settlement regarding the care of their children without a full trial, although some of these parents will require several attendances in court, often to be told by the presiding judge that a settlement would be in the best interests of their children (Robinson, 2009).

Providing family justice services and supports is a social challenge. Resources are finite, and parents involved in high-conflict cases make disproportionate use of dispute resolution resources, both "free" (i.e., paid by the government) and those for which they must pay, and they often ignore the advice of lawyers, mediators, and judges to focus on the interests of their children and settle their disagreements.

Violence and Spousal Abuse

Canadian courts and legislatures have increasingly come to recognize that spousal abuse should be a significant factor in determining post-separation parenting arrangements (Bala, Jaffe, & Crooks, 2007). There is, however, also a growing awareness of the complexity of the issue of spousal violence. While men are much more likely to use violence to control and intimidate their spouses, and most victims of serious domestic violence and homicide are women, in a significant number of relationships, the violence between the spouses may be characterized as mutual.

Most reports of spousal violence to police and the courts are well founded: false denials of abuse by violent men are more common than false allegations by women (Jaffe, Johnston, Crooks, & Bala, 2008). However, in some cases, alleged victims, primarily women, make unfounded or exaggerated reports of spousal violence to the police in order to have their spouses arrested and removed from the home. With police policies and training now focusing on "wife abuse," women can sometimes manipulate the criminal justice system into effectively evicting a father from the home, often thereby severing his relationship with his children, at least until the matter can be resolved by the courts (Kruk, 2008).

Even when allegations of spousal abuse are well founded, it is necessary to take a multi-factoral approach to determining what implications a history of violence should have on post-separation parenting (Jaffe et al., 2008). In some cases, a violent man poses a continuing threat to his former partner and children, and contact must be terminated as safety planning becomes the main priority. Other cases may entail significant concerns about the possibility of intimidation or inappropriate parenting, and a father's visits with a child may need to be supervised. In some cases, however, there may have been only one or two acts of spousal violence, perhaps an assault occurring after the discovery of adultery; while such acts are crimes, if there is no likelihood of recurrence and the children are not frightened of their father, it may be appropriate for the father to have an active role in the lives of his children, perhaps even as the custodial parent.

Access and Enforcement

A major concern of fathers in Canada is the difficulty of enforcing access rights. This is exacerbated by the fact that most government agencies enforce child support orders on behalf of custodial parents (mainly mothers), but non-custodial parents (mainly fathers) are left on their own to try to enforce access rights or their allocated parenting time with their children. Fathers' rights groups sometimes distort the extent of the problem, but for non-custodial parents (usually men), being unfairly denied a relationship with their children can be very frustrating and emotionally upsetting. Although programs have been established to try to help separated parents to understand the importance of children having continued involvement with both parents after separation, significant problems with enforcing access remain unresolved (Bala et al., 2010).

Alberta's Family Law Act (2003) is the most explicit and detailed legislation in Canada for the enforcement of a parent's time with his or her children. The legislation provides for assistance from government agencies to locate a child and for imposition of monetary penalties on parents who deliberately interfere with visitation rights. While the reality for most fathers, even in Alberta, is that court enforcement of the right to have contact with a child can be a frustrating and expensive process, Canadian courts are starting to take access problems more seriously and, in appropriate cases, may change custody so that the child can live with a parent who will support the child's relationship with the other parent (Bala et al., 2010).

Child Support

The push for family law legal reforms in the 1990s was largely focused on child support and the introduction of the Federal Child Support Guidelines (SOR/97-175, as amended) (D. W. Allen, 2009; Millar & Gauthier, 2002). Child support is an important aspect of children's well-being, regardless of custody and visitation arrangement (Amato & Gilbreth, 1999). Despite its association with positive outcomes for children, child support continues to be one of the most contentious and frequently litigated issues facing separating parents (Hart Wensley, 2004/2005). Fathers have long bemoaned that the Canadian child support tables are too high and become particularly onerous if they have a new family to support. Mothers have long decried that child support amounts are much too low to reflect the true costs of raising children and that these rates also fail to reflect the labour costs, both direct (e.g., laundry, meal preparation, child care) and indirect (e.g., inability to accept more work hours because of child care responsibilities) (Altman, 2003).

The Federal Child Support Guidelines came into effect in Canada in 1997. The introduction of the guidelines was intended to achieve four objectives: (a) to establish fair standards of support, (b) to reduce conflict, (c) to improve the efficiency of the legal process and encourage settlement, and (d) to ensure consistent treatment of spouses and children who are in similar circumstances. Concerns about child poverty were at the forefront in the production of these guidelines (Millar & Gauthier, 2002).

Generally, when one parent has primary custody, child support will be established by reference to a table that sets the amount of child support payable, based solely on the payor's income and the number of children. Child support becomes more complicated and less formulaic if each parent has the child at least 40% of the time (shared physical custody); there are also provisions to allow for variation in the table amount to take account of undue hardship of the payor or special expenses of the recipient (Colman, 2004; Whitehead, 2010). Juby et al. (2005) report that most families are reaching a child support agreement relatively soon after separation and that payments are being made regularly and on time, suggesting that the guidelines are meeting the objective of reducing conflict.

The guidelines are not without their faults and critics (D. W. Allen, 2009; Colman, 2004). While the legislation states that they are premised on the principle that both parents have financial responsibility for their children, the calculation of child support amounts generally only takes into account the income of the payor parent (usually fathers). Furthermore, the calculations do a poor job of accounting for the expenses that fathers incur when they spend time with their children (Colman, 2004). The guidelines have faced other criticisms from fathers, including (a) that the actual costs associated with raising a child have not been well established, particularly for children of high-income parents; (b) that custodial parents are overcompensated for expenditures on children and are not required to account for payments received; and (c) that an increase in the income of the custodial parent or the expenses of the payor (for example, due to the birth of children with a new partner) generally does not affect the amount of child support payable (D. W. Allen, 2009; Millar & Gauthier, 2002).

Québec has a more "pro-father" model of child support guidelines – applicable to all cases in that province, including federal Divorce Act cases – that addresses some of the shortcomings of the federal guidelines. First, the calculation of support takes into account the incomes of both the payor and the payee. Second, for every 1% increase in access time (over 20%), there is a reduction in child support. Amounts of child support payable in Québec, however, tend to be somewhat lower than amounts payable in similar circumstances in other provinces.

Research substantiates what many lawyers and judges have long suspected – mothers and fathers view child support and access as interrelated (Lin & McLanahan, 2007) even though within the law, they are treated as separate and distinct (Brownstone, 2009). In other words, mothers tend to view child support as the price for child access, and fathers view payment of child support as the basis for their entitlement to see their children. The association between child support and father-child contact has been well established by research – the more contact fathers have with their children, the more likely they are to pay child support, and vice versa (Juby et al., 2007). An emphasis on financial provision, however, at the expense of time for nurturance and care, is problematic both for non-resident fathers who need opportunities to actively parent their children and for their children (Lamb et al., 1997).

Fathers can feel disenfranchised from the legal system and their ex-spouse when more emphasis is placed on their ability to provide than on their ability to nurture their children (Mandell, 2002). And, as discussed earlier, given extensive government services, such as provincial child support enforcement agencies that enforce payments and punish those who fail to comply, it is reasonable for fathers to expect that their time with their children will also be actively enforced with appropriate services and resources (Bala & Bailey, 2004/2005).

Fathers and Their Children: New Presumptions for Policy and Practice

The notion of legal presumptions for the custody of children has been advanced by fathers' rights advocates as a way to better provide for the care of a child after separation. At the forefront is a demand that family law legislation be reformed to mandate a rebuttable presumption for the shared physical custody of children. In other words, the starting point for all custody negotiations would assume the equal sharing of children, unless there are proven facts of abuse or violence that would rebut the presumption (Kruk, 2008). In our view, this approach to post-separation child care arrangements is short-sighted and plays more to parents longing for expediency and simplified notions of equality without giving due consideration to what benefits children the most, based on their wishes and developmental needs, the degree of co-operation or conflict between parents, and how children and families actually change following separation and divorce (McIntosh, 2009).

To date, Canadian law has rejected this presumptive approach, in part because of the lack of good research on shared custody and a recognition of the complexity and uniqueness of families. With this in mind, it is time to work toward a broader array of approaches to assist families and, in turn, fathers in a more concrete way. Canadian society and its family justice system should do the following:

- Find ways to help fathers overcome structural, cultural, and socio-political limitations to their involvement with children. Lack of father-only paternity leave and a strong cultural tie-in to the mandatory nature of work establish patterns of father-child relationships that have long-term implications both within and outside partnered families (Daly, Ashbourne, & Hawkins, 2008).
- Recognize that fathers should not be denied the opportunity to parent their children after separation merely because they have assumed the mantle of primary breadwinner (Maccoby, 2005). Fathers can be primary

166   *Denise L. Whitehead and Nicholas Bala*

caregivers for their children, and decision making about child care arrangements should be free of gender bias.

- Ensure that parents have access to appropriate legal services. An increase in self-represented litigants due to lack of personal financial resources and the inadequacy of legal aid schemes inhibits family courts from acting efficiently and compromises parents' access to appropriate family law justice (Brownstone, 2009).
- Continue to reject a presumption for shared parenting. That approach is too simplistic to reflect the realities of what happens in families and with children, and caters too easily to parents' notions of fairness with little regard to the effects on children and the flexibility needed to adapt to change (McIntosh, 2009; McIntosh & Chisholm, 2008; Whitehead, 2012). For most families, some form of shared post-separation parenting is preferable, but there should be caution about imposing this arrangement where there are concerns about violence, abuse, or manipulation of children.
- Provide more supports for parents to make parenting plans outside of courts – such as parent education, mediation, parent coordinators, and mental health supports – so that parents can work through their own solutions and decisions about their children, both at the time of separation and over time as family circumstances and children change (Bala, 2012; Brownstone, 2009; Emery, Otto, & O'Donohue, 2005).
- Provide mechanisms within the legal system that can identify high-conflict families as early in the process as possible to provide early case management by experienced judges as well as other supports and services to help facilitate satisfactory resolutions for parents and their children (Bala et al., 2010).
- Recognize that contact and preservation of a relationship between fathers and children is just as important as enforcing child support awards. Resources such as access enforcement, parenting education, and mental health services must be made available to fathers to support ongoing positive parent-child relationships (Ashbourne et al., 2012; Bala, 2012; Bala & Bailey, 2004/2005).

Conclusions

An increased focus on father involvement has brought about significant change in perspectives, expectations, and fathering behaviours over the last three decades. It should, therefore, come as no surprise that this would also translate into a changing vision of the separated/divorced father. Slowly, separated and divorced fathers are finding a place within the family justice system and society. While men make their own choices about whether to maintain an active and engaged role in their children's lives, and sometimes choose to remain uninvolved, legal and structural factors have influenced these choices. At times, fathers have been left at the margins of their children's lives. Most fathers are no longer content to be merely visitors in their children's lives; a focus on provision of child support payments as the principal post-separation role of fathers is no longer satisfactory. Social and legal change is slowly begetting a new reality of post-separation fathering – an increasing number of fathers have primary responsibility for the care of children and many more fathers enjoy joint or shared co-parenting of their children.

It is now generally agreed that an adversarial legal system that is seen to produce only winners and losers has many undesirable features. Although court involvement is sometimes necessary, children are the biggest losers when parents are unable to communicate with each other and find common ground that nurtures each parent's relationship with the child. Post-separation fathering has much diversity, and the family justice system is slowly responding to this reality in a way that recognizes the needs and well-being of children. For some children, highly involved fathers after separation will reflect highly involved father-child relations from the pre-separated family. In other cases, father involvement may be tenuous or absent, reflecting a multitude of issues, not all of which can be satisfactorily addressed in a court of law. Fathers are very important, whether separated or not. Providing supports and services that enable parents to reach a resolution and develop a co-parenting plan is critical. Motivating both parents to focus on the needs and experiences of their children is the central imperative. Quality of time with children must always take precedence over quantity of time, and our laws, policies, and programs and services must support fathers in their quest for positive involvement with their children.

References

Allen, D. W. (2009). *The anatomy of Canada's Child Support Guidelines: The effects, details, and history of a feminist family policy.* Unpublished manuscript, Simon Fraser University. Abstract retrieved from http://papers.ssrn.com/sol3/papers.cfm?abstract_id=1441607.

Allen, S., & Daly, K. (2007). *The effects of father involvement: An updated research summary of the evidence.* Guelph, ON: Centre for Families, Work and Well-Being. Retrieved from http://www.fira.ca/cms/documents/29/Effects_of_Father_Involvement.pdf.

Altman, S. (2003). A theory of child support. *International Journal of Law, Policy and the Family, 17*(2), 173-210.

Amato, P. R. (1993). Children's adjustment to divorce: Theories, hypotheses, and empirical support. *Journal of Marriage and Family, 55*(1), 23-38.

Amato, P. R. (2003). Reconciling divergent perspectives: Judith Wallerstein, quantitative family research and children of divorce. *Family Relations, 52*(4), 332-339.

Amato, P. R., & Afifi, T. D. (2006). Feeling caught between parents: Adult children's relations with parents and subjective well-being. *Journal of Marriage and Family, 68*(1), 222-235.

Amato, P. R., & Booth, A. (1996, May). A prospective study of divorce and parent-child relationships. *Journal of Marriage and the Family, 58,* 356-365.

Amato, P. R., & Cheadle, J. (2005). The long reach of divorce: Divorce and child well-being across three generations. *Journal of Marriage and Family, 67*(1), 191-206.

Amato, P. R., & Gilbreth, J. G. (1999). Nonresident fathers and children's well-being: A meta-analysis. *Journal of Marriage and the Family, 61*(3), 557-573.

Amato, P. R., Meyers, C. E., & Emery, R. E. (2009). Changes in nonresident father-child contact from 1976 to 2002. *Family Relations, 58*(1), 41-53.

Amato, P. R., & Sobolewski, J. M. (2001). The effects of divorce and marital discord on adult children's psychological well-being. *American Sociological Review, 66,* 900-921.

Ambert, A. M. (2009, November). Divorce: Facts, causes and consequences. Ottawa, ON: The Vanier Institute of the Family. Abstract retrieved from http://www.vanierinstitute.ca/modules/news/newsitem.php?ItemId=96

Ashbourne, L. M. (2006). Young fathers. In D. S. Lero, L. M. Ashbourne, & D. L. Whitehead (Eds.), *Inventory of policies and policy areas influencing father involvement* (pp. 75-79). Guelph, ON: Father Involvement Research Alliance.

Ashbourne, L. M., Whitehead, D. L., & Hawkins, L. (2012). *Orienting services to separated/divorced fathers: A conceptual framework.* Manuscript submitted for publication.

Bala, N. (1999). A report from Canada's "gender war zone": Reforming the child-related provisions of the divorce act. *Canadian Journal of Family Law, 16,* 163-227.

Bala, N. (2012). Reforming family dispute resolution in Ontario: Systemic changes & cultural shifts. In M. Trebilcock, A. Duggan, & L. Sossin (Eds.), *Middle income access to justice* (pp. 269-315). Toronto, ON: University of Toronto Press.

Bala, N., & Bailey, N. (2004/2005). Enforcement of access and alienation of children: Conflict resolution strategies and legal responses. *Canadian Family Law Quarterly, 23,* 1-61.

Bala, N., Hunt, S., & McCarney, C. (2010). Parental alienation: Canadian court cases 1989-2008. *Family Court Review, 48*(1), 164-179.

Bala, N., Jaffe, P., & Crooks, C. (2007). Spousal violence and child-related cases: Challenging cases requiring differentiated responses. *Canadian Family Law Quarterly, 27,* 1-113.

Baum, N. (2003). The male way of mourning divorce: When, what, and how. *Clinical Social Work Journal, 31*(1), 37-50.

Baum, N. (2006). Postdivorce paternal disengagement: Failed mourning and role fusion. *Journal of Marital and Family Therapy, 32*(2), 245-254.

Boyd, S. B. (2000). Can child custody law move beyond the politics of gender? *University of New Brunswick Law Journal, 49,* 157-168.

Boyd, S. B. (2003). *Child custody, law, and women's work.* Don Mills, ON: Oxford University Press.

Boyd, S. B. (2006). "Robbed of their families"? Fathers' rights discourses in Canadian parenting law reform processes. In R. Collier & S. Sheldon (Eds.), *Fathers' rights activism and law reform in comparative perspective* (pp. 27-51). Portland, OR: Hart Publishing.

Brownstone, H. (2009). *Tug of war: A judge's verdict on separation, custody battles, and the bitter realities of family court.* Toronto, ON: ECW Press.

Collier, R., & Sheldon, S. (2006). Fathers' rights, fatherhood and law reform: International perspectives. In R. Collier & S. Sheldon (Eds.), *Fathers' rights activism and law reform in comparative perspective* (pp. 1-26). Portland, OR: Hart Publishing.

Colman, G. C. (2004). Contino v. Leonelli-Contino: A critical analysis of the Ontario Court of Appeal interpretation of section 9 of the child support guidelines. *Canadian Journal of Family Law, 20,* 291-320.

Cossman, B. (2001). *An analysis of options for changes in the legal regulation of child custody and access* (2001-FCY-2E). Ottawa, ON: Department of Justice Canada.

Daly, K., Ashbourne, L., & Hawkins, L. (2008). Work-life issues for fathers. In K. Korabik, D. S. Lero, & D. L. Whitehead (Eds.), *Handbook of work-family integration: Research, theory, and best practices* (pp. 249-264). San Diego, CA: Elsevier Academic Press.

Department of Justice Canada. (2002). *Final federal-provincial-territorial report on custody and access and child support: Putting children first.* Ottawa, ON: Author.

Dienhart, A. (2001). Make room for daddy: The pragmatic potentials of a tag-team structure for sharing parenting. *Journal of Family Issues, 22*(8), 973-999.

Emery, R. E., Otto, R. K., & O'Donohue, W. T. (2005). A critical assessment of child custody evaluations. *Psychological Science in the Public Interest, 6*(1), 1-29.

Erera, I., & Baum, N. (2009). Chat-room voices of divorced non-residential fathers. *Journal of Sociology and Social Welfare, 36*(2), 63-83.

Family Law Act, R.S.A. Chapter F-4.5 (2003).

Fidler, B., & Bala, N. (2010). Children resisting post-separation contact with a parent: Concepts, controversies and conundrums. *Family Court Review, 48*(1), 10-47.

Fidler, B., Bala, N., & Saini M. (2012). *Children resisting postseparation contact: A differential approach for legal and mental professionals.* New York, NY: Oxford University Press.

Geldhof, B. (2003). The real love that dare not speak its name. In A. Bainham, B. Lindley, M. Richards, & L. Trinder (Eds.), *Children and their families: Contact, rights and welfare* (pp. 171-200). Portland, OR: Hart Publishing.

Gill, R. (2004). *Shared custody arrangements: Pilot interviews with parents* (Background Paper No. 2004-FCY-SE). Ottawa, ON: Department of Justice Canada. Retrieved from http://www.justice.gc.ca/eng/pi/fcy-fea/lib-bib/rep-rap/2004/2004_5/p2.html.

Hallman, M., Dienhart, A., & Beaton, J. (2007). A qualitative analysis of fathers' experiences of parental time after separation and divorce. *Fathering, 5*(1), 4-24.

Hart Wensley, K. (2004/2005). Shared custody – section 9 of the federal child support guidelines: Formulaic? pure discretion? structured discretion? *Canadian Family Law Quarterly, 23,* 63-123.

Hawkins, D. N., Amato, P. R., & King, V. (2007). Nonresident father involvement and adolescent well-being: Father effects or child effects? *American Sociological Review, 72,* 990-1010.

Jaffe, P., Johnston, J., Crooks, C., & Bala, N. (2008). Custody disputes involving allegations of domestic violence: The need for differentiated approaches to parenting plans. *Family Court Review, 46,* 500-522.

Juby, H., Billette, J., Laplante, B., & Le Bourdais, C. (2007). Nonresident fathers and children: Parents' new unions and frequency of contact. *Journal of Family Issues, 28*(9), 1220-1245.

Juby, H., & Le Bourdais, C. (1998). The changing context of fatherhood in Canada: A life course analysis. *Population Studies, 52*(2), 163-175.

Juby, H., Le Bourdais, C., & Marcil-Gratton, N. (2003). *Linking family change, parents' employment and income, and children's economic well-being: A longitudinal perspective* (Research No. 2003-FCY-2E). Ottawa, ON: Department of Justice Canada.

Juby, H., Le Bourdais, C., & Marcil-Gratton, N. (2005a). *Moving on: The expansion of the family network after parents separate.* Ottawa, ON: Department of Justice Canada. Retrieved from http://www.justice.gc.ca/eng/pi/fcy-fea/lib-bib/rep-rap/2005/2004_9/index.html.

Juby, H., Le Bourdais, C., & Marcil-Gratton, N. (2005b). Sharing roles, sharing custody? Couples' characteristics and children's living arrangements at separation. *Journal of Marriage and Family, 67*(1), 157-172.

Juby, H., Marcil-Gratton, N., & Le Bourdais, C. (2005). *When parents separate: Further findings from the national longitudinal survey of children and youth* (No. 2004-FCY-6E). Ottawa, ON: Department of Justice Canada.

Kruk, E. (1994). The disengaged noncustodial father: Implications for social work practice with the divorced family. *Social Work, 39*(1), 15-25.

Kruk, E. (2008). *Custody, access and parental responsibility: The search for a just and equitable standard.* Guelph, ON: Father Involvement Research Alliance. Retrieved from http://www.fira.ca/cms/documents/181/April7_Kruk.pdf.

Lamb, M. E. (2000). The history of research on father involvement: An overview. *Marriage and Family Review, 29*(2-3), 23-42.

Lamb, M. E., Sternberg, K. J., & Thompson, K. A. (1997). The effects of divorce and custody arrangements on children's behavior, development, and adjustment. *Family and Conciliation Courts Review, 35,* 393-404.

Le Bourdais, C., Juby, H., & Marcil-Gratton, N. (2001). *Keeping contact with children: Assessing the father/child post-separation relationship from the male perspective* (CSR-2000-3). Ottawa, ON: Department of Justice Canada.

Lewis, J., & Welsh, E. (2005). Fathering practices in twenty-six intact families and the implications for child contact. *International Journal of Law in Context, 1*(1), 81-99.

Lin, I., & McLanahan, S. S. (2007). Parental beliefs about nonresident fathers' obligations and rights. *Journal of Marriage and Family, 69*(2), 382-398.

Maccoby, E. E. (2005). Editorial: A cogent case for a new child custody standard. *Psychological Science in the Public Interest, 6*(1), i-ii.

Mandell, D. (2002). *"Deadbeat dads": Subjectivity and social construction.* Toronto, ON: University of Toronto Press.

Manning, W. D., Stewart, S., & Smock, J. (2003). The complexity of fathers' parenting responsibilities and involvement with nonresident children. *Journal of Family Issues, 24,* 627-644.

Marshall, K. (2006). Converging gender roles. *Perspectives on Labour and Income, 7*(7), 5-17. Statistics Canada – Catalogue no. 75-001-XPE.

Marsiglio, W., Day, R. D., & Lamb, M. E. (2000). Exploring fatherhood diversity: Implications for conceptualizing father involvement. *Marriage and Family Review, 29*(4), 269-293.

Marsiglio, W., & Hinojosa, R. (2007). Managing the multifather family: Stepfathers as father allies. *Journal of Marriage and Family, 69*(3), 845-862.

McIntosh, J. E. (2009). Legislating for shared parenting: Exploring some underlying assumptions. *Family Court Review, 47*(3-4), 389-400.

McIntosh, J., & Chisholm, R. (2008). Cautionary notes on the shared care of children in conflicted parental separation. *Journal of Family Studies, 14*(1), 37-52.

Milan, A., Vezina, M., & Wells, C. (2007, September). *Family portrait: Continuity and change in Canadian families and households in 2006 census* (Catalogue No. 97-553-XIE). Ottawa, ON: Statistics Canada.

Millar, P., & Gauthier, A. H. (2002). What were they thinking? The development of child support guidelines in Canada. *Canadian Journal of Law and Society, 17*(1), 139-162.

Moloney, L. (2008). The elusive pursuit of Solomon: Faltering steps toward the rights of the child. *Family Court Review, 46*(1), 39-52.

Moyer, S. (2004). *Child custody arrangements: Their characteristics and outcomes* (2004-FCY-3E). Ottawa, ON: Department of Justice Canada.

R. v. R., 34 R.F.L. (2d) 277 (Alta.C.A.) (1983).

Rhoades, H. (2002). The "no contact mother": Reconstructions of motherhood in the era of the "new father." *International Journal of Law, Policy and the Family, 16,* 71-94.

Robinson, P. (2009). Parenting after separation and divorce: A profile of arrangements for spending time with and making decisions for children. *Juristat, 29*(4), 1-16.

Rotermann, M. (2007). Marital breakdown and subsequent depression. *Statistics Canada: Health Reports, 18*(2), 33-44.

Schmeeckle, M. (2007). Gender dynamics in stepfamilies: Adult stepchildren's views. *Journal of Marriage and Family, 69,* 174-189.

Scott, M. E., Booth, A., King, V., & Johnson, D. R. (2007). Postdivorce father-adolescent closeness. *Journal of Marriage and Family, 69*(5), 1194-1209.

Special Joint Committee on Child Custody and Access. (1998). *For the sake of the children: Report of the Special Joint Committee on Child Custody and Access.* Ottawa, ON: Department of Justice Canada.

Swiss, L., & Le Bourdais, C. (2009). Father-child contact after separation: The influence of living arrangements. *Journal of Family Issues, 30*(5), 623-652.

Talsky v. Talsky, 2 S.C.R. 292 (1976).

Trociuk v. British Columbia (Attorney General), 1 S.C.R. 835, 2003 SCC 34 (2003).

Whitehead, D. L. (2006). Separated and divorced fathers. In D. S. Lero, L. M. Ashbourne, & D. L. Whitehead (Eds.), *Inventory of policies and policy areas influencing father involvement* (pp. 105-113). Guelph, ON: Father Involvement Research Alliance.

Whitehead, D. L. (2010). Divorcing parenting from child support: Justice and care in the discourse of the rights and responsibilities of shared custody. *Fathering, 8*(2), 147-162.

Whitehead, D. L. (2012). *The shared custody experience: The adult child's perspective on transitions, relationships and fairness* (Doctoral dissertation). Retrieved from http://hdl.handle.net/10214/3595.

8
Fathering within Child Welfare

Susan Strega, Leslie Brown, Elizabeth Manning, Christopher Walmsley, Lena Dominelli, and Marilyn Callahan

Although there is much talk about the "involved father" in popular culture and considerable recent research exploring the role of fathers in child development, this increased attention to fathers seems to have had little impact in child welfare. "Fathering within Child Welfare" is the title of a multi-year research project funded by the Social Sciences and Humanities Research Council (SSHRC) that set out to understand this conundrum through examining child welfare practice, policy, and discourse with fathers whose children have come to the attention of child welfare authorities. We employed a variety of research strategies, including a quantitative study of child protection files (Strega et al., 2008); individual interviews with fathers (Strega, Brown, Callahan, Dominelli, & Walmsley, 2009); a review of policies, practices, and discourses (Brown, Callahan, Strega, Walmsley, & Dominelli, 2009a); and focus group interviews with child welfare social workers and support workers.

Our findings confirm that child welfare often fails to engage purposefully with fathers, either as risks or assets, and instead holds mothers responsible for most aspects of family functioning, including managing the behaviour of fathers. Child welfare law, policy, and discourse support these practices. Our research suggests that three major factors are at play: deeply entrenched child welfare traditions of engaging only with mothers; child welfare and contingent policies that foster father invisibility; and race and class biases about men. In this chapter, we explore these matters in two ways. First, we provide a description and critical analysis of the Canadian child welfare system with particular attention to matters of race, class, and gender. Second, we present the experiences of fathers with child welfare from their perspective. We conclude by discussing how child welfare systems and practices might usefully be changed.

Understanding the Context

Child Welfare in Canada

In Canada, child welfare services are designated as the responsibility of provinces and territories. These governments set the legislative framework and control the service delivery system, including protection services and support resources. In some Canadian jurisdictions (Ontario, for example), the government contracts with non-governmental organizations for the delivery of child protection services, while in other jurisdictions (British Columbia, for example) child protection is provided directly by government employees. In some provinces and territories, Indigenous child welfare authorities complement non-Indigenous services, with both operating under the same child welfare legislation. "Child protection" usually refers to the investigation and disposition of complaints of child maltreatment, while "child welfare" encompasses a broader array of support services and resources such as parent education. Most non-statutory services are provided through contractual relationships with non-government agencies, which are often considered part of the child protection system because they perform significant roles in monitoring and assessing families who come to the attention of protection authorities.

Although every jurisdiction in Canada has its unique child protection legislation and service delivery system, all Canadian child welfare laws reflect a shared ideology. Within this ideology, child maltreatment is explained as the result of the dysfunction of individual parents separate from the influence of structural, environmental, or historical conditions. While dysfunction was once ascribed to immorality, it is now more commonly explained as the result of psychological deficiencies, though as Swift and Callahan (2009) point out, concerns about immorality infuse current psychological explanations. Parents are understood to have an individual responsibility to care for, supervise, and protect their children, and if they fail to carry out this responsibility to the standard inscribed in law and policy, the state has an obligation to intrude into the private sphere of the family. This obligation is framed by the doctrine of *parens patriae* that historically, and currently, informs all Canadian child welfare legislation. Parens patriae, Latin for "protector" or "father of the people," allows the state to act as a substitute parent when doing so is in the best interests of the child (MacIntyre, 1993). Decisions to intrude are rationalized through referencing the "best interests of the child" standard enshrined in all Canadian child welfare legislation, though as Swift and Callahan note, these best interests are to be safeguarded individually and not through state commitments to adequately support or resource families. The notion of "personal responsibility" is now common throughout Canadian social policy (Swift, 2001), and rather than redressing an increasing gap between the rich and the poor, both federal and provincial governments have eliminated or reduced social spending and income security measures that might reduce child and family poverty (Banting, 2005). Concurrently, the concept of "risk" has become a fundamental organizing principle in child welfare, and most jurisdictions use some form of actuarial measurement such as risk estimation to assess family functioning and to justify state intervention (Swift & Callahan, 2009). These assessment processes exclude any consideration of systemic or structural factors, and view child protection through legal and judicial lenses rather than as the responsibility of governments and communities.

In Canada, the provision of resources and supports to families is generally contingent on a finding that a child has been or is likely to be harmed. However, in many European countries (for example, France and Sweden), child welfare systems are oriented to preserving and resourcing families and to collaborative rather than investigative processes (Cameron, Freymond, Cornfield, & Palmer, 2007). Indigenous people across Canada envision a similarly supportive and community-based system but have been largely constrained from implementing their ideas by the child welfare laws under which most Indigenous services operate (Mandell, Clouston Carlson, Fine, & Blackstock, 2007). The French and Swedish systems operate within a framework of universal income guarantees, extensive daycare provision, and a wide range of family support measures. When court systems are involved, the emphasis is usually on reaching a collaborative agreement with the family, including which supports the community or state might provide.

Race and Class Dimensions
Although theoretically any family might be involved with child welfare, child welfare interventions are, and always have been, disproportionately aimed at families already marginalized by race and poverty (Blackstock, Trocmé, & Bennett, 2004; Lindsey, 2003; Roberts, 2002; Swift, 1995). In particular, poor single-mother-led families and Indigenous children and families are vastly overrepresented in Canadian child welfare caseloads (Trocmé et al., 2005).

At present, there are three times as many Indigenous children in care today as there were at the height of the operation of residential schools in the 1940s (Mandell et al., 2007). It is estimated that across Canada, 38% of children currently in care (approximately 25,000 of 66,000) are Indigenous although Indigenous children constitute only 5% of the Canadian child population (Blackstock, 2009). Colonization and ongoing colonialism have created significant losses for Indigenous peoples in Canada, including, to name but a few, land, children, language, and spiritual practices (Bellefeuille & Ricks, 2003; Youngblood Henderson, 2000). Although the rest of Canadian children were historically viewed as dependent on their families, Indigenous children were denied this right through residential schools and the child welfare system, which "pathologized individual Aboriginal mothers and their families as deficient" (Thobani, 2007, 123).

Poverty is also significantly implicated in determining which families get caught up in child protection processes, and in Canada, it has increased markedly among both the working poor and families receiving social assistance over the last few decades (Banting, 2005). At 15.1%, Canada's child poverty rate is higher than average for Western industrialized democracies, ranking 13th among the 17 countries measured (Conference Board of Canada, 2009). The poverty rate for Indigenous children (40%) is more than twice that for non-Indigenous children (Silver, 2007). Members of other non-white groups also have a much higher likelihood of being poor: the incidence of poverty for members of these groups is double that for the Canadian population at large (Galabuzi, 2006, cited in Silver, 2007).

As the 2003 Canadian Incidence Study (Trocmé et al., 2005) demonstrates, determinations of child neglect are closely intertwined with poverty. Interpretations of the CIS-2003 data note that disproportionate poverty among Indigenous peoples leads to disproportionate numbers of investigations and substantiations of neglect (Trocmé et al., 2006). During the five-year period between 1998 and 2003, the number of substantiated neglect cases almost doubled (Trocmé et al., 2005). In the CIS-2003, 24% of all children experiencing substantiated maltreatment were reported to be living in families relying on benefits, employment insurance, or social assistance; only 41% of those experiencing neglect lived in homes where a caregiver had full-time employment (Trocmé et al., 2005). As in 1998, CIS-2003 found that children who experienced substantiated maltreatment of any kind were more frequently reported to reside in a home with a lone parent at the time of the investigation (39% lone female, 4% lone male; Trocmé et al., 2005).

Race and poverty are implicated in father exclusion in child welfare in a number of ways. Indigenous people and people of colour are significantly overrepresented among Canadians receiving welfare (Mirchandani & Chan, 2007), a phenomenon that Galabuzi (2001) relates in part to racial bias on the part of prospective employers. Low welfare rates coupled with severe penalties for those accused of welfare fraud lead to fathers hiding their presence and contributions in order to maintain benefits that provide for their children. Because welfare legislation defines spouse much more broadly than it is defined in other national and provincial legislation, mothers are cautious about mentioning any contributions, financial or otherwise, from fathers or other involved men. This serves to decrease men's support and contact with children. Welfare policies also lack provision for poor noncustodial fathers to maintain adequate space and resources to remain involved with their children, as rates are determined based on the number of children in the home or the size of the family unit, and children rarely reside with the father. The notion that providing for and financially supporting one's family determines whether a father is a "good father" continues to be pervasive among fathers, mothers, and service providers (Hauari & Hollingworth, 2009). While poverty does not disqualify men from being fathers, it influences how they are perceived by child protection workers and how they perceive themselves. Immigrant and refugee fathers, in particular, sometimes absent themselves from their families because they experience a lack of efficacy as parents in the Canadian context (Ali, 2008).

Indigenous mothers sometimes fail to identify the fathers of their children because they and their children are adversely affected by their children's loss of benefits under the Indian Act if the father does not have status under the act (M. Mann, 2005). Between 1985 and 1999, nearly one in five children born to registered Canadian Indians had no paternity designated (Clatworthy, 2004), a situation that is particularly serious given that in many Canadian provinces, Indigenous children make up more than half of the children in state care. Colonization disrupted the traditional roles of Indigenous fathers, and ongoing colonial practices continue to impact these men. Genocidal and assimilationist practices such as residential schools and the "Sixties Scoop," and their intergenerational sequelae, mean that many Indigenous men grow up without father figures or positive male role models (Manahan & Ball, 2007).

In contrast to the populations they serve, those who intervene with poor, Indigenous, and otherwise marginalized families are disproportionately white and middle class. Social location differences between child protection workers and clients are remarkable. The most recent extant survey reveals that workers are 94% white, 80% female, 97% English-speaking (i.e., English being their primary language), 70% between the ages of 26 and 44, and only 2% Indigenous (Fallon, MacLaurin, Trocmé, & Felstiner, 2003, 45). While these differences do not necessarily lead to the exclusion of Indigenous or visible minority fathers, racial and class disproportionality in who comes to the attention of child welfare authorities and how they are responded to is well documented (Ferguson & Hogan, 2004; Lavergne, Dufour, Trocmé, & Larrivée, 2008; Maiter, 2009).

Gender Dimensions
Concerns about the role of fathers in child development (Lamb & Tamis-LeMonda, 2004) and whether fathers have rights to ongoing contact with their children in cases of family breakdown (R. Mann, 2003) have had little impact in child welfare, where gender inequity is extensive. Our research, described below, along with that of others, confirms this observation (Strega et al., 2008). We reviewed a sample of child protection files dated between 1997 and 2005 from a child welfare authority in a mid-sized Canadian city to see how and if fathers were present and described. We assessed the type, purpose, and quantity of contacts with fathers, deliberately using a very

generous definition of "contact" in order to establish whether workers viewed the fathers as assets, risks, combinations of asset and risk, or irrelevant. We included all men attached to a family whether or not they were biological fathers. Contact of any sort with fathers was rare and occurred most often when the father was seen as an asset. In 52% of the cases, fathers were seen as irrelevant.

In common with most other Canadian jurisdictions, the province from which we drew our sample uses the gender-neutral term "parent" throughout its child welfare legislation and policy. Yet it appears that workers persistently read "parent" as "mother" and consistently regarded the mother as the presumptive parent. For example, despite policy instructing workers to interview alleged abusers, workers contacted fathers considered to be a risk to children only 40% of the time. Every "parenting capacity assessment" we found on file concerned itself solely with the mother even when a father was actively engaged in parenting. In situations where children were headed for permanent state care, child welfare authorities advised fathers to "get a lawyer" if they were interested in being custodial parents. This instruction reflects what Smart and Neale (1999) characterize as the responsibilities/rights division at the heart of child welfare: mothers have responsibilities (to physically and emotionally care for and protect their children) while fathers have rights (to access and visitation and possibly to custody).

While there are options available to workers who want to place children with fathers, such as making a temporary placement (declaring that the father's residence is a "place of safety," for example), workers rarely pursued these options. Those few fathers who ended up with custody did so serendipitously rather than through any effort on the part of child welfare authorities. Similarly, when fathers were violent toward children and/or mothers, workers expected mothers, but not fathers, to behave "protectively," often requiring mothers to leave the relationship or have their children apprehended under "failure to protect" clauses, even though child welfare legislation in most jurisdictions allows workers to apply for a restraining order (sometimes called a "protective intervention order") against any adult who might endanger a child.

Our findings accord with those of Coohey and Zang (2006) and Mayer, Dufour, Lavergne, Girard, & Trocmé (2003), who note that even when children have two parents, investigations into child neglect tend to focus solely on mothers' behaviours and responsibilities. Child protection workers engage with mothers and ignore fathers and father figures even when fathers are the identified source of the family's difficulties (Bancroft & Silverman, 2002; Nixon, 2001; Scourfield, 2003; Strega, 2006). Mothers are held to be at fault when children are physically or sexually assaulted by a father or father figure (Radhakrishna, Bou-Saada, Hunter, Catellier, & Kotch, 2001) and are required to act protectively in ways that are defined by the state (Krane, 2003). As

Sullivan, Juras, Bybee, Nguyen, and Allen (2000) note, child protection assessment and intervention focus on the "availability" of mothers and their parenting skills, while "assailants and fathers of the children have been virtually ignored" (590).

The introduction of "failure to protect" as the overarching lens through which child welfare views violence in the home has exacerbated both mother blaming and father exclusion. Since 1993, all Canadian jurisdictions have added "failure to protect," in some form or another, as a specific category of concern requiring child protection investigation and intervention. In six of 10 Canadian provinces, the failure to protect a child from being exposed to domestic violence is considered by itself to be sufficient grounds for finding that a child is in need of protection by child welfare authorities. In other jurisdictions, "failure to protect" is considered evidence of psychological or emotional abuse that could result in such a finding (Nixon, Tutty, Weaver-Dunlop, & Walsh, 2007). Similarly, clauses specific to sexual abuse by a father or father-figure require authorities to assess a mother's "ability" and "willingness" to protect the child (Krane, 2003).

These policies affect mothers and fathers disproportionately (Alaggia, Jenney, Mazucca, & Redmond, 2007). In 90% of domestic violence cases referred to child welfare, mothers are victims of the violence; in 8%, other adult family members are involved; and in 2%, the victims are fathers (Lavergne, Chamberland, Laporte, & Baraldi, 2003). In Canada, approximately one third of substantiated child maltreatment investigations involve some form of exposure to domestic violence, and 70% of investigations are substantiated (Black, Trocmé, Fallon, & MacLaurin, 2006; Lawson et al., 2006). Investigations can and often do result in children's removal from their homes and from the care of the "non-offending parent," usually a mother (Neilson, 2001). Although fathers are cast as protectors and providers in popular culture, when violence in the home is the concern, child welfare rarely positions fathers in these roles, nor are fathers considered potential resources or responsible for ensuring children's safety and well-being.

Explaining the Exclusion of Fathers

Father absence in child welfare is complex and not entirely accounted for by race, class, and gender factors. While poor fathers may voluntarily absent themselves from contact in the knowledge that mothers receive more money from welfare if they are not involved, they may also absent themselves in part from a sense of inability or failure to fulfill the basic Anglo-American cultural role available to men – that of economic provider to the family. Indigenous and visible minority men caught up in child welfare face both systemic racism and the racist beliefs held by social workers (Bernard Thomas & Este, 2005; Mussell, 2005; Roer-Strier, Strier, Este, Shimoni, & Clarke, 2005). Some fathers may believe that it is the mother's fundamental duty to care for the child and that such caring work is optional for men. Child protection workers collude with and foster these beliefs. Along with Scourfield (2003) and Swift (1995), we noted in our research the presence of what Scourfield describes as a "gendered occupational discourse" in child welfare work that supports avoiding men (Brown et al., 2009a). McKinnon, Davies, and Rains (2001), whose interest in fathers resulted from their research with adolescent teenage mothers, described among service providers three dominant and sometimes overlapping constructions of the men in these mothers' lives: men as violent and irresponsible, men as romantic attachments, and men involved in fathering. Similarly, Scourfield described six constructions of men in child welfare discourse: men as a threat, men as no use, men as irrelevant, men as absent, men as no different from women, and men as better than women. In the midst of these discourses, the space for engaging with men as fathers or potential fathers is small.

The Experiences of Fathers

As part of our research project, we set out to understand fathering within child welfare from the standpoint of fathers. Participants were recruited through fathering programs, advertising, and word of mouth. We conducted 11 qualitative interviews with fathers in two provinces. Our relatively small sample is congruent with existing disproportionalities in Canadian child welfare caseloads (Lavergne et al., 2008) in that a disproportionate number (5) were Indigenous and 10 of the 11 fathers were poor, with welfare benefits being the primary source of income for most. We did not interview any visible minority fathers. At the time of the interviews, the fathers ranged in age from 24 to more than 50 years old. All of the Indigenous fathers and some of the white fathers had been in state care for some part of their childhoods. All but one father had past or present problems with substance misuse. Five fathers had been incarcerated. All but two fathers had an educational level of Grade 8 or less. Four fathers had custody and full-time care of their children at the time of the interview, and those fathers who did not have children in their care were actively seeking, either on their own or together with the children's mother, to resume caring for their children.

Elsewhere, we report on our narrative analysis of the father interviews (Strega et al., 2009). For this chapter, we returned to these interviews and encoded the information into themes, using thematic analysis methods recommended by Luborsky (1994) and Braun and Clarke (2006). We generated initial codes, sorted the codes into potential themes, reviewed and refined emerging themes, defined and named each theme, and analyzed for subthemes within them. Finally, we chose examples intended to capture the essence of each theme. Two major themes emerged: see me, see the complexities; and work with me, not at me.

See Me, See the Complexities

Fathering within child welfare is complicated. Many men whose children have child welfare involvement are the cause of that involvement because of their violence or their substance misuse. Some have to learn how to be fathers in the absence of positive role models or past experience with caring for their children. All of the fathers we interviewed, including those without custody, were striving to be involved in their children's lives in positive ways. They wanted their potential and positive contributions to be recognized.

See Me as a Potential Parent

Time and again, the fathers described how they were overlooked by child welfare, at least initially, as viable parents. Some fathers were not contacted when their children were taken into care. Others were directed to use the court system to gain access to and custody of their children. The fathers we interviewed wanted to be seen by child welfare workers equally with mothers as potential parents. They wanted to be seen as individuals with strengths, parenting skills, supports, love for their children, and potential to grow as fathers. Len is an Indigenous father whose two older children, a son and a daughter, had been lost to the child welfare system.[1] When he had another daughter in a new relationship, he saw a second chance to be a father. His drinking and violence toward the child's mother interfered with his aspirations, but when the baby was taken from the mother because of her drinking, he wanted to demonstrate that he could be a custodial parent even though his history of violent behaviour complicated that possibility: "Assault and assault with a weapon, that makes me a high-risk father right off the bat, you know, so nobody wanted to deal nothing with me or anything else ... Now I got to prove, I got to prove." He was also discouraged from parenting because he was a father:

> Everybody was telling me, "Oh, no, you leave that to the mother," but she didn't have a mother. All she had was me. If I would have left it to her mother, she would still be, where would she be now? ... Nobody wanted me to do it. Nobody thought I could do it ... "How are you going to look after a baby?"

In rare situations, it was the social worker who saw a father as a possible parent despite the complications of violence and substance misuse. Bill, an Indigenous father of two girls, was visited in jail by a worker who wanted to explore his ability to become the sole parent of the youngest girl when that child was apprehended from her mother:

> [The child protection worker] asked me, "You know, would you be, would you want to be the father?" "Well I am the father," I told her. "But would

you want to take care of her?" While I was in jail, I was having visits with the baby ... They'd [worker and baby] come once a week or so.

Bill accepted the worker's challenge to make himself into a viable parent:

I had to learn fast. I grew up in a hurry. Like, I had to. My social life went down the drain 'cause I had no time for other people ... I quit drinking. I quit smoking ... I took a ton of parenting programs. I got a lot of support through agencies.

All the fathers interviewed commented on a father's role in supporting his children financially, suggesting that they were aware that the provider role continues to be the pervasive and positive role available to fathers in child welfare. Many fathers wrestled with and rejected a narrow definition of "provider" and opted for a more diverse range of fathering roles including nurturer, role model, caregiver, homemaker, concerned parent, learner, and so on. The fathers wanted to be seen as complex individuals occupying many roles, including attending to their children's hearts, minds, and souls. How fathers see themselves and the roles available to them significantly impacts how they father. The fathers in our research simultaneously resisted and felt bound by dominant fathering ideas. David – an Indigenous father with one child in state care, two children in the care of his former partner, and two daughters he was raising with his current partner – observed that "being a father isn't always about money. It's about how you love your children. How you show them this world. How you show them values and things ... Fathering is about teaching, supporting, guiding, and leading."

See Me as I Am Now
Fathers were diverse in terms of the extent to which they recognized the effects of their substance misuse and violence. Some denied that they were perpetrators of violence or significantly minimized the effects of their violence, even when it was extensively documented and they had been convicted of assault. Others were reflective about their roles in family violence and described how they had changed. Many fathers articulated that they felt as if they were only seen in past negative roles: for example, as substance abusers, perpetrators of violence, or deadbeat dads. All were trying to shrug off negative stereotypes and wanting to be seen in other ways. Because child welfare relies extensively on file documentation and workers change frequently, violence or substance misuse easily become immortalized as a father's identity. Andy, a young white father with full-time custody of his daughter, was questioned frequently by workers about an assault he committed when he was 16:

But does that make me violent towards my daughter? My daughter's never been in the hospital in the six years I've had her. She's soon to be six ... perfectly healthy little girl. She's flying through kindergarten, top of her class, so I mean nobody can challenge what I'm doing, you know, but I've been challenged and I've been attacked [by workers].

Fathers with histories of childhood abuse were concerned that workers would assume they would be violent with their own children. David made a conscious and deliberate choice to avoid the child welfare workers monitoring his family because "I'm scared that they're going to say, 'Well, he's no good' ... you know, if they look at my file. Oh, this and that, and oh, he's garbage." Fathers were also conscious of and concerned about child welfare biases. David's choice to not be seen by workers also related to his Indigeneity: "Who am I? I'm just another low-grade Indian or Métis or whatever, however I look." Some of the Indigenous fathers we interviewed spoke explicitly of the need to "act white" in order to be seen positively. Eddie, an Indigenous custodial father of three who had extensive dealings with child welfare, explained, "I need to behave like a Caucasian person."

Several of the fathers we interviewed described an experience of seeing themselves – coming face-to-face with "the man in the mirror" – as an essential part of their fathering journey. This experience moved them to take responsibility for their actions as part of being the best father they could be. Gerald, a non-custodial Indigenous father with six children in his care, most of them affected by fetal alcohol syndrome, commented that he felt bad "because it's my fault, too, the alcohol and not being there that much for them. But I'm here, I'm there now for them. They realize that I'm making changes." Jack, an Indigenous father raising six children on his own, acknowledged that "I had to work on myself first ... My children believe in me and I like that they believe in me. I want them to see me as a role model for them that I don't need alcohol in my life. I hope they see it that way too."

See the Ways I Am Making Family
Making family in the child welfare context is challenging. When children have been apprehended at birth or as babies, fathers may become full-time custodial parents with little previous experience in caregiving. Fathers have to manage relationships with child welfare workers and support workers, and sometimes with non-custodial mothers. Shortly after he received custody, Bill ran into his daughter's mother but was afraid of the impact that taking her home to visit their daughter might have: "You want to see her, you can see her, you can talk to her, you can hold her, you can do whatever, but you're not going to tell her that you're her mom and then take off and you don't come back again."

Sometimes children remain in care and fathers must accomplish their fathering in unconventional ways. Although all of Gerald's children were in permanent care, he and his partner continued to see themselves as parents: "We raised them [our children], through the phone or through visits." He was preparing for the day when the children would age out of care and be old enough to return home: "The only chance that we have of being a family is only when our older girls come in or when our grandchildren are coming in."

The fathers we interviewed drew from diverse supports, resources, mentors, and models to develop their own fathering methods and skills. Rather than trying to get child welfare out of his family's life, Eddie welcomed them in as if they were part of his extended family, able to play important roles in supporting him and his children: "I never told [child welfare] to go away. I said I need help here. I'm a single man. I've got kids here that are alcohol affected."

In some jurisdictions, child protection is moving away from adversarial responses to more collaborative work with families and the inclusion of extended family and community supports. For example, Walker (2010) reports on the success of a strengths-based approach that used positive influences in fathers' existing networks. Family development response and family group conferencing (sometimes known as family group decision making) can play important roles, especially for violent fathers, in assisting fathers to build their communication skills, work with people in authority in a more conciliatory way, and develop their own ways of being accountable. Some of the fathers we interviewed had benefited from these processes. Jack believed that the family group conference was instrumental in him becoming the custodial parent:

> The one reason why I think they never really went against me was because of the family group conferencing that we went through and all the people that were involved ... I didn't ever once try to lie to them or say anything to try to impress them ... I put my trust in the family conferencing.

Work With Me, Not at Me

"Work with me" distinguishes an approach to working with fathers that focuses on supporting and guiding rather than the judging and ruling encompassed by "work at me." We also use the phrase "work with me" to denote concepts of humility and listening to fathers. Most of the fathers we interviewed had experienced both approaches and, like Bill, distinguished between them. The phrase is, in fact, taken from our interview with Bill, who contrasted the styles of two different child protection workers. He described his first worker thus: "She's not against me. She's with me. That's the good thing about it ... It's caring instead of business-like caring where you have to care. She wants to care." He contrasted this with his experience with his second worker:

I have to prove to her of what I can do ... She doesn't want to work with me, she wants to work at me ... I don't feel comfortable talking to her. I figure if I tell her something, she writes it all down and then she uses it against me, which the other one [previous worker] would understand why I'm doing the stuff I'm doing.

Jumping Through Hoops

Fathers involved in child welfare are required to participate and engage with processes such as attending parenting classes, submitting to drug and alcohol testing, meeting with child protection workers, and undergoing various forms of treatment. These activities serve to verify that these men are indeed fathers or can be made into suitable fathers in the eyes of the state. The fathers we interviewed were aware of the importance of following child welfare's instructions. Isaac, a white father who had custody of his daughter after a long and rancorous battle with child welfare authorities, described some of the requirements:

I was there with my baby. I had my visits. I went every week. I was going to work at the time, so I was taking time off work and everything to come down and get my visits in with baby and stuff like that. In the meantime, they had me take – I had to go for anger management. I had to go for better parenting, better fathering. Oh jeez, I can't remember what else now. But anyhow, they wanted all these things.

Gerald commented on the futility of challenging child welfare's requirements: "It's like we can't argue with the agreements that they give us 'cause if we don't take it, then that's our problem. It's like we have no say."

Collaboration and Support

Working with fathers who have been neglectful or violent requires compassion and support along with clear boundaries and encouragement to take responsibility for their behaviour so that they might shift it, see the effects, and cultivate hope that they can be different. Jack, an Indigenous father whose family had all been forced into residential schools, made the additional point that workers had to put a father's behaviour in context: "Most of the social workers, they don't understand where you're coming from, and that is where it has to start. You have to understand where that person is coming from and where that person has been before you go and judge them on what they do now."

Several research participants had attended a specific support program and articulated how the empathetic but challenging connection offered was critical in their transformation and personal growth as fathers. Workers in this agency engaged in specific strategies to build trust with fathers who had been violent, including asking lots of questions, avoiding overwhelming fathers with information, allowing men to talk or be silent, validating their feelings, and allowing other fathers in the group to challenge their thinking. Len graduated from this agency's program for violent fathers and was now participating as a volunteer. He articulated the program's philosophy clearly:

> You've got to help someone and you can't help them by telling them what to do all the time. You can't help someone by saying, "Well, you are doing this bad." You've got to help someone by saying, you know, "Well, okay, we'll come with you. We'll be there together. I'll be there. If you're having difficulty with this let me know. I'll be there and I'll help you."

Moving Toward Father-Inclusive Practice

Failing to engage fathers in child welfare potentially deprives mothers and children of supports and resources, and potentially fails to protect mothers and children. It excludes men who may have significant contributions to make as fathers or who can become full-time custodial fathers when the alternative is state care. The fathers we interviewed did not want child welfare to ignore the risks they represented but to engage directly with them about these matters and support them in being the best fathers they could be. The advantages of addressing men's violence are clear. Fleming (2007), reviewing Australian research, documents an increase in positive outcomes for both mothers and children when workers hold men responsible for their violence. Salisbury, Henning, and Holdford (2009) administered questionnaires to more than 2,500 men in fathering roles who had been convicted of intimate partner assault. Although two thirds of the men exposed children to their violence, most believed it did not affect the children. Alternatively, Rothman, Mandel, and Silverman (2007) administered questionnaires to 464 fathers who had, on average, participated in 14 weeks of batterer intervention. A significant majority of these fathers (73% of biological fathers and 69% of social fathers) expressed concern about the impact of their violence on children. The current lack of focus on fathers in child welfare is not inevitable nor is it, as we have illustrated, absolute. During our focus group interviews with child protection teams, we were struck by the great variability in practice with fathers: some protection workers almost never engaged with fathers while others routinely sought them out, a finding echoed in Stanley, Miller, Foster, and Thomson's (2011) review of 46 UK child protection cases involving violent fathers. This suggests that the attitudes and beliefs that protection workers hold may be the most significant factors in predicting father inclusion, a finding supported in our interviews with fathers.

When the child protection gaze shifts to include fathers, it must include fathers in all of their complexity. The process of becoming a father in child welfare is not linear or singular, especially for men marginalized by race and class. Assessing the risk or danger that a particular father poses in the moment, or posed in the past, must be accompanied by support for change efforts (Perel & Peled, 2008; Scott & Crooks, 2004). As Featherstone, Rivett, and Scourfield (2007, 3) contend, "We should not approach work with men on the assumption that we are dealing with men as a risk or a resource, a perpetrator or a victim. Either/or should be replaced with both/and." Some jurisdictions provide advice to workers about how to engage fathers (Minnesota Department of Human Services, 2009), and some recent publications from the UK (see Ferguson & Hogan, 2004; Rivett, 2009) specifically address practice with violent fathers. Groves, Van Horne, and Lieberman (2007) and Brown, Strega, Dominelli, Walmsley, & Callahan (2009b) offer concrete ideas for revamping child welfare practices with these fathers. Relatively new practices in the Anglo-American child welfare paradigm such as family group conferencing and family development response can also support the *both/and* approach.

At the same time, seeing fathers (and mothers) wholly in terms of dangers and deficits continues to be reinforced by current child protection assessment procedures and processes (Swift & Callahan, 2009). Positive, engaged fathering in child welfare can best be supported by shifting away from the current individualized and investigatory paradigm toward Indigenous and other holistic perspectives because these approaches are based in the paradigm of community caring (Cameron et al., 2007) that we consider essential to transforming child welfare. We advocate this in concert with other researchers (see, for example, Featherstone et al., 2007; Ferguson & Hogan, 2004) whose work about vulnerable and/or marginalized men demonstrates how engaging fathers can strengthen families. We suspect that many fathers, like those we interviewed, are eager for child welfare to move away from mother-blame and into father-inclusive practice. In the words of one father:

These people need to start opening up their eyes a little bit more and looking at our perspective, our point of view, instead of always judging the woman ... This old-fashioned thinking doesn't get you nowhere but old-fashioned thinking. You want to fix your 1960s automobile, well, great, go ahead. You're not going to find no parts for it ... Vehicles, just like people, change. (Ken)

Note

1   All names are pseudonyms.

References

Alaggia, R., Jenney, A., Mazucca, J., & Redmond, M. (2007). In whose best interest? A Canadian case study of the impact of child welfare policies in cases of domestic violence. *Journal of Brief Therapy and Crisis Intervention, 7*(3), 1-16.

Ali, M. (2008) Loss of parenting self-efficacy among immigrant parents. *Contemporary Issues in Early Childhood, 9*(2), 148-160.

Bancroft, L., & Silverman, J. (2002). *The batterer as parent.* Thousand Oaks, CA: Sage.

Banting, K. (2005). Do we know where we are going? The new social policy in Canada. *Canadian Public Policy, 31*(4), 421-29.

Bellefeuille, G., & Ricks, F. (2003). A pathway to restoration: From child protection to community wellness. *Journal of Native Social Work, 5,* 23-43.

Bernard Thomas, W., & Este, D. (2005). Resiliency and young African Canadian males. In M. Ungar (Ed.), *Handbook for working with children and youth: Pathways to resilience across cultures and contexts* (pp. 433-454). Thousand Oaks, CA: Sage.

Black, T., Trocmé, N., Fallon, B., & MacLaurin, B. (2006). The Canadian child welfare system response to exposure to domestic violence investigations (CECW Information Sheet #39E). Toronto, ON: University of Toronto, Faculty of Social Work.

Blackstock, C. (2009). The occasional evil of angels: Learning from the experiences of Aboriginal peoples and social work. *First Peoples Child and Family Review, 4*(1), 28-37.

Blackstock, C., Trocmé, N., & Bennett, M. (2004). Child maltreatment investigations among Aboriginal and non-Aboriginal families in Canada: A comparative analysis. *Violence against Women, 10*(8), 901-916.

Braun, V., & Clarke, V. (2006). Using thematic analysis in psychology. *Qualitative Research in Psychology, 3,* 77-101.

Brown, L., Callahan, M., Strega, S., Walmsley, C., & Dominelli, L. (2009a). Manufacturing ghost fathers: The paradox of father presence and absence in child welfare. *Child and Family Social Work, 14,* 25-34.

Brown, L., Strega, S., Dominelli, L., Walmsley, C., & Callahan, M. (2009b). Engaging fathers in child welfare practice. In S. Strega and S. A. Esquao (Eds.), *Walking this path together: Anti-racist and anti-oppressive practice in child welfare* (pp. 238-256). Halifax, NS: Fernwood.

Cameron, G., Freymond, N., Cornfield, D., & Palmer, S. (2007). Positive possibilities for child and family welfare: Moving beyond the Anglo-American child protection paradigm. In G. Cameron, N. Coady, & G. Adams (Eds.), *Moving toward positive systems of child and family welfare: Current issues and future directions* (pp. 1-78). Waterloo, ON: Wilfrid Laurier University Press.

Clatworthy, S. (2004). Unstated paternity: Estimates and contributing factors. In J. P. White, P. Maxim, and D. Beavon (Eds.), *Aboriginal policy research: Setting the agenda for change* (Vol. 2, pp. 225-244). Toronto, ON: Thompson Educational Publishing.

Conference Board of Canada. (2009). *How Canada performs: Child poverty.* Retrieved from http://www.conferenceboard.ca/HCP/Details/society/child-poverty.aspx.

Coohey, C., & Zang, Y. (2006). The role of men in chronic supervisory neglect. *Child Maltreatment, 11*(1), 27-33.

Fallon, B., MacLaurin, B., Trocmé, N., & Felstiner, C. (2003). The Canadian incidence study of child abuse and neglect: A profile of a national sample of child protection workers. In K. Kufeldt & B. MacKenzie (Eds.), *Child welfare: Connecting research, policy and practice* (pp. 41-52). Waterloo: Wilfrid Laurier University Press.

Featherstone, B., Rivett, M., & Scourfield, J. (2007). *Working with men: Theory and practice in health and social welfare.* London, England: Sage.

Ferguson, H., & Hogan, F. (2004). *Strengthening families through fathers: Developing policy and practice in relation to vulnerable fathers and their families.* Waterford, Ireland: Waterford Institute of Technology, Centre for Social and Family Research.

Fleming, J. (2007). "If we get the mums and kids in we are doing well": Father absence in the context of child welfare, a review of the literature. *Children Australia, 32*(3), 13-20.

Galabuzi, G. (2001). *Canada's creeping economic apartheid: The economic segregation and marginalisation of racialised groups*. Toronto, ON: Centre for Social Justice Foundation for Research and Education.

Groves, B., Van Horne, P., & Lieberman, A. (2007). Deciding on fathers' involvement in their children's treatment after domestic violence. In J. Edleson & O. Williams (Eds.), *Parenting by men who batter: New directions for assessment and intervention* (pp. 65–84). New York, NY: Oxford University Press.

Hauari, H., & Hollingworth, K. (2009). Understanding fathering: Masculinity, diversity and change. London, England: Joseph Rowntree Foundation. Retrieved from http://www.jrf.org.uk/sites/files/jrf/understanding-fathering-diversity-full.pdf.

Krane, J. (2003). *What's mother got to do with it? Protecting children from sexual assault*. Toronto, ON: University of Toronto Press.

Lamb, M. & Tamis-LeMonda, C. (2004). The role of the father. In M. E. Lamb (Ed.), *The role of the father in child development* (4th Ed.) (pp. 1-31). Hoboken, NJ: John Wiley.

Lavergne, C., Chamberland, C., Laporte, L., & Baraldi, R. (2003). *Domestic violence: Protecting children by involving fathers and helping mothers* (CECW Information Sheet #6E). Montreal: Institut de recherche pour le développement social des Jeunes and Université de Montréal.

Lavergne, C., Dufour, S., Trocmé, N., & Larrivée, M. C. (2008). Visible minority, Aboriginal, and Caucasian children investigated by Canadian protective services. *Child Welfare, 87*(2), 59-76.

Lawson, A., Gardiner, S., Johansson, B., MacLaurin, B., Giray, E., & Crockford, T. (2006). *Addressing the effects of child maltreatment through the lens of domestic violence* (CECW Research in Brief #1). Toronto, ON: Faculty of Social Work, University of Toronto. Retrieved from http://dev.cwrp.ca/publications/651

Lindsey, D. (2003). *The Welfare of Children* (2nd ed.). New York, NY: Oxford University Press.

Luborsky, M. (1994). The identification and analysis of themes and patterns. In J. F. Gubrium & A. Sankar (Eds.), *Qualitative methods in aging research* (pp. 189-210). Thousand Oaks, CA: Sage.

MacIntyre, E. (1993). The historical context of child welfare in Canada. In B. Wharf (Ed.), *Rethinking child welfare in Canada* (pp. 13-36). Toronto, ON: Oxford University Press.

Maiter, S. (2009). Race matters: Social justice not assimilation or cultural competence. In S. Strega & S. A. Esquao (Eds.), *Walking this path together: Anti-racist and anti-oppressive child welfare practice* (pp. 62-77). Halifax, NS: Fernwood.

Manahan, C., & Ball, J. (2007). Aboriginal fathers support groups: Bridging the gap between displacement and family balance. *First Peoples Child and Family Review, 3*(4), 42-49.

Mandell, D., Clouston Carlson, J., Fine, M., & Blackstock, C. (2007). Aboriginal child welfare. In G. Cameron, N. Coady, & G. Adams (Eds.), *Moving toward positive systems of child and family welfare: Current issues and future directions* (pp. 115-160). Waterloo, ON: Wilfrid Laurier University Press.

Mann, M. (2005). *Indian registration: Unrecognized and unstated paternity*. Ottawa, ON: Status of Women.

Mann, R. (2003). Violence against women or family violence? In L. Samuelson & W. Antony (Eds.), *Power and resistance: Critical thinking about Canadian social issues* (pp. 41-64). Halifax, NS: Fernwood.

Mayer, M., Dufour, S., Lavergne, C., Girard, M., & Trocmé, N. (2006). Structures familiales, paternité et négligence: Des réalités à revisiter. *Revue de psychoéducation, 35*(1), 157-181.

McKinnon, M., Davies, L., & Rains, P. (2001). Taking account of men in the lives of teenage mothers. *Affilia, 16*, 80-99.

Minnesota Department of Human Services. (2009). *Working with fathers: A program improvement resource*. Retrieved from http://edocs.dhs.state.mn.us/lfserver/Legacy/DHS-5575A-ENG.

Mirchandani, K., & Chan, W. (2007). *Criminalizing race, criminalizing poverty: Welfare law enforcement in Canada*. Halifax, NS: Fernwood.

Mussell, B. (2005). *Warrior-caregivers: Understanding the challenges and healing of First Nations men*. Ottawa, ON: Aboriginal Healing Foundation.

Neilson, L. (2001). *Spousal abuse, children and the legal system: Final report for Canadian Bar Association Law for the Futures Fund.* Fredericton, NB: Muriel McQueen Fergusson Centre for Family Violence Research, University of New Brunswick.

Nixon, K. (2001). *Domestic violence and child welfare policy: An examination of Alberta's child welfare legislation and the impact on child welfare practice.* Unpublished master's thesis, University of Calgary, Calgary, AB.

Nixon, K., Tutty, L., Weaver-Dunlop, G., & Walsh, C. (2007). Do good intentions beget good policy? A review of child protection policies to address intimate partner violence. *Children and Youth Services Review, 29*(12), 1469-1486.

Perel, G., & Peled, E. (2008). The fathering of violent men: Constriction and yearning. *Violence against Women, 14*(4), 457-482.

Radhakrishna, A., Bou-Saada, I. E., Hunter, W. M., Catellier, D. J., & Kotch, J. B. (2001). Are father surrogates a risk factor for child maltreatment? *Child Maltreatment, 6*(4), 281-289.

Rivett, M. (2009). Working with violent male carers (fathers and stepfathers). In B. Featherstone, C.-A. Hooper, J. Scourfield, and J. Taylor (Eds.), *Gender and child welfare in society* (pp. 195-222). London, England: John Wiley.

Roberts, D. (2002). *Shattered bonds: The color of child welfare.* New York, NY: Basic Books.

Roer-Strier, D., Strier, R., Este, D., Shimoni, R., & Clarke, D. (2005). Fatherhood and immigration: Challenging the deficit theory. *Child and Family Social Work, 10,* 315-329.

Rothman, E. F., Mandel, D. G., & Silverman, J. G. (2007). Abusers' perceptions of the effect of their intimate partner violence on children. *Violence against Women, 13,* 1179-1191.

Salisbury, E., Henning, K., & Holdford, R. (2009). Fathering by partner-abusive men: Attitudes on children's exposure to interparental conflict and risk factors for child abuse. *Child Maltreatment, 14*(3), 232-242.

Scott, K., & Crooks, C. (2004). Effecting change in maltreating fathers: Critical principles for intervention planning. *Clinical Psychology: Science and Practice, 11*(1), 95-111.

Scourfield, J. (2003). *Gender and child protection.* Houndmills, England: Palgrave MacMillan.

Silver, J. (2007). Persistent poverty and the promise of community solutions. In L. Samuelson & W. Antony (Eds.), *Power and resistance: Critical thinking about Canadian social issues* (pp. 182-214). Halifax, NS: Fernwood.

Smart, C., & Neale, B. (1999). *Family fragments?* Cambridge, England: Polity Press.

Stanley, N., Miller, P., Foster, H. R., & Thomson, G. (2011). A stop–start response: Social services' interventions with children and families notified following domestic violence incidents. *British Journal of Social Work, 41*(2), 296-313.

Strega, S. (2006). Failure to protect? Child welfare interventions when men beat mothers. In R. Alaggia & C. Vine (Eds.), *Cruel but Not Unusual: Violence in Canadian Families* (pp. 237-266). Waterloo, ON: Wilfrid Laurier University Press.

Strega, S., Brown, L., Callahan, M., Dominelli, L., & Walmsley, C. (2009). Working with me, working at me: Fathers' narratives of child welfare. *Journal of Progressive Human Services, 20,* 72-91.

Strega, S., Fleet, C., Brown, L., Dominelli, L., Callahan, M., & Walmsley, C. (2008). Connecting father absence and mother blame in child welfare policies and practices. *Children and Youth Services Review, 30*(7), 705-716.

Sullivan, C., Juras, J., Bybee, D., Nguyen, H., & Allen, N. (2000). How children's adjustment is affected by their relationships to their mothers' abusers. *Journal of Interpersonal Violence, 15*(6), 587-602.

Swift, K. (1995). *Manufacturing "bad mothers": A critical perspective on child neglect.* Toronto, ON: University of Toronto Press.

Swift, K. J. (2001). The case for opposition: Challenging contemporary child welfare policy directions. *Canadian Review of Social Policy, 47,* 59-76.

Swift, K., & Callahan, M. (2009). *At risk: Social justice in child welfare and other human services.* Toronto, ON: University of Toronto Press.

Thobani, S. (2007). *Exalted subjects: Studies in making of race and nation in Canada.* Toronto, ON: University of Toronto Press.

Trocmé, N., Fallon, B., MacLaurin, B., Daciuk, J., Felstiner, C., Black, T., ... Cloutier, R. (2005). *Canadian Incidence Study of Reported Child Abuse and Neglect – 2003: Major findings*. Ottawa, ON: Minister of Public Works and Government Services Canada.

Trocmé, N., MacLaurin, B., Fallon, B., Knoke, D., Pitman, L., & McCormack, M. (2006). *Mesnmimk Wasatek, catching a drop of light. Understanding the overrepresentation of First Nations children in Canada's child welfare system: An analysis of the Canadian incidence study of reported child abuse and neglect (CIS-2003)*. Toronto, ON: Centre of Excellence for Child Welfare.

Walker, L. (2010). "His mam, my dad, my girlfriend, loads of people used to bring him up": The value of social support for (ex) offender fathers. *Child and Family Social Work, 15*(2), 238–247.

Youngblood Henderson, J. S. (2000). Postcolonial ghost dancing: Diagnosing European colonialism. In M. Battiste (Ed.), *Reclaiming Indigenous voice and vision* (pp. 57-76). Vancouver, BC: UBC Press.

9

The Experiences of Fathers of a Child with a Chronic Health Condition: Caregiving Experiences and Potential Support Interventions

John Beaton, David Nicholas, Ted McNeill, and Lisa Wenger

Over the last decade, research has clearly shown that fathers who are actively involved with their children play an important role in their children's development (see Allen, Daly, & Ball, this volume; Doherty, Kouneski, & Erikson, 1998; Pleck & Masciadrelli, 2004). However, the majority of this research has been conducted with families whose children do not have chronic health conditions and/or developmental delays. This is problematic, considering that about 4% of Canadian families have a child with some type of disability (Statistics Canada, 2007). Families who have a child with a disability often have different parenting experiences and encounter more stressful life events than do families without a child with a disability (Beckman, 1991; Dyson, 1997; Pelchat, Lefebvre, & Levert, 2007). Research involving heterosexual couples has shown that although mothers and fathers of children with disabilities tend to experience similar levels of stress (Pelchat et al., 2007), the respective types of stress may vary. Thus, fathering a child with a health condition appears to be a unique experience (Katz, 2002; Vrijmoet-Wiersma et al., 2008), warranting specific investigation and targeted policy and program support.

In the past, research with parents of children with disabilities tended to focus on mothers' perspectives while largely ignoring fathers' perspectives. Similarly, fathers generally receive less consideration or support from the health care system (Sterken, 1996) since mothers tend to be the primary caregivers who attend the majority of health care appointments (Brody & Simmons, 2007). Health care professionals may incorrectly assume that fathers are too busy, disinterested, or incompetent to care for the needs of a child with a chronic health condition. However, recent research with fathers in Canada consistently shows that many fathers today are extensively involved in the lives of their children (McNeill, 2004). With respect to their masculine identity and role, McNeill (2007) observed that fathers of children with chronic health conditions often "transcend traditional male stereotypes and embrace the opportunity for a more intimate and involved style of parenting" (409).

In this chapter, we examine the experiences of Canadian fathers who have a child with a chronic health condition within the larger context of the family system. Although there has been a growing interest among clinicians and researchers in the experience of fathering a child with conditions including arthritis, diabetes, cancer, heart disease, and cerebral palsy, the research to date is limited. To a certain extent, the voices of fathers with a child with a chronic health condition have been absent in the literature (or have been heard through mothers' voices), and subsequently, few studies of interventions for fathers exist. This speaks to a prevailing gap in terms of fatherhood-based research and adds to the critique that research guiding family-centred care is largely unbalanced in terms of omitting a member of the family – fathers.

In addressing this gap, this chapter aims to summarize and critically analyze research to date regarding these fathers' experiences. In addition to attempting to improve our understanding of the experience and role of fathers and the pursuit of ameliorative supports for fathers, we introduce several broad interventions that may offer appropriate and useful support for families. We begin with a general discussion about how a child with a chronic health condition impacts the entire family system. Most of the literature regarding children with chronic health conditions focuses only on the mother-child dyadic relationship, while excluding fathers' experiences and ignoring family system dynamics. Next, we summarize literature specifically about the experiences of fathers of children with chronic health conditions. Finally, we review the very few existing interventions for such fathers and make suggestions for future interventions.

Impact of Pediatric Chronic Health Conditions on Families

A diagnosis of a pediatric chronic health condition may be a life-changing experience for the child and her/his family, potentially affecting not only the child but also dyadic and triadic relationships within the family (e.g., parent-child, sibling, co-parenting, and couple relationships). For some families, diagnosis can be devastating, while for others, diagnosis and illness can serve as an impetus for growth and resilience. Diagnosis and illness can, for example, be a catalyst for parents to become involved differently in the care of their child; however, while some parents may become more involved, others may become less involved (Berge & Holm, 2007; Boss, 1999). There is little research that examines mechanisms that act as catalysts or deterrents for parental involvement or growth during child illness.

During the period of diagnosis and subsequent transition, family members may experience significant role ambiguity. Boss's (1999) concept of "ambiguous loss" is often discussed in relation to issues of physical suffering. Ambiguous loss is a stressful life event that can produce high levels of anxiety and continual stress, which can immobilize families. Boss identifies two types of ambiguous loss: (a) when someone is physically present but psychologically absent, and (b) when someone is psychologically present but physically absent. For example, when a child is diagnosed with a chronic illness, it may seem as though part of that child is psychologically absent yet physically present, or vice versa. Boss uses the term *boundary ambiguity* to refer to how individuals and families perceive an ambiguous loss event. Boundary ambiguity involves not knowing who is "in" or "out" of the family, or what role each family member now plays as a result of changing life events. When a child is diagnosed with a chronic illness, both the child and the family experience tremendous uncertainty and boundary ambiguity about their present and future, and about what might happen if the illness is terminal (Berge & Holm, 2007). Often, family members experience different types of ambiguity according to the nature and phase of the illness. Furthermore, mothers and fathers may have different experiences of managing and coping with a child's chronic health care issue and with their experience of role ambiguity and stress. Frequently, boundary ambiguity and stress in these families can lead to an increase in marital conflict, anxiety, and depression.

In addition to the psychological impacts on families with children with a chronic health condition, families can experience significant financial, work, school, and community challenges (Cashin, Small, & Solbert, 2008; Pelchat et al., 2007). Parents of a chronically ill child often have to quit their jobs or reduce their work hours, resulting in lowered income. At the same time, they may be dealing with an increase in costs associated with some therapy services for their child that are not covered by health care plans. It may also be challenging for parents to find appropriate community programs and school settings for their child. All of these challenges can potentially leave families feeling isolated and overwhelmed. Moreover, differing access to private insurance plans, coverage schemes, or other resources may leave poorer families at risk of receiving fewer or less timely services, with potentially debilitating impacts for these less financially advantaged families.

Fathers' Experiences of Parenting a Chronically Ill Child

There is increasing acceptance among Canadian researchers and health care providers not only that fathers' lives are profoundly impacted by their child's diagnosis of chronic illness but also that they may have *qualitatively different* experiences compared to those of mothers (see Cashin et al., 2008; McNeill, 2004; Nicholas, Gearing, et al., 2009; Pelchat et al., 2007). In their review of the international literature from 1980 to 2005, Pelchat and colleagues (2007) found that amidst some similarities, men and women tend to report different sources of stress and use diverse adjustment strategies when faced with a child's health condition. These differences are briefly explored here. The primary focus in the following discussion is on Canadian studies although other key studies are also included.

Sources of Stress

Although mothers generally assume greater responsibility for daily caregiving responsibilities for their child with a chronic illness (Hovey, 2005; Pelchat et al., 2007), research shows that fathers are also actively involved in maintaining family stability and care. In Canadian studies, fathers have often described themselves as providers, protectors, sources of strength, supports to their partners and ill child, and, in some families, the primary caregiver for the healthy children in the family (McNeill, 2004; Nicholas, Gearing, et al., 2009; Pelchat et al., 2007). Although literature comparing mothers and fathers indicates a range of differences and similarities in levels of distress (Pelchat et al., 2007), some trends have emerged. Specifically, women tend to report higher levels of parental stress related to higher caregiving expectations and the associated physical and emotional demands, while the stress reported by fathers tends to be related to the quality of their attachment to their child, a desire for normalcy for the family, limited time alone with their partner, and their ability to provide financially (Pelchat et al., 2007).

These trends in the literature are illustrated vividly in the findings of qualitative researchers seeking an understanding of fathers' experiences. In a study of men fathering a child with cancer, Nicholas, Gearing, and colleagues (2009) reported stories of devastation and efforts at managing the emotive elements associated with fears about an unknown and potentially precarious future for the child, as well as demonstrations of resilience in the face of that intensive and prolonged threat. The investigators found that fathers often struggled with concern for the future of their ill child and the needs of their healthy children. They reported role confusion and loss as they worried about their ability to remain productive at work and to fulfill their assumed roles of family provider and protector, and they struggled with a loss of connection with their partner as energies were focused toward the child and away from the partnership.

This ongoing sense of worry resonates with research from Cashin and colleagues (2008) and McNeill (2004), who found that fathers of ill children experienced uncertainty, boundary ambiguity, and an ever-present concern about their child's day-to-day safety, as well as fears about his or her medical and personal future (see also Goble, 2004). Fathers sought to balance these anxieties with a desire to enable a "normal" life for their child (Brody & Simmons, 2007; Cashin et al., 2008; Hovey, 2005; McNeill, 2004). Stressors for fathers have been found to shift over time from uncertainty before diagnosis, to the diagnosis and condition-specific learning, to developing competency and integrating the condition into daily life. (For findings on the phases of parental coping with a chronically ill child, see Cashin et al., 2008; Vrijmoet-Wiersma et al., 2008.)

Although most fathers are emotionally impacted by their child's illness (Brody & Simmons, 2007), research indicates that fathers feel an obligation to present themselves as physically and emotionally strong for the stability of their family, even when they feel weak (McNeill, 2004; Nicholas, Gearing, et al., 2009). Fathers may be reflecting traditional expectations of masculinity, such as stoicism and strength (McNeill, 2007) and a desire to serve as a protector in times of heightened stress, a response deemed by some fathers as "natural" (McNeill, 2004). As Nicholas, Gearing, and colleagues (2009) explain, many fathers allow themselves "little justification to grapple with and express their emotions, rendering them emotionally vulnerable and largely unsupported in their sorrow and pain" (266). With few acceptable outlets for their emotions, fathers can experience a sense of isolation as they struggle privately (McNeill, 2004). Thus, a father's distress can operate at two levels: first, his response to the difficulties posed by the situation, and second, his efforts to manage his emotional response.

Adjustment and Coping

In addition to detailing differences in terms of perceived stressors, Pelchat and colleagues (2007) found that fathers and mothers also tend to use different coping strategies. Although fathers experience acute emotional responses to their child's condition, they are less likely than mothers to discuss these openly or to report the use of emotional coping strategies (Pelchat et al., 2007). Instead, seeking to present themselves as a source of strength for the family, men are likely to use strategies of self-support and are more likely than women to employ avoidance strategies (McNeill, 2004; Nicholas, Gearing, et al., 2009; Pelchat et al., 2007). Both fathers and mothers tend to rely on behavioural strategies (including information gathering) and social supports, although men tend to be less likely to access the support of family and friends, or to solicit help from health professionals (Pelchat et al., 2007).

Self-support strategies can include pragmatic, action-oriented efforts to focus on what can be controlled or changed (e.g., the physical environment, one's own health) as well as cognitive efforts to maintain a positive attitude (Brody & Simmons, 2007; Cashin et al., 2008; McNeill, 2004; Nicholas, Gearing, et al., 2009; Pelchat et al., 2007). A spirit of pragmatism is evidenced in efforts men make to focus on what they can control or alter as they seek to bring normalcy to their child's life (McNeill, 2004). As illustrated by Cashin and colleagues (2008) in their study of fathers of children with asthma, men manifest ongoing concern for their child's safety by implementing physical changes in the home and modifying family activities in an effort to reduce or control triggers. In his study of fathers of children with juvenile rheumatoid arthritis, McNeill (2004) found that fathers prided themselves on their efforts to "just deal with it" (537). This emphasis on practicality and self-sufficiency is illustrated by a father in the study by Cashin and colleagues, who observed, "It's a part of life. So you have to say, 'Fine. That's the cards that were dealt to me'" (381).

Fathers' cognitive attempts to "adapt" and, in some cases, focus on the "silver lining" have been framed as an expression of spiritual or philosophical belief, a search for meaning in the experience, and as a direct attempt to balance a perceived negative outlook held by their partner (McNeill, 2004; Nicholas, Gearing, et al., 2009). As a father in McNeill's (2004) study described, "My wife and I have arguments, and there are times that my wife has negative thoughts, and I try to convince her to look at the positive side of it" (536). This suggestion of relational and positive-oriented coping efforts has also been identified by Benn and McColl (2004), who found that parents tend to use complementary coping strategies and seek to accommodate different approaches that enable equilibrium in the relationship.

Recent research examining the ways in which mothers and fathers co-construct their parenting roles has contributed to our understanding of the couple as a unit. McNeill, Nicholas, Beaton, and Montgomery (2008) propose the concepts of "complementarity" and "symmetry" to explain how parents organize themselves. Complementarity refers to arrangements in which each parent has distinct, specialized roles with little overlap between parents, while symmetry applies to situations where parenting roles are more shared and the parents work together as a "tag team" with considerable overlap of what each does to provide care for their child. It is not an either/or prospect for most parents; in fact, most parents are neither complementary nor symmetrical but combine aspects of both approaches according to their skills, preferences, and/or availability. Complementarity and symmetry can be expressed as a continuum. Understanding individual parenting behaviour partly as a reflection of the context in which it occurs rather than solely as an expression of individual character is a more informative and richer way of understanding complex processes and parenting arrangements.

Utilization of Support
Despite increasing attention to the experiences of fathers of children with health conditions, there remains a lack of research focused specifically on the development and evaluation of paternal-oriented supports and resources. At least two issues are at play in fathers' use of supports related to their child's illness: their comfort in soliciting support and their access to effective and relevant services.

Turning first to solicitation, although fathers have been shown to place high value on connections with friends, family, and health providers as they seek to obtain information, reframe their situation, and continue moving forward amidst the challenges associated with parenting an ill child (Brody

& Simmons, 2007; Cashin et al., 2008; Nicholas, Gearing, et al., 2009), re-search indicates that in general, men tend to make more limited use of formal support services for a range of needs (Addis & Mahalik, 2003). In explaining this general pattern of reluctance, researchers often emphasize the social construction of masculinity, particularly the prioritization of stoicism, self-reliance, and denial of vulnerability (Smith, Braunack-Mayer, & Wittert, 2006). The nature of these dynamics are largely unknown in terms of the specific construction of fathers' caregiving identity, but patterns of avoiding or delaying help-seeking have been observed in relation to men's experiences with a range of physical and emotional challenges, including stressful life events (Addis & Mahalik, 2003; Moller-Leimkuhler, 2002). In addition, little research has been conducted on how best to encourage men's use of support services (Robertson, Douglas, Ludbrook, Reid, & van Teijlingen, 2008).

These patterns, however, are neither universal nor static. Cultural expecta-tions and norms of masculinity vary across context and communities (Addis & Mahalik, 2003; O'Brien, Hunt, & Hart, 2005), as do those related to re-sponsible fatherhood (Coltrane & Adams, 2008; LaRossa, 1997). Compared to fathers of 20 years ago, those of today are likely to feel less restricted emotionally and are more likely to ascribe to roles beyond that of "bread-winner," including greater involvement in all aspects of their children's care (Palkovitz, 2002). As men endorse different models of masculinity and father involvement rooted in values of care and nurturance, they may explore different kinds of support for their own and their children's health.

Beyond a general reluctance to solicit or receive help, men also tend to have more limited informal and formal support systems than women (Katz, 2002; McNeill, 2004; Nicholas, Gearing, et al., 2009; Pelchat et al., 2007). Pelchat and colleagues (2007) report that in comparison with women, men appear to experience their child's illness as more stigmatizing and, in some cases, perceive male friends as less adept at providing the emotional support they need. And within the partnership, some men have described feeling limited in their expression by fears that demonstrating their emotions will increase the burden experienced by their partner (McNeill, 2004).

In regard to formal supports, research indicates that fathers are significantly less likely than mothers to take a leave from work to care for their ill child (Chung et al., 2007). In addition to the influence of social norms that con-tinue to emphasize maternal responsibilities for caregiving (Maume, 2008; McKay & Doucet, 2010), this pattern has been linked to a tendency among men to remain in the workforce during a child's acute and chronic illness to ensure that family income remains as stable as possible (Nicholas, 1998) and that financial obligations can be met throughout health crises and prolonged care needs of the child. Families with chronically ill children often need to ensure that the parent with the most earning potential remains active in the workforce. For families in poverty or with jobs that do not

The Experiences of Fathers of a Child with a Chronic Health Condition   197

provide adequate sick leave or parental benefits, this challenge can be par-ticularly acute (Heymann, Toomey, & Furstenberg, 1999). Given continued trends of higher average wages for employed men, despite some narrowing of the gap (Drolet, 2011), the parent with the most earning potential is often the father. In addition to the myriad potential structural, familial, and per-sonal reasons why a father might be less involved in the care of the child, these dynamics can limit a man's access to child and family support programs, particularly those offered during work hours. The accompanying lack of exposure and direct communication with health providers can further a cycle in which professionals tend to stereotype men as having fewer emo-tional needs than women as they devote the majority of their attention and supports to mothers (Pelchat et al., 2007).

Health care practitioners need to be responsive to and supportive of men as fathers experience, understand, and attend to their child's illness and care needs, and as they integrate this experience into their lives and that of their family. This attentiveness must go beyond single points of clinical interaction and include an ongoing, integrated, multi-factorial trajectory of assessment complemented by responsive and proactive supports that are specifically geared to fathers' (as well as other family members') emerging needs and priorities. Models of paternal need and program/system responsiveness have yet to be developed and tested in the context of pediatric chronic illness. More research is needed to determine what types of support are helpful for fathers and, similarly, what intervention programs would be accessed and valued.

Potential Intervention Models

Fathers' care of their children is necessarily located within the social context of co-parenting, the family, and the health care system. This perspective is grounded in the broader rubric of family-centred care, which is strongly advocated in family social science and pediatric health care. Family-focused researchers and pediatric health care scholars have developed health models in order to study families, health, and illness. A family-centred model was proposed by McDaniel, Hepworth, and Doherty (1992), who envisioned a responsive bio-psycho-social model for working with families on health-related issues. This model suggested careful attention to the biological, psych-ological, and social aspects of health and illness as experienced by the patient and family. Rolland (1994) expanded this model, using both family systems and family development theoretical frameworks to provide therapists with a series of specific questions and focuses to address with families dealing with physical health issues. Rolland emphasized that different types and phases of illness develop over time and in unique ways. Walsh (1998) developed a family resilience framework that is somewhat different from other models by focusing on the strengths of families and their ability to demonstrate resilience when encountering crises such as chronic health conditions. Interprofessional practice has recently emerged in the family-centred care discourse (Nicholas, Fleming-Carroll, & Keatings, 2009). Increasingly, considering the family at the core of the health care team is proposed as critical to ensuring inclusion and adaptability of care to the presenting needs, priorities, and strengths of family members, including fathers. Yet while the term *family-centred care* is used routinely in family social science and pediatric health care discourses, until recently little was known specifically about how fathers experience and are involved in the care of their ill child or the meanings they ascribe to their fathering role in this circumstance, and little attention has been directed to these fathers' self-identified needs and priorities.

Father-Based Discussion or Support Groups

Steinglass (1998) demonstrated that multiple-family "discussion groups" facilitate conversations about health care from single families to several families dealing with a chronic health care issue. This approach appears to draw on mutual aid frameworks in which social support is both provided and received as parents support one another. Increasingly, clinical programs offer opportunity for family members to connect with another "peer" or "mentor" family that has also experienced pediatric illness (see Doherty & Mendenhall, 2006; Nicholas & Keilty, 2006). Peer support constitutes an important resource, potentially allowing fathers to share their experiences with other fathers and to find common ground for connection and reciprocal social support.

Recent research demonstrates the benefits of social support for fathers of children with chronic health conditions (Nicholas & Keilty, 2006). Effective interventions appear to include groups for fathers (e.g., Holmbeck et al., 1997; Nicholas, 2003). Over 25 years ago, Konopka (1983) advocated for support groups for fathers because "such groups serve to provide [fathers] with information, afford them relief from anxiety, and develop some insight into themselves and their relationships with their children" (209). Stein (1983) concurs that groups offer fathers the opportunity to "change [their] belief systems and affective experiences" (150) through social exchange and emotional and informational support. The additional and common experiences associated with pediatric illness provide rich topical currency for group discussion among fathers (Nicholas, 2003). However, there are significant challenges to engaging fathers to attend support groups.

The authors' clinical experiences and the research and practice literature suggest that interventions for fathers require thoughtful development of content, process, and structure that reflect the particular needs, goals, and communication styles of specific populations of men (Nicholas, McNeill, Montgomery, Stapleford, & McClure, 2003). For instance, in a recent Canadian-based online group for fathers of children with spina bifida,

The Experiences of Fathers of a Child with a Chronic Health Condition 199

patterns of masculine communication process and group dynamics were observed that appear distinct from models of experiential and affective exploration common among traditional support interventions within clinical programs (Nicholas et al., 2003). Accordingly, current supports may fail to optimally balance multiple considerations such as men's preferred communication or relational exchange approaches with their simultaneous need for targeted support related to their child's condition and their possible priority of remaining strong for their partner and family.

Beyond intervention content, intervention methods conducive to reaching fathers merit further development in clinical practice and research. As an example, online technology in the provision of support to fathers has been used by some practitioners in an effort to overcome scheduling and geographic limitations often imposed within conventional support resources, meetings, or programs in clinical settings (Nicholas, 2003; Nicholas et al., 2003). Increasing evidence suggests that the benefits of online support, offering accessibility and convenience for fathers, outweigh concerns about erroneous information sharing or risk to confidentiality (Galinsky, Schopler, & Abell, 1997; Nicholas, 2003). Notwithstanding the potential suitability of this medium for supporting fathers, there is an urgent need for the development of tested strategies to mitigate any potential harm and to ensure informed consent related to online interventions.

Family-Centred Intervention Models

Recognizing the many challenges that exist in the structural and social environments in which ill children and families are embedded, it is essential to consider these relevant broader social conditions. These conditions are generally referred to as the social determinants of health, and they have the potential to exert a powerful influence on individuals and families. For example, if a father experiences high levels of stress associated with poverty, discrimination, an unsupportive employer, or inadequate working conditions, then achieving his role as a caring father is likely to be more complicated. Another social determinant of health is illustrated by the higher rate of child health conditions among poor and marginalized families. These are issues of social justice that need to be considered. An additional consideration is the role of agencies and hospitals in raising awareness about the risk factors associated with the social determinants of health and in advocating for policy and program changes that will support fathers and families (McNeill & Nicholas, 2008).

Clearly, greater awareness of these broad social forces is warranted, which, in turn, invites consideration of resources that meaningfully address fathers' needs and priorities. To that end, interventions are needed that attend to structural imbalances and gaps in the health system as it relates to fathers. Consistent with an increased call for responsiveness to fathers' potential need for clinical and targeted support, there has been a simultaneous and strong call in Canada and the United States in recent years for community building and civic renewal. For instance, the community development literature shows an increased awareness that family clinicians and academics need to promote active citizenship and stronger communities (Doherty & Beaton, 2000; Doherty & Carroll, 2002). Doherty and Carroll (2002) have called for a new type of health community practice that is driven less by clinician-defined problems and expertise, and more by community-defined problems and families' own expertise. It is believed that academics, researchers, clinicians, and health care organizations on their own lack sufficient knowledge to create effective programs and that significant involvement from family members and their communities is needed. Accordingly, fathers, mothers, and children bring important knowledge and potential support to one another and therefore should be included as both educators and learners in the development of supportive programs, which should include the opportunity to develop leadership abilities that will sustain the work and nurturance sought by a given initiative.

These assumptions about interventions reflect foundational principles of the families and democracy model (FDM) developed by Doherty, Beaton, Carroll, and Mendenhall and their colleagues at the University of Minnesota in the late 1990s (see Doherty & Beaton, 2000; Doherty & Carroll, 2002). From the foundational principles of the FDM, Doherty and Mendenhall (2006) created the citizen health care model (CHM) through their work with families affected by diabetes. This innovative way of engaging families around health care issues fosters community-building skills among individuals and families, who are encouraged to see themselves as "citizens" of health care. This approach challenges traditional provider-consumer models of health care by encouraging creative partnerships between professionals and those who live with health issues for the benefit of the larger community as well as those living with the health condition and their families. The CHM offers promise in potentially engaging and supporting fathers and their families, with a particular focus on participation and engagement in ways that may be particularly salient for fathers and/or render opportunities for fathers to express and tangibly work toward change in terms of their experiences and the many personal and family challenges and losses related to their child's chronic illness.

The CHM uses a collaborative approach, which is critical to inclusive partnerships among fathers, families, and clinicians. This approach espouses quality and mutuality of relationships with an ultimate aim of social change. No doubt, many families only have energy and resources to focus on their own health challenges and concerns. Yet these models not only address personal and familial struggles but also allow fathers the possibility of being a part of a larger effort of working with others to make a better world for themselves, their child, their family, and others in the wider community. The application and evaluation of these and other models with fathers and families are priorities for advancing interventional innovation.

Conclusion

Increasingly, Canadian clinicians and researchers are demonstrating the value of understanding and attending to the experiences and manifestations of stress among fathers of chronically ill children from a family system and family-centred care perspective. Until recently, relatively little empirical inquiry systematically examined the experiences of fathers of children with chronic health conditions. Recent scholarship identifies both comparable and diverse stresses, concerns, and priorities between caregiving mothers and fathers. Understanding fathers' concerns and experiences as they relate to their child's illness calls for more research and clinical innovation, including greater attention to the development and evaluation of resources that are conducive to fathers' needs, challenges, sensitivities, and ways of being. Without specific programs that target fathers' experiences of caring for chronically ill children, there may be a tendency to continue to miss fathers' needs and to obscure their central roles in the lives of their ill or disabled child.

This gap in the literature invites the empirical investigation of relevant factors, including fatherhood contexts, child condition and age, cultural background, socio-economic status, family constellation, and fatherhood identities; this investigation also needs to include the experiences of stepfathers (see Zarelli, 2009), single dads, gay fathers, and other fatherhood groups. Attention to the contextual factors in the social environment that shape a father's role is essential for a richer understanding of his experiences and parenting behaviour. Premature assumptions about a father's "character" without consideration of his social context can result in simple and reductive stereotypes. Intervention and longitudinal research is needed to understand and attend to experiences of fatherhood, including how this experience unfolds over time and across the trajectory of child and family development. In particular, research is needed to examine the challenges and experiences of marginalized populations of fathers caring for their ill or disabled children, including Indigenous, refugee, transgendered, and young fathers.

Incorporating support for fathers that is more accessible and effective is strongly recommended. Online applications of augmentative psycho-education and support appear promising in terms of improving outreach and fostering connection between fathers. In so doing, however, careful analysis needs to examine who is reached and how effectively. Examining which groups of fathers are helped by which type of intervention must be a priority in a program of intervention research. This research should not reduce fathers to a homogenized group with identical needs. It may be possible to create a typology of fathers with chronically ill children based on various continua of variability, and to design and evaluate the types of supports and clinical interventions that appear to benefit particular types of fathers in particular child, family, and community contexts.

Fathers of children with health conditions remain under-recognized in clinical, support-provision, and family system discourses. Given the father's critical role in the lives of his ill child and family, and the stressful impact of pediatric chronic health conditions, targeted clinical innovations that increase fathers' and their families' well-being are clearly warranted. Optimizing support to fathers offers the potential to buffer an intensely stressful experience relating to their child's chronic illness and, ultimately, to foster adaptation and growth. Such efforts offer the possibility of less individual suffering and a better quality of life, with potential vicarious beneficial impacts on the ill child and the family as a whole.

In terms of Canadian health and social policy planning for families with children with chronic health conditions, policies are substantially different across provinces and territories, and generally have not been sufficiently far-reaching. Policies tend to be broad in scope and often do not address the unique challenges of families with chronically ill children. Rather than being family centred, family support policy is often more focused on mothers and children, with little consideration for fathers' situations or needs (see Lero, Ashbourne, & Whitehead, 2006). To foster more support for fathers, policies are warranted that specifically focus on father involvement as a core of pediatric health care. Research needs to be directed toward understanding and measuring impacts of proactive policy supports that may benefit fathers, such as flexible workplace environments, government funding for paternal child-health leave, and income-protection opportunities. Research about fathers' experiences in various family configurations, clinical research on interventions, and exploration of father-inclusive policy reforms can contribute to stronger systems of family-centred supports, health service delivery, and social change for fathers and families with children with chronic health conditions.

References

Addis, M., & Mahalik, J. (2003). Men, masculinity, and the contexts of help seeking. *American Psychologist, 58*(1), 5-14.

Beckman, P. J. (1991). Comparison of mothers' and fathers' perceptions of the effect of young children with and without disabilities. *American Journal on Mental Retardation, 95*(5), 585-595.

Benn, K. M., & McColl, M. A. (2004). Parental coping following childhood acquired brain injury. *Brain Injury, 18*(3), 239-255.

Berge, J. M., & Holm, K. E. (2007). Boundary ambiguity in parents with chronically ill children: Integrating theory and research. *Family Relations, 56*, 123-134.

Boss, P. (1999). *Ambiguous loss: Learning to live with unresolved grief.* Cambridge, MA: Harvard University Press.

Brody, A. C., & Simmons, L. A. (2007). Family resiliency during childhood cancer: The father's perspective. *Journal of Pediatric Oncology Nursing, 24*(3), 152-165.

Cashin, G. H., Small, S. P., & Solbert, S. M. (2008). The lived experience of fathers who have children with asthma: A phenomenological study. *Journal of Pediatric Nursing, 23*(5), 372-385.

Chung, J., Garfield, C. F., Elliott, M. N., Carey, C., Eriksson, C., & Shuster, M. A. (2007). Need for and use of family leave among parents of children with special health care needs. *Pediatrics, 119*(5), 1047-1055.

Coltrane, S., & Adams, M. (2008). *Gender and families.* Lanham, MD: Rowman & Littlefield.

Doherty, W. J., & Beaton, J. M. (2000). Family therapists, community, and civic renewal. *Family Process, 39,* 149-161.

Doherty, W. J., & Carroll, J. S. (2002). The Families and Democracy Project. *Family Process, 41,* 579-590.

Doherty, W. J., Kouneski, E., & Erickson, M. (1998). Responsible fathering: An overview and conceptual framework. *Journal of Marriage and the Family, 60*(2), 277-292.

Doherty, W. J., & Mendenhall, T. J. (2006). Citizen health care: A model for engaging patients, families, and communities as coproducers of health. *Families, Systems, and Health, 24*(3), 251-263.

Drolet, M. (2011). Why has the gender wage gap narrowed? *Perspectives on Labour and Income 23*(1), 3-13. Statistics Canada – Catalogue no. 75-001-X.

Dyson, L. (1997). Fathers and mothers of school-age children with developmental disabilities: Parental stress, family functioning and social support. *American Journal on Mental Retardation, 102*(3), 267-279.

Galinsky, M. J., Schopler, J. H., & Abell, M. D. (1997). Connecting group members through telephone and computer groups. *Health and Social Work, 22,* 181-188.

Goble, L. A. (2004). The impact of a child's chronic illness on fathers. *Issues in Comprehensive Pediatric Nursing, 27*(3), 153–162.

Heymann, S. J., Toomey, S., & Furstenberg, F. (1999). Working parents: What factors are involved in their ability to take time off from work when their children are sick? *Archives of Pediatric and Adolescent Medicine, 153,* 870-874.

Holmbeck, G., Gorey-Ferguson, L., Hudson, T., Seefeldt, T., Shapera, W., & Turner, T. (1997). Maternal, paternal, and marital functioning in families of preadolescents with spina bifida. *Journal of Pediatric Psychology, 22*(2), 167-181.

Hovey, J. K. (2005). Fathers parenting chronically ill children: Concerns and coping strategies. *Issues in Comprehensive Pediatric Nursing, 28,* 83-95.

Katz, S. (2002). Gender differences in adapting to a child's chronic illness: A causal model. *Journal of Pediatric Nursing, 17*(4), 257-269.

Konopka, G. (1983). *Social group work: A helping process.* Englewood Cliffs, NJ: Prentice Hall.

LaRossa, R. (1997). *The modernization of fatherhood: A social and political history.* Chicago, IL: University of Chicago Press.

Lero, D. S., Ashbourne, L. M., & Whitehead, D. L. (2006). *Inventory of policies and policy areas influencing father involvement.* Guelph, ON: Centre for Families, Work and Well-Being, University of Guelph.

Maume, D. J. (2008). Gender differences in providing urgent childcare among dual-earner parents. *Social Forces, 87*(1), 273-297.

McDaniel, S., Hepworth, J., & Doherty, W. J. (Eds.). (1992). *Medical family therapy: A biopsychosocial approach to families with health problems.* New York, NY: Basic Books.

McKay, L., & Doucet, A. (2010). "Without taking away her leave": Canadian case study of couples' decisions on fathers' use of paid parental leave. *Fathering, 8*(3), 300-320.

McNeill, T. (2004). Fathers' experience of parenting a child with juvenile rheumatoid arthritis. *Qualitative Health Research, 14*(4), 526-545.

McNeill T. (2007). Fathers of children with a chronic health condition: Beyond gender stereotypes. *Men and Masculinities, 9*(4), 409-424.

McNeill, T., & Nicholas, D. (2008). Our system of health. In J. Turner & F. Turner (Eds.), *Canadian social welfare* (pp. 258-269). Toronto, ON: Pearson Education Canada.

McNeill, T., Nicholas, D., Beaton, J., & Montgomery, G. (2008). *Unpacking how mothers and fathers construct their roles for caring for a child with a disability or chronic health condition.*

Presentation at the Society for Social Work Leaders in Health Care Annual Conference, Montreal, QC.

Moller-Leimkuhler, A. (2002). Barriers to help-seeking by men: A review of sociocultural and clinical literature with particular reference to depression. *Journal of Affective Disorders, 71,* 1-9.

Nicholas, D. B. (1998). *The lived experience of mothers caring for their child with end stage renal disease.* Unpublished doctoral dissertation, University of Toronto, Ontario.

Nicholas, D. B. (2003). Participant perceptions of online groupwork with fathers of children with spina bifida. In N. Sullivan, E. S. Mesbur, N. C. Lang, D. Goodman, & L. Mitchell (Eds.), *Social work with groups: Social justice through personal, community and societal change* (pp. 227-240). Binghamton, NY: Haworth Press.

Nicholas, D. B., Fleming-Carroll, B., & Keatings, M. (2009). Examining organizational context and a developmental framework in advancing interprofessional collaboration: A case study. *Journal of Interprofessional Care, 24*(3) 319-322.

Nicholas, D. B., Gearing, R. E., McNeill, T., Fung, K., Lucchetta, S., & Selkirk, E. K. (2009). Experiences and resistance strategies utilized by fathers of children with cancer. *Social Work in Health Care, 48,* 260-275.

Nicholas, D. B., & Keilty, K. (2006). An evaluation of dyadic peer support for caregiving parents of children with chronic lung disease requiring technology assistance. *Social Work in Health Care, 44*(3), 246-259.

Nicholas, D. B., McNeill, T., Montgomery, G., Stapleford, C., & McClure, M. (2003). Patterns of peer communication among men in an online group for fathers of children with spina bifida. *Social Work with Groups, 26*(2), 65-80.

O'Brien, R., Hunt, K., & Hart, G. (2005). "It's caveman stuff, but that is to a certain extent how guys still operate": Men's accounts of masculinity and help-seeking. *Social Science and Medicine, 61*(3), 503-516.

Palkovitz, R. J. (2002). *Involved fathering and men's adult development: Provisional balances.* Mahwah, NJ: Lawrence Erlbaum.

Pelchat, D., Lefebvre, H., & Levert, M. J. (2007). Gender differences and similarities in the experiences of parenting a child with a health problem: Current state of knowledge. *Journal of Child Health Care, 11*(2), 112–131.

Pleck, J., & Masciadrelli, B. (2004). *Paternal involvement by U.S. residential fathers: Levels, sources, and consequences.* Hoboken, NJ: John Wiley.

Robertson, L. M., Douglas, F., Ludbrook, A., Reid, G., & van Teijlingen, E. (2008). What works with men? A systematic review of health promoting interventions targeting men. *BMC Health Services Research, 8*(1), 141. doi:10.1186/1472-6963-8-141.

Rolland, J. S. (1994). *Families, illness, and disability: An integrative treatment model.* New York, NY: Harper Collins.

Smith, J., Braunack-Mayer, A., & Wittert, G. (2006). What do we know about men's help-seeking and health service use? *Medical Journal of Australia, 184*(2), 81-83.

Statistics Canada. (2007). *Participation and Activity Limitation Survey (PALS).* Ottawa, ON: Author. Retrieved from http://www.statcan.gc.ca/cgi-bin/imdb/p2SV.pl?Function=getSurvey&SDDS=3251&lang=en&db=imdb&adm=8&dis=2.

Stein, T. S. (1983). An overview of men's groups. *Social Work with Groups, 6,* 149-161.

Steinglass, P. (1998). Multiple family discussion groups for patients with chronic medical illness. *Families, Systems, and Health, 16,* 55-70.

Sterken, D. J. (1996). Uncertainty and coping in fathers of children with cancer. *Journal of Pediatric Oncology Nursing, 13*(2), 81-88.

Vrijmoet-Wiersma, C. M. J., van Klink, J. M. M., Kolk, A. M., Koopman, H. M., Ball, L. M., & Egeler, R. M. (2008). Assessment of parental psychological stress in pediatric cancer: A review. *Journal of Pediatric Psychology, 33*(7), 694-706. doi:10.1093/jpepsy/jsn007

Walsh, F. (1998). *Strengthening family resilience.* New York, NY: Guilford Press.

Zarelli, D. A. (2009). Role-governed behaviors of stepfathers in families with a child with chronic illness. *Journal of Pediatric Nursing, 24*(2), 90-100.

Part 3
Toward Social Change: Policy
and Practice Issues for Fathers

10

Fathers and Parental Leave in Canada: Policies and Practices

Lindsey McKay, Katherine Marshall, and Andrea Doucet

Given that parental leave enables fathers to temporarily exit the workforce to take up caring for their newborn children, it carries the potential to increase father involvement and contribute to gender equality in the home and in the labour market. Working mothers in Canada gained the right to job-protected maternity leave in 1971, with fathers following in 1990 with access to shared-entitlement parental leave and in 2006, in Québec only, to paternity leave. While mothers still use the majority of leave time, fathers' use of leave has risen significantly in the last decade. More than one in four Canadian fathers now take some time off of paid employment on the arrival of a newborn child. In 2000, only 3% of eligible fathers took paid leave; in 2008, 33% of eligible fathers took paid leave – 12% of fathers outside Québec and 82% of Québécois fathers.[1] These statistics raise several key questions: What explains the rise in fathers' use of leave benefits relative to that of mothers, both in Canada as a whole and in Québec? What enables and inhibits fathers from taking leave? And which fathers take leave among identifiable subpopulations: for example, low- versus high-income fathers, Indigenous fathers, newcomer fathers, fathers employed in standard versus non-standard jobs, and so on?

The sociological interest in explaining fathers' use – and lack of use – of leave benefits is led by European scholars, who have identified a number of influences on fathers' use of parental leave, including loss of household income, role expectations, program design, employment characteristics, workplace culture, educational level, partners' willingness to share leave, and men's interest in shared parenting (Haas, 2003; Haas, Allard, & Hwang, 2002; O'Brien, 2009; Whitehouse, Diamond, & Baird, 2007). Chronholm (2002) found in self-reported interviews that the reasons fathers took leave were to establish a close relationship with their child, to facilitate their partner working or studying, and to achieve greater gender equality. It is widely acknowledged that national contexts – especially child-rearing patterns, parental leave, and child care policy – must be taken into account when

208   *Lindsey McKay, Katherine Marshall, and Andrea Doucet*

attempting to explain leave-taking patterns (Kammerman & Moss, 2009; Moss, 2009).

Canada shares with other OECD countries the long-term demographic and social trend of a declining fertility rate and rise in dual-earner families. Paid leave benefits in Canada (and Québec) are not universal; they are an earned entitlement based on employment. Parents therefore require a minimum level of attachment to insurable employment to qualify for leave provisions of any sort. With Canada being a federal state, jurisdictional divisions complicate the full complement of parental leave provisions, most notably by having two government-sponsored wage-compensation programs: one in Québec and one in the rest of the country. Until 2006, there was one program for all parents: Parental Leave Benefits, located within the federal Employment Insurance (EI) program. In 2006, Québec created a separate Québec Parental Insurance Plan (QPIP). This context adds to the complexity and opportunity for explanations of fathers' use of parental leave.

In this chapter, we draw on quantitative and qualitative evidence to demonstrate that public policy influences fathers' leave-taking decisions but that those decisions are also shaped by at least three factors: mothers' desired leave preference and duration, mothers' eligibility for parental leave (or not), and fathers' employment status in a labour market that carries gendered expectations in relation to fathers and infant care. In other words, fathers' embeddedness in couple relationships and the paid workforce play a strong role in their use of leave. We also identify what is known about the diversity of fathers who qualify and take leave, and those who do not. Our contribution unfolds as follows: First, we provide a brief background of the context within which children are born and of the two parental leave benefit programs (Canada and Québec). Second, we describe our data sources. Third, we present a profile of fathers who take leave and an analysis of fathers' leave taking as heavily influenced by public policy, negotiations with mothers, and employment situations.

The Child-Rearing and Public Policy Context

Most Canadian parents are raising children with an opposite-sex partner in a situation where both are employed. Work hours and individual earnings of each parent bear an influence on parental leave decisions. Statistics Canada data indicate that the labour-market patterns of families with dependent children continue to evolve as a result of changes in family formation, women's increased labour-force participation rate, and the average paid work hours of both women and men (Marshall, 2009). The proportion of couples with both partners working at least part-time has remained steady for some time (68%) in 2008. However the proportion of couples with dual earners working full-time continues to increase, up from 70% in 1997 to 74% in 2008. As a consequence, "fewer families have a parent at home, either full-time or part-time, to help manage the household, to provide child care, and, increasingly, to provide elder care" (Marshall, 2009, 12).

Paid-leave programs provide dual-earner parents with the opportunity to take time away from their jobs in order to care for their infant children. With wives' average employment hours increasing relative to those of husbands, the wage gap is narrowing and the financial contribution of spouses is becoming more equal. The larger trend is toward gender convergence in the distribution of paid work and housework within heterosexual couples (Marshall, 2006). However, differences still exist. For example, husbands in dual-earner couples earned, on average, $1,040 per week in 2008 compared to only $740 for wives (Marshall, 2009; Perusse, 2003). For this reason, fathers' leave taking is more likely to have a greater negative impact on household earnings than mothers' leave taking.

One Country, Two Paid Leave Benefit Programs

The full complement of parental leave provisions includes the right to job-protected leave and government- and/or employer-sponsored wage compensation during leave. As Pulkingham and Van der Gaag (2004) point out, Canada has a tripartite parental leave system consisting of (a) provincial/territorial job-protected unpaid leave, (b) federal or Québec government wage-compensation programs (also known as paid leave benefits), and (c) employer-sponsored wage-compensation benefits to top up EI/QPIP. For all three aspects of this system, only parents who qualify receive this form of support in raising their children. Parents with standard "good jobs" (high wages, full-time, permanent, and with benefits) have far greater job protection and access to benefits, and higher wage-replacement rates, than parents with precarious "bad jobs" (low wages, part-time, non-permanent, and without benefits). At the systemic level, labour-market stratification translates into inequities in parental leave along class, race, and gender lines under the federal (EI) program and, although less so, under the Québec government program (for an analysis of the evolution of leave benefits, see Doucet, McKay, & Tremblay, 2009; Phipps, 2006).

Where Canadian parents reside matters in terms of the rules governing job-protected unpaid and paid leave. Eligibility, duration, and rights (accrual of seniority and maintenance of benefits) are established under federal/provincial/territorial employment standards legislation and therefore vary by jurisdiction (Women's Network PEI, 2005). This means that regardless of income or hours, new or contract-based workers are less likely to have the right to job-protected leave in Nova Scotia, Alberta, and the three territories; in all of these jurisdictions, 12 months of continuous employment with a single employer is required. At the other end of the spectrum, British Columbia, New Brunswick, and Québec have no length-of-employment requirement. All other provinces fall in between.

Residence also matters for access, use, and rate of government-sponsored wage-compensation parental leave benefits: Québécois parents have fared far better than parents in the rest of Canada since the introduction of QPIP in 2006. The generic term parental leave refers in actuality to three types of leave: maternity, paternity, and *parental leave*. Maternity leave for mothers and paternity leave for fathers are non-transferable individual entitlements. Parental leave and adoption leave are shared entitlements that parents can divide how they wish (one taking it all or both taking a number of weeks either concurrently or consecutively). Table 10.1 below shows the similarities and differences between EI and QPIP (Human Resources and Skills Development Canada, 2007).

Table 10.1

Comparison of Canada (EI) and Québec (QPIP) parental leave benefit plans since 2006

	Canada EI	Québec Basic Plan	Québec Special Plan
Eligibility	600 hours	$2,000 earnings	
Self-employed workers	Starting in 2011	Covered	
Waiting period	2 weeks per couple	None	
Weeks by wage-replacement rate (% of average earnings)			
Maternity	15 at 55%	18 at 70%	15 at 75%
Paternity	None	5 at 70%	3 at 75%
Parental (shared)	35 at 55%	32 (7 at 70% + 25 at 55%)	25 at 75%
Total weeks per couple	50	55	43
Adoption (shared)	35 at 55%	(12 at 70% + 25 at 55%)	28 at 75%
Low-income replacement rate (net annual income < $25,921)	Up to 80%	Up to 80%	
Maximum insurable earnings (adjusted annually)	$447/week	$894.22/week	

Source: Adapted from "Employment Insurance Maternal and Parental Benefits," Service Canada, 2011, http://www.servicecanada.gc.ca/eng/sc/ei/benefits/maternityparental.shtml, and "Québec Parental Insurance Plan," Emploi et Solidarité sociale, Québec, 2012, http://www.rqap.gouv.qc.ca/index_en.asp.

A defining feature of maternity/parental leave benefits outside Québec is the location of the benefits within the EI program. In 2001, new legislation significantly modified Canada's parental leave scheme by adding 25 weeks of paid parental leave to make a total of 35 weeks. When mothers take maternity leave plus all of the parental leave, this change doubled their total compensated care time from 25 weeks to 50 weeks.[2] While this change was important, QPIP went much further in enhancing parental leave.

Québec's 2006 Parental Insurance Plan contains four major differences from EI: (a) lower eligibility criteria ($2,000 earnings instead of 600 hours) and inclusion of the self-employed; (b) three to five weeks of non-transferable paternity leave ("daddy weeks"); (c) more flexibility, with two plan options (the Basic Plan – longer leave with lower benefits – or the Special Plan – shorter leave with higher benefits); and (d) higher income-replacement rates and earnings ceiling (70% and 75% of wages, depending on the plan, and maximum insurable income up to $62,000 instead of $42,300). In both plans (Basic and Special), families earning less than a net family income of $25,921 qualify for a family supplement that increases the wage-replacement rate to 80%.

Prior to the introduction of QPIP in 2006, roughly one third of all Canadian mothers were consistently ineligible for parental leave. Reasons for ineligibility included not being in the paid workforce, often due to full-time care work for older children; self-employment; and not working the requisite number of hours, which was common for part-time and contract workers (Bertrand & Bédard, 2002; Marshall, 2003). However, recent data show that the Québec system now gives greater accessibility than the Canadian EI system. In 2008, a higher proportion of Québécois mothers claimed paid leave benefits than other Canadian mothers – 79% versus 64%. Mothers reported that among fathers who do not claim benefits, roughly 20% are ineligible, which probably comprises mainly self-employed fathers outside Québec.

At the other, high end of the spectrum, employer-sponsored wage-compensation top-up payments are offered to about one in five mothers across the country. From 2000 to 2008, top-up recipients reported having an employer top-up for an average of 16 to 19 weeks, suggesting that most receive a top-up to their maternity leave benefits only (Marshall, 2010). Statistics Canada does not collect top-up data on fathers.

Data Sources

This chapter draws on two complementary data sets, one quantitative and one qualitative. The quantitative data provide national information on the coverage of parental leave benefits and are derived from Statistics Canada's annual Employment Insurance Coverage Survey (EICS). The survey is administered to a sub-sample of individuals from the Labour Force Survey

(LFS), which excludes residents of the Yukon, Northwest Territories, and Nunavut; persons living on Indian Reserves; full-time members of the Canadian Armed Forces; and inmates of institutions. The maternity and parental benefits section of the EICS, which was introduced in 2000, is designed in part to determine the proportion of mothers who receive paid benefits and the reason why some mothers do not receive benefits, and to collect information about the extent to which parents share parental benefits. All information regarding the father's use of parental leave, including the number of weeks taken and the reasons for non-participation, are limited to answers given by the mother. Selected labour-market and demographic information on fathers is available and originates from the LFS. The monthly LFS collects information on labour-market activity during a one-week period from all household members aged 15 years and over.

The maternity and parental benefits section of the EICS is administered to all mothers with a child aged 0 to 12 months. Proxy responses are not permitted. The survey covers the civilian, non-institutionalized population 15 years of age and over living in the 10 provinces. All records are weighted, and estimates are representative of the Canadian population. Calculated coefficients of variation ensure that the estimates are reliable. In 2008, more than 1,100 married or common-law mothers were interviewed, representing a weighted count of roughly 353,000. The response rate for the EICS was 86% in 2008.

The qualitative data are from a small-scale interpretive study conducted from 2006 to 2008 by Doucet and McKay that builds on Doucet's decade-long program of qualitative work on involved fathering in Canada (e.g., Doucet, 2006). We conducted in-depth couple interviews with 25 heterosexual couples and one gay couple. With three multiple births in our sample, there were 49 children born from 45 births. All couples had at least one child under the age of three, and all the fathers took some leave from work to care for at least one of their children in their first year, ranging from 14 days to exiting the labour force to be the primary caregiver. Access to parental leave benefits varied within the sample, ranging from some parents not qualifying for EI/QPIP for any or one of their children, to both parents qualifying for each child, to at least one parent qualifying plus receiving a 93% employer-sponsored wage-replacement top-up. Those who did not qualify were students, contract workers, self-employed workers, or at-home parents; those who did qualify and received top-up benefits tended to hold full-time, permanent positions in the private or public sector.

Parents were recruited through posters put up at community centres and daycares, and through "snowballing" via social networks. Almost all lived around Ottawa-Gatineau, 16 in Ontario and 10 in Québec, and, with a few exceptions, the parents were white, middle-class dual earners (which reflects the population that qualifies for parental leave benefits). Interviews followed a loosely framed "aide memoire" of several themes that encouraged narrative flexibility and flow. The themes comprise (a) a description of leave arrangements and caregiving for each child, (b) how decisions were made for the father to take leave from work, (c) responses and reactions of employers and extended family, (d) fathers' experiences on leave, (e) family background, and (f) the division of labour between parents in sharing care work and housework. A background questionnaire was used to collect demographic, socio-economic, and employment information.

Both researchers conducted interviews, either together or separately.[3] We both took field notes and we conducted the qualitative analysis together, first by working with interview transcripts while being guided loosely by a set of readings called the Listening Guide (see Doucet & Mauthner, 2008; Mauthner & Doucet, 1998, 2003). These in-depth readings led to the establishment of a coding scheme, which we applied through the qualitative analysis software program ATLAS.ti. Interviewee names used in this chapter are pseudonyms.

Findings

Which Fathers Take Leave?

Before analyzing the influences on fathers' use of leave, we needed to identify which fathers take leave. The EICS is the only representative data set available to probe the diversity among fathers who take leave, do not take leave, and are not qualified for leave. As mentioned earlier, mothers report that 20% of fathers do not take leave because they are ineligible. There is a dearth of currently available data on the characteristics of ineligible fathers.

In 2008, 33% of eligible fathers in Canada's 10 provinces claimed paid leave benefits – 82% in Québec and 12% outside Québec (see Table 10.2 below). Selected socio-economic variables indicate no substantial differences between eligible fathers who claim benefits and those who do not. At the time of the survey, roughly the same proportion of claimers and non-claimers were employed (91% vs. 95%, respectively) and working full-time (96% vs. 97%), and claimers and non-claimers with paid jobs were earning similar hourly wages ($26.20 vs. $25.50). Furthermore, fathers who claimed benefits had an average age of 34, and 57% of them had completed college or university, while fathers who did not claim benefits averaged 33 years of age and 53% had higher education attainment. Data on other distinctions among fathers, such as immigration status, Aboriginal status, occupation, class of work, sector of employment (public or private), and unionization, among other variables in the LFS, are currently not available in the EICS.

What Influences Fathers' Use of Leave Benefits?

Findings from both the qualitative and quantitative data sets suggest that a father's decision to claim paid parental leave benefits is based on policy,

214   *Lindsey McKay, Katherine Marshall, and Andrea Doucet*

financial implications, and the father's position as an embedded subject, most importantly as a partner and a worker. Each of the following sections starts with quantitative findings and builds on those with findings from the qualitative study. In the qualitative research conducted by Doucet and McKay, fathers' reasons for taking leave and taking less leave time than mothers reflect three sets of relations within which heterosexual coupled men are embedded: the father's relationship to the infant's mother; the mother's relationship to parental leave benefits; and the father's relationship to the labour market and his employer.

When mothers in the 2008 Employment Insurance Coverage Survey were asked the main reason why their partner did not file for paid benefits, half (48%) reported that it was the preferred arrangement of the mother and/or family, selecting the "mother wants to stay home" response. Mothers also reported the following reasons, although less frequently: "impossible to take time off work" (18%), "money-related reasons" (18%), and, less frequently, "didn't know he could" (8%), "not interested" (4%), and "other" (5%) (Statistics Canada, 2008). It is noteworthy that almost one in five mothers reported financial concerns ("money-related reasons") as the main reason why the father did not claim benefits. Most families are likely to suffer a greater reduction in income if the father claims benefits since, as we demonstrated earlier, men, on average, earn more than women (Marshall, 2009).

Fathers' Leave in Relation to Mothers' Leave
In more than three quarters of Canadian couples with newborns, at least one partner claimed some parental leave benefits in 2008. Of these couples, the majority (87%) used all the paid benefit weeks available, with mothers claiming most of the time. Among fathers who claimed benefits, the duration and timing of their leave varied by benefit plan (EI vs. QPIP) and mothers' eligibility. An analysis of EICS data finds that in 2008, fathers in Québec claimed an average of 7 weeks of paid leave while fathers outside Québec claimed 13 weeks (see Table 10.2). The average duration of leave for fathers in Québec has fallen since the introduction of the QPIP, probably reflecting the large take-up of fathers who use the 3 to 5 weeks of non-transferable paternity leave only and do not use any of the shareable 25 to 32 weeks of parental leave. However, across all provinces, fathers with spouses not in receipt of paid benefits claimed for the longest average duration – 17 weeks.

Since fathers from Québec claim benefits for a relatively short time, it is not surprising to find that most fathers (73% in 2007/2008) claim paid leave benefits at the same time as the mother does. In fact, under one of the two options, the longer-duration Basic Plan, 3 of the 55 weeks must be taken together to fall within the 52-week benefit period. Outside Québec, only one quarter of fathers claim benefits at the same time as the mother. Half of leave-taking fathers outside Québec claim benefits when the mother does

Table 10.2

Take-up rate and average weeks taken among eligible fathers of paid paternity or parental leave

		Canada	Québec	Elsewhere
Fathers who claimed (%)	2004	12	22q[a]	9
	2005	18	32	13
	2006	23	56	11
	2007	31	83	11
	2008	33	82	12
Average no. of weeks off[b]	2005	12	13q	11
	2006	11	7	17
	2007	10	7	16
	2008	9	7	13

a *q* = High coefficient of variation
b Fathers' time off was not collected in 2004.
Source: Adapted from Statistics Canada, Employment Insurance Coverage Survey, unpublished data.

not. This scenario probably involves couples in which the father is the only parent eligible, and rather than have the family lose the right to any benefits, he participates (the mother may or may not be at home at the same time). This means that eligible fathers outside Québec are more likely to claim benefits when the mother is not in receipt of EI (suggesting ineligibility) than when she is – 18% versus 10%, respectively, in 2008. The remaining quarter of fathers outside Québec claim at a separate time from the mother, thus enabling a situation where at least one parent can be at home with the child for the entire one-year benefit period.

Findings from the qualitative study confirmed the pattern identified using EICS data: fathers took paternity leave whereas their use of shared parental leave was residual to that of mothers. Asking fathers and mothers the reasons for their decisions revealed a strong moral commitment to the idea that being a good father meant not "taking away" mothers' leave time. Mothers overwhelmingly claimed ownership to parental leave as a de facto extended maternity leave. All but two of 25 heterosexual couples deferred decision making and preference over use of leave to the mother: what she wanted was seen as her right. Under EI, mothers would say, "I took 5 weeks off mine to give it to him." Fathers shared this perception, stating the reason they took leave as "she gave it to me." Fathers in heterosexual couples viewed only individual entitlement leave as their own. Only one father asserted his desire to split leave time 50-50. As his wife, Arianna, put it, "We bartered.

He wanted six and six and I wasn't really ready. I wanted the whole year but I thought we'd try it. So we went to nine and three."

Fathers took all the leave they could that did not reduce mothers' desired leave duration. Parents aimed to maximize the duration of leave while minimizing the reduction in earnings while on leave. This resulted in a strategy of sequencing leave entitlements, using individual-entitlement leave first and leaves that had the least impact on earnings (e.g., paid vacation days). Notably, when one parent was not eligible for EI or QPIP, shared-entitlement parental leave became, in effect, individual-entitlement leave. Fathers in Québec told us that they appreciated QPIP paternity leave because it "didn't take away" from the mother.

A dimension captured neither in survey data nor in international literature on parental leave is birth mothers' exclusive ability to breastfeed. That is, biological sex rather than socially inscribed gender differences are relevant to who provides care for a newborn. For the mainly middle-class parents in the qualitative study, this translated into an expressed strong commitment – by mothers and fathers – to exclusive nursing, in accordance with recommendations from both the World Health Organization and Health Canada for an optimum period of six months or more. Given that maternity leave only covers 15 to 18 weeks, mothers in the qualitative study drew on shared parental leave to stay home to breastfeed for six months or longer. Breastfeeding, seen as in the best interest of the child, was therefore a powerful rationale for the mother to take more, if not all of the shared parental leave time.

Fathers' Leave in Relation to Employment

Like mothers, fathers' standing in the labour market influences their right to job-protected parental leave, access to EI/QPIP wage-replacement leave benefits, and an employer top-up. One in five mothers reported in the EICS that the main reason their spouse did not claim benefits was because it was "impossible to take time off work." This finding gives some indication that the nature of fathers' self-employed or paid work can be a hindrance to a father's propensity to file for benefits.

In the qualitative study, we identified a number of factors in relation to paid work that influenced fathers to take leave, including fathers' earnings, employment status, employer, and type of work or workplace culture. Generally, as mentioned, fathers took all the leave they could that did not impinge on mothers' desired leave. Furthermore, they acted on their right to paternity/parental leave entitlement when it was affordable and seen by employers as legitimate.

Affordability   Among fathers living outside Québec, results from a regression analysis[4] using EICS data show that differences in individual characteristics are not associated with a father's use of benefits but that his average earnings and eligibility for benefits, vis-à-vis the mother, are significant. For couples in which the mother claims benefits and earns the same or more than the father, fathers are significantly more likely to claim some of the benefits. This strongly suggests that some families take into account how much the family will lose if the father versus the mother stays home before deciding who takes the leave. Income lost to the household is more significant under EI, with a wage replacement at 55%, than under QPIP, with a wage-replacement rate at 70% (Basic Plan) or 75% (Special Plan). If the income loss is equal or higher if the mother stays home, couples are more likely to share the benefits. High-earning mothers may also return to work earlier due to greater job satisfaction or being in demand at their jobs. Of the minority of couples who did not claim all available benefits, the EICS data show that one third (35%) gave financial concerns as the reason for doing so. An additional 50% stated that they either preferred to work or had other work-related reasons for not claiming all available benefits, while the remaining 15% gave other reasons.

In the qualitative study, two cases illustrate challenges for lower-income fathers that may inhibit accessing and using parental leave. One father described how he scrambled during his wife's pregnancy to change jobs (from self-employment to insured employment) and work enough hours to qualify for EI parental leave. Another father in Ottawa took only five of 35 weeks of parental leave in order to keep his older child's child care spot. Because of a municipal child care subsidy rule that parents must care for children at home if they are home for more than five weeks, he would have had to take the first child out of child care to care for his newborn; given the two-year wait list, his eldest would never have regained his spot. Although it lies beyond the scope of this chapter, the child care shortage in both provinces was found to affect parental leave, in this case by significantly reducing leave duration.

By contrast, fathers in the qualitative study who took longer leaves had access to paid vacation days, time in lieu of overtime, and/or high wage-replacement individual-entitlement leave benefits (as the only parent eligible for EI with a employer-sponsored top-up, or as an eligible candidate for QPIP paternity leave). These fathers were predominantly employed in permanent, unionized jobs in the public sector. They received a top-up over and above EI/QPIP, raising their wage-replacement rate to either 75% or, more commonly, 93%. One of these fathers, Matthew, whose wife did not qualify for EI, said, "I would be insane not to take it."

Our findings concur with research on Nordic parents, which identifies economic cost as a reason for fathers' minimal use of leave provisions. Higher-earning fathers must continue working for the family to pay the bills while the mother is off work (Haas, 2003). Concomitantly, mothers' lower employment status and weaker labour-market attachment contribute to maternal dominance of shared parental leave. Some observers argue that compensation rules in Sweden have the effect of favouring the lower-paid worker in a couple, who tends to be the woman, taking time off work (Seward, Yeatts, & Zottarelli, 2002). The gender gap in income is also reported as a reason why men take no more than "daddy days" since "families suffer less economically if mothers rather than fathers stay home" (Haas, 2003, 108). However, Haas (2003) cites government calculations showing that in the long run, the average family loses little income if the father takes leave because of the high level of compensation, tax breaks, and long-term economic gain from shortening mothers' leave time. There is no similar investigation of the long-term financial impact of parental leave decisions in Canada.

Legitimacy Fathers in other OECD countries have reported that employers, supervisors, and co-workers frown on parental leave based on the view that a man's role is to earn the family income, devote himself to paid work as his primary pursuit in life, and demonstrate loyalty to employers by working long hours (Seward et al., 2002). In research conducted in Sweden by Haas et al. (2002), men were more likely to use parental leave in workplaces that held an organizational culture that reflected an ethic of caring, promoted equal employment opportunity for women, and held father-friendly policies that were actually utilized; Haas and colleagues also found that it was more difficult to leave a small firm with a high degree of teamwork. This research is consistent with findings by Duvander, Ferrarini, and Thalberg (2005), also in Sweden, showing that it was more difficult for fathers to use parental leave when they worked at small, private, and male-dominated workplaces.

As mentioned earlier, no differences were found in the EICS between eligible Canadian fathers who claim and do not claim paid benefits in terms of being employed or working full-time, nor did hourly earnings, age, or education make a difference. Future quantitative data regarding fathers' workplaces may help explain fathers' use of parental leave. It would be valuable to compare take-up among fathers based on sector of employment (public vs. private), firm size, occupation, industry, unionization, and job tenure.

In the qualitative study, workplace culture made a difference to fathers' take-up of parental leave. Overall, fathers who worked for the federal government expressed greater ease in requesting and taking paternity or parental leave. This was attributed to collective agreement entitlements as well as a culture in which managers regularly accommodate a variety of different types of leaves (for example, language training, secondments, and sick leave). Also, a precedent of at least one other father taking leave empowered fathers to request leave. Nonetheless, there were vast differences reported by fathers in the degree of "family-friendliness" among departments within the federal government. Moreover, the attitude of one's immediate manager made a difference. One father's manager told him not to miss the opportunity to take parental leave. By comparison, Douglas, a federal employee, described managers in his department as showing "not active support but resigned acceptance" to fathers' leave.

Particular workplace cultures also influenced fathers' perceptions of how their leave taking would be received by their employer, and this, in turn, influenced their decision. A number of men expressed concern about losing their jobs; in fact, one father in the qualitative study was fired after he took nine weeks of parental leave. In his view, he was not falling into the career track the company had in mind for him. Daniel told us:

> I think they thought my priorities were elsewhere, that I wasn't there until all hours ... When I announced that I was planning on taking nine weeks, they were, I think, on the surface quite supportive but ... it was such a big ordeal, like, oh, this had never been done before. Women all the time, they were very supportive and hold baby showers, they had one for me as well, but ... I just wasn't fitting into their bigger long-term plans.

Another father, worried about being laid off, reduced his desired leave time and took the leave during a slower work period. This strategy accommodated the employer's schedule rather than that of the infant or family.

Couples reported in the interviews that while it has become the norm for mothers to take a year of leave, with rare exceptions, employers do not expect or encourage fathers to take leave. Consistent with the cultural practice of referring to parental leave as maternity leave, managers tend to see this period of infant care as reserved for mothers. Fathers expressed worry that taking leave "sent the wrong message" that they were not committed to their jobs. Pat and his wife, Hannah, shared parental leave, taking six months together to care for their twins and, two years later, about six months sequentially to care for their second child. Pat said, "We've got an ideal situation for men to take leave at work ... and yet even in that situation, men will only take two or three months." When asked why they don't take longer leaves, he explained, "It's because we're not there yet ... we're just not ... because they don't want to make waves, and there's been precedence, I mean I did it, and other people after me did it ... but still they're afraid ... they don't want to be seen as crusaders."

Overall, the fathers interviewed were more likely to take leave from work when doing so was affordable and perceived as legitimate, and did not threaten to permanently disrupt their ability to earn money. In relation to employers, QPIP enabled fathers to take leave for two reasons: the higher wage compensation and maximum insurance earnings ceiling reduced the impact on household earnings, and individual entitlement legitimized requests for leave from work. The "use-it-or-lose-it" terms of the three or five weeks of paternity leave emboldened fathers to assert their right to leave. To summarize, in order to take parental leave and/or to take longer leave durations than is currently the case in Canada, fathers must overcome, through entitlement gains and/or cultural change, the infant-care gender expectations that employers generally hold.

Conclusion

While Canada currently stands as one of the countries in the world with father-friendly parental leave policies, especially in Québec, the take-up is complex and characterized by high numbers with short duration for Québécois fathers and low numbers with comparatively long leave times for Canadian fathers in the other provinces. As explored in this chapter, a father's leave-taking patterns are influenced not only by public policy but also by how this policy intersects with his relationship to his spouse and to his paid employment. We have argued that these factors explain what enables and inhibits fathers from taking leave and therefore the significant differences in parental leave take-up between mothers and fathers, and between Canada (EI) and Québec (QPIP).

First, fathers' leave-taking patterns are determined in relation to mothers' leave time. This subject position is reflected in an agreed deference to mothers' preferences and a commitment to breastfeeding, both of which are shaped by ideas of the practices that constitute a "good father." Second, fathers' leave-taking decisions relate to mothers' eligibility. We demonstrated that fathers are more likely to claim shared-entitlement parental leave (and more of it) when they are partnered with mothers without benefits. Thus, fathers take leave so that the parental leave is not lost to the family. Third, we highlighted how fathers negotiate leave as primary family breadwinners, as they remain in over two thirds of Canadian families. Since most fathers earn higher incomes than their partners, the loss of income for taking leave has a greater impact on family income and acts as a disincentive to fathers to take leave. Finally, fathers make parental leave decisions in relation to the labour market and to the particular culture in their workplace; even government jobs exhibited differences between departments and, even more minutely, between work groups as to the support that fathers received. With strong social, community, and workplace norms still leaning toward mothers as primary caregivers for infants, fathers can feel scrutinized and penalized by employers and colleagues for taking leave.

Although Canadian fathers' use of parental leave breaks from the traditional division of labour between men and women in the home, take-up patterns actually reinforce these roles, at least in the first year of a child's life. All but a small proportion of fathers take temporary leave such that it does not disrupt the mother-infant dyad or their breadwinning potential. While over 80% of fathers in Québec take leave, the duration of this leave remains short and largely in tandem with that of the mother. A positive interpretation of this would be that fathers are taking advantage of public policy, especially "daddy weeks" in Québec, to spend time at home caring for a newborn or, where older siblings are present, facilitating the move to a larger family unit. A negative interpretation would be that gender divisions continue to affect infant care in Canada. However, the question of whether short-term gender differences in parental leave take-up leads to long-term gender divisions of labour in Canadian households is one that requires further longitudinal research (see Doucet, 2009).

Another negative interpretation, noted throughout our analysis, would be to recognize that socio-economic class also influences who is eligible for and able to afford to take leave. In Canada, parents who work in standard insurable employment with access to and higher compensation from EI/QPIP benefits and employer top-ups are the ones who are most supported, thus leading to a situation of "parental-leave rich" and "parental-leave poor" households (O'Brien, 2009). This being said, we demonstrated that Québec has broadened access and take-up, putting Québécois parents in a much better situation than parents in the rest of the country. Also of note is that although our analysis found no differences among eligible claiming and non-claiming fathers, the dearth of representative data prevents us from analyzing subpopulations of fathers by occupation, employment status, and diversity.

While differences in class and gender remain in regard to who can take parental leave and how much is actually taken, the data show that Canada's move to a father focus in parental leave policy does induce more men to share in infant care, at least for some part of the first year. As the Québec case demonstrates, non-transferable paternity leave is very effective in ensuring that fathers use leave provisions. It is also clear that qualifying for leave and being able to afford to take leave present further barriers to fathers' use of parental leave. While the federal EI program began matching Québec's provisions for self-employed workers as of January 2011, if fathers' take-up rates in other provinces are to approach those of Québec, other features similar to those provided in Québec will have to be adopted: higher replacement rates, lower eligibility requirements, and non-transferable leave provisions.

In looking to similar policies in Nordic countries such as Sweden, commentators have noted that fathers' participation in infant care has indeed increased after three decades of dual-earner family policy. Nevertheless, systemic gender differences remain in paid and unpaid labour. Understanding the impacts of Canadian fathers' take-up of parental leave and whether and how the length of time taken by men matters to Canadian families and society requires greater longitudinal attention as well as comparative work on households in which fathers do and do not take parental leave.

Notes

1 Unless otherwise noted, quantitative data are drawn from the Employment Insurance Coverage Survey, Statistics Canada. It refers only to parents who are eligible for benefits (the survey excludes parents without insurable earnings) and is reported by mothers.

2 At the same time, the required number of annual employment hours was cut from 700 to 600, and the 14-day unpaid waiting period before payment commences was changed from applying to each parent when leave is shared to one waiting period per couple.

3 Seventeen interviews were conducted in person, with the broad majority done together with both authors present. Due to geographical distance, nine interviews were done by Doucet by telephone. Four interviews were conducted by Doucet and a second francophone interviewer, Josée Charlebois. French interviews were then translated into English.

4 Using 2008 EICS data, logistic regression was used to examine the probability of a father claiming paid parental leave benefits. Independent variables included father's education, mother's education, household income, mother's receipt of employer top-up, mother's receipt of paid benefits, and the ratio of mother's earnings to father's. Similar results were found in a previous analysis of EICS data (Marshall, 2006).

References

Bertrand, J.-F., & Bédard, M. (2002). *EI benefit coverage of the unemployed according to work pattern prior to unemployment* (No. SP-568-02-03E). Ottawa, ON: Human Resources Development Canada, Strategic Policy, Applied Research Branch.

Chronholm, A. (2002). Which fathers use their rights? Swedish fathers who take parental leave. *Community, Work and Family, 5*(3), 343-364.

Doucet, A. (2006). *Do men mother? Fathering, care, and domestic responsibility*. Toronto, ON: University of Toronto Press.

Doucet, A. (2009). Dad and baby in the first year: Gendered embodiment. *The Annals of the American Academy of Political and Social Sciences, 624*(1), 78-98.

Doucet, A., & Mauthner, N. S. (2008). What can be known and how? Narrated subjects and the Listening Guide. *Qualitative Research, 8*(3), 399-409.

Doucet, A., McKay, L., & Tremblay, D.-G. (2009). Canada and Québec: Two policies, one country. In S. B. Kammerman & P. Moss (Eds.), *The politics of parental leave policies: Children, parenting, gender and the labour market* (pp. 33-50). Bristol, England: Policy Press.

Duvander, A.-Z., Ferrarini, T., & Thalberg, S. (2005). *Swedish parental leave and gender equality: Achievements and reform challenges in a European perspective*. Stockholm, Sweden: Institute for Future Studies.

Haas, L. (2003). Parental leave and gender equality: Lessons from the European Union. *Review of Policy Research, 20*(1), 89-114.

Haas, L., Allard, K., & Hwang, P. (2002). The impact of organizational culture on men's use of parental leave in Sweden. *Community, Work and Family, 5*(3), 319-341.

Human Resources and Skills Development Canada (HRSDC). (2007). *Child care spaces recommendations: Report from the Ministerial Advisory Committee on the Government of Canada's Child Care Spaces Initiative*. Ottawa, ON: Human Resources and Skills Development Canada. Retrieved from http://www.hrsdc.gc.ca/eng/publications_resources/social_policy/mac_report/child_care_spaces_strategy.pdf.

Kammerman, S. B., & Moss, P. (Eds.). (2009). *The politics of parental leave policies: Children, parenting, gender and the labour market*. Bristol, England: Policy Press.

Marshall, K. (2003). Benefiting from extended parental leave. *Perspectives on Labour and Income, 15*(2), 15-21. Statistics Canada – Catalogue no. 75-001-XPE.

Marshall, K. (2006). Converging gender roles. *Perspectives on Labour and Income, 7*(7), 5-17. Statistics Canada – Catalogue no. 75-001-XPE.

Marshall, K. (2009). The family work week. *Perspectives on Labour and Income, 21*(2), 21-29. Statistics Canada – Catalogue no. 75-001-XPE.

Marshall, K. (2010). Employer top-ups. *Perspectives on Labour and Income, 22*(1), 43-50. Statistics Canada – Catalogue no. 75-001-X.

Mauthner, N. S., & Doucet, A. (1998). Reflections on a voice-centred relational method of data analysis: Analysing maternal and domestic voices. In J. Ribbens & R. Edwards (Eds.), *Feminist dilemmas in qualitative research: Private lives and public texts* (pp. 119-144). London, England: Sage.

Mauthner, N. S., & Doucet, A. (2003). Reflexive accounts and accounts of reflexivity in qualitative data analysis. *Sociology, 37*(3), 413-431.

Moss, P. (Ed.). (2009). *International review of leave policies and related research 2009* (Employment Relations Research Series No 102). London, England: Department for Business Innovation and Skills.

O'Brien, M. (2009). Fathers, parental leave policies, and infant quality of life: International perspectives and policy impact. *The Annals of the American Academy of Political and Social Science 624,* 190-213.

Perusse, D. (2003). New maternity and parental benefits. *Perspectives on Labour and Income, 4*(3), 1-4. Statistics Canada – Catalogue no. 75-001-XIE.

Phipps, S. (2006). *Working for working parents: The evolution of maternity and parental benefits in Canada.* Montreal, QC: Institute for Research on Public Policy (IRPP).

Pulkingham, J., & Van der Gaag, T. (2004). Maternity/parental leave provision in Canada: We've come a long way, but there's further to go. *Canadian Woman Studies, 23*(3-4), 116-125.

Seward, R. R., Yeatts, D. E., & Zottarelli, L. K. (2002). Parental leave and father involvement in child care: Sweden and the United States. *Journal of Comparative Family Studies, 33*(3), 387-399.

Statistics Canada. (2008). [Employment Insurance Coverage Survey]. Unpublished data.

Whitehouse, G., Diamond, C., & Baird, M. (2007). Fathers' use of leave in Australia. *Community, Work and Family, 10*(4), 387-407.

Women's Network PEI. (2005). *Looking beyond the surface: An in-depth review of parental benefits.* Retrieved from http://www.hrsdc.gc.ca/eng/labour/employment_standards/fls/submissions/formal_briefs/brief44/page00.shtml.

11
Looking Forward: Father Involvement and Changing Forms of Masculine Care

Kerry Daly and Jessica Ball

Scholarly efforts to understand father involvement have often focused on trying to understand core activities, commitments, and beliefs held by fathers. The chapters in this book indicate the importance of going beyond monolithic thinking of what constitutes "father involvement" to demonstrate the importance of examining father involvement as a complex and contested set of constructions, values, and behaviours that are emerging in response to changing social, political, and economic conditions. As several chapters in this volume have explicated, examining the changing nature of father involvement in its many forms cannot be separated from the changing nature of masculinities (and femininities, for that matter!), changing gender relationships, and changing patterns of family life, including queer parenting, parenting apart or together, and separation between biological and social fathering.

As we look to the future of father involvement scholarship, we must continue to explore father involvement as a diverse, multi-faceted, and complex experience. Although fathers have many common experiences when parenting their children, they also face many unique challenges associated with the ways in which their identities, social and economic circumstances, and patterns of family life intersect and change over time. In the same way that hegemonic masculinity can blur the "many masculinities" associated with class, ethnicity, and sexual orientation, so too does a hegemonic perspective on father involvement render invisible the different struggles and opportunities encountered by fathers in a wide array of social and cultural circumstances. To promote social inclusion, future father-involvement scholarship should provide a forum for making visible and understanding fathering experiences that have been marginalized and poorly understood (Long, 2007). While the current volume has deliberately set out to highlight diverse populations of fathers, there are populations of fathers whose experiences, behaviours, and viewpoints are not represented explicitly, including stepfathers, adoptive fathers, and fathers from different stages of the life cycle. There is still much work to be done.

Fathering Research and Social Change

Many of the studies in this book have illustrated varied approaches to partnership and engagement as part of conducting community-based research. This collaborative approach can play a critical role both in understanding the diverse nature of father involvement activities and as a catalyst for change in public attitudes, service delivery, and social policy. The development of scholarship in these areas not only makes visible the different forms of father involvement but also provokes active engagement in a broader process of social transformation related to parenting – one that involves a new, more nuanced language for fathering and a deeper appreciation of the many pathways through which fathers make a difference in children's lives.

Part of the value of community-engaged research approaches is the recognition of the linkages between fathering activities and the community contexts and processes in which they are embedded. The micropolitics of gendered parenting must be understood within the politics of ethnicity, physical ability, social class, and sexual orientation. When we consider the many different populations of fathers and fathering styles portrayed in this volume, it is apparent that fathers' participation in family and community life can take many forms. For example, fathers of children with chronic health conditions participate in various communities of care, from the formal health care system to other supportive communities (Beaton, Nicholas, McNeill, & Wenger, this volume). At a broader level, fathers at all stages, including young fathers (Pratt, Lawford, & Allen, this volume), express their generative concern by seeking to successfully integrate their children into the many communities of which they are a part. Recent research has documented the importance of fathers in sport and leisure activities (Kay, 2009), which offer opportunities to understand how fathers "participate" in community by interacting with their children in public spaces and how fathers and children are active agents in the construction of community relationships, events, and opportunities. Moreover, through the experience of active fathering, men often learn to be mentors to children and youth in the community through sports, clubs, and faith-based organizations (Marsiglio, 2009).

Diversity, invisibility, and the embeddedness of fathering activity in relationships and communities have been central themes in this volume. Underlying all of these themes, however, is a fundamental question about how fathers provide care to their children. To even raise the question in a way that includes the words *men* and *care* in the same phrase is to invoke a disruption in our dominant ways of thinking about gender that so often associate care activities with women's work. In this final chapter, we explore the ways in which the changing practices of diverse father involvement can lead us to different understandings of masculine forms of care through fathering activity and the navigation of care practices in parenting relationships.

Men, Father Care, and Masculinities

In order to understand father care and the many forms of masculinity, it is important to begin with the persistence of a patriarchal legacy that stubbornly upholds a set of structural values and practices that reinforce male power and privilege. In spite of many changes in gendered practices – including parenting – there is an ongoing divide in cultural ideals between the masculine values of control, strength, and rationality, and the feminine values of co-operation, mutuality, and caring (Johnson, 2005). Although the literature on gender contains extensive discourse about the socially constructed nature of these values and ideals, evidence suggests that in addition to being moulded by early and ongoing socialization, gendered practices also have a biological basis. For example, meta-analytic research examining evidence of the biological underpinnings of women's and men's pro-social behaviour, including parenting, indicate that higher levels of oxytocin (as well as reduced cortisol and testosterone) are associated with behaviours that produce parental bonding, nurturance, and intimacy, whereas higher levels of testosterone are associated with dominance and competition (Eagly, 2009). Although men and women overall demonstrate very similar *levels* of pro-social behaviour, these neurochemical processes are linked to very different *styles* of pro-social activity: women are more likely to provide and seek emotional support to others and to focus on emotions while providing support whereas men are more often linked to agentic behaviour, which is often directed to strangers and to the support of social collectives (e.g., through providing for the family) (Eagly, 2009). Hence, if we are going to examine directions for men's patterns of care with children, it is useful to acknowledge at the outset two prevalent but intertwined forces: the biology of sex differences and the social structure of dominant norms and values. Our purpose is not to explore either of these in detail but rather to indicate their significance for understanding the way in which men and women are socially, historically, and biologically positioned to provide care. We treat these not as obdurate forces but rather as important but malleable conditions for understanding how and why father care is changing.

There are a number of indications that fathers are changing their level of involvement with children and the kind of care that they provide. As Ravanera and Hoffman (this volume) point out, both the percentage of Canadian fathers providing care and the amount of time they spend with their children have increased. These rises are consistent with other time-diary studies in industrialized countries that show steady increases over the past four decades in fathers' total child care time (Bianchi, Robinson, & Milkie,

2006). As discussed in Chapter 3, fathers who spend more time with their children make a positive difference in children's cognitive, social, and emotional developmental outcomes. Although this influence appears to be direct and is more readily measured as a direct effect, it is mediated by a number of systemic relationships and processes (Allen, Daly, & Ball, this volume).

Underlying the shift to greater father involvement generally are changes in the relationship that many men have toward care activities. As we see fathers spending more time in child care activities with deepening levels of engagement and responsibility, we have fresh opportunities to examine some underlying changes in how men think about their relationships with children, women, and other men; their participation in activities of care; and the values, priorities, and decisions they make about how to live. Nevertheless, the focus on measuring "time spent with children" offers little in terms of understanding the nature of care activities associated with involvement. Moreover, these aggregate data offer little insight into the ways in which different kinds of fathers either make or resist changes in their contributions to care.

As research on assessing father involvement continues to grow, calls for this work to become more differentiated are increasing. As Pleck (2010) argues, our measures of involvement need to do a much better job of understanding the nature of care within measures of engagement. Specifically, we need to focus on positive father-involvement activities that deal with direct forms of care, including warmth and responsiveness, enrichment activity, monitoring and control, and playing (Pleck, 2010). Pleck also stresses the importance of examining indirect forms of care that were previously associated with the responsibility dimension. These forms of care are "undertaken for the child" but not with the child (65). Fathers' indirect care includes purchasing and arranging goods and services for the child like shopping or arranging child care (material indirect care), managing or arranging friendships and community connections (social indirect care), and taking initiative and seeing what is needed (process responsibility) (Pleck, 2010). Research on the responsibility dimension of care has been challenging because it is often a form of invisible work that is not readily measured. Nevertheless, research on process responsibility (i.e., planning and anticipating activities/ needs) and other forms of indirect care has demonstrated the prevalence of mothers maintaining the primary role in the management and orchestration of family life (Coltrane, 2000; Daly, 2002; Doucet, 2006), characterized most simply by fathers playing the role of "helping their wives" by responding to their requests for assistance with housework and child care (Coltrane, 1996). However, as Doucet (2006) points out, fathers who take on the primary care of their children (e.g., stay-at-home and joint custodial fathers) fill a broader range of responsibility roles, with almost half of the men in her study seeing themselves as "assistants" to mothers who tend to do the primary administrative work of parenting, one quarter seeing themselves as equal partners in coordinating activities, and one quarter seeing themselves as playing the primary responsibility role (usually construed as filling in the gap when wives had very busy work lives).

Our dominant models of care provision in Euro-Western cultures are steeped in a tradition of maternal child care activities and the lexical equivalence of mothering and nurturance. But this appears to be changing. As men develop their own confidence, skill, and rewards as fathers, they embrace the role more fully, and in so doing, they can expand beyond the traditional restrictions of stereotyped masculinity, which has reinforced their roles as providers, protectors, and disciplinarians at the expense of their roles as nurturers, emotional partners, and engaged companions.

Related to this is a gendered tradition that tends to view care activities as a choice for fathers, whereas for mothers, the performance of direct care activities is a deeply embedded moral expectation. In the field of family therapy, attention has been directed toward unpacking and reforming the practice of mother blaming, which is a reflection of the tendency to hold mothers morally accountable when care is in some way deficient. Men, on the other hand, may be cast as deficient or incompetent, but this is more likely an occasion for joking or lightheartedness than blame. It reflects the willingness to excuse fathers for this incompetence because parenting is not seen as their primary responsibility.

This tendency to see father care as a choice rather than as a responsibility is nowhere more apparent than in the work-life domain, where workplace flexibility strategies and policies often assume women as the primary beneficiaries and men as very occasional users. Even then, men who choose to take advantage of these strategies to provide family care can be viewed with suspicion or ridicule. Furthermore, as McKay, Marshall, and Doucet (this volume) indicate, fathers are often seen as "taking away mother's leave time" because parental leave decisions are, by default, made by mothers as a result of the desire to breastfeed, a moral expectation that the mother "should" stay home, assumed responsibility, and their underlying sense of entitlement. Choice for men to exercise care through parental leave is typically only possible if mothers forfeit their opportunity to do so and if men are willing to contend with a social and work environment that sends messages of suspicion and ridicule.

For men, the relationship between father care and masculinity is problematic for a variety of reasons. First, we continue to operate within a cultural context where certain forms of masculinity are dominant and more socially acceptable, while others are marginalized and more frequently subjected to question, ridicule, or stigmatization. At the same time, men are slowly changing their commitment to and participation in various forms of care activity that erode stereotypical patterns and expectations of masculinity in favour of expanding meanings of what it means to be a man (Daly, Ashbourne, & Brown, 2009). These expanded meanings are rooted in men's discoveries about the way in which involvement with children can sharpen their own emotional awareness, change their values and priorities, and redefine the meaning of work and play (Daly et al., 2009). Through the process of learning to be positively involved with their children, these fathers are also learning and modelling new and broader ways of thinking about masculinity, thus generating a spiralling process of psychological and social transformation. As Doucet (2006) asks: "Does fathers' caregiving disrupt the smooth surface of hegemonic masculinity?" (38). As the fathers portrayed in the foregoing chapters are opening pathways to new forms of masculinity, the answer arising from the stories in this volume would be "yes!"

Men Navigating Care in Parenting Relationships

As these changes in parental involvement have evolved, the notion of "interchangeability" between women and men has often been held out as a cultural ideal. In other words, in order to manage the complexities of dual-earner families, separated and divorced parenting, gay- and lesbian-headed families, fathering children who live in several different families, or families who are coping with a chronically ill child, there is a growing need for parents to be able to seamlessly trade off duties of care with a broad spectrum of skills as opposed to highly specialized or complementary roles. Interchangeability has given rise to all kinds of questions in the literature, including "Do men mother?" "Are fathers essential?" and "Is there anything unique about fathering and mothering?" These are critical and provocative empirical questions that not only get at the possible differences and similarities between mothers and fathers but also raise more questions about the complex constructions that underlie the very meaning of masculinity and femininity. Furthermore, given our highly gendered legacy of women being at the centre of networks of care (see Doucet & Hawkins, this volume), men and women approach this interchangeability from radically different starting points: for women, it is a question of making room for men in care activities; for men, it is a question of establishing a niche through demonstration of credible and competent caregiving.

Given our focus on father involvement and the potential importance of father involvement for children, interchangeability creates some challenges. On the one hand, interchangeability is arguably a socially desirable goal that means focusing less on gender and more on the parenting skills that can be adapted by male and female, gay and straight parents in their efforts to optimize children's developmental outcomes. It is apparent that warmth, responsiveness, positive engagement, mutually supportive adult relationships, and authoritative parenting all play a role in contributing to positive child development (Allen et al., this volume; Pleck, 2010). In contrast with biologically rooted arguments (see Eagly, 2009) that women and men are predisposed to different forms of pro-social behaviour, other research argues that these are not "gender-exclusive parenting abilities" (Biblarz & Stacey, 2010) but rather interchangeable skills and learned capabilities. In this regard, the principle of interchangeability points to a promising way forward for supporting fathers in which the goal would be to help men develop parenting competencies while at the same time encouraging their comfort and confidence as fully capable parents whether parenting solo, in a gay marriage, or in a heterosexual relationship. Fully embracing the identity of a confident parenting partner would mean that men no longer "babysit" their children when their partners are absent; rather, they assume the responsibility, anticipate the needs, plan the activities, and respond to their children's requests in ways that reflect their skills and abilities.

While interchangeability may be an ideal, it is not immediately evident that it is often realized in practice. Research consistently shows a number of asymmetries between the parenting activities of mothers and fathers. In heterosexual families, for example, women spend more time with children and are more involved in the direct provision of care to children (Ravanera & Hoffman, this volume). Comparisons of lesbian parents and heterosexual parents, although based on limited research, suggest that lesbian co-parents demonstrate greater parenting ability (i.e., communication, caretaking, and intimacy) compared to married heterosexual parents, due in part to women exceeding men in parenting investment and skills (Biblarz & Stacey, 2010). Also, the tradition of having women play a primary caregiving role has resulted in a tendency toward gatekeeping whereby mothers are seen to manage and mediate relationships and activities between fathers and their children (Allen & Hawkins, 1999). This may be rooted in the propensity of women to play a greater role in the responsibility dimension of providing care, which involves the mental work of planning and orchestrating family activities (Daly, 2002; Doucet, 2006). The implication is that men are often cast in a supporting, "second string" kind of role that is rooted in a "deficit" or "role inadequacy" model. In a more positive vein, mothers play a key role in encouraging greater father involvement (Cowan & Cowan, 2000). Recent research has found that fathers who receive support from their spouse were more likely to view their paternal caregiving role as important and were subsequently more likely to get involved in caregiving activities (Wong, Mangelsdorf, Brown, Neff, & Schoppe-Sullivan, 2009).

While this research clearly points to the important role that mothers play in either supporting or directing men in care activities, it highlights the continued presence of a hierarchical relationship within heterosexual couples that makes it difficult to realize the ideal of interchangeability. Although research focusing on gay fathers might provide some insight into issues of roles, interchangeability, and hierarchy, this area of research is limited and inconclusive (Biblarz & Stacey, 2010). Currently, most men in heterosexual families continue to navigate parenting care within the context of an asymmetrical relational dynamic where they are expected to play up to a set of standards and expectations for providing care rather than being in a position to construct these standards for themselves. Nevertheless, as evidenced in families that work non-standard shifts (Presser, 1995) or where men are required to step up to the plate with primary responsibility for parenting (e.g., gay male parenting, custody after divorce, or death of a co-parent), fathers have tended to demonstrate a high capacity for warmth, care, and nurturance – all qualities that have been conventionally associated with mothering. As this discussion suggests, many questions remain with respect to the interaction of nature and nurture, biology and learning care, and ultimately the potential to realize the current cultural ideal of interchangeability. What is apparent, however, is that women and men are shifting their commitments to care in ways that reflect the malleability of underlying biology, cultural norms, and power dynamics within families.

Involving Fathers in Social Change

The studies in this book draw attention to the varied ways in which diverse populations of men provide care to children. As outlined in Chapter 2, national time-diary studies indicate that fathers continue to increase their contributions to care through increases in participation rates and in the time that they devote to caring for children and contributing to the unpaid work in the home. This reflects the effort to dismantle the traditional gendered division of labour in the home (Edwards, Doucet, & Furstenberg, 2009) referred to in Chapter 1 of this volume. As the discussions of indirect effects in Chapter 3 suggest, men's traditional contributions to the financial well-being of the family play an important role in shaping child development outcomes. Mutual emotional support between co-parenting partners is also key in creating an environment in which children can thrive and feel secure in a household led by a strong relationship. The authors of Chapter 9 report that fathers of children with a chronic health condition expressed their care by ensuring financial stability during times of intense medical testing or treatment, carrying out physical work in the home to ensure that it was safe, maintaining a positive attitude, and supporting the mother. Chapter 8 describes how fathers involved in the child welfare system expressed their care through their participation in programs designed to heal and provide an opportunity for reflection on their values and commitments related to children. In Chapter 5, the authors discuss how young dads were committed to many forms of generative care that they demonstrated through their commitment to positive choices in the future, monitoring their current behaviour in order to be a responsible parent, and finding a renewed sense of purpose in relation to their child. Chapter 7 discusses how separated and divorced dads express care through keeping a focus on the best interests of the child and being active partners in a fair co-parenting plan. And for the Aboriginal fathers in Chapter 6, it was often the "long and winding road" of learning how to communicate, play, and accept the responsibilities of fatherhood that enabled them to develop care relationships with their children.

As fathers demonstrate their capacity for and commitment to care, they become more publicly available models of masculine care. In a cultural landscape that is inclined to uphold gender stereotypes and to ridicule fathers who are less than perfectly competent, it is important that men demonstrate through their care actions – for each other and the communities within which they are embedded – portrayals of successful and satisfied fathers. These everyday models can play transformative roles in resetting the standard of capable and responsible fathering, a standard that can fill a long-standing gap left by previous generations of absent fathers or the paucity of strong, accessible, and engaged father models in the media. Of critical importance for achieving this goal is that we disrupt traditional and prescriptively narrow concepts of what good fathers do and open out to a range of possibilities for fathers to demonstrate their competent and caring engagement.

Throughout this book, the relational context within which men provide care to children has been strongly emphasized. The process of change and negotiation in parenting highlights the systemic dynamics of masculine models of care. Given mothers' traditionally central role in providing care, in order to work through the complex set of challenges involved in fundamentally redefining parental territory, a unilateral move on the part of men is not sufficient. Rather, transforming gendered care requires men to engage in ongoing negotiations with mothers and other care providers. If this involves men taking on more tasks and responsibilities associated with care, it may also involve women letting go of some of these responsibilities in order to make room for greater father involvement.

Although there is important work to be done in supporting fathers to deepen and broaden the forms of care they provide to children, perhaps our most meaningful indicator of progress will come when gender truly does not matter. Although the research strongly points to evidence suggesting that the gender of the parents does not matter in regard to healthy child development (Biblarz & Stacey, 2010), it appears that biology does matter (albeit in complex, interactive ways), and we continue to live a culture where it matters a great deal. Mothering and fathering are ultimately about two kinds of developmental concerns: one focusing on the child with a concern for optimizing healthy and adaptive outcomes for children and the other on parents' ability to learn care and demonstrate concern for the next generation as part of their own healthy adult development and successful adaptation. Both women and men stand to benefit from embracing a standard of care for children that is devoid of unwelcome and destructive gender stereotypes, free from unnecessary gendered territorial boundaries, and open to the fulsome possibilities of committed shared parenting.

Looking Forward: Directions for Research and Programs in Canada

This volume has highlighted some developments in understanding and supporting positive father involvement in Canada. A number of promising steps forward have been taken, while many gaps remain. The community of scholars and practitioners focused on father involvement in Canada (as demonstrated by the authors in this volume) recognizes the need to appreciate the diversity of fathers in Canada and to refine our understanding of what fatherhood means to them and their aspirations for their roles in relation to children and family life. Associated with avoiding a monolithic and prescriptive image of what positive father involvement entails, scholars and some fathers themselves are asking critical questions about one of Canada's most cherished values, that of social inclusion. As Long (2007) contends, a socially inclusive approach to providing support for fathers in Canada requires a new way of thinking about who these men are, what father/parenthood actually means to them, and what challenges and obstacles they face in being positively involved in the lives of their children. Negotiating the tension between recognizing the diversity of Canadian fathers and working toward greater social inclusion for fathers in family policy, programs, and life in communities will be a preoccupying theme in future work on father involvement.

Directions for Government Investment in Research

One of the goals in putting this book together was to highlight some of the scholarship on father involvement that has been developing in Canada over the last decade. Although good work has been done, Canadian research on father involvement is in the early stages. For the present volume, we encouraged authors to include Canadian research when it was available; however, the relevant literature often came from other countries. Canada has made some fruitful investments in father involvement research – most notably the FIRA-CURA project that is threaded throughout this volume. Now the federal government and other granting agencies need to build on this foundation of research. For example, steps need to be taken to modify the way in which some of our national data sets are structured. As noted by Ravanera and Hoffman (this volume), the serious limitations in how we gather data on fathers limit our understanding of fathering trends and practices, both domestically and internationally. Also, although the past preference for qualitative research to uncover dimensions of fathers' experiences that have remained invisible and to generate fresh insights is understandable, more quantitative research is now needed that could offer broader perspectives on trends in fathering practices, attitudes, and milieus in Canada. As well, there is an immediate need for a funded program of community-engaged research to assess what kinds of outreach and intervention programs are effective for supporting involvement of different populations of fathers in various contexts and at different stages of their own and their child's development.

Pathways to Meaningful Supports for Fathers

While parenting programs for heterosexual couples, maternal care programs for expectant and new mothers, and mother-child programs are readily available in nearly every community in Canada, few programs or resources address the specific needs and interests of fathers. Initiatives in Canada that are specifically designed to support father involvement are rare; they have been championed by individuals or small groups who worked tirelessly to get them started, and they are constantly at risk of being disbanded due to a lack of public support. Sustained government investment is needed in a variety of father outreach and support initiatives that are culturally and linguistically relevant and that address the diverse situations, needs, and goals of fathers in Canadian communities.

Finding skilled facilitators, particularly men with fathering experience, to lead father support programs remains a challenge, and again, funding has not been readily available to offer training in father support. Scholars and community partners involved in FIRA have advocated for public investments in fathering education as well as regularly scheduled in-service training for social service and health practitioners to strengthen their preparedness and their skills in reaching out to and working effectively with fathers. Little progress has been made on this frontier to date. A recent survey (Hodgins, 2009) of all undergraduate courses offered in public post-secondary universities and colleges in social sciences, education, and human services found not one course that focused specifically on fatherhood, and only one course that focused specifically on fathers and mothers. Numerous courses are geared to families, but coverage of fathers' specific experiences, needs, and contributions is sparse. Credentialed practitioners need to be offered opportunities to become aware of some of fatherhood's unique challenges as compared to motherhood, and the diversity of fathers' experiences, goals, and needs.

On a positive note, anecdotal reports indicate that support for fathers is being provided in a variety of ways through programs that are not ostensibly targeting father involvement. In fact, Canada's orientation to public health and education aims – conceptually, if not always in practice – to bring sectors together and integrate services and supports for family members through a number of community-based entry points. While integration of father support within broader community supports for children and families

– such as Aboriginal Head Start, Best Babies, and Community Action Program for Children – has many advantages in terms of a delivery approach, the feasibility and sustainability of this integrated approach depends on a sustained government commitment to funding the father involvement component.

As outlined in Chapter 1, a number of father involvement initiatives have been developed to support fathers. Nevertheless, research is needed on the effectiveness of various types of fathering programs and their implications for parenting relationships. For example, while the ideal of interchangeability would point to the importance of parenting programs without reference to gender, father involvement initiatives that focus on programs for fathers are typically developed on the belief that the kinds of information and support men need – and the kinds of programs they will respond to – are likely to be different from those for mothers.

Given the research pointing to the positive effects of father involvement on fathers' mental health and self-concept (Palkovitz, 2002; WHO, 2007), advocates for government investment in fathering programs could legitimately emphasize health benefits for fathers as much as salutogenic impacts of father involvement for children. For example, in an analysis of a diverse sample of fathers in the FIRA thematic study, fathers often talked about how their children contribute to their sense of growing maturity, responsibility, and engagement and help them learn about and deal with their own emotions in the context of their parenting activities (Daly et al., 2009). The findings suggested the potential to turn the tables and focus on children's impact on their fathers, more than on fathers' contributions to children's development, as a promising approach to understanding and reaching out to fathers. Programs for fathers might be framed as ways for fathers to build relationships with their children, appreciate their own growth and development as adults, and have an opportunity to learn from other men.

At this stage in the development of understanding and supporting father involvement in Canada, a central goal is to generate public dialogue about the conditions that shape father involvement and to make recommendations for policy reforms that provide a social environment that is more conducive to fathers' involvement from conception and sustained over time.

Conclusion

By the late 1990s in Canada, many fathers and staff in family resource programs based in communities were actively seeking information, resources, and connections to programs dealing with fathers (Taylor, Brown, & Beauregard, 1999). Obstacles included the overall lack of services for fathers and the lack of good referral systems. Taylor and colleagues (1999) emphasized that "across Canada, people who do innovative work with fathers remain isolated from one another" (134). They noted that fathers, practitioners, volunteers, and investigators alike were craving opportunities to share information and support a program of action to support father involvement. Over the past decade, Canada has built a vital and sustainable network of people interested in making more visible the diversity of fathers' experiences and their contributions to children's health and development, and in creating more spaces and supports for fathers to learn fatherhood, to enjoy and benefit from fatherhood, and to contribute to children's quality of life. This is a foundation on which to build programs of research and social action that can offer support for expectant and new fathers and families, and provide direction for practitioners working in child- and family-serving agencies about how to make visible and enhance the diverse ways in which fathers can contribute to children's well-being and quality of life.

References

Allen, S. M., & Hawkins, A. J. (1999). Maternal gatekeeping: Mothers' beliefs and behaviors that inhibit greater father involvement in family work. *Journal of Marriage and the Family, 61*(1), 199-212.

Bianchi, S., Robinson, J., & Milkie, M. (2006). *Changing rhythms of American family life.* New York, NY: Russell Sage Foundation.

Biblarz, T. J., & Stacey, J. (2010). How does the gender of parents matter? *Journal of Marriage and Family, 72,* 3-22.

Coltrane, S. (1996). *Family man.* New York, NY: Oxford Univeristy Press.

Coltrane, S. (2000). Research on household labour: Modelling and measuring the social embeddedness of routine family work. *Journal of Marriage and the Family, 62,* 1208-1233.

Cowan, C. P., & Cowan, A. (2000). *When partners become parents* (2nd ed.). Mahwah, NJ: Erlbaum.

Daly, K. J. (2002). Time, gender and the negotiation of family schedules. *Symbolic Interaction, 25,* 323-342.

Daly, K. J., Ashbourne, L., & Brown, J. (2009). Fathers' perceptions of children's influence: Implications for involvement. *The Annals of the American Academy of Political and Social Science, 624,* 61-77.

Doucet, A. (2006). *Do men mother? Fathering, care and domestic responsibility.* Toronto, ON: University of Toronto Press.

Eagly, A. H. (2009). The his and hers of prosocial behavior: An examination of the social psychology of gender. *American Psychologist, 64,* 644-658.

Edwards, R., Doucet, A., & Furstenberg, F. (2009). Fathering across diversity and adversity: International perspectives on policy interventions. *The Annals of the American Academy of Political and Social Science, 624,* 6-11.

Hodgins, D. (2009). *Survey of courses related to family, parenting, and fatherhood in 80 Canadian universities and colleges.* Unpublished report, School of Child and Youth Care, University of Victoria.

Johnson, A. G. (2005). *The gender knot: Unravelling our patriarchal legacy* (2nd ed.). Philadelphia, PA: Temple University Press.

Kay, T. (2009). *Fathering through sport and leisure.* London, England: Routledge.

Long, D. (2007). *All dads matter: Towards an inclusive vision for father involvement initiatives in Canada.* Guelph, ON: Father Involvement Research Alliance. Retrieved from http://www.fira.ca/cms/documents/176/April7.Long.PDF.

Marsiglio, W. (2009). Men's relations with kids: Exploring and promoting the mosaic of youth and fathering. *The Annals of the American Academy of Political and Social Science, 624,* 118-138.

Palkovitz, R. (2002). *Involved fathering and men's adult development.* Mahwah, NJ: Lawrence Erlbaum.

Pleck, J. (2010). Paternal involvement: Revised conceptualization and theoretical linkages with child development outcomes. In M. E. Lamb (Ed.), *The role of the father in child development* (5th ed., pp. 58-93). New York, NY: Wiley.

Presser, H. (1995). Job, family and gender: Determinants of non-standard work schedules among employed Americans in 1991. *Demography, 32,* 577-598.

Taylor, A., Brown, F., & Beauregard, B. (1999). Engaging fathers in becoming involved with their children. In E. Lowe (Ed.), *Linking research to practice: Second Canadian forum* (pp. 130-135). Ottawa, ON: Canadian Child Care Federation.

WHO (World Health Organization). (2007). *Fatherhood and health outcomes in Europe.* Copenhagen, Denmark: Author.

Wong, M. S, Mangelsdorf, S. C., Brown, G. L., Neff, C., & Schoppe-Sullivan, S. J. (2009). Parental beliefs, infant temperament, and marital quality: Associations with infant-mother and infant-father attachment. *Journal of Family Psychology, 23*(6), 828-838.

Contributors

James W. Allen is a doctoral candidate in the Lifespan Development program of the Department of Psychology at the University of Victoria in British Columbia. His research interests centre on social-cognitive and personality development from childhood to young adulthood, narrative, identity development, and socio-cultural influences on development, particularly among First Nation youth in Canada.

Sarah Allen received a PhD in Family Relations from the University of Guelph. She is currently adjunct teaching faculty at Montana State University in the College of Letters and Sciences, University Studies, and the Health and Human Development Department. She has published articles in academic journals and contributed chapters to textbooks and other edited volumes that focus on fathering, mothering, work and family relationships, and the meaning and processes of home. Sarah has also been involved in various fathering initiatives in Canada and the United States. These include web design and development for the Fatherwork website at Brigham Young University, research and writing for the Fatherhood Involvement Initiative – Ontario Network (FII-ON), and research for Health Canada's "My Daddy Matters" project, which identified best practices in the delivery of fathering services across Canada.

Nicholas Bala is a professor of law at Queen's University and one of Canada's leading experts in legal issues related to families and children. He addresses such issues as high-conflict separations, parental alienation, domestic violence, parental rights and responsibilities after divorce, child abuse, child witnesses, and juvenile justice. Much of his research work is interdisciplinary; he collaborates with psychologists, criminologists, and social workers to better understand the effect of the justice system on families and to make recommendations to improve legal responses to the problems faced by children and parents. His work is often quoted by all levels of court in Canada, including the Supreme Court, and is cited by courts in the United States and the United Kingdom. He frequently presents at education programs for judges, lawyers, social workers, and other professionals.

Jessica Ball, MPH, PhD, is a professor in the School of Child and Youth Care at the University of Victoria. She is the director of a grant-funded program of research and education on the cultural nature of child and family development (www.ecdip.org) and has led several innovative education programs and research projects involving community-university partnerships to co-generate concepts and practices. Dr. Ball spent 12 years in Southeast Asia working in community mental health, youth health risk prevention, school psychology and teacher education, and early childhood care and development programs. Dr. Ball is affiliated with the Canadian Father Involvement Research Alliance and was a co-principal investigator in the first national study of fatherhood, leading the Indigenous fathers component of the study. Dr. Ball is the author or co-author of over 100 journal articles and book chapters, and of three books.

John Beaton is an associate professor and Chair of the Department of Family Relations and Applied Nutrition at the University of Guelph. He has taught primarily in the Couple and Family Therapy program, training graduate students to be therapists. He is a clinical member and approved supervisor with the American Association of Marriage and Family Therapy. His research and clinical interests lie primarily in the areas of men's health, fatherhood, and community intervention. He has a number of publications in social science journals in the areas of fatherhood, intergenerational family relationships, and community intervention. More recently, he has developed a passion for addressing men's and children's physical health issues with a community action research approach.

Leslie Brown is Associate Dean of Research for the Faculty of Human and Social Development at the University of Victoria. Her scholarly and professional activities strive to support children, families, and communities. Co-editor of *Research as Resistance: Critical, Indigenous and Anti-oppressive Approaches* (2005) and principal of the BC Indigenous Child Welfare Research Network (www.uvic.ca/icwr), she has a strong interest in liberatory, decolonizing approaches to research.

Marilyn Callahan is a professor emeritus at the School of Social Work, University of Victoria. She has written extensively in the area of child welfare with an emphasis on the experiences of those who are affected most by child welfare policy and practices, including mothers, grandmothers, young women in care, fathers, and social workers. Her latest book, *At Risk: Social Justice in Child Welfare and Other Human Services,* examines the application of risk assessment with an emphasis on how it transforms child welfare into a set of management practices focused on surveillance and punishment.

Kerry Daly is Dean of the College of Social and Applied Human Sciences, a Professor in the Department of Family Relations and Applied Nutrition, and one of the founding directors of the Centre for Families, Work and Well-Being – all at the University of Guelph in Ontario. He received his PhD in Sociology from McMaster University, Hamilton, Ontario. He was the principal investigator for the Father Involvement Research Alliance (FIRA) CURA project from 2004 to 2009. His current research interests focus on the changing practices of fatherhood, the ways in which families negotiate and navigate time pressures in their lives, and the challenges families face in trying to harmonize their work and family life.

Lena Dominelli is a professor of Applied Social Sciences at Durham University in England. She is an experienced educator, practitioner, and researcher, and has published extensively in the fields of sociology, social policy, and social work. Her current research interests include climate change and environmental social work, globalization, social and community development, social change, women's well-being and welfare, motherhood, fatherhood, child well-being, and children's rights. Among her most recent books are *Green Social Work* (2012), *Social Work in a Globalising World* (2010), *Introducing Social Work* (2009), *Critical Practice in Social Work* (2009), *Practising Social Work in a Complex World* (edited with R. Adams and M. Payne, 2009), and *Anti-Racist Social Work* (2008).

Andrea Doucet is the Canada Research Chair in Gender, Work, and Care, and a Professor of Sociology and Gender Studies at Brock University. Her research and writing focuses on gender and care work, mothering and fathering, parental leave policies, embodiment, reflexive sociology, and knowledge construction processes. Her book, *Do Men Mother?* (2006), was awarded the John Porter Tradition of Excellence Book Award from the Canadian Sociology Association. She is currently working on two book projects, one on breadwinning mothers and caregiving fathers, and a co-authored book, *Narrative Analysis: The Listening Guide Approach* (with Natasha Mauthner). She is the editor of the international journal *Fathering*.

Linda Hawkins is the co-founder and current director of the Institute for Community Engaged Scholarship and the Research Shop at the University of Guelph, Ontario, which builds capacity for research engagement among community, faculty, and students. She was previously executive director of the Centre for Families, Work and Well-Being, with numerous interdisciplinary partnership projects related to gender work and care. She worked as the coordinator for the Father Involvement Research Alliance from its inception to 2009.

John Hoffman is a National Magazine Award-winning journalist and knowledge translation specialist. Canada's leading popular media writer on fatherhood, John has written well over 50 magazine articles and seven educational booklets for and about fathers. He has served as communications coordinator for the Father Involvement Research Alliance (FIRA) since 2006 and was a member of FIRA's Steering Committee.

Heather L. Lawford received her PhD in Psychology from Concordia University in Montreal. She is an Assistant Professor in Psychology at Bishop's University in Sherbrooke, Quebec. Her research interests are in parent-child relationships and moral and identity development in adolescence.

Elizabeth (Eli) Manning is an MSW graduate from the School of Social Work at the University of Victoria. Her thesis – entitled "Who Are the Men in 'Men Who Have Sex with Men'?" – interrogates the sex and gender constructions of men in HIV/AIDS research and discourse. In her doctoral work in gender, sexuality, and women's studies at Simon Fraser University, she continues to pursue her academic interests in HIV, post-structuralist strategies, and anti-racist and anti-colonialist practices.

Katherine Marshall has a BA in sociology from the University of British Columbia and an MA in women's studies from Carleton University in Ottawa, Ontario. She has spent most of her career doing research and analysis at Statistics Canada and has written extensively for their flagship publication, *Perspectives on Labour and Income*. Her areas of research include employment patterns of families, alternative work arrangements, and workplace benefits.

Lindsey McKay is a PhD Candidate in the Department of Sociology and Anthropology at Carleton University in Ottawa, Canada. Her research focuses on stratification and power, health and illness, and gender and social policy. She has authored several publications on parental leave with Andrea Doucet. Her dissertation examines the social relations of organ transplantation.

Ted McNeill, PhD, RSW, is an associate professor (status only) in the Factor-Inwentash Faculty of Social Work at the University of Toronto. He has extensive experience in the child health field, working with interprofessional teams to optimize health outcomes of children and their families. His academic interests include child and family adaptation to health conditions, parenting, positive father involvement, and the social determinants of health, including the toxic effects of poverty on children's health. These issues are part of his continuing interest in families, health, and social justice.

David Nicholas is an associate professor in the Faculty of Social Work, University of Calgary, Alberta. He brings a background in quality-of-life research with a focus on family experience related to childhood disability and chronic health conditions. Currently, he is principal investigator in studies examining both mothers' and fathers' caregiving roles and experiences related to autism, and he has led studies examining fathering in the context of childhood cancer, chronic kidney disease, and life-limiting conditions. Dr. Nicholas holds research funding from the Canadian Institutes for Health Research and the Social Sciences and Humanities Research Council of Canada.

Michael W. Pratt is a professor of psychology in the developmental area at Wilfrid Laurier University in Waterloo, Ontario. His research and teaching interests include narrative, personality and identity development, civic and environmental engagement, and generativity in the family context across the lifespan.

Zenaida R. Ravanera is coordinator of the Population Change and Lifecourse Strategic Knowledge Cluster. She is also an Adjunct Research Professor in the Department of Sociology; research associate at the Centre for Population, Aging, and Health; and information officer of the Research Data Centre at the University of Western Ontario in London. She obtained her MBA from Xavier University and her PhD in demography from Vrije Universiteit Brussel. Her research interests include timing and trajectories of life course events, social capital and family structures, social integration of immigrants, and the interrelation of work and family life. She co-edited *Canada's Changing Families: Implications for Individuals and Society* (with Kevin McQuillan, 2006).

Susan Strega is an associate professor in the School of Social Work, University of Victoria. She is the co-editor, with Sohki Aski Esquao, of *Walking This Path Together: Anti-racist and Anti-oppressive Child Welfare Practice* (2009) and the co-editor, with Leslie Brown, of *Research as Resistance: Critical, Indigenous and Anti-oppressive Approaches* (2005). Her research interests include male violence, child welfare, and discourse analysis. She is a former child protection worker and a former youth in care.

Christopher Walmsley is a professor in the School of Social Work and Human Service at Thompson Rivers University, Kamloops, BC. A member of the Fathering in Child Welfare Research Group, he is the father of one daughter, author of *Protecting Aboriginal Children* (2005), and co-editor (with Diane Purvey) of *Child and Family Welfare in British Columbia: A History* (2005). He is currently editing a collection on social issues in small cities and researching the life and professional experience of Elder African-Canadian social workers.

Lisa M. Wenger has a PhD from the Department of Family Relations and Human Development at the University of Guelph, Ontario. Drawing on a background in community-based health research, her research interests orient around the social and cultural dimensions of health and illness, with a focus on enhancing psycho-social interventions for men with cancer. Currently a post-doctoral fellow in the School of Nursing at the University of British Columbia, she continues her doctoral research on men, cancer, and help-seeking.

Denise L. Whitehead is a lawyer (JD, Osgoode Hall, of the Ontario Bar) and is completing her PhD in Family Relations and Human Development at the University of Guelph, Ontario. Her socio-legal research focuses on policy and practice issues that affect separated families. She contributed to an innovative inventory of policies as they relate to father involvement, including separated/divorced fathers. Her primary research focus is shared custody. She has examined the social and legal interplay between child support and shared custody, and her dissertation research involved in-depth interviews with young adults who spent time in shared custody as children; she examined their perspectives on transitions, relationships, and fairness.

Index

Note: "(t)" following a page number indicates a table

Aboriginal children: in child welfare system today, 173; effects of non-involved fathers, 130; influence on fathers, 135, 143; interned in residential schools, 128-29, 173-74; mental and physical health, 127; taken by child welfare system, 129

Aboriginal communities: constructs of masculinity, 134; family-based or matriarchal historically, 128, 134; fatherhood programs, 142; healing movement, 134, 135, 140

Aboriginal families: and child welfare interventions today, 173, 177; complicated and extended arrangements, 128, 132, 133; effects of colonization, 96, 128-30, 133, 134, 135, 144, 173, 175; effects of residential school system, 8, 129-30; historical precedence in society, 128; income vulnerability, 3, 127; policy and programming needs, 138-41; prevalence in Canada, 9; socio-economic characteristics, 126-28

Aboriginal fathers: complicated family arrangements, 132, 138; effects of colonization, 133, 134, 135; effects of residential school system, 8, 96, 129-30, 135; experiences as children, 133-34; experiences as fathers, 133-36; in FIRA study, 12, 92, 114; invisibility of, 96; lack of programming for, 10, 17, 135; lack of research on, 10, 137-38; policy and programming needs, 138-44; similarities and differences with other fathers, 12; socio-economic characteristics, 37-38, 46, 126-28, 132

Aboriginal Head Start, 235

Aboriginal Healing Foundation, 140

Aboriginal mothers: not designating paternity to protect children's status, 175

Aboriginal women: importance in Aboriginal society, 128, 134; importance in care networks, 100; importance in father involvement, 134

access rights after separation/divorce: and "best interest of child," 158, 159; enforcement of, 162-63, 166; legally separate from child support, 164-65; recommendations, 165-66

adoption: parental leave for, 210; by same-sex male couples, 18

adoptive fathers: demographic characteristics, 43-44

age, of child: at parental separation/divorce, 150

age, of fathers (*see also* young fathers): cohort numbers, 28(t), 29, 38-39; at fatherhood, 29-30; and generative stages of development, 108, 109-10, 111-12; taking parental leave, 213

age, of mothers: at motherhood, 29-30

Alberta: Aboriginal children in child welfare, 129; Family Law Act (2003), 160, 163; parental leave, 209

Association of Research on Mothering, 89

Australia: child care by fathers, 34

Best Babies, 235

"best interest of the child": as basis for both mother and father advocacy groups, 159; as basis of child welfare assessments, 161, 172; as basis of custody assessments, 158, 160; and breastfeeding as basis for parental leave, 216; and need for father involvement, 150; and parental conflict, 161

boundary ambiguity: among parents of children with special needs, 192, 193

British Columbia: father involvement programming, 20-21; parental leave, 211; Surrey's school libraries, inclusiveness, 18

British Columbia study on Aboriginal fathers: findings, 133-36; implications for policies and programs, 138-44; implications for research and theory, 136-38; methodology, 130-31; participants, 131-33

Canadian Household Panel Survey, 47

child abuse: and child welfare assessments, 176, 177, 180; experienced by fathers, 181; in residential schools, 129

child care: of children with special needs, 190, 192; decision-making about, 9, 157, 166; gender divisions in, 3, 8, 92, 226-28; and masculinity, 26, 34, 226-29; social expectations for mothers, 5; as support service for men and women, 92; in traditional Aboriginal families, 128

child support payments: calculations, 163-64; contentious issue, 163; effects on child development, 60-61, 163; legally separate from access rights, 164-65

child welfare system: father exclusion explanations, 177-78; father invisibility, 66; fathers' experiences, 178-84; gender biases in parent assessments, 175-77; ideology of parental dysfunction, 172; lack of consideration of external factors, 172-73; legislation and delivery of services, 172; race and class dimensions, 173-75; recommendations for, 144, 184-85; removal of Aboriginal children in 1960s-80s, 129, 175; risk assessments, 173

childrearing patterns: and use of parental leave, 207, 208-9

children (see also Aboriginal children): direct effects of father involvement, 54-57; effects of generative father on, 118-19; effects of separation/divorce, 150-53, 155-56; "illegitimate," and custody law, 158; indirect effects of father involvement, 57-66; influence on fathers, 52; multiple pathways of father influences, 7-8, 50-52, 66-67

children with special needs: prevalence, 3, 190; vulnerability to poverty, 3

chronic illness in child. See children with special needs; fathers of children with special needs

chronological model: applied to Aboriginal fathers, 137; as context for conceptualizing father involvement, 7-9

citizen health care model, 200-1

cognitive development of child: effects of father absence, 75(t); effects of father involvement, 55, 69-70(t); effects of poverty, 58

colonization: long-term effects on Aboriginal families, 96, 128-30, 133, 134, 135, 144, 173, 175

common-law families: Aboriginal, 37, 127; immigrant, 36; numbers of, 28(t)

Community Action Program for Children, 235

crime: and Aboriginal men, 127, 144; and children of lone parents, 151

cultural factors (see also specific subpopulations); in Aboriginal fathering, 128, 134; effects on child development, 64-65; and fatherhood roles, 10; in immigrant fathering, 64-65; in poverty rates, 174

custody arrangements: and child development, 63; child support payments, 60-61, 163-65; difficulty of research on, 41-43, 143-44; enforcing access rights, 162-63, 166; and gender equity, 93; high-conflict parents, 161-62; legal history, 158; legal reform movements, 159-61; policy recommendations, 165-66; research needs, 97; settlements vs. court orders, 154, 160; shared parenting, 154, 156-57, 159-60, 165-66; and spousal abuse, 162

Dad Central Ontario, 20

Daddies and Papas 2B, 18

decision making: about family and parenting, 9; in joint legal custody, 157, 166

disability (see children with special needs): fathers of children with special needs

diversity: cultural, 10, 64-65; of family forms, 93, 94-96; of fathers, and research, 96-97, 224-25; in feminist research, 90, 91, 94; of forms of masculinity, 1, 224; and policies and programs, 14, 94; recognizing in research, 93-94, 225; and social inclusion, 9-12; and terminology, 94-96; of types of father involvement, 6, 9-10, 12, 26, 93-94, 111, 136, 225

divorce. See separated/divorced fathers

Divorce Act (Canada), 160

domestic violence: and custody law, 162; difficulty of measuring, 21n2; and gendered child welfare assessments, 176-77, 179, 180-81, 183, 184-85; and issues of feminism and active fathering, 93; rates of, 4

ecological model, 7-8, 50-52, 66-67, 68
education: of Aboriginal fathers, 38(t); of fathers, effects on child development, 59-60; of fathers vs. non-fathers, 30, 31(t), 32; of fathers taking parental leave, 213; of immigrant fathers, 36(t), 37; of lone fathers, 40, 41(t); on reserves, 129
embeddedness: defined, 6; of fathering in relationships and communities, 225
emotional development of child: effects of father absence, 75-76(t); effects of father involvement, 55-56, 70-72(t); effects of parental separation/divorce, 150-52; effects of poverty, 58; and father's generative action, 113-14
Employment Insurance Coverage Survey, 212-13
Employment Insurance (EI) program: compared to QPIP, 210-11, 210(t), 221; inequities in parental leave, 209; parental leave requirements and provisions, 208, 210-11, 210(t), 222n1
employment status: of Aboriginal fathers, 38(t); of Aboriginal men, 127; effects on child development, 59-60; of fathers vs. non-fathers, 30, 31(t), 32; and fathers' use of parental leave, 216; of immigrant fathers, 36(t), 37; of lone fathers, 40, 41(t); and paid and unpaid work hours, 32, 33(t), 34
Erikson model of generativity, 107, 108-9
ethnicity. *See* race/ethnicity

"**f**ailure to protect" as child welfare lens, 177
families. *see also specific subpopulations*; of children in child welfare system, 173, 181-82, 185; of children with special needs, 3, 190, 191-92, 197-98, 199-201; common-law couples, 2-3, 4; defined by Statistics Canada, 21n1; diversity of, 93, 94-96; married couples, 2, 4; in multi-directional model of father involvement, 51-52; research from women's viewpoint, 92
father absence: effects on child development, 57-58, 63, 75-77(t)
father involvement: among Aboriginal fathers (*see* Aboriginal fathers); among

fathers of children with special needs (*see* fathers of children with special needs); among separated/divorced fathers (*see* separated/divorced fathers); from before birth, 12; in child welfare system, 179-84; direct effects on child development, 54-57; diversity of, 6, 9-10, 12, 26, 93-94, 111, 136, 225; and familial and social systems, 6-8; indirect effects in child development, 57-66; lack of policies for, 136; lack of programming for, 18-19, 136; from life course perspective, 153; measuring and interpreting, 5, 52-54; as multidimensional construct, 52, 54; over generations, 7-9; over life of child, 5, 13; and parental leave, 207, 222; and social assistance policies, 174; and social inclusion, 10; when father never lived with mother, 151
Father Involvement Initiative – Ontario Network. *See* Dad Central Ontario
Father Involvement Network – British Columbia, 20-21
Father Involvement Research Alliance (FIRA): attention to diversity in family forms, 94-96; attention to diversity in fathering, 93-94, 96-97; definitions of *father* and *parent*, 95; history, goals, and projects, 19-20; methodology, 114; research on active fathering, 91; research informed by feminism, 89, 92, 93, 101-2; research tension around "essential father," 99-100; research tension around patriarchal privilege, 97-99; subpopulations of fathers studied, 12, 92, 114
fatherhood: contextual factors in experiences, 111-12; effects of generativity on, 117-18, 120-23; and masculinity, 1, 15-18, 91, 224, 228-29; as predictor of generativity, 112-14; socio-economic benefits, 32, 34, 35(t); types of, 1
Fatherhood Responsibility Movement, 99
fathers (*see also specific subpopulations*): age at fatherhood, 29-30; ages of, 28(t), 29, 38-39; child welfare exclusion, 174-78; child welfare experiences, 178-84; child welfare inclusion, 184-85; common-law arrangements, 28(t); defined, 26, 27, 95; diversity of, and research, 96-97, 224-25; effects of relationship with partner, 7, 61-64, 151-52; engagement of, 12-14; as essential, 16-17, 67, 99-100; family responsibilities and workforce participation, 8-9, 32, 33(t), 34, 58, 59; "invisible," 44-45, 66, 96, 224; involving in social change, 231-32; living arrangements,

28(t); as marginalized, 96, 98; married, 28(t); numbers of, 2, 27, 28(t), 29; in popular media, 4-5, 16, 18, 127-28, 144; research involvement, 10-11; similarities and differences in specific subpopulations, 12; stay-at-home, 3; work hours, 3, 9, 209

fathers of children with special needs: coping strategies, 194-95; in FIRA study, 12, 92, 114; invisibility of, 96; lack of programming for, 95, 202; lack of research on, 10, 190, 191, 201; levels of involvement, 190-91; potential intervention models, 197-201; recommendations, 201-2; research needs, 201-2; similarities and differences with other fathers, 12; sources of stress, 193-94, 201; use of supports and resources, 195-97

fathers' rights groups: on child support guidelines, 164; on enforcing child access rights, 163; on equality of access rights, 158, 159, 165; seeking presumption of equal-time sharing, 159-60; vocal in research, 96, 97, 101

fathers' use of parental leave: compared to mothers, 214-16, 219, 220-21; father characteristics, 213; increasing prevalence, 207; influences on, 213-14, 216-21; take-up rate and average duration, 214-15, 215(t)

Federal Child Support Guidelines, 163-64

feminist research: contributions to fatherhood research, 93-97, 101; defined, 91; experience with diversity, 94, 101; tensions in linking with fatherhood research, 89-90, 93, 97-100, 101-2

fertility rate decline, 208

First Nations. *See* Aboriginal families; Aboriginal fathers

France: child protective services, 173

gay, bisexual, transgendered, and transsexual fathers (*see also* same-sex couples): and concepts of masculinity, 17-18; difficulty of identifying numbers of, 45; in FIRA study, 12, 92, 114; invisibility of, 96; lack of programming for, 17; lack of research on, 10, 68; parenting expectations, 17-18; parenting roles, 230-31; similarities and differences with other fathers, 12; and terminology, 95-96

gender: and child welfare assessments, 175-77; of children, and separation/divorce custody arrangements, 155, 157-58; and division of labour in families, 3, 8-9, 91; and domestic violence, 4-5, 162; and

experiences of parenting a child with special needs, 193-94; and father involvement research, 94-99; and generative development, 113; and healthy development of child, 232-33; and parenting expectations, 4, 15-17, 65, 226-28; and use of parental leave, 214-16, 217-18

generative action, 109

generative concern or motivation, 109, 120

generative narration: and identity growth, 110; in McAdams model, 109; themes in young fathers' experiences, 115-16

generative plans or strivings, 109

generativity: and Aboriginal fathers, 137; and contextual factors in fathering, 111-12; effects on fathering, 117-18, 121; effects of generative fathering on children, 118-19; fatherhood and policy implications, 123; fatherhood as predictor of, 112-14, 121-22; findings of FIRA study, 114-17, 121; future research, 122-23; and men's anticipation of fatherhood, 119-20; recent research, 109-10; stages of, 108

Germany: child care by fathers, 34

health. *See* mental health; physical health of child

health care system: and families of children with special needs, 190, 199-200, 225

historical factors: in Aboriginal families/fathering, 8, 96, 128-30, 133, 134, 135-37, 144, 173, 175; in custody law, 158; in expectations from separated/divorced fathers, 153-58; in fathering experiences, 96, 109; in gender-role expectations, 8, 10, 14

home ownership: by Aboriginal fathers, 38(t); by fathers vs. non-fathers, 30, 31(t); by immigrant fathers, 36(t), 37; by lone fathers, 40, 41(t)

homelessness: of Aboriginal men, 127, 132

hospitalization rates: Aboriginal children, 127; Aboriginal men, 127

housework: by fathers, 33(t), 34, 209

identity: effects of fathering on, 112, 113, 114-15, 117, 120-21; growth through generative narration, 110; lost by children in child welfare system, 129; of separated/divorced fathers, 152

immigrant families: and parenting roles, 5; prevalance in Canada, 9; wealth and income vulnerability, 3 immigrant fathers (*see also* refugee fathers): effects on child development, 64-65; in FIRA study, 12, 92, 114; invisibility of, 96; lack of programming for, 17; lack of research on, 10; numbers of, 35-36; self-perceived efficacy in Canadian context, 175; similarities and differences with other fathers, 12; socio-economic characteristics, 35, 36(t), 37, 46

income: of Aboriginal fathers, 38(t); effects on child development, 57-59, 60; of families of children with special needs, 192; of fathers vs. non-fathers, 31(t); and fathers' use of parental leave, 216-18; of husbands vs. wives, 209; of immigrant fathers, 36(t), 37; inequalities of, 3; of lone fathers, 40, 41(t); on reserves, 129; stability of, 6; of teenaged fathers, 39

Indigenous peoples. *See* Aboriginal families

individual/personal factors: in fathering experiences, 111

interchangeability of care, 229-31

international comparisons: child poverty, 174; family supports where child at risk, 173; father involvement in child care, 34, 221, 226; paternal leave, 218, 220

Inuit. *See* Aboriginal families; Aboriginal fathers

job protection with parental leave: geographic inequities, 209-10; provincial/territorial programs, 209; requirements and provisions, 209-10; socio-economic inequities, 209

land reallocation (Aboriginal), 128, 129, 173

LGBTQ. *See* gay, bisexual, transgendered, and transsexual fathers

libraries: social inclusiveness, 18

lone fathers: Aboriginal, 37, 38(t), 127; defined, 40; immigrants, 36(t), 37; marital status, 40; numbers of, 3-4, 28(t), 154; socio-economic characteristics, 46; teenaged, 39

lone mothers: Aboriginal, 127; and child welfare interventions, 173; income, 58; numbers of, 9, 154

lone-parent households: Aboriginal families, 127-28; and child welfare interventions, 174; effects on child development, 57-58, 150-51; numbers of, 3, 154; rising prevalence of, 1, 3

Loyola Generativity Scale, 109

Manitoba: Aboriginal children in child welfare, 129

marital status: of Aboriginal couples, 127; of Aboriginal fathers, 37, 38(t); of fathers vs. non-fathers, 32; of immigrant fathers, 36(t), 37; of lone fathers, 40; of teenaged fathers, 39

marriage, heterosexual: declining longevity, 1

marriage, same-sex: legalization, 17-18; rising numbers of, 3

masculinity: diversity of forms, 1, 224; and interchangeability of child care, 229; reconceptualizing in terms of parenting, 15-18, 91; and societal structure, 228-29

McAdams model of generativity, 109, 110

media: depictions of Aboriginal fathers, 127-28, 144; depictions of fatherhood, 4-5, 16, 18

medicine wheel teachings, 137

men: effects of fatherhood expectations on generativity, 119-20; effects of fathering on development, 110-12, 120-21; fatherhood as predictor of generativity, 112-14; as innately different from women, 99; privileges in society, 96-99, 226-29

mental health: Aboriginal children, 127; Aboriginal men, 127; separated/divorced fathers, 152

Menzies' Intergenerational Trauma Model, 137

Métis. *See* Aboriginal families; Aboriginal fathers

mothers (*see also* lone mothers): age at motherhood, 29-30; ambivalence about father involvement, 4; in child welfare assessments, 175-77; and custody law, 158; defined, 95; as facilitators of father involvement, 7, 62-63, 151-52; family responsibilities and workforce participation, 8-9, 26, 32, 33(t), 34, 93; as gatekeepers of father involvement, 5, 15, 26, 62, 151; heading lone-parent households, 3; parental leave ineligibility, 211; in popular media, 4; psycho-social effects of separation/divorce, 152; research and advocacy for, 92; use of parental leave compared to fathers, 207, 214-16, 219, 220-21; work hours, 8-9, 209

mothers of children with special needs: coping strategies, 194-95; levels of involvement, 190; sources of stress, 192

National Population Health Survey: limitations, 46-47

neglect: and gendered child welfare assessments, 176; and removal of Aboriginal children from family, 127, 174
New Brunswick: parental leave, 211
new fathers: in FIRA study, 12, 91, 92, 114; generative development, 110; invisibility of, 96; lack of programming for, 95; value of early parenting classes, 66
Northwest Territories: parental leave, 209
Norway: child care by fathers, 34
Nova Scotia: parental leave, 209
Nunavut: parental leave, 209

outreach: lack of research investment, 19, 234; through father-supportive programs and practices, 12-15

parental alienation, 62-63, 161-62
parental leave: for adoptive births, 210; in context of shared childrearing, 208-9; EI requirements and provisions, 208, 210-11, 222n2; employer top-up programs, 209, 211; ineligibility for, 211, 213; inequities of gender, race, and class, 98, 209; international comparisons, 221-22; job-protection provisions, 209-10; legal history, 207; QPIP requirements and provisions, 208, 210-11; in Sweden, 218
parental leave use by fathers: father characteristics, 213, 221; influences, 207, 213-20, 221-22; in Québec compared to rest of Canada, 220, 221
parental relationship: effects of caring for child with special needs, 193, 195; effects on development of child, 61-64, 151-52; effects on fatherhood involvement, 7, 151-52; high-conflict, and custody arrangements, 62-63, 161-62; and role expectations, 65, 229-31
parenting and adult development. *See* generativity
parenting classes: father-friendly, 65-66
parents: defined, 95
people of colour: and child welfare interventions, 174
physical health of child: Aboriginal children, 127; effects of father absence, 76-77(t); effects of father involvement, 56, 74(t); effects of parents' relationship, 61-64; effects of poverty, 58
policies: for Aboriginial fathers, 139; on child care, and use of parental leave, 207; Euro-centric, 136; for families of children with special needs, 202; focused on labour-market involvement, 6; historic, of colonization, 128-29; implications of

generativity research, 123; importance of recognizing diversity, 14, 94; inclusion of father input, 10-11; mother-centric, 136, 141; promoting gender equity in parenting, 4, 5, 92-93; supportive of fathers, 12-15, 65-66
population health model, 7, 20
poverty: in Aboriginal families, 127, 174; among Canada's children compared to other countries, 174; and child support guidelines, 163; and child welfare interventions, 173, 174-75; effects on child development, 57-58; in lone-parent households, 127, 151
Prince Edward Island: adoption restrictions, 18
programs: Euro-centric, 136; father-supportive, 65-66, 234-36; mother-centric, 13, 14-15, 136, 141-43; recommendations from and for Aboriginial fathers, 139-44; supporting gender equity in parenthood, 92-93; supportive of fathers, 12-15, 18-21
Promise Keepers, 99
ProsPère, 19

Québec: child support guidelines, 164; father involvement programming, 19; fathers' use of parental leave, 207, 213, 214-15, 215(t), 220-21; parental leave legislation (*see* Québec Parental Insurance Plan [QPIP])
Québec Parental Insurance Plan (QPIP): compared to EI, 210-11, 210(t), 221; inequities in parental leave, 209; requirements and provisions, 207, 208, 210-11

race/ethnicity: and child welfare interventions, 173-75, 177; and definition of masculinity, 224; effects on child development, 58, 64-65; and lack of non-Euro-centric programs and policies, 136
rape: in custody law, 158
refugee fathers (*see also* immigrant fathers): effects on child development, 64; self-perceived efficacy in Canadian context, 175; similarities and differences with other fathers, 12
repartnering after divorce, 155-56
research on changing families: largely focused on women, 92
research on fatherhood (*see also* Father Involvement Research Alliance [FIRA]): community-based perspectives, 92, 225; father involvement in, 10-11; importance

of women's participation, 91; need for government investment, 19, 233; and social change, 225-26; theories resulting from, 5, 52-53; in underrepresented sub-populations, 12, 136

research needs: Aboriginal fathers, 10, 136-38; better data sets, 27, 37, 38-39, 41, 43, 44-47, 233; broadly, 1-2, 11; custody arrangements, 97; father demographics, 45-47; father supports, 234-35; father-child influences, 66-67; fathers of children with special needs, 201-2; GLBTQ fathers, 18, 68; immigrant fathers, 10

reserves: lone-father households, 127; policy and programming needs, 140-41; tertiary education and income generation restrictions, 129

residential school system: attendance by men in Ball study, 132; effects on Aboriginal families/fathers, 8, 96, 129-30, 173-74

rural and remote areas: lack of family supports and services, 3

same-sex couples (*see also* gay, bisexual, transgendered, and transsexual fathers): having children, 4, 17-18, 45; and interchangeability of care roles, 230-31; male vs. female, 3

Saskatchewan: Aboriginal children in child welfare, 129

school attendance: by Aboriginal children, 127; by children in lone-parent households, 151; by teenaged fathers, 39

schools: social inclusiveness, 18

separated/divorced fathers: child access rights, 158, 159, 162-63, 164-65, 166; child support payments, 60-61, 163-65; custody arrangements, 40, 41-43, 63; custody conflicts, 161-62; and custody law in history, 158; custody law and policy recommendations, 165-66; and custody law reform, 159-61; difficulty of research on, 41-43, 153-54; diversity of, 3, 151; effects on child development, 62-63, 150-51; and fathers' rights advocacy, 96-97, 101, 158, 159-60, 163, 164, 165; in FIRA study, 12, 92, 98, 114; "invisibility," 44-45, 66; numbers of (*see* fathers: numbers of); ongoing relationship with child, 154-56; psycho-social needs, 152-53; repartnering, 155-56; similarities and differences with other fathers, 12; social supports and services for, 152

sexual orientation: and definition of masculinity, 224

shared parenting: equal-time advocacy, 159-60, 165; legal expectations, 156-57

single-earner families: wealth and income vulnerability, 3

single-parent households. *See* lone-parent households

social assistance: receipt of, and child welfare interventions, 174

social capital: effects on child development, 57; of fathers vs. non-fathers, 34-35

social change: involving fathers in, 231-32; and research on fatherhood, 225-26

social determinants of health: and families of children with special needs, 199

social development of child: effects of father absence, 76(t); effects of father involvement, 56, 72-74(t); effects of parental separation/divorce, 150-52; effects of parents' relationship, 61-64; and father's generative action, 113-14

social inclusion: of different types of fathers, need to promote, 224; effects on fatherhood, 10; obstacles, 19; school libraries and GLBTQ parents, 18

social workers: dissimilarities with clients, 175

societal factors: in Aboriginal fatherhood, 127-28, 134, 136, 137; in fatherhood experiences, 8-9; in fathers' experiences, 111; in parenting expectations, 4, 5, 15-18, 65, 226, 228; in separated/divorced fatherhood, 153

socio-economic characteristics: of Aboriginal fathers, 37-38; and age at parenthood, 30; and definition of masculinity, 224; effects on child development, 57-60; of families of children with special needs, 199; and fathers vs. non-fathers, 30, 31(t), 32; of fathers taking parental leave, 213, 216-18, 221; of immigrant fathers, 36(t); of lone fathers, 40, 41(t); of young fathers, 38-39

Special Joint Committee on Child Custody and Access, 159-60

spousal abuse: and custody law, 162

stay-home parents: fathers as, 26

stepfathers: demographic characteristics, 43-44

stigma: Aboriginal fathers, 16, 127

stress: in parents of children with special needs, 193-94

substance use: among Aboriginal children, 127; among Aboriginal men, 130, 133-34,

136; among fathers of children in child welfare system, 179, 180-81, 183

suicide rates: Aboriginal children, 127; Aboriginal men, 127

supports and services: for families of children with special needs, 199-201; father-supportive, 10-11, 65-66, 234-36; for fathers of children with special needs, 196-97, 198-99; mother-centric, 6, 135; in rural and remote areas, 3; for separated/divorced fathers, 152; for separated/divorced parents, 166

Sweden: child care by fathers, 34, 221; child protective services, 173; parental leave, 218

teenaged fathers (*see also* young fathers): socio-economic characteristics, 38-39, 46

terminology: *Aboriginal*, 145n1; in child welfare legislation, 176; in federal Divorce Act, 160; recognizing diversity, 94-96

Trans Fathers 2B, 18

two-earner families: numbers increasing, 3, 26, 208-9; and use of parental leave, 209

two-parent households: importance of parents' relationship, 7, 61-64

United States: child care by fathers, 34; father involvement policies and practices, 16; longitudinal studies on fathers, 46

urban areas: Aboriginal people in, 129; Aboriginal program and policy needs, 141, 143-44; lone-parent Aboriginal families in, 127

well-being of child: effects of father absence, 75-76(t); effects of father involvement, 55-56, 70-72(t); effects of father's earnings, 58-59; effects of parents' relationship, 61-64; effects of poverty, 58

women: diversity of, and feminist research, 90, 91; education and income increasing, 26; generative development, 113; income compared to men, 3, 26, 209; as innately different from men, 99; numbers in labour market increasing, 3, 26, 208-9; participation in fatherhood research, 91; underprivileges in society, and father involvement research, 96-100

workplaces: culture of, and fathers' use of parental leave, 218-20; mother-centric policies, 98; parental leave policies, 209, 211

young fathers: in FIRA study, 12, 92, 98, 114-17; generative development, 111-12, 120, 121; generative narratives, 114-17; income and identity, 60; invisibility of, 96; lack of programming for, 10; lack of research on, 10; socio-economic characteristics, 29, 38-39, 46, 115; stereotyped as incompetent, 109

young mothers: Aboriginal, 127

young parents: socio-economic characteristics, 127

Yukon: parental leave, 209